Hegel's Dialectic of Desire and Recognition

SUNY Series in the Philosophy of the Social Sciences
Edited by Lenore Langsdorf

Hegel's Dialectic of Desire and Recognition

TEXTS AND COMMENTARY

Edited by John O'Neill

STATE UNIVERSITY OF NEW YORK PRESS

Published by
State University of New York Press, Albany

© 1996 State University of New York

Printed in the United States of America

For information, address State University of New York Press,
State University Plaza, Albany, N.Y., 12246

Production by Cathleen Collins
Marketing by Bernadette LaManna

Library of Congress Cataloging in Publication Data

Hegel's dialectic of desire and recognition : texts and commentary /
    edited by John O'Neill.
        p.   cm. — (SUNY series in the philosophy of the social
    sciences)
    Includes bibliographical references and index.
    ISBN 0-7914-2713-7. — ISBN 0-7914-2714-5 (pbk.)
    1. Hegel, Georg Wilhelm Friedrich, 1770-1831.   I. Hegel, Georg
Wilhelm Friedrich, 1770-1831.   II. O'Neill, John, 1933-
III. Series.
B2948.H354   1996
193--dc20   95-5523
                                                                            CIP

10 9 8 7 6 5 4 3 2 1

FOR TOM

Dialectics is the self-consciousness of the objective context of delusion; it does not mean to have escaped from that context. Its objective goal is to break out of the context from within. The strength required from the break grows in dialectics from the context of immanence; what would apply to it once more is Hegel's dictum that in dialectics an opponent's strength is absorbed and turned against him, not just in the dialectical particular, but eventually in the whole.

—Adorno, *Negative Dialectics*

Contents

Acknowledgments   ix

Introduction: A Dialectical Genealogy of Self, Society,
and Culture in and after Hegel   1
John O'Neill

Part I. Lordship and Bondage

1   Lordship and Bondage   29
    G. W. F. Hegel

2   Critique of Hegel   37
    Karl Marx

Part II. Desire and Recognition

3   Desire and Work in the Master and Slave   49
    Alexandre Kojève

4   Self-Consciousness and Life:
    The Independence of Self-Consciousness   67
    Jean Hyppolite

5   The Existence of Others   87
    Jean-Paul Sartre

Part III. Alienation and Recognition

6   Hegel's Economics During the Jena Period   101
    Georg Lukács

7   Labor and Interaction: Remarks on Hegel's
    Jena *Philosophy of Mind*   123
    Jürgen Habermas

8   Hegel's Dialectic of Self-Consciousness   149
    Hans-Georg Gadamer

Part IV. Dialectics of Desire and Recognition

  9   Of Human Bondage: Labor and Freedom
      in the *Phenomenology*   171
      Howard Adelman

 10   Labor, Alienation, and Social Classes
      in Hegel's *Realphilosophie*   187
      Shlomo Avineri

 11   Master and Slave: The Bonds of Love   209
      Jessica Benjamin

 12   Hegel and Lacan: The Dialectic of Desire   223
      Edward S. Casey and J. Melvin Woody

 13   The Concept of Recognition in Hegel's Jena Manuscripts   233
      Henry S. Harris

 14   Notes on Hegel's "Lordship and Bondage"   253
      George Armstrong Kelly

 15   The Struggle for Recognition: Hegel's Dispute
      with Hobbes in the Jena Writings   273
      Ludwig Siep

 16   Self-Sufficient Man: Dominion and Bondage   289
      Judith N. Shklar

 17   The Metaphor in Hegel's *Phenomenology of Mind*   305
      Henry Sussman

Index   329

Acknowledgments

I am grateful to the authors and publishers for permission to use material from the following works or journals:

G. W. F. Hegel, "Lordship and Bondage." From *Phenomenology of Spirit*, trans. A. V. Miller (1977), 110–19. Oxford University Press, 1977.

Karl Marx, "Critique of Hegel." From *Karl Marx: Early Texts*, trans. David McLellan (1971), 161–78. Blackwell Publishers and with the translator's permission.

Alexandre Kojève, "Desire and Work in the Master Slave." From *Introduction to the Reading of Hegel*, by Alexandre Kojève, 39–57. Edited by Allan Bloom and translated by James H. Nichols Jr., 1969 by Basic Books, Inc. Reprinted by permission of Basic Books, Inc., Publishers, New York.

Jean Hyppolite, "Self-Consciousness and Life." From *Genesis and Structure of Hegel: Phenomenology of Spirit*, by Jean Hyppolite, translated by Hazel E. Barnes. Pp. 235–45. Reprinted with permission of the Philosophical Library, Inc., New York, and Routledge, Loundon.

Georg Lukács, "Hegel's Economics during the Jena Period." From Georg Lukács, *The Young Hegel: Studies in the Relations between Dialectics and Economics*, trans. Rodney Livingston (1975). Pp. 319–37. Reprinted with permission of The Merlin Press, Ltd., London.

Jürgen Habermas, "Labor and Interaction: Remarks on Hegel's Jena *Philosophy of Mind*." From *Theory and Practice*, by Jürgen Habermas. Copyright (c) 1973 by Beacon Press. Pp. 142–69. Reprinted by permission of Beacon Press.

Hans Georg Gadamer, "Hegel's Dialectic of Self-Consciousness." From Hans-Georg Gadamer, *Hegel's Dialectic: Five Hermeneutical Studies*, trans P. Christopher Smith (1976). Pp. 54–74. Reprinted with permission of Yale University Press.

Howard Adelman, "On Human Bondage: Labour, Bondage and Freedom in the Phenomenology." From *Hegel's Social and Political Thought*, ed. Donald Phillip Verene (Atlantic Highlands, N.J.: Humanities Press, 1980). Pp. 119–35. Reprinted by permission of the author.

Schlomo Avineri, "Labor, Alienation and Social Classes in Hegel's *Realphiloso-phie*." From *The Legacy of Hegel: Proceedings of the Marquette Hegel Symposium 1970*, edited by J. J. O'Malley, K. W. Algozin, H. P. Kainz, and C. C. Rise (1973), Pp. 196–215. Reprinted with permission of Kluwer Academic Publishers, Dordrecht.

Jessica Benjamin, "Master and Slave: The Bonds of Love." From *The Bonds of Love* by Jessica Benjamin. Pp. 53–67. Copyright (c) 1988 by Jessica Benjamin. Reprinted by permission of Pantheon Books, a division of Random House, Inc.

Edward S. Casey and J. Melvin Woody, "Hegel and Lacan: The Dialectic of Desire." From *Interpreting lacan*, edited by Joseph H. Smith and William Kerrigan. Copyright (c) 1983 by Forum on Psychiatry and the Humanities of The Washington School of Psychiatry. Pp. 77–88. Reprinted by permission of Yale University Press.

Henry S. Harris, "The Concept of Recognition in Hegel's Jena Manuscripts." *Hegel-Studien* 20 (1977): 229–48. Reprinted by permission of Bouvier Verlag, Bonn.

George Armstrong Kelly, "Notes on Hegel's 'Lordship and Bondage.' *Review of Metaphysics* 19:4 (June 1966): 189–217. Reprinted with permission of *The Review of Metaphysics*.

Ludwig Siep, "The Struggle for Recognition: Hegel's Dispute with Hobbes in the Jena Writings." Translated by Charles Dudas from "Der Kampf um Anerkennung: Zu Hegels Auseinandersetzung mit Hobbes in den Jenaer Schriften *Hegel-Studien* 9 (1974): 155–207. Reprinted with permission by Bouvier Verlag, Bonn.

Judith N. Shklar, "Self-Sufficient Man: Dominion and Bondage." From *Freedom and Independence: A Study of the Political Ideas of Hegel's Phenome-nology of Mind*, by Judith N. Shlar (Cambridge University Press, 1976). Pp. 59–73. Reprinted with permission of Cambridge University Press.

Henry Sussman, "The Metaphor in Hegel's *Phenomenology of Mind*." *Clio* 11:4 (1982): 361–86. Reprinted by permission of the author.

Jean-Paul Sartre, "The Existence of Others," From *Being And Nothingness*. Translated and with an Introduction by Hazel E. Barnes. Pp. 235–245. Copyright © 1953 Philosophical Library, Inc., New York and Routledge, London.

Introduction

A DIALECTICAL GENEALOGY OF SELF, SOCIETY, AND CULTURE IN AND AFTER HEGEL

John O'Neill

Against the current drift into cultural and political minoritarianism, I believe that without Hegel and Marx in our toolbox we are doomed to flounder in a world marked by the split between postmodern indifference and premodern passion.[1] Inasmuch as postmodernism pronounces itself to be post-Hegelian and post-Marxist—if not post-Freudian—I think we are called to account for this remarkable shedding of intellectual weight as something akin to cultural anorexia.[2] How did Hegelianism-Marxism fall so low in the current market of ideas? The answer, paradoxically, can come only by asking the ghosts themselves what it was that killed them. So we must let them speak—as we do in the present collection of texts and commentaries. I hope that they help convince us that we cannot afford to trash our Hegelian-Marxist culture because it contains the very engine of cultural renewal that has always been the mark of any great cultural apparatus.

The texts here suggest a persistent topos in Western philosophy, namely, the narrative of the rise of human consciousness from within the world of nature and a historical society that recognizes itself through such a story. This narrative of the struggle over recognition and desire may be regarded as the secular sequel to the biblical narrative of a failed

---

1. John O'Neill, "Critique and Remembrance," in *On Critical Theory,* ed. John O'Neill (Washington, D.C.: University Press of America, 1989), 1–11.
2. John O'Neill, *The Poverty of Postmodernism* (New York: Routledge, 1995).

1

recognition between the Creator and the creation. In this sequel, life, labor, and language are each subject to a historicized dialectic of (unconscious) desire and (class) recognition, developed in the Hegelian-Marxist and in the Freudian version of the economy of recognition, reciprocity, and alienation. We can find a persistent concern with the issue of human reciprocity and alienation (to put it most simply) throughout the human sciences. Within this history, I have reconstructed a genealogy of the dialectic of recognition that derives from:

- the Hegelian-Marxist master-slave relation
- French commentary by Kojève, Hyppolite, Sartre, and Lacan that has been central to existential philosophy, politics, psychoanalysis, and literature with the result that the latter disciplines have reworked their original sources in remarkable ways
- German commentary by Lukács, Habermas, Gadamer, and Siep as well as Avineri, Harris, and Kelly, which has considerably clarified the background in political economy and hermeneutics required to situate the Hegelian master-slave dialectic within the history of bourgeois society and the attempt to elaborate an emancipatory critique of its social relationships
- some contemporary commentary in which the problematic of the master-slave dialectic is translated into the recognition-scene of critical hermeneutics weighted by Freudo-Lacanian concepts of the split-self, misrecognition, and alienation

The overall effect of these selections is to show how the Hegelian-Marxist topos is a contested one, shot through with the problematic of difference in class, race, and gender, and thus how it constitutes a model of de-canonization along the lines of contemporary debate in the academy.

From Hegel to Freud/Lacan we can discern a persistent attempt to analyze the reproduction and resolution of the cultural knotting of subject who must "split," so to speak, in order to become a social subject. Hegel describes this dialectic in terms of the dynamics of an intra-subjective division and an intersubjective exchange. Marx translated this dialectic into class-division, alienation, and communism, while Freud recast it in the dynamics of transference, religious illusion, and civilizational discontent. In each case, the certainties of narcissism, solipsism, and possessivism—and their institutional displacements—are inserted into an expanding cycle of dialectical reciprocity without which "we" can make no progress. As Hegel shows in the Introduction to the *Phenomenology*, to ask what something or other means is either to ask for the thought (*Gedanke*) behind an expression (*Vorstellung*), or else to ask for an instance or example (*Beispiel*) of the thought. The passage—translation or recollection—involved in either case is itself exemplary of the self-transformation of consciousness as narrated in the *Phenomenology*.

It is the destiny of sensuous experience to be raised to the level of the concept just as the concept itself must find instantiation in the sensuous. Spirit (*Geist*) is at home (*zu Hause*) in the contents of the world not as one more thing in the world but as the example or model (*Vorbild*) of all things. In short, the world and the spirit presuppose interpretation. In Hegel, however, interpretation cannot be based on mimesis, since that model lacks the dynamic force of transformation that Hegel locates in the soul's incorporation of meaning in order to emphasize the activity of self-production and appropriation (*Aneignung*) in the interpretative act (*Meinen*):

> We may be permitted here, in this appeal to universal experience, to anticipate with a reference to the practical sphere. In this connection we may answer those who thus insist on the truth and certainty of the reality of objects of sense, by saying that they had better be sent back to the most elementary school of wisdom, the ancient Eleusinian mysteries of Ceres and Bacchus; they have not yet learnt the inner secret of the eating of bread and the drinking of wine. For one who is initiated into these mysteries not only comes to doubt the being of things of sense, but gets into a state of despair about it altogether; and in dealing with them he partly himself brings about the nothingness of those things, partly he sees these bring about their own nothingness. Even animals are not shut off from this wisdom, but show they are deeply initiated into it. For they do not stand stock still before things of sense as if these were things *per se*, with being in themselves; they despair of this reality altogether, and in complete assurance of the nothingness of things they fall-to without more ado and eat them up. And all nature proclaims, as animals do, these open secrets, these mysteries revealed to all, which teach what the truth of things of sense is.[3]

Hegel's pun on the "inability" of opinion to mean (*Meinen*) what it says—its inability to hold onto "mine" without "thine"— turns off the

---

3. G. W. F. Hegel, *The Phenomenology of Mind*, trans. J. B. Baillie (London: George Allen and Unwin, 1947), 158–59.

capacity of language to transform commonsense, rational, and mythical discourse.[4] As Sussman's commentary shows so well, however, there is a constant return of the repressed evinced in the double pun on alimentary, reproductive, and spiritual transformation, in which communication and communion are themselves redoubled. Neither can be reduced to the other—there is no community without the body and no body without community, just as there is no communion without the body and no body without communion.[5]

In sense-certainty we are (un)certain of the primacy of sensation ("*Like*, man, I'm *seeing* this whale") or of the primacy of the object ("Man, I'm *talking* whale; I saw this—like—huge, *really* huge whale!"). As soon as we ask, "Where, what sort, with whom?" sense-certainty is mortified by the rejection of its insistent language: it is puzzled by the request for the observance of laws and convention, of communication that it had hoped to bypass. This occurs because there is no *punctum* outside language. Thus, "*Like*, man, I'm walking along this street. . ." or "*Like*, there's this car, and I'm walking along this street. . .," in striving to place the object "immediately" in consciousness or to present the *punctum* of consciousness as an object on the same level as its object, can only stage itself through the impersonal, "*man*," or "*you know*," that is, by invoking the collective speech whose grammar it seeks to forget. In short, naive realism cannot say what it means—"Like, I mean. . ."—without translation into what "we" mean; thus, it suffers that first reversal (*umkehren*) that substance and subject will experience throughout the course of Hegel's developmental phenomenology of mind and society. Sensory realism cannot say what it means without resort to classification—a more complex language game—just as opinion can clarify itself only through appeal to more complex levels of understanding and explanation: "Language. . . is the more truthful; in it we ourselves refute directly and at once our own 'meaning'; and since universality is the real truth of sense-certainty, and language merely expresses *this* truth, it is not possible at all for us even to express in words any sensuous existence which we 'mean'."[6]

The limits of expression and knowledge are the limits of our language. So far from being the ultimate referent of language, our

---

4. Donald Phillip Verene, *Hegel's Recollection: A Study of Images in the Phenomenology of Spirit* (Albany: State University of New York Press, 1985).

5. John O'Neill, *The Communicative Body: Studies in Communicative Philosophy Politics and Sociology* (Evanston: Northwestern University Press, 1989).

6. *Phenomenology of Mind*, 152.

sensations are rule governed. Language has no foundational language games such as are proposed by sensory realists. Similarly, our perceptual acts, like seeing, imply a grammar in which they are linked to imagination and thinking. The latter are in turn presupposed in the act of perceiving an object in some relevant aspect, since any object is a unity of both internal and external properties.[7]

During the Jena years, Hegel himself had been tempted by a kind of speechlessness rather different from that of the sensate realist. It derived from his experience of the inadequacy of language to express either the divinity or the sublimity of nature, as well as its inability to capture the harmony in the Greek spirit. Yet, even in his awe before the waterfall at Reichenbach, Hegel had begun to grasp the living principle of contradiction as the endless identity through change that constitutes the waterfall. In fact, he saw that the encounter between himself and the waterfall could only be experienced in their mutual reflection:

> To understand is to dominate. To endow objects with life is to make them into gods. To look at a brook, how it must fall according to the laws of gravity to deeper places, and how it is limited and compressed by the bottom and the banks, this is to understand its to give it a soul, to participate in it as something equal, means to make it into a god.[8]

Here Hegel's own language begins to join philosophy and poetry, just as the child joins its parents and the tool joins reason and the body. So Hegel calls speech "the tool of reason, the child of intelligent being." All three are modes of alienation, *Entaüsserung*, that exteriorization of the spirit through which it produces its self-contents.

We are now a long way from Hegel's initial despair over the incapacity of language to capture experience, leaving us in estrangement (*Entfremdung*) from the source of our life and being. It is this experience that Hegel reenacts, so to speak, in his opening phenomenology of the language games of realism, solipsism, and skepticism, each of which threaten to return consciousness to silence. Hegel's account of the transition from consciousness to self-consciousness is taken by most

---

7. P. T. Geach, *Mental Acts* (London: Routledge, 1957); David Lamb, "Sense and Meaning in Hegel and Wittgenstein," in *Hegel and Modern Philosophy*, ed. David Lamb (London: Croom-Helm, 1987), 70–101.

8. Hegel, *Theologische Jugendschriften*, ed. Herman Nohl (Tübingen, 1907), 376.

commentators to occur through the experience of desire. Yet, as Navickas[9] and Loewenberg[10] have remarked, Hegel's account of how desire operates in the first stage of the constitution of self-consciousness is not easily understood. We have seen how Hegel arrives at consciousness as a structure—within—difference, as a living entity with subject and object polarities that continually conceals any exclusivity in either object—awareness or self-awareness. The sensory ego can never be satisfied on the level of appetite—"he eats like a pig"—because the growth of the living body is a more complex structure of differentiation and integration, involving higher levels of endo-/exo/structuring. Hence, the senses are subject to fading and exhaustion in the wake of the embodied subject even before we encounter the higher level of intersubjectivity that Hegel calls the "highway of despair" so far as natural awareness is concerned.

The commensurability of subject and object-consciousness appears to break down in the experience of desire since in canceling its object the desiring consciousness merely reproduces its object as the very essence of desire. Consciousness is therefore obliged to treat the object of its desire as something living, endowed with an opposing consciousness, that is, as the genus "life" in which our own life is lived out. Having achieved primacy over the object, self-consciousness has still to press on with the articulation of its own self-determination. To achieve this, self-consciousness must both split and integrate its awareness of its self *qua* "self" and its awareness of objects as "other" than itself but only as objects of thought. This structure is exemplified in the operation of desire in which I propose to myself an object that, in this very act, exerts upon me an irresistible attraction. I am, so to speak, my desire and I am not my desire. To integrate this conflict between the self and "its" desires, rather than to remain in endless subjection to the insatiability of desire on the level of appetite (I can never eat the one meal that will satisfy hunger), consciousness must propose to itself an object of desire that will shut down its enslavement to desire:

> It is in these three moments that the notion of self-consciousness first gets completed: (a) pure undifferentiated ego is its first immediate object. (b) This immediacy is itself, however, thoroughgoing mediation: it has its being only by cancelling the independent object, in other words it is Desire. The satisfaction of

---

9. Joseph Navickas, *Consciousness and Reality: Hegel's Philosophy of Subjectivity* (The Hague: Martinus Nijhoff, 1976).
10. Jacob Loewenberg, *Hegel's Phenomenology: Dialogues on the Life of the Mind* (Lasalle, Ill.: Open Court, 1965).

THE MASTER-SLAVE DIALECTIC

Transitions

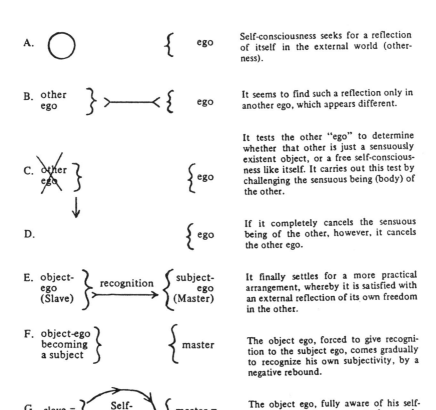

A. Self-consciousness seeks for a reflection of itself in the external world (otherness).

B. other ego / ego — It seems to find such a reflection only in another ego, which appears different.

C. other ego / ego — It tests the other "ego" to determine whether that other is just a sensuously existent object, or a free self-consciousness like itself. It carries out this test by challenging the sensuous being (body) of the other.

D. ego — If it completely cancels the sensuous being of the other, however, it cancels the other ego.

E. object-ego (Slave) — recognition → subject-ego (Master) — It finally settles for a more practical arrangement, whereby it is satisfied with an external reflection of its own freedom in the other.

F. object-ego becoming a subject / master — The object ego, forced to give recognition to the subject ego, comes gradually to recognize his own subjectivity, by a negative rebound.

G. slave = master / Self-recognition / master = slave — The object ego, fully aware of his self-conscious freedom, ceases to be an object-ego, ceases to be a Slave. The subject-ego must therefore also cease to be "Master" of the Slave.

All the preceding transitions should be understood in terms
of the following ultimate transition:

ego ⟷ ego

H. In this transition, which does not take place until the end of the first part of the *Phenomenology*, the mutual recognition of egos replaces the various kinds of one-sided recognition; and intersubjectivity in the fullest sense ensues.

desire is indeed the reflexion of self-consciousness into itself,
is the certainty which has passed into objective truth. But (c)
the truth of this certainty is really twofold reflexion, the
reduplication of self-consciousness. Consciousness has an object
which implicates its own otherness or affirms distinction as
a void distinction, and therein is independent. The individual
form distinguished, which is only a living form, certainly
cancels its independence also in the process of life itself: but
it ceases along with its distinctive difference to be what it is.
The object of self-consciousness, however, is still independent
in this negativity of itself: and thus it is for itself genus,
universal flux or continuity in the very distinctiveness of its
own separate existence; it is a living self-consciousness.[11]

Self-consciousness, then, must now encounter as its other a self-
consciousness that can accord to it the same "self" that it is aware of
in its own case. The transitions involved so far are nicely summarized
by Kainz[12] on the previous page.

Before we can reach the level of the master-slave dialectic, there must
occur a doubling of the subject/object-relation on the level of sociology
as well as of epistemology. Henceforth, consciousness exists in a *double
entente* of mutual recognition, that is, *intrasubjectivity is intersubjectivity*, the achievement of identity accorded to each by the other rather
than as a self-insistent stance excluding all others except as objects of
self-appropriation. Admittedly, even intersubjectively aware consciousnesses at first confront one another in creaturely isolation, more sure
of themselves than of any other, more attached to their own life and
survival than to anything else, as Siep and Harris show in their commentaries. Yet this very situation is unstable since, unless there is a
conscious decision to risk "one's" life in the potential conflict with
another "self" making the same decision, one will surely die—or be
enslaved, as Sklar shows in her commentary. In short, self-consciousness
must seek freedom as something higher than its own independence, since
in the worst possible scenario only *one* self might survive the life-and-
death struggle. This negative freedom would return us to the very impossibility of self-possession that the *Phenomenology* has so far demonstrated, and that finds its example in the stoic and the skeptic. Here
Sklar's commentary is important inasmuch as it makes clear that the

11. *Phenomenology of Mind*, 226.
12. Howard P. Kainz, *Hegel's Phenomenology, Part I: Analysis and Comments*
(Tuscaloosa, Ala.: The University of Alabama Press, 1976), 86.

unending pursuit of the self by itself can only forge knowledge and community on the level of collective sacrifice. The figures of the epic hero. the stoic and the skeptic and the unhappy consciousness, are ridden by death, passivity, and uncreative consumption. Even so, Hegel sought to retain the hero's freedom in the face of necessity by translating the hero into the figure of the Athenian citizen whose freedom is given through the law. Of course, the Greco-Roman world remained politically divided, "dreaming" of its unity on the level of culture[13] to be pursued in the Enlightenment and the French Revolution.

We cannot remove the equivocations in Hegel's concept of desire (*Begierde*), except to remark that he characterizes its operation in both presocial and social terms that must not be conflated, as Kelly's commentary reminds us. We might say that it is only from the standpoint of the social self that its natural, precontractual self can be imagined— and then only as a spur to the imagination, to remind it of the impossibility of life before or after society. The importance of the commentary on the Jena period (Avineri, Habermas, Harris, and Lukács) is to show that there is neither reason nor freedom in the state of nature. Likewise, self-consciousness can only stage the life-and-death struggle as a *role* for itself that presupposes a common discourse for the display of rational, independent selves whose limit is sheer violence. Siep asks in his commentary whether Hegel is harking back to Hobbes in locating reason's mastery in the animal passions. I suggest the difference lies in their concept of imagination, which remains sensate in Hobbes but in Hegel is also related to recollection (*Erinnerung*) and language.[14] In Hegel the sensate repetition of animal desire is mediated in human beings by the intention of tools that transform desire through cultural and institutional modes of appropriation and recognition.

We might say that for Hegel, Hobbes' fantasy of origins—*exeundum e statu naturae*—remains an impossible originary fantasy without the mediation of language, and the intersubjective structures of which it is the originary condition. As we see from the commentary by Siep and Harris, this sublates the Hobbesian distinction between man as the material of society, ruled by fear, and man as the subject of society, the product of the laws that rule Leviathan. We can reflect on this in the

---

13. Stanley Rosen, *G. W. F. Hegel: An Introduction to the Science of Wisdom* (New Haven: Yale University Press, 1974).
14. Jacques Taminiaux, "Hegel and Hobbes," in his *Dialectic and Difference: Finitude in Modern Thought*, ed. James Decker and Robert Crease (Atlantic Highlands, N.J.: Humanities Press, 1985), 1–37.

conflict between Creon and Antigone. In the struggle between life and death, between the family and the state, reasons of state are confronted with the reasons of the heart, if not the unconscious of androgyny. Here the father may not sacrifice the daughter/son to the law that reinstates his power. Rather, what confronts Creon is Antigone's appeal for reciprocity between generations so that the life of the state is not exhausted in its conflicts as it is when these are viewed only in the present time. What Creon has to learn is that Antigone is not threatening the state on the level of parity of the ruler and ruled but on the level of life where everyone is ruled by death—to which we can respond only in honoring the rituals of burial.

Reciprocity is not simply the reversal of its constituent terms: it is the ethical internalization by both terms of the relationship they bear to one another. In other words, reciprocity is the life of the collectivity in-and-for-us. In the episode on "Lordship and Bondage" a symmetric relationship is shows to dissolve into a conflict forces over life and labor. Whether the servant's renunciation of honor and his apprenticeship to the practical arts and sciences is a model for the priestly renunciation operative in the episode on the "Unhappy Consciousness," what is experienced here is the transformation of physical force into self-restraint and social service. "Civilization" has opened up the master-slave relation to the possibility of the craft of reflection with its proper orientation toward public-mindedness.[15] Thus, we have the employment of a distinction between a substructural level of "need" and a superstructural level of "recognition," to which Hegel adds a third level of the specifically political or collective virtue (*Gemüt, Tapferkeit*), in which—despite Habermas's claim to an original critique—we may see the origins of his notion of *Mundigkeit* (political maturity) that is achieved in the ideal speech community as a model polis.

For this reason I believe it is important that Hegel thought less of the hierarchy involved in the shift from need to intersubjective communication than of the need for a political pedagogy that would encourage people to keep the collectivity in mind:

> For Schiller this was the task of aesthetic imagination (in the broad sense): for Hegel it was the task of philosophy in general and of a philosophy of *Sittlichkeit* in particular. In Hegel's case, however, this process of coordination and self-evaluation had very definite correlates in the objective world of experience.

---

15. Lawrence Dickey, *Hegel: Religion, Economics and the Politics of Spirit, 1770–1807* (Cambridge: Cambridge University Press, 1987).

That is because he regarded self-evaluation as a collective process to which a people must subject itself if it were to become a truly political and truly human entity. Thus, if Schelling had moved the point of indifference from external nature to internal man, Hegel was committed to moving it from a point internal to man to a point that would be external to him in the sense that it would be located in the world of a shared socio-economic and political experience. There, it was to become a subject of collective debate: and out of that debate, in which intuitions could become concepts and concepts intuitions, was to emerge, for better or worse, the political character of a people. In that context, Hegel's conception of the point of indifference is a point of departure for, rather than the culmination of, thinking about the Absolute.[16]

It must be stressed that Hegel sees the first estate as a product of the social division of labor through which it acquires the task, or "calling," of thinking the public mind, or of thinking in public how men should reproduce themselves not only on the level of need but on the level of humanity. So far from constituting a political elite, Hegel's first estate represents a moral group organized on the basis of a covenant theology to offer a countervailing force to the economism of the bourgeoisie. Now although Hegel locates the "voice" of what we may call the ideal political community in the first group, this group is constituted by its members' cultivation of "indifference" toward immediate needs and pleasures and by its reflective concept of an enlightened public.

In Hegel, education, *Bildung*, is operative as both a psychological and a sociological process that raises the need for unity from its barest intuition on the level of life's struggle to its full political conception:

> For Hegel, *Bildung* brings the collectivity to a social point of indifference. It is the point where all things—body and spirit, the one and the many, intuitions and concepts, universals and particulars, subjectivity and objectivity, the organic and inorganic, the infinite and the finite—converge in one very pregnant textual and historical moment of "dramatic action." In a simple phrase, it is what Hegel called the moment of "living indifference," the point where "all natural difference is nullified" such that "the individual intuits himself as himself in every other individual." This moment, Hegel suggests, is when the idea of

---

16. Ibid., 268.

individual." This moment, Hegel suggests, is when the idea of
"a people" becomes a practicable political possibility. A people,
he tells us, is neither a "mass" nor a "plurality." Rather, it is
a "living indifference" with the potential for "organic totality"
within itself. By that Hegel means the people have the possibility of becoming "self-constituting," of becoming a "cause" for
itself. And should it realize that possibility it will be drawing
nearer to "the Absolute," to true *Sittlichkeit*, "rising" toward the
organic "from below," as he put it. In other words, "the people"
are now the objective, social carrier of the "intuition" that had
longed for unity, true *Sittlichkeit*. And were a people to try to
realize itself as such, Hegel thought, it would open itself to the
future and begin the kind of "pilgrimage" that leads ultimately
to religious recollectivization.[17]

By now we are well into Hegel's later phenomenology of objective spirit
and the mutuality of civic and state institutions. I do not mean to suggest
that all this flows "directly" from the master-slave dialectic. It does so
"dialectically" and how it does—both in Hegel's mind and in the history
that he interpreted—is meant to be considered more closely through the
commentaries by Lukács, Avineri, Habermas, and Harris, without imposing any unified thesis upon them.

Hegel's master-slave dialectic was, of course, subjected to Marx's
world-shaking "misreading."[18] We shall try to convey the main lines of
Marx's appropriation of Hegel, while again leaving it to the reader to
estimate from the commentaries by Lukács, Habermas, and Avineri
exactly what is fair to Hegel even on Marx's own ground of economic
history. In a few words, Hegel and Marx are agreed that there is no history
(though there may be time) of nature outside human society, and that
all history is the history of the social development of the human mind
and its sensorium. What Marx adds to this is that it is the history of
social relations that determines the generality of the sciences and arts
rather than any objective natural referent outside human society. All
history is "prehistory" until this pragmatic notion of the history of
material and cultural institutions has emerged. This is not the history
of a fall or of the soul's alienation in the body, but rather the slow history
of how it is anyone becomes human in mind and body, in work, language,
and politics. Once this shift in human consciousness has occurred, the

---

17. Ibid., 273.
18. Harold Bloom, *The Anxiety of Influence: A Theory of Poetry* (New York:
Oxford University Press, 1973).

history of nature is the history of second nature endlessly refashioned in the order of political economy and the history of the civilized arts and sciences.

Human nature is the historical and civil achievement of ways of thought, perception, language, and labor through which we mediate our own humanity.[19] Understood in this way, alienation is a necessary moment in the history of our lived-being:

> But man is not only a natural being, he is a human natural being. This means that he is a being that exists for himself, thus a species-being that must confirm and exercise himself as such in his being and knowledge. Thus human objects are not natural objects as they immediately present themselves nor is human sense, in its purely objective existence, human sensitivity and human objectivity. Neither nature in its objective aspect nor in its subjective aspect is immediately adequate to the human being. And as everything natural must have an origin, so man too has his process of origin, history, which can, however, be known by him and thus is a conscious process of origin that transcends itself. History is the true natural history of man.[20]

The human world involves at every level of sensation, perception, thought, and action a *social praxis* in which man's inner and outer worlds are mutually articulated. The human eye is civilized by what it sees in the field of art as is the human ear by the music to which it listens. In each case, what is proper to human physiology is inserted into a hermeneutical field whose own historical articulation includes the relatively autonomous praxes of optics, acoustics, art, and music:

> Only through the objectively unfolded richness of man's essential being is the richness of subjective human sensibility (a musical ear, an eye for beauty of form—in short, senses capable of human gratification, senses affirming themselves as essential powers of man) either cultivated or brought into being. For not only the five senses but also the so-called mental senses—the practical senses (will, love, etc.)—in a word, human sense—the human nature of the senses—comes to be by virtue of its object,

19. John O'Neill, "Naturalism in Vico and Marx: A Discourse Theory of the Body Politic," in his *For Marx Against Althusser: And Other Essays* (Washington, D.C.: University Press of America, 1982), 97–108.
20. Karl Marx, *Early Texts*, trans. and ed. David McLellan (Oxford: Basil Blackwell, 1971), 169.

by virtue of humanized nature. *The forming of the five senses
is a labour of the entire history of the world down to the
present.* (emphasis added)[21]

In many ways Marx overstressed his difference from Hegel. Avineri's
commentary rightly points to Hegel's concept of the transsubjective and
nonindividual nature of property as what pertains to the person who
is recognized as such by others. This is a remarkable extraction from
the possessive individualism that is otherwise thought to be under-
written by the device of contract. Similarly, in his commentary Lukács
calls attention to Hegel's concept of labor as the transformation of
individual appetites into creative social work presupposing recognition
of the other and the outline of a civil society, as found in his *Philosophy
of Right.* Yet Hegel was also aware of the problematic of early indus-
trialism—as Lukács, Avineri, Habermas, and Harris show in their citations from the works of the Jena period. I have included this commentary
precisely because it shows how Hegel struggled with the social division
of labor, property relations, commerce, money, commodity exchange, and
alienation, yet did not abandon the enterprise of philosophical anthropology to the supposed natural necessities of political economy.

In view of the current concept of postindustrialism to which the
relevance of Hegel and Marx is generally denied, I think it is imperative
to hold on to the relevant difference between Hegel's concept of civil
society and Marx's concept of class society:

> The class nature of political power is to Marx a sin against the
> state's claim for expressing the universal as against the partic-
> ularism and egotism of civil society. For Hegel, the institution-
> alization of class relationships into the political structure is the
> way through which the atomism of civil society is being inte-
> grated into a comprehensive totality. . . . While for Marx classes
> represent a division of labor that has to be overcome, for Hegel
> they stand for the integration of this division, regrettable, yet
> necessary, into a meaningful whole. (Avineri, 196)

Of course we cannot simply appropriate Hegel's concept of civil society—
certainly not in its Platonic or quietist aspects, pointed out by Lukács
and Avineri. Yet for his recognition of the civic task of reconciling difference in modern society I believe we cannot do without Hegel. Here

---

21. Karl Marx, *The Economic and Philosophic Manuscripts of 1844*, trans. Martin
Milligan and ed. Dirk J. Struik (New York: International Publishers, 1964), 141.

we may notice again the difference between the Hegelian and Hobbesian concepts of fear. The latter cancels itself in a greater authority, wereas in Hegel fear is an educative force on the level of both individual and society. Hegelian desire, likewise, is not presocial but mediated by other selves, through language and work.

In the French Hegelian-Marxist discussions of the master-slave dialectic a considerable first step was taken by Kojève in his "reading" of the *Phenomenology*, which percolated into the work of Sartre, Merleau-Ponty, Hyppolite, and Lacan on the themes of recognition, desire, and death that are, of course, central to Lacanian psychoanalysis (to which we shall return later). Kojève's reading of Hegel is remarkable for its decisive anthropologization of desire or as the metonomy of desire of a desiring other who freely renounces his or her desire in an act that constitutes the arbitrary premise of human history:

> Generally speaking, by accepting the four premises mentioned above, namely: (1) the existence of the revelation of given being by speech, (2) the existence of a desire engendering action that *negates*, transforms, given being, (3) the existence of *several* desires, which can desire one another mutually, and (4) the existence of a *possibility* of difference between the desires of (future) masters and desires of (future) slaves—by accepting these four premises, we understand the possibility of a *historical* process, of a *history*, which is, in its totality, the history of the fights and the work that finally ended in the wars of Napoleon and the table on which Hegel wrote the *Phenomenology* in order to *understand* both those wars and that table. Inversely, in order to explain the possibility of the *Phenomenology*, which is written on a *table* and which explains the wars of Napoleon, we must suppose the four premises mentioned. (Kojève, 50–51)

Kojève reads everything in the *Phenomenology* through the master-slave figure—a reading strategy that must be weighed in our own approach to it (see the commentaries by Sussman and Kelly) if we are not to lose sight of the more subtle dialectic of reason and violence in, for example, Merleau-Ponty's *Humanism and Terror* (1969) or Sartre's later *Critique of Dialectical Reason* (1976). Here the "end of history" is preserved in order to avert the fall into relativism while nevertheless trying to avoid the equally violent fall into scientism—two moves that underlie the ideology of the end of historical narratives.

Hyppolite's commentary focuses on the dialectic of subjective and intersubjective desire at the heart of consciousness seeking mutual recognition through another self-consciousness in a life-and-death struggle:

In this new experience, the life element, the medium of life, becomes a new self-consciousness (the specific figure of the slave) and immediate self-consciousness (that of the master) poses itself facing it. Whereas in the prior experience the life element was only the form of the emergence of differentiated self-consciousnesses, it is now integrated to a type of self-consciousness. The two moments of self-consciousness, self and life, confront each other now as two unique figures of consciousness. This is the case throughout the *Phenomenology*. Just as master and slave oppose each other as two figures of consciousness. so noble consciousness and base consciousness, and sinning consciousness and judging consciousness, oppose each other until finally the two essential moments of every dialectic are simultaneously distinguished and united as universal consciousness and individual consciousness. (Hyppolite, 78)

Inasmuch as Sussman comments at length upon the similarities between Hegel's dialectic of recognition and Freud's dialectic of misrecognition taken up in Lacan (1968)—here it may be worth recalling how Hyppolite[22] later came close to reading the *Phenomenology* as the discovery of the *historical unconscious* in the mind's history of its self-revelation, unfolding in:

(a) Self-consciousness as *misrecognition* of itself in the figures of solipsism, complete, flattery, hypocrisy: and

(b) as misrecognition that simultaneously involves partial recognition so they can chafe against each other until self-consciousness discovers its own truth.

If I suppress the other I suppress myself. Hyppolite moves the master-slave dialectic, which had arisen on the level of understanding, to a higher level of self-consciousness. Here the separation between the uncontrollable circumstances of life and the freely/contingent act of living toward death is internalized in the figure of the unhappy consciousness as the prototype of the failure of speculative consciousness to provide its own mirror:

(a) this is the experience of an embodied self whose nature is appropriable only through *appetitive desire*—and

---

22. Jean Hyppolite, "Hegel's Phenomenology and Psychoanalysis," in *New Studies in Hegel's Philosophy*, ed. Warren Steinkraus (New York: Holt, Rinehart and Winston, 1977), 57–70.

(b) the mutually recognized desire of self/other, or *anthropo-genetic desire*: so that

(c) self-consciousness desires its own desire: but it can achieve this only in the circuit of *others* who likewise desire their own desire in

    (i) mimetic rivalry—struggle to death;

    (ii) repression of desire—service, work, cultures

    (iii) sublimation of desire/*Bildung*.

It is Sartre who reverses the commonplaces of the master-slave dialectic. In Sartre, desire is social rather than presocial; the self is *solitary* and its language and emotions only *contingently* connected through insurmountable conflicts with others over whom it can establish no priority—contrary to the truce in the master-slave relation. If anything unifies Sartrean consciousness, it is its experience of nausea, its overwhelming disconnectedness. Yet Sartre allows the possibility of losing oneself in a melody or an "affair" (a love story)—perhaps even in the decision to write *La Nausée*. Such temptations are, however, to be scrupulously distinguished from the "bad faith" in both ascriptive and achieved identities (servant, leftist, professor) since—this side of God—human beings can never be what they "are." For all else, Sartre would say, I am an open wound in the world of others and this wound cannot be sutured either by Hegel's optimistic epistemology, in which I can know myself in the other for whom I am at first an object, or by Hegel's optimistic ontology, where an overarching totality is postulated in order to reconcile its own conflicting elements. On the contrary, my encounter with the other always dissolves these two options. Only through embracing the conflict that is emblematic of intrasubjectivity can I begin to work through the "original choices" that have patterned my life and its relationships and thus assume responsibility for the original violence in my passions, my knowledge and my relationships.

Although Sartre later attempts to reconcile subjectivity and collectivity in the complex structures of his *Critique of Dialectical Reason*, we may see in his earlier work the movement of the master-slave dialectic into its most forceful figure that I shall call *the recognition-scene of philosophy/psychoanalysis*, which looks back to Hegel and forward to Lacan (see commentary by Casey and Woody). It should be said that it is Hegel's dialectical concept of language and life that is borrowed by Lacan to redeem Freud's early biologism and to place psychoanalysis beyond all egological figures of consciousness from Descartes to Sartre. Hegel, so to speak, shows consciousness its mirror in the world, society, and history just as Marx later showed consciousness its true face in the mirror of production—and it is these two mirrors that are triangulated by Lacan's "mirror stage," that is, the infant's first misrecognition of its unified self reflected in a mirror.

Lacan regards the specular self as the originary model of alienation that is repeated on the levels of language and sexual difference in endless circuits of unfulfilled desire that cannot be broached either in incest or from the dead ends of sadomasochism (as we see in Benjamin's commentary on the *Story of O*). Nor can the subject of desire ever be absorbed in history since Lacan regards the individual's history as a history of the repression and subversion of (un)conscious desire that forever bars the way to *jouissance*, keeping death at the door of life:

> Symbols in fact envelop the life of man in a network so total that they join together, before he comes into the world, those who are going to engender him "by flesh and blood"; so total that they bring to his birth, along with the gifts of the stars, if not with the gifts of the fairies, the shape of his destiny; so total that they give the words that will make him faithful or renegade, the law of the acts that will follow him right to the very place where he is not yet and even beyond his death; and so total that through them his end finds its meaning in the last judgement, where the Word absolves his being or condemns it— unless he attain the subjective bringing to realization of being-for-death.[23]

Once philosophy becomes inseparable from literature and psychoanalysis (see commentary by Sussman and Benjamin) we may ask whether desire can ever again be reconciled in the other or whether "we" are forever condemned to the mirror play of the self's misrecognition in the other—master or mother, slave or lover, writer or reader:

> The fantasy of erotic domination embodies both the desire for independence and the desire for recognition. This inquiry intends to understand the process of alienation whereby these desires are transformed into erotic violence and submission. What we shall see, especially in voluntary submission to erotic domination, is a paradox in which the individual tries to achieve freedom through slavery, release through submission to control. Once we understand submission to be the *desire* of the dominated as well as their helpless fate, we may hope to answer the

---

23. Jaques Lacan, *Écrits: A Selection*, trans. Alan Sheridan (New York: W. W. Norton, 1977), 68.

central question, How is domination anchored in the hearts of those who submit to it?[24]

Can we still hold on to the romance of recognition and reconciliation at the end of a tortuous history or of a painful analysis? Here the initial problems we considered around solipsism appear to be swamped in narcissism. This may be due to the Freudian conception of origins in the infant fusion with the mother body whose own desire, like that of the father, may be "elsewhere." Here, if Adelman's commentary (supported by Hyppolite, Kelly, and Harris) on the Abraham story is considered, Freud may have restarted human history. In the biblical account, the misery of the "first man" arises because Adam is "nobody" and can only project his desires upon "Eve" as a first body. What the couple has to learn, as Benjamin also argues in her commentary, is to desire each in the other, to overcome narcissistic self-projection and the vicissitudes of sadomasochism in the labor and sacrifice of love.

The Bible account of the master-slave dialectic in effect sketches the structuralist account of the relation between the imaginary of Adam and Eve and the symbolic law, or real of reproductive labor. This is what permits Lacan to tease us with the taunt that "there are no sexual relations." What he means is that—to connect with our introductory remarks—there are no relations on the level of the imaginary that are social; it is only in the circuit of the symbolic that we are social beings. Whether we attribute the latter insight to Marx or to Lacan, it is insightful to turn the master-slave trope into a hermeneutic or deconstructive rule for resistance to the enslaving function of ideologies, canons, and classic texts. Thus, the text is not the mirror of either authorial or critical intention because, as Gadamer[25] has shown us, it is the text and its tradition that puts *us* into question. In effect, this recognition of our answerability to a tradition (literary, political, or scientific) modifies the contemporary dominance of "gaze hermeneutics," which so easily invokes an empty specularity that privileges contemporary ideologies of alienation and exclusion. Thus, the split-subject of language and interpretation must learn to struggle with interpretation on the levels of combat, play, and agony—all of which move in the light of the recognition of a potential reconciliation of the ratio of recognition and misrecognition—but within the limits of our respect for an unconscious residue of desire that cannot understand itself.

---

24. Jessica Benjamin, *The Bonds of Love: Psychoanalysis, Feminism, and the Problem of Domination* (New York: Pantheon, 1975), 52.
25. Hans-Georg Gadamer, *Truth and Method* (New York: Seabury Press, 1975).

It is essential to the practice of hermeneutics that we yield to a factor of dispossession distributed on the levels of language, difference, and capital, so that the ethics of communication is not brutalized in authoritarian commentary. We owe this insight to Habermas's reading of Hegel—if not to Hegel's critique of Kant's ethics of intra-/intersubjectivity. To expand upon the remarks in Habermas's commentary in the present text, Habermas argues that we need to take into account three domains of subject/object mediation, each with specific dialectics whose interaction determines the concept of the inter-/intrasubjectivity of spirit:

> Spirit is the communication of individuals (*Einselner*) in the medium of the universal, which is related to the speaking individuals as the grammar of a language is, and to the acting individuals as is a system of recognized norms. It does not place the moment of universality before that of singularity, but instead permits the distinctive links between these singularities.[26]

The communicative dialectic is not an event of conflict but the practical process through which a conflict is reconstituted from its originally split-off elements into a differentiated but reciprocal unity in which the relation of force is replaced by the relation of mutual recognition:

> The result is not the immediate recognition of oneself in the other, thus not reconciliation, but a position of the subjects with respect to each other on the basis of mutual recognition—namely, on the basis of the knowledge that the identity of the "I" is possible solely by means of the identity of the other, who in turn depends on my recognition, and who recognizes me.[27]

Kant's categorical imperative merely serves to universalize a solitary will and entirely abstract from the process of social interaction that is a constitutive feature of the moral community. Kant's moral message lacks, so to speak, an ethical medium. In Hegel's terms, moral consciousness must be achieved through the socialization processes intrinsic to the operation of language, labor, and society. In practice these systems interpenetrate one another. But while language is presupposed in the exchange of labor, the recognition of property and contracts, it cannot be reduced to the strategic discourse of material control and emancipation.

Finally, with the preceding considerations in mind, it may be useful in evaluating the current appeal of the psychoanalytic turn in the master-

---

26. Jürgen Habermas, *Theory and Practice* (Boston: Beacon, 1973), 146.
27. Ibid., 149.

slave trope to recall some comments by Ricoeur[28] upon the limits of a Freudian hermeneutics of culture (more expansively defended in Sussman's commentary). Against the divided, absent, and even dead subject of language and culture celebrated in postmodern abandonments of the Hegelian-Marxist narrative of subject and community reconciliation, Ricoeur adopts the following position on the subject of interpretation. He insists that the subject is never the subject(one) it supposes. This is because the split is not enough to define the subject in its telos, nor even the origins of the desire that projects it. Moreover, in Freud there is no archaeology of the subject except in contrast with its teleology which, as Hegel shows, is mediated through the figures of the mind that projects symbolic culture (spirit). Whereas Hegel links the teleology of mind to an archaeology of its life and desires, Freud fails to thematize the teleology of the soul in relation to the thematic of its archaeology of the unconscious. In Hegel—and I think the same is true in Marx— the progressive figuration of self-consciousness begins in desire, which is humanized from the standpoint of an intersubjective relation that moves into progressively more general institutions of humanity. But in Freud analysis is ruled by a principle of archaism, an inability to move beyond the death instinct and its vicissitudes within a primitive mythology. Despite current attempts to read psychoanalysis into Hegelianism, Freud failed to integrate the two economies of pleasure and recognition, that is, of (a) the desire to *have* what the father has, and (b) the desire *to be* like the father.

Thus, whereas Freud reduced the dialectic of desire to a movement of regression (a return to narcissism), any adequate theory of desire, sublimation, and creative work, Ricoeur argues, must reconstitute the grounds of desire that are productive of the cultural sublime in a threefold structure of the passions:

> I propose to reexamine the trilogy of fundamental feelings that I borrowed from the Kantian anthropology—the trilogy of the passions of having, power, and valuation or worth [*avoir, pouvoir, valoir*]—and to redo the exegesis of the three "quests" that the moralist knows only under the distorted mask of fallen figures— the "passions" of possession, domination, and pretension, or, in another language, of avarice, tyranny, and vanity [*Habsucht, Herrschsucht, Ehrsucht*].... I would like to show that this

---

28. Paul Ricoeur, *Freud and Philosophy: An Essay on Interpretation* (New Haven: Yale University Press, 1970).

threefold quest pertains to a phenomenology in the style of
Hegel and to an erotics in the style of Freud.

   It should be emphasized that the three spheres of meaning
through which the trajectory of feeling passes as it moves from
having, to power, and to worth, constitute regions of human
meanings that are in essence nonlibidinal. . . . By what, then,
are they constituted? It seems to me this is where the Hegelian
method is of help. One way of modernizing the Hegelian enterprise would be to constitute through progressive synthesis the
moments of "objectivity" that guide the human feelings as they
center on having, power, and worth. Such moments are indeed
moments of objectivity: to understand these affective factors,
which we name possession, domination, and valuation, is to
show that these feelings internalize a series of object-relations
that pertain not to a phenomenology of perception, but to an
economics, a politics, a theory of culture. The progress of this
constitution of objectivity should guide the investigation of the
affectivity proper to man. At the same time that they institute
a new relationship to things, the properly human quests of
having, power, and worth institute new relationships to other
persons, through which one can pursue the Hegelian process
of the reduplication of consciousness and the advancement of
self-consciousness.[29]

Here Ricoeur throws open the master-slave dialectic to a broad inquiry
into the dialectics of intra- and intersubjectivity that might well be
aligned with Habermas's project of a communicative model of knowledge—interests and ethics.

   It is hoped that teachers and students will find in the following pages
that marvelous experience offered in a year's teaching where the texts
chosen may serve to rework the master-slave discourses that operate in
the pedagogic situation itself. Inasmuch as student and teacher will be
alerted to the risks of bad faith on either side of their relationship, a step
will be taken through these readings toward the wider world where
sexism, racism, and ageism are major dimensions of mastery and servitude. At the same time, by recognizing the claims of minority groups
upon a political center (nomadic capitalism) that we regard as everywhere
and nowhere, we must be careful not to proliferate fragmentation without any hope of collective reconciliation. It is in relation to this risk

---

29. Ibid., 507–8.

that the Hegelian (and Marxist) tradition still has much to offer.[30] For many social critics, however, Hegel now stands as yet another philosopher we must learn to "forget" as we whirl around on the postmodern roller coaster of signs without referents, texts without authors, and interpretation without community.[31] Postmodernism affects to be both post-Hegelian and post-Marxist. The *Phenomenology of Spirit* and *Capital* are to be broken up, fragmented, and forgotten like the Berlin Wall. They stood for a totality of knowledge and power whose Enlightenment appeal is now so hollowed that it takes little more than Lyotard's finger to poke out the cracked eye of history: "The grand narrative has lost its credibility, regardless of what mode of unification it uses, regardless of whether it is a speculative narrative or a narrative of emancipation."[32]

We are now urged to abandon any standpoint upon our humanity that is not acutely modified by its encounter with other viewpoints whose claim upon our attention relativizes all perception, belief, and value. Western philosophy and politics have exhausted themselves molding the dead language all-knowing father or spirit. Postmodernists shuck off modernism by refusing to carry the old gods any further unto the settlements of the new age. Of course, we still mean to improve ourselves; at least, we are anxious not to court disaster. Yet we now place our faith nowhere else than in the last of all institutions—in the market, where everything exchanges without reference to anything but its exchangeability. Here history and politics are junk. Like junk, they nevertheless mimic the goods of the market because they find buyers whose world is not of this world and who cling to the possession of past ages in defiance of the market's law of fashion.

Marx's laws of history now rot like an abandoned railroad, a miserable reminder of a journey that went nowhere. Today we realize that history has no locomotive. There is no journey: the passengers have fled from the highway into the local markets to make their fortune without the guide books of philosophy—Each little piggy off to market. Such, at any rate, is the mininarrative reinvented to gather the events precipitated by the collapse of nonmarket regimes in Central and Eastern Europe. Meanwhile in Asia and in North and South America, the market is globalizing itself to achieve a force that has no counterpart in the local markets that are the fancy of minoritarian philosophy and politics.

---

30. *The Poverty of Postmodernism.*
31. John H. Smith, "U-Topian Hegel: Dialectic and Its Other in Poststructuralism," *The German Quarterly*, Spring 1987: 237–261.
32. Jean-François Lyotard, *The Postmodern Condition: A Report on Knowledge* (Minneapolis: The University of Minnesota Press, 1984).

Against such trends, I believe it may be useful to think of Hegel as the philosopher of cultural memory and to think of Marx and Freud as the analysts of how we collectively and individually refine ourselves from age to age rather than succumb to the cultural sirens that call for dumping the past and reinventing ourselves from moment to moment:

> Forgetfulness closes history whereas remembrance keeps open both the past and the utopian future of man. Remembrance is the womb of freedom and justice and must be cultivated long before men are able to name their slavery within the discourse of rational freedom and consensus. Remembrance is therefore cultivated as much in collective ritual, art and music as in rational discussion. Remembrance is the bodily infrastructure of political knowledge and action. It holds injustice to account and sustains the utopian hope that underlies the will to freedom and equality. Remembrance is musical, it generates literature, art, song, and poetry as well as the scientific culture of revolution. Remembrance is at the heart of what I have called wild sociology or wild politics. I have in mind by this the necessary recognition of the claims of that anonymous labor in the history of man's senses and intellect which have left us a world without any vision of human solidarity.[33]

Hegel can teach us how it is we move from "my" (*mein*) to "meaning" (*meinen*), just as Freud can show us how to shift from the illogic of the dream, symptom, or joke to the narrative of the family romance and the recuperation of desire. In Hegel language is the therapeutic agent, provided we deconstruct its reifications and totalizations (realism, solipsism, stoicism) that resist the actual history of our socialization (*Bildung*). In Freud, the deconstructive or analytic task is to reveal how the body of language is sexualized and the mind released only in sublimation—or through imaginative leaps of recollection that undo our cultural and psychic neuroses. We may nevertheless conclude with a wonderful passage from Marx in which he envisages a parallelism of the *two mirrors of humanity* in which the work of each is reflected in the other and in turn amplifies the enjoyment of self-expression:

> Supposing that we had produced in a human manner; each of us would in his production have doubly affirmed himself and his fellow men. I would have: (1) objectified in my production my individuality and its peculiarity and thus both in my activity

---

33. John O'Neill, ed., *On Critical Theory* (New York: Seabury, 1976), 4–5.

enjoyed an individual expression of my life and also in looking at the object have had the individual pleasure of realizing that my personality was objective, visible to the senses and thus a power raised beyond all doubt. (2) In your enjoyment or use of my product I would have had the direct enjoyment of realizing that I had both satisfied a human need by my work and also objectified the human essence and therefore fashioned for another human being the object that meets this need. (3) I would have been for you the mediator between you and the species and thus been acknowledged and felt by you as a completion of your own essence and a necessary part of yourself and have thus realized that I am confirmed both in your thought and in your love. (4) In my expressions of my life I would have fashioned your expression of your life, and thus in my own activity have realized my own essence, my human, my communal essence.

In that case our products would be like so many mirrors, out of which our essence shone.

Thus, in this relationship what occurred on my side would also occur on your.[34]

Here I think Marx offers us a model of reciprocity and recognition that should govern all forms of human endeavor, in work, in art, in science, and in everyday life. It is above all a mirror of the ideal academy, in teaching and in learning.

---

34. Karl Marx, *Early Texts*, 202.

PART I

Lordship and Bondage

LIST OF HEGEL'S WORKS CITED

GW — *Gesammelte Werke* (Hamburg: Meiner, 1968).

SW — *Sämtliche Werke*, ed. Georg Lasson and Johannes Hoffmeister (Leipzig and Hamburg: Meiner Verlag, 1905–).

PG — *Phänomenologie des Geistes*, SW, II.

PM — *The Phenomenology of Mind*, trans. J. B. Baillie, rev. 2nd ed. (London: George Allen and Unwin, 1949).

PS — *The Phenomenology of Spirit*, trans. A. V. Miller with analysis of the text and foreword by J. N. Findlay (Oxford: Clarendon, 1977).

PE — *Phénoménologie de l'esprit*, trans. Jean Hyppolite (Paris: Aubier, vol., I, 1939; vol. II, 1941).

Erste Druckschriften, SW, I.

Jenenser Logik, Metaphysik, und Naturphilosophie, SW, XVIIIa.

Jenenser Realphilosophie I, SW, XIX.

Jenenser Realphilosophie II, SW, XX.

Encyclopädie der philosophischen Wissenschaften, SW, V, VI.

System der Sittlichkeit, in Schriften zur Politik und Rechtsphilosophie, SW, VII.

"Über die wissenschaftliche Behandlungsarten des Naturrechts," in *Schriften zur Politik und Rechtsphilosophie*, SW, VII.

Theologische Jugendschriften, ed. Herman Nohl (Tübingen, 1907).

Early Theological Writings, trans. T. M. Knox (Chicago, 1948).

CHAPTER 1

Lordship and Bondage

G. W. F. Hegel

178. Self-consciousness exists in and for itself when, and by the fact that, it so exists for another; that is, it exists only in being acknowledged. The notion of this its unity in its duplication embraces many and varied meanings. Its moments, then, must on the one hand be held strictly apart, and on the other hand must in this differentiation at the same time also be taken and known as not distinct, or in their opposite significance. The twofold significance of the distinct moments has in the nature of self-consciousness to be infinite, or directly the opposite of the determinateness in which it is posited. The detailed exposition of the notion of this spiritual unity in its duplication will present us with the process of recognition.

179. Self-consciousness is faced by another self-consciousness; it has come *out of itself*. This has a twofold significance: first, it has lost itself, for it finds itself as an *other* being; second, in doing so it has superseded the other, for it does not see the other as an essential being, but in the other sees its own self.

180. It must supersede this otherness of itself. This is the supersession of the first ambiguity, and is therefore itself a second ambiguity. First, it must proceed to supersede the *other* independent being in order thereby to become certain of *itself* as the essential being; second, in so doing it proceeds to supersede its *own* self, for this other is itself.

181. This ambiguous supersession of its ambiguous otherness is equally an ambiguous return *into itself*. For first, through the supersession, it receives back its own self, because, by superseding *its* otherness, it again becomes equal to itself; but second, the other self-consciousness equally gives it back again to itself, for it saw itself in the other, but

supersedes this being of itself in the other and thus lets the other again
go free.

182. Now, this movement of self-consciousness in relation to another
self-consciousness has in this way been represented as the action of one
self-consciousness, but this action of the one has itself the double
significance of being both its own action and the action of the other as
well. For the other is equally independent and self-contained, and there
is nothing in it of which it is not itself the origin. The first does not
have the object before it merely as it exists primarily for desire, but as
something that has an independent existence of its own, which, therefore, it cannot utilize for its own purposes, if that object does not of its
own accord do what the first does to it. Thus, the movement is simply
the double movement of the two self-consciousnesses. Each sees the
other do the same as it does; each does itself what it demands of the
other, and therefore also does what it does only in so far as the other
does the same. Action by one side only would be useless because what
is to happen can only be brought about by both.

183. Thus, the action has a double significance not only because
it is directed against itself as well as against the other, but also because
it is indivisibly the action of one as well as of the other.

184. In this movement we see repeated the process that presented
itself as the play of forces, but repeated now in consciousness. What in
that process was *for us*, is true here of the extremes themselves. The
middle term is self-consciousness that splits into the extremes; and each
extreme is this exchanging of its own determinateness and an absolute
transition into the opposite. Although, as consciousness, it does indeed
come *out of itself*, yet, though out of itself, it is at the same time kept
back within itself, is *for-itself*, and the self outside it, is for *it*. It is aware
that it at once is, and is not, another consciousness, and equally that
this other is *for-itself* only when it supersedes itself as being-for-itself,
and is for-itself only in the being-for-self of the other. Each is for the other
the middle term, through which each mediates itself with itself and
unites with itself; and each is for-itself, and for-the-other, an immediate
being on its own account, which at the same time is such only through
this mediation. They *recognize* themselves as *mutually recognizing* one
another.

185. We have now to see how the process of this pure notion of
recognition, of the duplicating of self-consciousness in its oneness,
appears to self-consciousness. At first, it will exhibit the side of the
inequality of the two, or the splitting-up of the middle term into the
extremes which, as extremes, are opposed to one another, one being only
recognized, the other only *recognizing*.

186. Self-consciousness is, to begin with, simple being-for-self, self-equal through the exclusion from itself of everything else. For it, its essence and absolute object is "I"; and in this immediacy, or in this [mere] being, of its being-for-self, it is an *individual*. What is "other" for it is an unessential, negatively characterized object. But the "other" is also a self-consciousness; one individual is confronted by another individual. Appearing thus immediately on the scene, they are for one another like ordinary objects, *independent* shapes, individuals submerged in the being [or immediacy] of *life*—for the object in its immediacy is here determined as life. They are, *for each other*, shapes of consciousness that have not yet accomplished the movement of absolute abstraction, of rooting out all immediate being, and of being merely the purely negative being of self-identical consciousness; in other words, they have not as yet exposed themselves to each other in the form of pure being-for-self, or as self-consciousnesses. Each is indeed certain of its own self, but not of the other, and therefore its own self-certainty still has no truth. For it would have truth only if its own being-for-self had confronted it as an independent object, or, what is the same thing, if the object had presented itself as this pure self-certainty. But according to the notion of recognition this is possible only when each is for the other what the other is for it, only when each in its own self through its own action, and again through the action of the other, achieves this pure abstraction of being-for-self.

187. The presentation of itself, however, as the pure abstraction of self-consciousness consists in showing itself as the pure negation of its objective mode, or in showing that it is not attached to any specific existence, not to the individuality comm on to existence as such, that it is not attached to life. This presentation is a twofold action: action on the part of the other, and action on its own part. In so far as it is the action of the *other*, each seeks the death of the other. But in doing so, the second kind of action, action on its own part, is also involved; for the former involves the staking of its own life. Thus, the relation of the two self-conscious individuals is such that they prove themselves and each other through a life-and-death struggle. They must engage in this struggle, for they must raise their certainty of being *for-themselves* to truth, both in the case of the other and in their own case. And it is only through staking one's life that freedom is won; only thus is it proved that for self-consciousness, its essential being is not [just] being, not the *immediate* form in which it appears, not its submergence in the expanse of life, but rather that there is nothing present in it that could not be regarded as a vanishing moment, that it is only pure *being-for-self*. The individual who has not risked his life may well be recognized as a *person*, but he has not attained to the truth of this recognition as an independent

self-consciousness. Similarly, just as each stakes his own life, so each must seek the other's death, for it values the other no more than itself; its essential being is present to it in the form of an "other," it is outside of itself and must rid itself of its self-externality. The other is an *immediate* consciousness entangled in a variety of relationships, and it must regard its otherness as a pure being-for-self or as an absolute negation.

188. This trial by death, however, does away with the truth that was supposed to issue from it, and so, too, with the certainty of self generally. For just as life is the *natural* setting of consciousness, independence without absolute negativity, so death is the *natural* negation of consciousness, negation without independence, which thus remains without the required significance of recognition. Death certainly shows that each staked his life and held it of no account, both in himself and in the other; but that is not for those who survived this struggle. They put an end to their consciousness in its alien setting of natural existence, that is to say, they put an end to themselves, and are done away with as *extremes* wanting to be *for-themselves*, or to have an existence of their own. But with this there vanishes from their interplay the essential moment of splitting into extremes with opposite characteristics; and the middle term collapses into a lifeless unity that is split into lifeless, merely immediate, unopposed extremes; and the two do not reciprocally give and receive one another back from each other consciously, but leave each other free only indifferently, like things. Their act is an abstract negation, not the negation coming from consciousness, which supersedes in such a way as to preserve and maintain what is superseded, and consequently survives its own supersession.

189. In this experience, self-consciousness learns that life is as essential to it as pure self-consciousness. In immediate self-consciousness the simple "I" is absolute mediation, and has as its essential moment lasting independence. The dissolution of that simple unity is the result of the first experience; through this there is posited a pure self-consciousness, and a consciousness that is not purely for-self but for-another, that is, is a merely *immediate* consciousness, or consciousness in the form of *thinghood*. Both moments are essential. Since to begin with they are unequal and opposed, and their reflection into a unity has not yet been achieved, they exist as two opposed shapes of consciousness; one is the independent consciousness whose essential nature is to be for itself, the other is the dependent consciousness uhose essential nature is simply to live or to be for another. The former is lord, the other is bondsman.

190. The lord is the consciousness that exists *for-itself*, but no longer merely the notion of such a consciousness. Rather, it is a consciousness existing *for-itself* that is mediated with itself through another conscious-

ness, that is, through a consciousness whose nature it is to be bound up with an existence that is independent, or thinghood in general. The lord puts himself into relation with both of these moments, to a *thing* as such, the object of desire, and to the consciousness for which thinghood is the essential characteristic. And since he is (a) *qua* the notion of self-consciousness an immediate relation of *being-for-self*, but (b) is now at the same time mediation, or a being-for-self that is for-itself only through another, he is related (a) immediately to both, and (b) mediately to each through the other. The lord relates himself mediately to the bondsman through a being [a thing] that is independent, for it is just this which holds the bondsman in bondage; it is his chain from which he could not break free in the struggle, thus proving himself to be dependent, to possess his independence in thinghood. But the lord is the power over this thing, for he proved in the struggle that it is something merely negative; since he is the power over this thing and this again is the power over the other [the bondsman], it follows that he holds the other in subjection. Equally, the lord relates himself mediately to the thing through the bondsman; the bondsman, *qua* self-consciousness in general, also relates himself negatively to the thing, and takes away its independence; but at the same time the thing is independent vis-à-vis the bondsman, whose negating of it, therefore, cannot go the length of being altogether done with it to the point of annihilation; in other words, he only *works* on it. For the lord, on the other hand, the *immediate* relation becomes through this mediation the sheer negation of the thing, or the enjoyment of it. What desire failed to achieve, he succeeds in doing, namely, to have done with the thing altogether, and to achieve satisfaction in the enjoyment of it. Desire failed to do this because of the thing's independence; but the lord, who has interposed the bondsman between it and himself, takes to himself only the dependent aspect of the thing and has the pure enjoyment of it. The aspect of its independence he leaves to the bondsman, who works on it.

191. In both of these moments the lord achieves his recognition through another consciousness; for in them, that other consciousness is expressly something unessential, both by its working on the thing, and by its dependence on a specific existence. In neither case can it be lord over the being of the thing and achieve absolute negation of it. Here, therefore, is present this moment of recognition, namely, that the other consciousness sets aside its own being-for-self, and in so doing itself does what the first does to it. Similarly, the other moment too is present, that this action of the second is the first's own action; for what the bondsman does is really the action of the lord. The latter's essential nature is to exist only for himself; he is the sheer negative power for whom the thing

is nothing. Thus, he is the pure, essential action in this relationship, while the action of the bondsman is impure and unessential. But for recognition proper the moment is lacking, that what the lord does to the other he also does to himself, and what the bondsman does to himself he should also do to the other. The outcome is a recognition that is one-sided and unequal.

192. In this recognition the unessential consciousness is for the lord the object, which constitutes the *truth* of his certainty of himself. But it is clear that this object does not correspond to its notion, but rather that the object in which the lord has achieved his lordship has in reality turned out to be something quite different from an independent consciousness. What now really confronts him is not an independent consciousness, but a dependent one. He is, therefore, not certain of *being-for-self* truth of himself. On the contrary, his truth is in reality the unessential consciousness and its unessential action.

193. The *truth* of the independent consciousness is accordingly the servile consciousness of the bondsman. This, it is true, appears at first *outside* of itself and not as the truth of self-consciousness. But just as lordship showed that its essential nature is the reverse of what it wants to be, so too servitude in its consumation will really turn into the opposite of what it immediately is; as a consciousness forced back into itself, it will withdraw into itself and be transformed into a truly independent consciousness.

194. We have seen what servitude is only in relation to lordship. But it is a self-consciousness, and we have now to consider what as such it is in- and for-itself. To begin with, servitude has the lord for its essential reality; hence the *truth* for it is the independent consciousness that is *for-itself*. However, servitude is not yet aware that this truth is implicit in it. But it does in fact contain within itself this truth of pure negativity and being-for-self, for it has experienced this as its own essential nature. For this consciousness has been fearful, not of this or that particular thing or just at odd moments, but its whole being has been seized with dread. In that experience it has been quite unmanned, has trembled in every fiber of its being, and everything solid and stable has been shaken to its foundations. But this pure universal movement, the absolute melting-away of everything stable, is the simple, essential nature of self-consciousness, absolute negativity, *pure being-for-self*, which consequently is *implicit* in this consciousness. This moment of pure being-for-self is also *explicit* for the bondsman, for in the lord it exists for him as his *object*. Furthermore, his consciousness is not this dissolution of everything stable merely in principle; in his service he *actually* brings this about.

Through his service he rids himself of his attachment to natural existence in every single detail; and gets rid of it by working on it.

195. However, the feeling of absolute power both in general, and in the particular form of service, is only implicitly this disolution, and although the fear of the lord is indeed the beginning of wisdom, consciousness is not therein aware that it is a being-for-self. Through work, however, the bondsman becomes conscious of what he truly is. In the moment that corresponds to desire in the lord's consciousness, it did seem that the aspect of unessential relation to the thing fell to the lot of the bondsman, since in that relation the thing retained its independence. Desire has reserved to itself the pure negating of the object and thereby its unalloyed feeling of self. But that is the reason why this satisfaction is itself only a fleeting one, for it lacks the side of objectivity and permanence. Work, on the other hand, is desire held in check, fleetingness staved off; in other words, work forms and shapes the thing. The negative relation to the object becomes its *form* and something *permanent*, because it is precisely for the worker that the object has independence. This *negative* middle term or the formative *activity* is at the same time the individuality or pure being-for-self of consciousness that now, in the work outside of it, aquires an element of permanence. It is in this way, therefore, that consciousness, *qua* worker, comes to see in the independent being [of the object] its *own* independence.

196. But the formative activity has not only this positive significance that in it the pure being-for-self of the servile consciousness acquires an existence; it also has, in contrast with its first moment, the negative significance of *fear*. For, in fashioning the thing, the bondsman's own negativity, his being-for-self, becomes an object for him only through his setting at nought the existing *shape* confronting him. But this objective *negative* moment is none other than the alien being before which it has trembled. Now, however, he destroys this alien negative moment, posits *himself* as a negative in the permanent order of things, and thereby become *for-himself*, someone existing on his own account. In the lord, the being-for-self is an "other" for the bondsman, or is only *for*-him [i.e., is not his own]; in fear, the being-for-self is present in the bondsman himself; in fashioning the thing, he becomes aware that being-for-self belongs to him, that he himself exists essentially and actually in his own right. The shape does not become something other than himself through being made external to him; for it is precisely this shape that is his pure being-for-self, which in this externality is seen by him to be the truth. Through this rediscovery of himself by himself, the bondsman realizes that it is precisely in his work wherein he seemed to have only an alienated existence that he acquires a mind of his own. For this

reflection, the two moments of fear and service as such, as also that of formative activity, are necessary, both being at the same time in a universal mode. Without the discipline of service and obedience, fear remains at the formal stage, and does not extend to the known real world of existence. Without the formative activity, fear remains inward and mute, and consciousness does not become explicitly *for-itself*. If consciousness fashions the thing without that initial absolute fear, it is only an empty self-centered attitude; for its form or negativity in not negativity per se, and therefore its formative activity cannot give it a consciousness of itself as essential being. If it has not experienced absolute fear but only some lesser dread, the negative being has remained for it something external, its substance has not been infected by it through and through. Since the entire contents of its natural consciousness have not been jeopardized, determinate being still *in principle* attaches to it; having a "mind of one's own" is self-will, a freedom that is still enmeshed in servitude. Just as little as the pure form can become essential being for it, just as little is that form, regarded as extended to the particular, a universal formative activity, an absolute notion; rather it is a skill that is master over some things, but not over the universal power and the whole of objective being.

CHAPTER 2

Critique of Hegel

Karl Marx

Hegel has committed a double error.

The first is most evident in the *Phenomenology*, the birthplace of the Hegelian philosophy. When he considers, for emample, wealth and the power of the state as beings alienated from man's being, this happens only in their conceptual form. . . . They are conceptual beings and thus simply an alienation of pure, that is, abstract, philosophical thought. The whole process therefore ends with absolute knowledge. What these objects are alienated from and what they affront with their pretention to reality, is just abstract thought. The philosopher, who is himself an abstract form of alienated man, sets himself up as the measure of the alienated world. The whole history of externalization and the whole recovery of this externalization is therefore nothing but the history of the production of abstract, that is, absolute thought, logical, speculative thought. Alienation, which thus forms the real interest of this externalization and its supersession is the opposition inside thought itself of the implicit and the explicit, of consciousness and self-consciousness of object and subject, that is, it is the opposition inside thought itself of abstract thought and sensuous reality or real sensuous experience.

All other oppositions and their movements are only the appearance, the cloak, the exoteric form of these two opposites that alone are interesting and that give meaning to other, profane contradictions. What is supposed to be the essence of alienation that needs to be transcended is not that man's being objectifies itself in an inhuman manner in opposition to itself but that it objectifies itself in distinction from, and in opposition to, abstract thought.

The appropriation of man's objectified and alienated faculties is thus first only an appropriation that occurs in the mind, in pure thought, that is, in abstraction. It is the appropriation of these objects as thoughts and thought processes. Therefore in the *Phenomenology* in spite of its thoroughly negative and critical appearance and in spite of the genuine criticism, often well in advance of later developments, which is contained within it, one can already see concealed as a germ, as a secret potentiality, the uncritical positivism and equally uncritical idealism of Hegel's later works, this philosophical dissolution and restoration of existing empirical reality. Second, the vindication of the objective world for man (for example, the knowledge that sense perception is not abstract sense perception but human sense perception; that religion, wealth, etc., are only the alienated reality of human objectification, of human faculties put out to work and therefore only the way to true human reality), this appropriation or the insight into this process appears in Hegel in such a way that sense perception, religion, state power, and so on, are spiritual beings; for spirit alone is the true essence of man and the true form of spirit is thinking spirit, logical, speculative spirit. The human character of nature and of historically produced nature, the product of man, appears as such in that they are products of abstract mind, and thus phases of mind, conceptual beings. The *Phenomenology* is thus concealed criticism that is still obscure to itself and mystifying; but in so far as it grasps the alienation of man, even though man appears only in the form of mind, it contains all the elements of criticism concealed, often already prepared and elaborated in a way that far surpasses Hegel's own point of view. The "unhappy consciousness," the "honest consciousness," the struggle of the "noble and base consciousness" and so on., these single sections contain the elements, though still in an alienated form, of a criticism of whole spheres like religion, the state, civil life, and the like. Just as the essence, the object appears as a conceptual being, so the subject is always consciousness or self-consciousness, or rather the object only appears as abstract consciousness, man only as self-consciousness. Thus, the different forms of alienation that occur are only different forms of consciousness and self-consciousness. Since the abstract consciousness that the object is regarded as being, is only in itself a phase in the differentiation of self-consciousness, the result of the process is the identity of consciousness and self-consciousness, absolute knowledge, the process of abstract thought that is no longer outward-looking but only takes place inside itself. In other words, the result is the dialectic of pure thought.

Therefore, the greatness of Hegel's *Phenomenology* and its final product, the dialectic of negativity as the moving and creating principle, is on the one hand that Hegel conceives of the self-creation of man as a process, objectification as loss of the object, as externalization and the transcendence of this externalization. This means, therefore, that he grasps the nature of labor and understands objective man, true, because real, man as the result of his own labor. The real, active relationship of man to himself as a species-being or the manifestation of himself as a real species-being, that is, as a human being, is only possible if he uses all his species powers to create (which is again only possible through the cooperation of man and as a result of history), if he relates himself to them as objects, which can only be done at first in the form of alienation.

We shall now describe in detail the one-sidedness and limitations of Hegel using as a text the final chapter of the *Phenomenology* on absolute knowledge, the chapter that contains both the quintessence of the *Phenomenology*, its relationship to speculative dialectic, and also Hegel's attitude to both and to their interrelations.

For the moment we will only say this in anticipation: Hegel adopts the point of view of modern economics. He conceives of labor as the self-confirming essence of man. He sees only the positive side of labor, not its negative side. Labor is the means by which man becomes himself inside externalization or as externalized man. The only labor that Hegel knows and recognizes is abstract, mental labor. Thus, Hegel conceives of what forms the general essence of philosophy, the externalization of man who knows himself or externalized science that thinks itself, as the essence of labor and can therefore, in contrast to previous philosophy, synthesize its individual phases and present his philosophy as the philosophy. What other philosophers have done—to conceive of single phases of nature and man's life as phases of self-consciousness, indeed, of abstract self-consciousness—this Hegel knows by doing philosophy. Therefore, his science is absolute.

Let us now proceed to our subject.

Absolute knowledge. Last chapter of the *Phenomenology*.

The main point is that the object of consciousness is nothing but self-consciousness or that the object is only objectified self-consciousness, self-consciousness as object. (Positing that man = consciousness.)

It is necessary, therefore, to overcome the objects of consciousness. Objectivity as such is considered to be an alien condition not fitting man's nature and self-consciousness. Thus, the reappropriation of the objective essence of man, which was produced as something alien and determined by alienation, not only implies the transcendence of alienation, but also of objectivity. This means that man is regarded as a non-objective, spiritual being.

Hegel describes the process of the overcoming of the object of consciousness as follows:

The object does not only show itself as returning into the self: that is according to Hegel the one-sided conception of this process. Man is equated with self. But the self is only man abstractly conceived produced by abstraction. It is the self that constitutes man. His eye, his ear, and so on, take their niture from his self; each of his faculties belongs to his self. But in that case it is quite false to say: self-consciousness has eyes, ears, and faculties. Self-consciousness is rather a quality of human nature, of the human eye, and so on, human nature is not a quality of self-consciousness.

The self, abstracted and fixed for itself, is man as abstract egoist, egoism raised to its pure abstraction in thought (we will return to this point later).

For Hegel, the human essence, man, is the same as self-consciousness. All alienation of man's essence is therefore nothing but the alienation of self-consciousness. The alienation of self-consciousness is not regarded as the expression of the real alienation of man's essence reflected in knowledge and thought. The real alienation (or the one that appears to be real) in its inner concealed essence that has first been brought to the light by philosophy, is nothing but the appearance of the alienation of the real human essence, self-consciousness. The science that comprehends this is therefore called "phenomenology." Thus, all reappropriation of the alienated objective essence appears as an incorporation into self-consciousness. Man making himself master of his own essence is only self-consciousness making itself master of objective essence. The return of the object into the self is therefore the reappropriation of the object.

Universally expressed, the overcoming of he object of consciousness implies:

1. That the object presents itself to consciousness as about to disappear.
2. That it is the externalization of self-consciousness that creates "thingness."
3. That this externalization has not only a negative but also a positive significance.
4. That this significance is not only implicit and for us but also for self-consciousness itself.
5. For self-consciousness, the negative aspect of the object or its self-supersession has a positive significance, or, in other words, it knows the nullity of the object because it externalizes itself, for in this externalization it posits itself as object or establishes the object as itself, in virtue of the indivisible unity of being-for-itself.

6. At the same time, this other phase is also present that self-consciousness has just as much superseded and reabsorbed this alienation and objectivity and thus is at home in its other being as such.
7. This is the movement of consciousness and consciousness is therefore the totality of its phases.
8. Similarly, consciousness must have related itself to the object in all its determinations, and have conceived it in terms of each of these determinations. This totality of determinations makes the object intrinsically a spiritual being, and it becomes truly so for consciousness by the perception of every one of these determinations as the self, or by what was earlier called the spiritual attitude toward them.

Concerning 1. That the object as such presents itself to the consciousness as about to disappear is the above-mentioned return of the object into the self.

Concerning 2. The externalization of self-consciousness posits thingness. Because man is equated with self-consciousness, his externalized objective essence thingness is equated with externalized. (Thingness is what is an object for man and the only true object for him is the object of his essence or his objectified essence. Now since it is not real man as such—and therefore not nature, for man is only human nature—is made the subject, but only self-consciousness, the abstraction of man, thingness can only be externalized self-consciousness.) It is quite understandable that a natural, living being equipped and provided with objective, that is, material faculties should have real, natural objects for the object of its essence and that its self-alienation should consist in the positing of the real, objective world, but as something exterior to it, not belonging to its essence and overpowering it. There is nothing incomprehensible and paradoxical in that. Rather, the opposite would be paradoxical. It is equally clear that a self-consciousness, that is, its externalization can only post thingness, that is, only an abstract thing, a thing of abstraction and no real thing. It is further clear that thingness is not something self-sufficient and essential in contrast to self-consciousness, but a mere creation established by it. And what is established is not self-confirming, but only confirms the act of establishment that has for a moment, but only a moment, crystallized its energy into a product and in appearance given it the role of an independent and real being.

When real man of flesh and blood, standing on the solid, round earth and breathing in and out all the powers of nature posits his real objective faculties, as a result of his externalization, as alien objects, it is not the positing that is the subject; it is the subjectivity of objective faculties whose action must therefore be an objective one. An objective being has an objective effect and it would not have an objective effect if its being did not include an objective element. It only creates and posits objects because it is posited by objects, because it is by origin natural. Thus, in the act of positing it does not degenerate from its "pure activity" into creating an object; its objective product only confirms its objective activity, its activity as an activity of an objective, natural being.

We see here how consistent naturalism or humanism is distinguished from both idealism and materialism and constitutes at the same time their unifying truth. We see also how only naturalism is capable of understanding the process of world history.

(Man is a directly natural being. As a living natural being he is on the one hand equipped with natural vital powers and is an active natural being. These powers of his are dispositions, capacities, instincts. On the other hand, man as a natural, corporeal, sensuous, objective being is a passive, dependent, and limited being, like animals and plants, that is, the objects of his instincts are exterior to him and independent of him and yet they are objects of his need, essential objects that are indispensable for the exercise and confirmation of his faculties. The fact that man is an embodied, living, real, seatient, objective being means that he has real, sensuous objects as the objects of his life-expression. In other words, he can only express his being in real, sensuous objects. To be objective, natural and sentient and to have one's object, nature, and sense outside oneself or oneself to be object, nature, and sense for a third person are identical.) Hunger is a natural need; so it needs a natural object outside itself to satisfy and appease it. Hunger is the objective need of a body for an exterior object in order to be complete and express its being. The sun is the object of the plant, an indispensable object that confirms its lift, just as the plant is the object of the sun in that it is the expression of the sun's life-giving power and objective faculties.

A being that does not have its nature outside itself is not a natural being and has no part in the natural world. A being that has no object outside itself is not an objective being. A being that is not itself an object for a third being has no being for its object, that is, has no objective relationships and no objective existence.

A non-objective being is non-being.

Imagine a being that is neither itself an object nor has an object. First, such a being would be the only being, there would be no being outside it, it would exist solitary and alone. For as soon as there are objects outside myself, as soon as I am not alone, I am something distinct, a different reality from the object outside me. Thus, for this third object, I am a reality different from it, that is, its object. Thus, an object that is not the object of another being supposes that no objective being exists. As soon as I have an object, this object then has me as an object. But a non-objective being is an unreal, nonsensuous being that is only thought of, that is, an imaginary being, a being of abstraction. To be sensuous, that is, to be real, is to be an object of sense, a sensuous object, thus to have sensuous objects outside oneself, to have objects of sense perception. To be sentient is to suffer.

Man as an objective, sentient being is therefore a suffering being, and, since he is a being who feels his sufferings, a passionate being. Passion is man's faculties energetically striving after their object.

But man is not only a natural being; he is a human natural being. This means that he is a being that exists for himself, thus a species-being that must confirm and exercise himself as such in his being and knowledge. Thus, human objects are not natural objects as they immediately present themselves nor is human sense, in its purely objective existence, human sensitivity and human objectivity. Neither nature in its objective aspect nor in its subjective aspect is immediately adequate to the human being. And as everything natural must have an origin, so man too, has his process of origin, history, which can, however, be known by him and thus is a conscious process of origin that transcends itself. History is the true natural history of man. . . .

Third, since the positing of thingness is itself only an appearance, an act that contradicts the essence of pure activity, it must again be transcended and thingness be denied.

Concerning 3, 4, 5, 6. (3). This externalization of consciousness has not only negative but also positive significance and (4) this significance is not only implicit and for us, but also for self-consciousness itself. (5) For self-consciousness the negative aspect of the object or its self-transcendence, has a positive significance or, in other words, it knows the nullity of the object because it externalizes itself, for in this externalization it knows itself as object, or in virtue of the indivisible unity of being for itself, establishes the object for itself. (6) At the same time, this other phase is also present that self-consciousness has just as much superseded and reabsorbed this alienation and objectivity and thus is at home in its other being as such.

We have already seen that the appropriation of the alienated objective essence or the supersession of objectivity regarded as alienation, which must progress from indifferent strangeness to a really inimical alienation, means for Hegel at the same time, or even principally, the supersession of objectivity, since what offends self-consciousness in alienation is not the determinate character of the object but its objective character. The object is thus a negative, self-annulling being, a nullity. This nullity has for consciousness not only a negative but also a positive meaning, for this nullity of the object is precisely the self-confirmation of its non-objectivity and abstraction. For consciousness itself the nullity of the object has a positive significance because it knows this nullity, objective being as its own self-externalization; because it knows that this nullity only exists through its self-externalization. . . .

The way that consciousness is and that something is for it, is knowledge. Knowledge is its only act. Thus, something exists for it in so far as it knows this something. Knowing is its only objective relationship. It knows the nullity of the object, that is, that the object is not distinct from itself, the nonbeing of the object for itself, because it recognizes the object as its own self-externalization. In other words, it knows itself, knows knowledge as object, because the object is only the appearance of an object, a mirage, that essentially is nothing but knowledge itself that opposes itself to itself and is thus faced with a nullity, something that has no objectivity outside knowledge. Knowing knows that in so far as it relates itself to an object it is only exterior to itself, alienates itself. It knows that it only appears to itself as an object or that what appears to it as an object is only itself.

On the other hand, says Hegel, there is implied this other aspect: that consciousness has equally superseded this externalization and objectivity and taken it back into itself and thus is at home in its other being as such.

In this discussion we have assembled all the illusions of speculation.

First, self-consciousness at home in its other being as such. It is, therefore, if we here abstract from the Hegelian abstraction and substitute man's self-consciousness for self-consciousness, at home in its other being as such. This implies, for one thing, that consciousness, knowing as knowing, thinking as thinking, pretends to be directly the opposite of itself, sensuous reality, life; it is thought overreaching itself in thought (Feuerbach). This aspect is entailed in so far as consciousness as mere consciousness is not offened by alienated objectivity but by objectivity as such.

The second implication is that in so far as self-conscious man has recognized the spiritual world (or the general spiritual mode of existence of his world) as self-externalization and superseded it, he nevertheless confirms it again in this externalized firm and declares it to be his true being, restores it, pretends to be at home in his other being as such. Thus, for example, after the supersession of religion and the recognition of it as the product of self-alienation, man nevertheless finds himself confirmed in religion as such. Here is the root of Hegel's false positivism or his merely apparent criticism. This is what Feuerbach has characterized as the positing, negation, and restoration of religion or theology, although it should be understood to have a wider application. Thus, reason finds itself at home in unreason as such. Man who has recognized that he has been leading an externalized life in law, politics, and so on, leads his true human life in this externalized life as such. Thus, the true knowledge and the true life is the self-affirmation and self-contradiction in contradiction with itself and with the knowledge and the nature of the object.

So there can be no more question of a compromise on Hegel's part with religion, the state, and so on, for this falsehood is the falsehood of his very principle.

If I know religion as externalized human self-consciousness, then what I know in it as religion is not my self-consciousness, but the conirmation in it of my externalized self-consciousness. Thus, I know that the self-consciousness that is part of my own self is not confirmed in religion, but rather in the abolition and supersession of religion.

Therefore, in Hegel the negation of the negation is not the confirmation of true being through the negation of apparent being. It is the confirmation of apparent being or self-alienated being in its denial or the denial of this apparent being as a being dwelling outside man and independent of him, its transformation into a subject.

Therefore, supersession plays a very particular role in which negation and conservation are united.

PART II

Desire and Recognition

CHAPTER 3

Desire and Work in the Master and Slave

Alexandre Kojève

There is no human existence without consciousness or without self-consciousness—that is, without revelation of being by speech or without desire that reveals and creates the I. That is why in the *Phenomenology*—that is, in phenomenological anthrophology—the elmentary possibility of revelation of given being by speech (implied in the chapter "Sensual Certainty") on the one hand, and on the other action that destroys or negates given being (action that arises from and because of desire), are two irreducible givens, which the *Phenomenology* presupposes as its premises. But these premises are not sufficient.

The analysis that uncovers the constituent role of desire enables us to understand who human existence is possible only with an animal existence as its basis: a stone or a plant (having no desire) never attains self-consciousness and consequently philosophy. But animals do not attain it either. Animal desire, therefore, is a necessary, but not a sufficient, condition of human and philosophical existence. And here is why.

Animal desire—hunger, for example—and the action that flows from it, negate, destroy the natural given. By negating it, modifying it, making it its own, the animal raises itself above this given. According to Hegel, the animal realizes and reveals its superiority to plants by eating them. But by feeding on plants, the animal depends on them and hence does not manage truly to go beyond them. Generally speaking, the greedy emptiness—or the I—which is revealed by biological desire is filled—by the biological action that flows from it—only with a natural, biological content. Therefore, the I, or the pseudo-I, realized by the action satisfaction of this desire, is just as natural, biological, material, as that toward which the desire and action are directed. The animal raises itself above the nature that is negated in its animal desire only to fall back into it immediately by the satisfaction of this desire. Accordingly, the animal attains only *Selbst-gefühl*, sentiment of self, but not *Selbst-bewusstsein*, self-consciousness—that is, it cannot speak of itself, it cannot say, "I . . ." And this is so because the animal does not really transcend itself as given—that is, as body; it does not rise *above* itself in order to *come back* toward itself; it has no distance with respect to itself in order to contemplate itself.

For self-consciousness to exit, for philosophy to exist, there must be transcendence of self with respect to self as given. And this is possible, according to Hegel, only if desire is directed not toward a given being, but toward a nonbeing. To desire being is to fill oneself with this given being, to enslave oneself to it. To desire nonbeing is to liberate oneself from being, to realize one's autonomy, one's freedom. To be anthropogenetic, then, desire must he directed toward a nonbeing—that is, toward another desire, another greedy emptiness, another *I*. For desire is absence of being (to be hungry is to be deprived of food); it is a nothingness that *nihilates* in being, and not a being that *is*. In other words, action that is destined to satisfy an animal desire, which is directed toward a given, existing thing, never succeeds in realizing a human, self-conscious I. Desire is human—or, more exactly, "humanizing," "anthropogenetic"—only provided that it is directed toward an other desire and an other desire. To be human, man must act not for the sake of subjugating a thing, but for the sake of subjugating another desire (for the thing). The man who desires a thing humanly acts not so much to possess the thing as to make another recognize his right—as will be said later—to that thing, to make another recognize him as the owner of the thing. And he does this—in the final analysis—in order to make the other recognize his superiority over the other. It is only desire of such a recognition (*Anerkennung*), it is only action that flows from, such a desire, that creates, realizes, and reveals a human, nonbiological I.

Therefore, the *Phenomenology* must accept a third irreducible premise: the existence of several desires that can desire one another mutually, each of which wants to negate, to assimilate, to make its own, to subjugate, the other desire as desire. This multiplicity of desires is just as "undeducible" as the fact of desire itself. By accepting it, one can already foresee, or understand ("deduce"), what human existence will be.

If, on the one hand—as Hegel says—self-consciousness and man in general are, finally, nothing but desire that tries to be satisfied by being recognized by another desire in its exclusive right to satisfaction, it is obvious that man can be fully realized and revealed—that is, be definitively satisfied—only by realizing a universal recogniztion. Now if—on the other hand—there is a multiplicity of these desires for universal recognition, it is obvious that the action that is born of these desires can—at least in the beginning—be nothing but a life and death fight "Kampf auf Leben und Tod"). A fight, since each will want to subjugate the other, *all* the others, by a negating, destroying action. A life-and-death fight because desire that is directed toward a desire directed toward a desire goes beyond the biological given, so that action carried out for the sake of this desire is not limited by this given. In other words, man will risk his biological life to satisfy his nonbiological desire. And Hegel says that the being that is incapable of putting its life in danger in order to attain ends that are not immediately vital—that is, the being that cannot risk its life in a fight for recognition, in a fight for pure prestige— is *not* a truly human being.

Therefore, human, historical, self-conscious existence is possible only where there are, or—at least—where there have been, bloody fights, wars for prestige. And thus it was the sounds of one of these fights that Hegel heard while finishing his *Phenomenology*, in which he became conscious of himself by answering his question, "What am I?"

But it is obvious that the three already mentioned premises in the *Phenomenology* are not sufficient to explain the possibility of the Battle of Jena. Indeed, if *all* men were as I have just said, every fight for prestige would end in the death of at least one of the adversaries. That is to say, finally, there would remain only one man in the world, and to Hegel— he would no longer be, he would not be, a human being, since the human reality is nothing but the fact of the recognition of one man by another man.

To explain the fact of the Battle of Jena, the fact of the history that that battle completes, one must therefore posit a fourth and last irreducible premise in the *Phenomenology*. One must suppose that the fight ends in such a way that *both* adversaries remain alive. Now, if this is to occur, one must suppose that one of the adversaries gives in to the other and submits to him, recognizing him without being recognized by him. One must suppose that the fight ends in the victory of the one who is ready to go all the way over the one who—faced with death— does not manage to raise himself above his biological instinct of preservation (identity). To use Hegel's terminology, one must suppose that there is a victor who becomes the becomes the master of the vanquished; or, if one prefers, a vanquished who becomes the slave of the victor. The existence of a difference between master and slave or, more exactly, the possibility of a difference between future master and future slave is the fourth and last premise of the *Phenomenology*.

The vanquished has subordinated his human desire for recognition to the biological desire to preserve his life: this is what determines and reveals—to him and to the victor—his inferiority. The victor has risked his life for a nonvital end: and this is what determines and reveals—to him and to the vanquished—his superiority over biological life and, consequently, over the vanquished. Thus, the difference between master and slave is realized in the existence of the victor and of the vanquished, and it is recognized by both of them.

The master's superiority over nature, founded on the risk of his life in the fight for prestige, is realized by the fact of the slave's work. This work is placed between the master and nature. The slave transforms the given conditions of existence so as to make them conform to the master's demands. Nature, transformed by the slave's work, serves the master, without his needing to serve it in turn. The enslaving side of the interaction with nature falls to the lot of the slave: by enslaving the slave and forcing him to work, the master enslaves nature and thus realizes his freedom in nature. Thus, the master's existence can remain exclusively warlike: he fights, but does not work. As for the slave, his existence is reduced to work (*Arbeit*, which he executes in the master's service (*Dienst*). He works, but does not fight. And according to Hegel, only action carried out in another's service is work (*Arbeit*) in the proper sense of the word: an essentially human and humanizing action. The being that acts to satisfy its own instincts, which—as such—are always natural, does not rise above nature: it remains a natural being, an animal. But by acting to satisfy an instinct that is *not* my own, I am acting in relation to an idea, a nonbiological end. And it is this transformation of nature in relation to a nonmaterial idea that is work in the proper sense of the word: work that creates a nonnatural, technical, humanized world adapted to the human desire of a being that has demonstrated and realized its superiority to nature by risking its life for the nonbiological end of recognition. And it is only this work that could finally produce the table on which Hegel wrote his *Phenomenology* and which was a part of the content of the I that he analyzed in answering his question, "What am I?"

Generally speaking, by accepting the four premises mentioned above, namely: (1) the existence of the revelation of given being by speech, (2) the existence of a desire engendering an action that negates, transforms, given being, (3) the existence of several desires, which can desire one another mutually, and (4) the existence of a possibility of difference between the desires of (future) masters and the desires of (future) slave—by accepting these four premises, we understand the possibility of a historical process, of a history, which is, in its totality, the history of the fights and the work that finally ended in the wars of Napoleon and the table on which Hegel wrote the *Phenomenology* in order to understand both those wars and that table. Inversely, in order to explain the possibility of the *Phenomenology*, which is written on a table and which explains the wars of Napoleon, we must suppose the four premises mentioned.[1]

In fine, then, we can say this: man was born and history began with the first fight that ended in the appearance of a master and a slave. That is to say that man—at his origin—is always either master or slave; and that true man can exist only where there is a master *and* a slave. (If they are to be human, they must be at least *two* in number.) And universal history, the history of the interaction between men and of their interaction with nature, is the history of the interaction between warlike masters and working slaves. Consequently, history stops at the moment when the difference, the opposition, between master and slave disappears: at the moment when the master will cease to be master, because he will no longer have a slave; and the slave will cease to be slave, because he will no longer have a master (although the slave will not become master in turn, since he will have no slave).

Now, according to Hegel, it is in and by the wars of Napoleon, and, in particular, the Battle of Jena, that this completion of history is realized through the dialectical overcoming (*Aufheben*) of both the master and the slave. Consequently, the presence of the Battle of Jena in Hegel's consciousness is of capital importance. It is because Hegel hears the sounds of that battle that he can know that history is being completed or has been completed, that—consequently—*his* conception of the world is a *total* conception, that *his* knowledge is an *absolute* knowledge.

---

1. We could try to deduce the first premise from the other three: speech (*Logos*) that reveals being is born in and from the slave's self-consciousness (through work). As for the fourth premise, it postulates the act of freedom. For nothing predisposes the future master to mastery, just as nothing predisposes the future slave to slavery; each can (freely) create himself as master or slave. What is given, therefore, is not the difference between master and slave, but hte free act that creates it. Now, the free act is by definition "undeducible." Here, then, we have what is indeed an absolute premise. All we can say is that without the primordial free act that creates mastery and slavery, history and philosophy could not exist. Now, this act in turn presupposes a multiplicity of desires that desire one another mutually.

However, to know this, to know that he is the thinker who can realize the absolute science, he must know that the Napoleonic Wars realize the dialectical synthesis of the master and the slave. And to know this, he must know on the one hand, what the essence (*Wesen*) of the master and the slave is; and, on the other, how and why history, which began with the "first" fight for prestige, ended in the wars of Napoleon. . . .

History, that universal human process that conditioned the coming of Hegel, of the thinker endowed with an absolute knowledge, a process that that thinker must understand in and by a *phenomenology* before he can realize this absolute knowledge in the "system of science"— universal history, therefore, is nothing but the history of the dialectical— that is, active—relation between master and slavery. Hence, history will be completed at the moment when the synthesis of and master and the slave is realized, that synthesis that is the shole man, the citizen of the universal and homogeneous state created by Napoleon.

This conception, according to which history is a dialectic or an interaction of master and slavery, permits us to understand the meaning of the division of the historical process into three great periods (of very unequal lengths, incidentally). If history begins with the fight after which a master dominates a slave, the first historical period must certainly be the one in which human existence is entirely determined by the existence of the master. Throughout this period, then, it is mastery that will reveal its essence by realizing its existential possibilities through action. But if history is only a dialectic of mastery and slavery, this latter too must be entirely revealed by being completely realized through action. Therefore, the first period must be completed in which human existence will be determined by slavish existence. Finally, if the end of history is the synthesis of mastery and slavery and the understanding of that synthesis, these two periods must be followed by a third, during which human existence, in some sense neutralized, synthetic, reveals itself to itself by actively realizing its own possibilities. But this time, these possibilities also imply the possibility of understanding oneself fully and definitively—that is, perfectly.

But of course, . . . in order to understand what history is, it is not sufficient to know that history has three periods. One must also know what each of them is, one must understand the why and the how of each of them and of the transition from one to another. Now, to understand this, one must know what is the *Wesen*, the essential-reality, of mastery and slavery, what is the essence of the two principles which, in their interaction, are going to realize the process being studied.

Let us begin with the master.

The master is the man who went all the way in a fight for prestige, who risked his life in order to be recognized in his absolute superiority by another man. That is, to his real, natural biological life he preferred something ideal, spiritual, nonbiological: the fact of being *anerkannt*, of being recognized in and by a consciousness, of bearing the name of "master," of being called "master." Thus, he "brought to light," proved (*bewąhrt*), realized, and revealed his superiority over biological existence, over *his* biological existence, over the natural world in general and over everything that knows itself and that he knows to be bound to this world, in particular, over the slave. This superiority, at first purely ideal, which consists in the mental fact of being recognized and of knowing that he is recognized as the master by the slave, is realized and materialized through the slave's work. The master, who was able to force the slave to recognize him as master, can also force the slave to work for him, to yield the result of his action to him. Thus, the master no longer needs to make any effort to satisfy his (natural) desires. The enslaving side of this satisfaction has passed to the slave: the master, by dominating the working slave, dominates nature and lives in it as master. Now, to preserve oneself in nature without fighting against it is to live in *Genuss*, in enjoyment. And the enjoyment that one obtains without making any effor is lust, pleasure. The life of the master, to the extent that it is not bloody fighting, fighting for prestige with human beings, is a life of pleasure.

At first glance, it stems that the master realizes the peak of human existence, being the man who is fully satisfied (*befriedigt*), in and by his real existence, by what he is. Now in fact, this is not at all the case.

What is this man, what does he *want* to be, if not a master? It was to become master, to be master, that he risked his life, and not to live a life of pleasure. Now, what he wanted by engaging in the fight was to be recognized by another—that is, by someone *other* than himself but who is like him, by another man: But in fact, at the end of the fight, he is recognized only by a slave. To be a man, he wanted to be recognized by another man. But if to be a man is to be master, the slave is not a man, and to be recognized by a slave is not to be recognized by another master. He would have to be recognized by another master. But this is impossible, since—by definition—the master prefers death to slavish recognition of another's superiority. In short, the master never succeeds in realizing his end, the end for which he risks his very life. The master can be satisfied only in and by death, *his* death or the death of his adversary. But one cannot be *befriedigt* (fully satisfied) by what *is*, by what *is*, in and by death.) For death *is* not, the dead man *is* not. And what *is*, what lives, is only slave. Now, is it worthwhile to risk one's life in order to know that one is recognized by a slave? Obviously not. And that is why, to the extent that the master is not made brutish by his pleasure and enjoyment, when he takes account of what his true end and the motive of his actions—that is, his warlike action—are, he will *not*, he will *never* be *befriedigt*, satisfied by waht *is*, by what *he* is.

In other words, mastery is an existential impasse. The master can either make brutish in pleasure or die on the field of battle as master, but he cannot live consciously with the knowledge that he is satisfied by what he is. Now, it is only conscious satisfaction, *Befriedigung*, that can complete history, for only the man who knows he is satisfied by what he is no longer strives to go beyond himself, to go beyond what he is and what is, through action that transforms nature, through action that creates history. If history must be completed, if absolute knowlelge must be possible, it is only the slave who can do it, by attaining satisfaction. And that is why Hegel says that the "truth" (= revealed reality) of the master is the slave. The human ideal, born in the master, can be realized and revealed, can become *Wahrheit* (truth), only in and by slavery.

To be able to stop and understand himself, a man must be satisfied. And for this, of course, he must cease to be a slave. But to be able to cease being slave, he must have been a slave. And since there are slaves only where there is a master, mastery, while itself an impasse, is "justified" as a necessary stage of the historical existence that leads to the absolute science of Hegel. The master appears only for the sake of engendering the slave who "overcomes" (*aufbebt*) him as master, while thereby "overcoming" himself as slave. And this slave who has been "overcome" is the one who will be satised by what he *is* and will understand that he is satisfied in and by Hegel's philosophy, in and by the *Phenomenology*. The master is only the "catalyst" of the history that will be realized, completed, and "revealed" by the slave or the ex-slave who has become a citizen.

But let us first see what the slave is in the beginning, the slave of the master, the slave not yet satisfied by the citizenship that realizes and reveals his freedom.

Man became a slave because he feared death. To be sure, on the one hand this fear (*Furcht*) reveals his dependence with respect to nature and thus justifies his dependence with respect to the master, who dominates nature. But on the other hand, this same fear—according to Hegel—has a positive value, which conditions the slave's superiority to the master. Through animal fear of death (*Angst*) the slave experienced the dread or the terror (*Furcht*) as nothingness, of his nothingness. He caught a glimpse of himself as nothingness, he understood that his whole existence was but a "surpassed," "overcome" (*aufgehoben*) death—a nothingness maintained in being. Now—we have seen it and shall see it again—the profound basis of Hegelian anthropology is formed by this idea that man is not a being that *is* in an eternal identity to itself in space, but a nothingness that *nihilates* as time in spatial being, through the *negation* of this being—through the negation or transformation of the given, starting from an idea or an ideal that does not yet exist, that is still nothingness (a "project")—through negation that is called the *action (Tat)* of fighting and of work *(Kampf und Arbeit)*. Hence the slave, who—through fear of death—grasps the (human) nothingness that is at the foundation of his (natural) being, understands himself, understands man, better than the master does. From the "first" fight, the slave has an intuition of the human reality, and that is the profound reason that it is finally he, and not the master, who will complete history by revealing the truth of man, by revealing his reality through Hegelian science.

But—still thanks to the master—the Slave has another advantage, conditioned by the fact that he works and that he works in the service *(Dienst)* of another, that he serves another by working. To work for another is to act contrary to the instincts that drive man to satisfy his own needs. There is no instinct that forces the slave to work for the master. If he does it, it is from fear of the master. But this fear is not the same as the fear he experienced at the moment of the fight: the danger is no longer immediate; the slave only knows that the master can kill him; he does not see him in a murderous posture. In other words, the slave who works for the master represses his instincts in relation to an idea, a concept.[2] And that is precisely what makes his activity a specifically *human* activity, a work, an *Arbeit*. By acting, he negates, he transforms the given, nature, *his* nature; and he does it in relation to an idea, to what does not exist in the biological sense of the word, in relation to the idea of a master—that is, to an essentially social, human, historical notion. Now, to be able to transform the natural given in relation to nonnatural idea is to possess a technique. And the idea that engenders a technique is a scientific idea, a scientific concept Finally, to possess scientific concepts is to be endowed with understanding, *Verstand*, the faculty of abstract notion.

Understanding, abstract thought, science, technique, the arts—all these, then, have their origin in the forced work of the slave. Therefore, the slave, and not the master, is the one who realizes all that has to do with these things; in particular Newtonian physics (which so impressed

---

2. According to Hegel, concept *(Begriff)* and understanding *(Verstand)* are born of the slave's work, whereas sensual knowledge *(sinnliche Gewissheit)* is an irreducible given. But one could try to deduce *all* human understanding from work.

Kant), that physics of force and of law, which—according to Hegel—are in the final analysis the force of the victor in the fight for prestige and the law of the master who is recognized by the slave.

But these are not the only advantages procured by work; work will also open the way to freedom or—more exactly—to liberation.

Indeed, the master realized his freedom by surmounting his instinct to live in the fight. Now, by working for another, the slave, too, surmounts his instincts, and—by thereby raising himself to thought, to science, to technique, by transforming nature in relation to an idea—he, too, succeeds in dominating nature and his "nature"—that is, the same nature that dominated him at the moment of the fight and made him the slave of the master. Through his work, therefore, the slave comes to the same result to which the master comes by risking his life in the fight: he no longer depends on the given, natural conditions of existence; he modifies them, starting from the idea he has of himself. In becoming conscious of this fact, therefore, he becomes conscious of his freedom (*Freiheit*), his autonomy (*Selbständigkeit*). And, by using the thought that arises from his work, he forms the abstract notion of the freedom that has been realized in him by this same work.

To be sure, in the slave properly so-called this notion of freedom does not yet correspond to a true reality. He frees himself mentally only thanks to forced work, only because he is the slave of a master. And he remains in fact this slave. Thus, he frees himself, so to speak, only to be a slave freely, to be still more a slave than he was before having formed the idea of freedom. However, the insufficiency of the slave is at the same time his perfection: this is because he *is* not acatually free, because he has an idea of freedom, an idea that is not realized but that can be realized by the conscious and voluntary transformation of given existence, by the active abolition of slavery. The master, on the other hand, *is* free; his idea of freedom is not abstract. That is why it is not an idea in the proper sense of the word: an *ideal* to realize. And that is why the master never succeeds in going beyond the freedom that is realized in himself and the insufficiency of that freedom. Progress in the realization of freedom can be carried out only by the slave, who begins with a non-realized ideal of freedom. And it is because he has an ideal, an abstract idea, that progress in the realization of freedom can be completed by an understanding of freedom, by the birth of the absolute idea (*absolute Idee*) of human freedom, revealed in and by absolute knowledge.

Generally speaking, it is the slave, and only he, who can realize a progress, who can go beyond the given and—in particular—the given that he himself is. On the one hand, as I just said, possessing the idea of freedom and not being free, he is led to transform the given (social) conditions of his existence—that is, to realize a historical progress. Further-more—and this is the important point—this progress has a meaning for him that it does not and cannot have for the master. The master's free-dom, engendered in and by the fight, is an impasse. To realize it, he must make it recognized by a slave, he must transform whoever is to recognize it into a slave. Now, my freedom ceases to be a dream, an illusion, an abstract idea, only to the extent that it is universally recognized by those whom I recognize as worthy of recognizing it. And this is precisely what the master can never obtain. His freedom, to be sure, is recognized. Therefore, it is real. But it is recognized only by slaves. Therefore, it is insufficient in its reality; it cannot satisfy him who realizes it. And yet, as long as it remains a master's freedom, the situation cannot be other-wise. On the other hand, if—at the start—the slave's freedom is recog-nized by no one but himself, if, consequently, it is purely abstract, it can end in being realized and in being realized in its perfection. For the slave recognizes the human reality and dignity of the master. Therefore, it is sufficient for him to impose his liberty on the master in order to attain the definitive satisfaction that mutual recognition gives and thus to stop the historical process.

Of course, in order to do this, he must fight against the master, that is to say—precisely—he must cease to be a slave, surmount his fear of death. He must become other than what he is. Now, in contrast to the warlike, master who will always remain what he already *is*—that is, master—the working slave can change, and he actually does change, thanks to his work.

The human action of the master reduces to risking his life. Now, the risk of life is the same at all times and in all places. The risk itself is what counts, and it does not matter whether a stone axe or a machine gun is being used. Accordingly, it is not the fight as such, the risk of life, but *work* that one day produces a machine gun, and no longer an axe. The purely warlike attitude of the master does not vary throughout the centuries, and therefore it cannot engender a historical change. Without the slave's work, the "first" fight would be reproduced indefi-nitely: nothing would change in it; it would change nothing in the master; hence nothing would change in man, through man, for man; the world would remain identical to itself, it would be nature and not a human, historical world.

Quite different is the situation created by work. Man who works transforms given nature. Hence, if he repeats his act, he repeats it in different conditions, and thus his act itself will be different. After making the first axe, man can use it to make a second one, which, by that very fact, will be another, a better axe. Production transforms the means of production; the modification of means simples production; and so on. Where there is work, then, there is necessarily change, progress, historical evolution.[3]

Historical evolution. For what changes as a result of work is not only the natural world; it is also—and even especially—man himself. Man, in the beginning, depends on the given, narural conditions of his existence. To be sure, he can rise above these conditions by risking his life in a fight for prestige. But in this risk he somehow negates the totality of these conditions, which are still the same; he negates the totality of these conditions, which are still the same; he negates them en masse, without modifying them, and this negation is always the same. Accordingly, the freedom that he creates in and by this act of negation does not depend on the particular forms of the given. It is only by rising above the given conditions through negation brought about in and by work that man remains in contact with the concrete, which varies with space and time. That is why he changes himself by transforming the world.

The scheme of historical evolution, therefore, is as follows:

At the start, the future master and the future slave are both determined by a given, natural world independent of them: hence, they are not yet truly human, historical beings. Then, by risking his life, the master rises himself above given nature, above his given (animal) "nature," and becomes a human being, a being that creates itself in and by its conscious negating action. Then, he forces the slave to work. The latter changes the real given world. Hence, he, too, raises himself above nature, above his (animal) "nature," since he succeeds in making it other than it was. To be sure, the slave, like the master, like man in general, is determined by the real world. But since this world has been changed, he changes as well.[4] And since it was *he* who changed the world, it is *he* who changes himself, whereas the master changes only through the slave. Therefore, the historical process, the historical becoming of the human being, is the product of the working slave and not of the warlike master. To be sure, without the master, there would have been no history;

---

3. A manufactured object incarnates an idea (a "project") that is independent of the material *hic et nunc*; that is why these objects can be "exchanged." Hence the birth of an "economic," specifically human world, in which money, capital, interest, salary, and so on appear.

4. Animals also have (pseudo) techniques: the first spider changed the world by weaving the first web. Hence it would be better to say: the world changes essentially (and becomes human) through "exchange," which is possible only as a result of work that realizes a "project."

but only because without him there would have been no slave and hence no work.

Therefore—once more—thanks to his work, the slave *can* change and become other than he is, that is, he can—finally—cease to be a slave. Work is *Bildung*, in the double meaning of the word: on the one hand, it forms, transforms the world, humanizes it by making it more adapted to man; on the other, it transforms, forms, educates man, it humanizes him by bringing him into greater conformity with the idea that he has of himself, an idea that—in the beginning—is only an abstract idea, an ideal. If then, at the start, in the given world the slave had a fearful "nature" and had to submit to the master, to the strong man, it does not mean that this will *always* be the case. Thanks to his work, he can become other; and, thanks to his work, the world can become other. And this is what actually took place, as universal history and, finally, the French Revolution and Napoleon show.

This creative education of man by work (*Bildung*) creates history— that is, human time. Work *is* time, and that is why it necessarily exists *in* time: it requires time. The transformation of the slave, which will allow him to surmount his dread, his fear of the master, by surmounting the terror of death—this transformation is long and painful. In the beginning, the slave who—by his work—raised himself to the abstract idea of his freedom, does not succeed in realizing it, because he does not yet dare to act with a view to this realization, that is to say, he does not dare to fight against the master and to risk his life in fight for freedom.

Thus it is that, before realizing freedom, the slave imagines a series of ideologies, by which he seeks to justify himself, to justify his slavery, to reconcile the idea of freedom with the fact of slavery.

The first of these slave's ideologies is stoicism. The slave tries to persuade himself that he is *actually* free simply by *knowing* that he is free—that is, by having the abstract idea of freedom. The real conditions of existence would have no importance at all: no matter whether one be a Roman emperor or a slave, rich or poor, sick or healthy; it is sufficient to have the idea of freedom, or more precisely, of autonomy, of absolute independence of all given conditions of existence. (Whence—in parentheses—the modern variant of stoicism, of which Hegel speaks in chapter 5 of *Phenomenology*: freedom is identified with freedom of thought; the State is called free when one can speak freely in it; so long as *this* freedom is safeguarded, nothing need be changed in that state.)

Hegel's criticism, or, more exactly, his explanation of the fact that man did not stop at this stoic solution that is so satisfying at first sight, can appear unconvincing and bizarre. Hegel says that man abandons stoicism because, as a stoic, he is bored. The stoic ideology was invented to justify the slave's inaction, his refusal to fight to realize his libertarian ideal. Thus, this ideology prevents man from acting: it obliges him to be content with talking. Now says Hegel, all discourse that remains discourse ends in boring man.

This objection—explanation—is simplistic only at first sight. In fact, it has a profound metaphysical basis. Man is not a being that *is*: he is a nothingness that *nihilates* through the negation of being. Now, the negation of being is action. That is why Hegel says, "The *true* being of man is his action." Not to act, therefore, is not to be as a truly human being; it is to be as *Sein*, as given, natural being. Hence, it is to fall into decay, to become brutish; and this metaphysical truth is revealed to man through the phenomenon of boredom: the man who—like a thing, like an animal, like an angel—remains identical to himself, does not negate, does not negate himself, that is, does not act, is bored. And only man can be bored.

However that may be, it was the boredom caused by stoic chatter that forced man to seek something else. In fact, man can be satisfied only by aaction. Now, to act is to transform what is real. And to transform what is real is to negate the given. In the slave's case, to act effectively would be to negate slavery—that is, to negate the master, and hence to risk his life in a fight against the master. The slave does not yet dare to do this. And with boredom driving him to action, he is content to activate his thought in some sense. He makes it negate the given. The stoic slave becomes the skeptic-nihilist slave.

This new attitude culminates in solipsism: the value, the very reality of all that is not I is denied, and the universality and radicalism of this negation makes up for its purely abstract, verbal character.

Nevertheless, man does not succeed in remaining in this skeptical-nihilistic attitude. He does not succeed because in fact he contradicts himself through his very existence: how and why is one to live when one denies the value and the being of the world and of other men? Thus, to take nihilism seriously is to commit suicide, to cease completely to act and—consequently—to live. But the radical skeptic does not interest Hegel, because, by definition, he disappears by committing suicide, he ceases to be, and consequently he ceases to be a human being, an agent of historical evolution. Only the nihilist who remains alive is interesting.

Now, this latter must eventually perceive the contradiction implied in his existence. And, generally speaking, the awareness of a contradiction is what moves human, historical evolution. To become aware of a contradiction is necessarily to want to remove it. Now, one can in fact overcome the contradiction of a given existence only by modifying the given existence, by transforming it through action. But in the slave's case, to transform existence is, again, to fight against the master. Now, he does not want to do this. He tries, therefore, to justify by a new ideology this contradiction in skeptical existence, which is, all things considered, the stoic—that is, slavish—contradiction, between the *idea* or the *ideal* of freedom and the *reality* of slavery. And this third and last slave's ideology is the Christian ideology.

At this point, the slave does not deny the contradictory character of his existence. But he tries to justify it by saying that *all* existence necessarily, inevitably, implies a contradiction. To this end he imagines an "other world," which is "beyond" (*jenseit*) the natural world of the senses. Here below he is a slave, and he does nothing to free himself. But he is right, for in *this* world *everything* is slavery, and the master is as much a slave here as he is. But freedom is not an empty word, a simple abstract idea, an unrealizable ideal, as in stoicism and skepticism. Freedom is real, real in the beyond. Hence no need to fight against the master, since one already *is* free to the extent that one participates in the beyond, since one is freed by that beyond, by the intervention of the beyond in the world of the senses. No need to fight to be recognized by the master, since one is recognized by a God. No need to fight to become free in this world, which is just as vain and stripped of value for the Christian as for the skeptic. No need to fight, to act, since—in the beyond, in the only, world that truly counts—one *is* already freed and equal to the master (in the service of God). Hence one can maintain the stoic attitude, but with good reason this time. And without being bored, too, for now one does not eternally remain the same: one changes and one *must* change, one must always go beyond oneself in order to rise above oneself as something given in the real empirical world, in order to attain the transcendental world, the beyond that remains inaccessible.

Without fighting, without effort, therefore, the Christian realizes tha slave's ideal: he obtains—in and through (or for) God—equality with the master: inequality is but a mirage, like everything in this world of the senses in which slavery and mastery hold sway.

Certainly an ingenious solution, Hegel will say. And not at all astonishing that man through the centuries could believe himself "satisfied" by this pious reward for his work. But, Hegel adds, all this is too good—too simple, too easy—to be true. In fact, what made man a slave was his refusal to risk his life. Hence, he will not cease to be a slave, as long as he is not ready to risk his life in a fight against the master, as long as he does not accept the idea of his death. A liberation without a bloody fight, therefore, is metaphysically impossible. And this metaphysical impossibility is also revealed in the Christian ideology itself.

Indeed, the Christian slave can affirm his equality with the master only by accepting the existence of an "other world" and a transcendent God. Now, this God is necessarily a master, and an absolute master. Thus, the Christian frees himself from human master only to be enslaved to the Divine master. He does free himself—at least in his idea—from the human master. But although he no longer has a master, he does not cease to be a slave. He is a slave without a master, he is a slave in *himself*, he is the pure essence of slavery. And this "absolute" slavery engenders an equally absolute master. It is before *God* that he is the equal of the master. Hence he is the master's equal only in absolute salvery. Therefore, he remains a servant, the servant of a Master for whose glory and pleasure he works. And this new Master is such that the new Christian slave is even more a slave than the pagan slave.

And if the slave accepts this new Divine Master, he does it for the same reason that he accepted the human master: through fear of death. He accepted—or produced—his first slavery because it was the price of his biological life. He accepts—or produces—the second, because it is the price of his *eternal* life. For the fundamental motive of the ideology of the "two worlds" and the duality of human existence is the slavish desire for life at any price, sublimated in the desire for an eternal life. In the final analysis, Christianity is born from the slave's terror in the face of nothingness, his nothingness; that is, for Hegel, from the impossibility of bearing the necessary condition of man's existence—the condition of death, of finiteness.[5]

Consequently, to overcome the insufficiency of the Christian ideology, to become free from the absolute Master and the beyond, to realize freedom and to live in the world as a human being, autonomous and free—all this is possible only on the condition that one accept the idea of death and, consequently, atheism. And the whole evolution of the Christian world is nothing but a progress toward the atheistic awareness of the essential finiteness of human existence. Only thus, only by "overcoming" Christian theology, will man definitively cease to be a slave and realize this idea of freedom which, while it remained an abstract idea—that is, an ideal, engendered Christianity.

This is what is effected in and by the French Revolution, which completes the evolution of the Christian world and inaugurates the third historical world, in which realized freedom will finally be conceived

---

5. There is no human (conscious, articulate, free) existence without fighting that implies the risk of life—that is, without death, without finiteness. "Immortal man" is a "squared circle."

(*begriffen*) by philosophy: by German philosophy, and finally by Hegel. Now, for a revolution to succeed in overcoming Christianity really, the Christian ideal must first be realized in the form of a world. For, in order that an ideology may be surpassed, "overcome" by man, man must first experience the realization of this ideology in the real world in which he lives. The problem, therefore, is to know how the pagan world of mastery can become a Christian world of slavery, when there has been no fight between masters and slaves, when there has been no revolution properly so-called. For if these had taken place, the slave would have become the free worker who fights and risks his life; hence, he would cease to be a slave and consequently could not realize a Christian, essentially slavish, world.

CHAPTER 4

Self-Consciousness and Life

THE INDEPENDENCE OF SELF-CONSCIOUSNESS

Jean Hyppolite

INTRODUCTION: THE MOVEMENT OF SELF-CONSCIOUSNESS

Self-consciousness, which is desire, can reach its truth only by finding another living self-consciousness. Three moments—the two self-consciousnesses posed in the element of externality and also externality itself, the *Dasein* of life—give rise to a dialectic that leads from the battle for recognition to the opposition between master and slave, and from that opposition between master and slave, and from that opposition to liberty. Indeed, in accordance with an ever-recurring pattern in the *Phenomenology*, this dialectic that arises in the midst of externality transposes itself to the interior of self-sconsciousness itself. Just as the forces discovered by understanding, which appeared to be alien to each other, proved to be a unique force divided within itself—each force being itself and its other—so the duality of living self-consciousness becomes the splitting and reproduction of self-consciousness within itself. The independence of the master and the harsh education of the slave become the self-mastery of the stoic who is always free, regardless of circumstance or the hazards of fortune, or the skeptic's experience of absolute liberty, which dissolves every position except that of the I itself. Finally, the truth of this stoic or skeptic liberty comes to be expressed in unhappy consciousness which is always divided within itself a consciousness both of absolute self-certainty and of the nothingness of that certainty. Unhappy consciousness is the truth of this entire dialectic. It is the pain felt by pure subjectivity that no longer contains its substance within itself. Unhappy consciousness, the expression of the pure subjectivity

67

of the I, leads back, trough the movement of self-alienation, to consciousness of substance. But this consciousness is not the consciousness described at the beginning of the *Phenomenology*, for being is now self, itself alienated. Self-consciousness has become reason.[1]

We shall follow this movement: the positing of self-consciousness as desire, the relation among self-consciousnesses in the element of life and the movement that recognizes self in the other, and, finally, the internalization of this movement in the three stages of stoicism, skepticism, and unhappy consciousness.

POSITING SELF-CONSCIOUSNESS AS DESIRE: DEDUCTION OF DESIRE

"Self-consciousness is desire in general" (*PE*, I, 147; *PG*, 135; *PM*, 220). In the practical part of the *Science of Knowledge*, Fichte discovered impulse (*Trieb*) to be at the base of theoretical consciousness as well as of practical consciousness, and he showed that the first condition of this sensuous instinct was "an instinct for instinct," a pure action in which the I strives to rediscover the "thetic" identity of self-consciousness. . . . Why is self-consciousness desire in general? And, as we might ask in contemporary terms, what is the intentionality of this desire? What is the new structure of the subject-object relation that is being described here? Hegel deduces desire, and the necessity of the presentation of self-consciousness as desire, in a few dense lines. The starting point of this deduction is the opposition between self-knowledge and knowledge of an other. Consciousness was knowledge of an other, knowledge of the sensuous world in general; self-consciousness, on the contrary, is self-knowledge, and is expressed in the identity I = I (*Ich bin Ich*). The I that is an object is an object for itself. It is simultaneously subject and object; it poses itself for itself. "The I is the content of the relation and the very movement of relating. At the same time, it is the I that opposes itself to an other and exceeds that other, an other that for it is only itself" (*PE*, I, 146; *PG*, 134; *PM*, 219). This seems far removed from what is commonly called "desire." But let us note that this self-knowledge

---

1. In the chapter on phrenology, Hegel himself clearly summarizes this development from unhappy consciousness to reason: "Unhappy self-consciousness has alienated its independence and has struggled until it has transformed its *being-for-itself* into a *thing*. Thus, it has returned from self-consciousness to consciousness, that is, to the consciousness for which the object is a *being*, a *thing*. But that which is a thing is self-consciousness which, therefore, is the category, the unity of the I and being [the category]" (*PE*, I, 284; *PG*, 252; *PM*, 369).

is not primary; self-consciousness is "reflection issuing from the being of the sensuous world and of the perceived world; it is essentially this return into itself starting from being-other" (*PE*, I, 146; *PG*, 134; *PM*, 219). Unlike Fichte, we do not pose the *Ich bin Ich* in the absoluteness of a thetic act in relation to which antithesis and synthesis would be secondary. The reflection of the I, which takes the sensuous world, the being-other, as its starting point, is the essence of self-consciousness, which, therefore, exists only through this return, only through this movement. "*Qua* self-consciousness, it is movement" (*PE*, I, 146; *PG*, 134; *PM*, 219). However, when we consider only the abstraction I = I, we have merely an inert tautology. The movement of self-consciousness, without which it would not exist, requires otherness, that is, the world of consciousness that in this way is that preserved for self-consciousness. But it is preserved not as a being-in-itself, as an object that consciousness passively reflects, but as a negative object, as the object that must be negated in order that through this negation of the being-other self-consciousness establish its own unity with itself. We must distinguish two moments. "In the first moment self-consciousness exists as consciousness, and the complete extension of the sensuous world is maintained for it, but maintained only insofar as it is related to the second moment, that is, the unity of self-consciousness with itself" (*PE*, I, 147; *PG*, 134; *PM*, 220). That is what we mean when we say that the sensuous world, the universe, stands before me now as no more than phenomenon, or manifestation (*Erscheinung*). The truth of that world now lies in me and not in it; that truth is the self of self-consciousness. I need only establish that unity by the movement that negates being-other and then reconstitutes the unity of the I with itself. The world no longer subsists in-itself; it subsists only in relation to self-consciousness, which is its truth. The I is the truth of being, for being exists only for the I that appropriates it and thus poses itself for itself. "This unity must become essential to self-consciousness, which is to say that self-consciousness is desire in general" (*PE*, I, 147; *PG*, 135; *PM*, 220). Desire is this movement of consciousness that does not respect being that negates it, appropriating it concretely and making it its own. Desire presupposes the phenomenal character of the world that exists for the self only as a means. The difference between perceiving consciousness and desiring consciousness can be put in metaphysical language even though neither consciousness is aware of this metaphysics. This difference can be glimpsed in the first chapter of the *Phenomenology*, the chapter on "Sensuous Certainty":

> Not even the animals are excluded from this wisdom but, rather, they show themselves to be profoundly initiated in it. For they

do not stand before sensuous things as though these were in-
itself; they despair of this reality and, absolutely convinced of
the nothingness of sensuous things, they grab them without
further ado and consume them. Like the animals, the rest of
nature celebrates the revealed mysteries that teach what the
truth of sensuous things is. (*PE*, I, 90–91; *PG*, 87–88; *PM*, 159)

THE MEANING OF DESIRE

Self-consciousness, then, is not "the inert tautology, I = I"; it presents
itself as engaged in a debate with the world. For self-consciousness, this
world is what disappears and does not subsist, but this very disappearance
is necessary for self-consciousness to pose itself. Self-consciousness,
therefore, is, *desire*, in the most general meaning of the word. And the
intentional object of desire is of a diiferent order than the object intended
by sensuous consciousness. Hegel describes this new structure of consciousness in a precise, although very condensed, manner. We should
recall that in his first essays on then philosophy of spirit, especially in
the *System der Sittlichkeit* written in Jena, Hegel had constructed a kind
of philosophical anthropology in which objects were grasped not so much
in their independent being as in their being-for-consciousness: as objects
of desire, as material for work, as expressions of consciousness. In the
same vein, the philosophies of spirit of 1803–4 and 1805–6 studied instruments, language, and so on, in an attempt to describe, and to present
in an original dialectic, the human world as a whole and the surrounding
world as a human world. All these dialectics must be presupposed if we
are to understand the transition from desire to the encounter between
self-consciousnesses, an encounter that is the precondition of social and
spiritual life. The individual object of desire—this fruit I wish to pluck—
is not an object posed in its independence. Insofar as it is an object of
desire we can just as well say of it that it exists as that it does not exist.
It exists, but soon it will no longer exist; its truth is to be consumed
and negated, in order that self-consciousness might gather itself up
through this negation of the other. From this arises the ambiguity that
characterizes the object of desire, or, rather, the duality of the end intended by desire.

> Henceforth, consciousness, *qua* self-consciousness, has a double
> object: one is the immediate, the object of sensuous certainty
> and of perception, which for self-consciousness is characterized
> by negativity (that is, this object is merely phenomenon, its
> essence being to disappear); the other is precisely itself, an object

that is true essence and that is present at first only in opposition to the first object. (*PE*, I, 147; *PG*, 135; *PM*, 220)

The end point of desire is not, as one might think superficially, the sensuous object—that is only a means—but the unity of the I with itself. Self-consciousness is desire, but what it desires, although it does not yet know this explicitly, is itself: it desires its own desire. And that is why it will be able to attain itself only through finding another desire, another self-consciousness. The teleological dialectic of the *Phenomenology* gradually unfolds all the horizons of this desire, which is the essence of self-consciousness. Desire bears first on the objects of the world, then on life, an object already closer to itself, and, finally, on another self-consciousness. Desire seeks itself in the other: man desires recognition from man.

DESIRE AND LIFE

We have translated *Begierde*, the word Hegel uses, as "desire" [*désir*] rather than as "appetite" [*appétit*], for this desire contains more than appears at first; although insofar as it bears on the various concrete objects of the world, it merges initially with sensuous appetite, it carries a much wider meaning. Fundamentally, self-consciousness seeks itself in this desire, and it seeks itself in the other. This is why desire is in essence other than it immediately appears to be. At each stage of the *Phenomenology* a certain notion of objectivity is constituted, a truth appropriate to that stage. It is less a matter of thinking individual objects than of determining the characteristics of a certain kind of objectivity. At the stage of sensuous certainty we deal not with this or that particular sensuous "this" but with the sensuous "this" in general. At the level of perception we deal not with this or that perceived object but with the perceived object in general. Similarly, at the level of self-consciousness, objectivity is defined in a new way. What self-consciousness discovers as its other can no longer be the merely sensuous object of perception, but must be an object that has already rejected back on itself. "Through such a reflection back on itself the object has become life." And, Hegel adds, "That which self-consciousness distinguishes from itself by considering it as an existent not only has, insofar as it is posed as an existent, the mode of sensuous certainty and of perception, but also is being reflected back on itself; the object of immediate desire is some living thing" (*PE*, I, 147–48; *PG*, 135; *PM*, 220). In other words, life is the medium in which self-consciousness experiences and seeks itself. Life constitutes the first truth of self-consciousness and appears as its other.

As we ourselves have grasped it as the result of the previous dialectic, it is the term that corresponds to self-consciousness. At the level of self-consciousness, truth is possible only as a truth that experiences and manifests itself in the midst of life. All the more must we emphasize the duality of self consciousness and life. . . . Life in general is genuinely the other of self-consciousness. What does this opposition mean, concretely? What I, as self-consciousness, find facing me (*Gegenstand*) is life, and life is simultaneously irremediably other and the same. When in his early works Hegel describes the consciousness of Abraham, he shows how reflection shatters a prior and immediate unity. Abraham separates himself from himself. His life, and life in general, appears to him as an other than himself; yet it is also what is closest to him, what is most intimate and most distant.[2] To desire life, to wish to live—and all particular desires appear to aim at this goal—is only, it seems, to desire to be oneself. Yet this life that is myself—and biological life especially— escapes me absolutely. Considered as other, it is the element of substantiveness with which I cannot completely merge insofar as I am a subject; it is "the universal, indestructible substance, the fluid essence that is equal to itself" (*PE*, I, 148; *PG*, 140; *PM*, 227). But self-consciousness as reflection signifies the break with life, a break the full tragedy of which will be experienced by unhappy consciousness. This is why Hegel's abstract text has such concrete implications. "But, as we have seen, this unity is also the act of rebounding away from itself, and this concept splits, giving birth to the opposition between self-consciousness and life" (*PE*, I, 148; *PG*, 135; *PM*, 221). Self-consciousness, "specificity" in Hegel's terminology, opposes universal life; it claims to be independent of it and wishes to pose itself absolutely for-itself. Nevertheless, it will encounter the resistance of its object. Thus, the object of consciousness is as independent at in-itself as consciousness is: "Self-consciousness that exists uniquely for-itself and which immediately characterizes its object as negative—self-consciousness that is at first desire—will experience instead the independence of that object" (*PE*, I, 148; *PG*, 135; *PM*, 221).

OTHERNESS IN DESIRE

How does this experience, in the course of which I discover that the object is independent of me, present itself? We can say that it is born at first from the continuous reproduction of desire and of the object. The object is negated and desire is quenched, but then desire arises again

---

2. *Early Theological Writings*, 182ff.; and *Theologische Jugendschriften*, 371ff.

and another object presents itself to be negated. The specificity of the objects and the desires matters little; the monotony of their reproduction has a necessity: it reveals to consciousness that the object is needed so that self-consciousness can negate it. "In order for this suppression [*Aufheben*] to be, this other, too, must be" (*PE*, I, 152; *PG*, 139; *PM*, 225). Desire in general, then, is characterized by a necessary otherness. This otherness appears to be merely provisional in the case of this or that particular desire; its essentiality results from the succession of desires. "Indeed, the essence of desire is an other than self-consciousness, and this truth becomes present to self-consciousness through the experience of the succession of desires" (*PE*, I, 153; *PG*, 139; *PM*, 225).

During the course of this experience, I discover that desire is never exhausted and that its reflected intention leads me to an essential otherness. Yet self-consciousness is also absolutely for itself. It must therefore satisfy itself, but it can do so only if the object itself presents itself to it as a self-consciousness. In this case indeed, and only in this case, "the object is I as well as object." Otherness. . . is maintained. At the same time, the I finds itself—which is the most profound aim of desire—and it finds itself as a being. Life is only the element of substantiveness, the other of the I. But when life becomes for me another self-consciousness, a selfl-consciousness that appears to me at once alien and the same, a self-consciousness in which desire recognizes another desire and bears on it, then in this splitting and reproduction of itself self-consciousness reaches itself. Here already we have the concept of spirit, which is why Hegel says here that spirit is present for us. "In this way the concept of spirit is already present for us. Consciousness will later experience what spirit is—that absolute substance which, in the complete freedom and independence of its oppositions, that is, of the various self-consciousnesses existing for it, constitutes their unity: the I that is a we, and the we that is an I" (*PE*, I, 154; *PG*, 140; *PM*, 227).

This movement from desiring self-consciousness to the multiplicity of self-consciousnesses suggests several comments: first of all, about the meaning of a deduction of this kind. "Deduction" is obviously an inappropriate word here, because the dialectic is teleological, that is, through exploring the horizons of desire it discovers the meaning of that desire and poses its conditions. The condition of self-consciousness is the existence of other self-consciousnesses. Desire is able to pose itself in being, to reach a truth and not merely remain at the subjective stage of certainty, only if life appears as another desire. Desire must bear on desire and discover itself as such in being; it must discover itself and be discovered; it must appear to itself as an other and appear to an other. In this way, we can understand the three moments that Hegel distinguishes in the concept of self-consciousness: "(a) its first immediate object is the pure, undifferentiated I, but (b) this immediateness itself is absolute mediation; that is, it exists only as the act of suppressing the independent object, only as desire." The satisfaction of desire is indeed the return to the first immediate object, the I, but it is a return one degree removed. It is no longer certainty but a truth; it is the I posed in the being of life and no longer presupposing itself. For this reason, "(c) the truth of this certainty is rather divided reflection, the splitting and reproduction of self-consciousness" (*PE*, I, 153; *PG*, 140; *PM*, 226). In this way, Hegel returns to the definition of spirit as opposed to nature and to life that he gave in his Jena philosophy. "In nature, spirit is spirit to itself, as spirit unaware of itself as absolute spirit, as absolute self-reflection which is not that absolute reflection for itself, which is not for itself the unity of a double knowledge discovering itself."[3] This unity of a double knowledge discovering itself is realized in the movement of the recognition of self-consciousnesses. One more thing needs to be said here, at least in order to characterize Hegel's venture: it would have been possible to present the duality of self-consciousnesses and their unity in the element of life as the dialectic of love. The importance attributed to love by the German romantics, by Schiller, for example, and by Hegel in his early works, is well known. Love is the miracle through which two become one without, however, completely suppressing the duality. Love goes beyond the categories of objectivity and makes the essence of life actually real by preserving difference within union. But in the *Phenomenology*, Hegel takes a different tack. Love does not dwell sufficiently on the tragic nature of separation; it lacks "the seriousness, the torment, the patience, and the labor of the negative" (*PE*, I, 18; *PG*, 20; *PM*, 81). For this reason the encounter between self-consciousnesses appears in the *Phenomenology* as a struggle between them for recognition. Desire is less the desire that characterizes love than that of one desiring consciousess for the virile recognition of another desiring consciousness. The movement of recognition, thus, will manifest itself through the opposition between self-consciousnesses. Each consciousness, indeed, will have to show itself as it is to be, that is, as raised above life, which conditions it and by which it is still imprisoned.

THE CONCEPT OF RECOGNITION

What consciousness, as understanding, contemplated outside itself as the interplay of forces, which is only the experience of the mutual action

---

3. Jena *Logic*, 193.

of causes, has now moved to the heart of consciousness. Each force, each cause, seemed to act outside consciousness and, reciprocally, to be solicited by the outside. But understanding discovered that each force contained within itself what appeared to be alien to it. Such, for example, was Leibniz's monad. This process has now moved from the in-itself to the for-itself. Each force, each self-consciousness, knows now that what is external to it is internal to it and vice versa. This truth is now no longer thought by an alien understanding, but by consciousness itself, which, for itself, splits, reproduces, and opposes itself. "What in the interplay of forces was for-us, now is for the extremes themselves. . . . As consciousness, each extreme indeed moves outside itself, but its being-outside-itself is at the same time kept within itself; it is for-itself, and its being-outside-itself is for-it" (PE, I, 157; PG, 142–43; PM, 231).[4]

This dialectic expresses what Hegel calls "the concept of the mutual recognition of self-consciousnesses." This concept is at first for-us, or in-itself. It expresses infinity realizing itself at the level of self-consciousness, but then it is for self-consciousness itself, for self-consciousness that undergoes the experience of recognition. This experience expresses the emergence of self-consciousness into the medium of life. Each self-consciousness is for-itself and, as such, it negates all otherness. It is desire but a desire that poses itself in its absoluteness. Yet it is also for-an-other, specifically, for an other self-consciousness. It presents itself as "immersed in the being of life," and it is not for the other self-consciousness what it is for itself. For itself, it is absolute self-certainty; for the other, it is a living object, an independent thing in the medium of being; a given being, it is, therefore, seen as "an outside." Now this disparity must disappear—on each side—for each self-consciousness is both a living thing for the other and absolute self-certainty for itself. And each can find its truth only through having itself recognized by the other as what it is for-itself and by manifesting itself on the outside as it is within. But in manifesting itself, each will discover an equivalent manifestation on the part of the other.

"The movement, thus, is wholly and simply the movement of two self-consciousnesses. Each sees the other do what it does itself; each does

---

4. The ontological relation of consciousness is also indicated in the following passage: "Each extreme is a middle term for the other extreme, a middle term by means of which it enters into a relation with itself and gathers itself up. Both for itself and for the other extreme, each extreme is an immediate essence which exists for-itself but which is for-itself only through this mediation." In other words, I am for-myself only in being for-the-other and only because the other is for-me.

what it requires of the other and therefore does what it does insofar as the other does it too" (*PE*, I, 156–57; *PG*, 142; *PM*, 230).

Self-consciousness, then, comes to exist ("exist," here, does not mean merely the *Dasein* that is characteristic of things) only by means of an "operation" that poses it in being as it is for itself. And this operation is essentially an operation on and by another self-consciousness. I am a self-consciousness only if I gain for myself recognition from another self-consciousness and if I grant recognition to the other. This mutual recognition, in which individuals recognize each other as reciprocally recognizing each other, creates the element of spiritual life—the medium in which the subject is an object to itself, finding itself completely in the other yet doing so without abrogating the otherness that is essential to self-consciousness. The concept of self-consciousness is indeed "the concept of infinity realizing itself in and by consciousness"; that is, it expresses the movement by means of which each term itself becomes infinite, becomes other while remaining self. This dialectic was already present in the development of life, but it was only in-itself; each term indeed became other, but its identity was so internal to it that it never manifested itself. Now self-consciousness itself opposes itself within being and yet recognizes itself in this opposition as the same. We must consider again the difference between a being that is merely alive and a self-consciousness. Self-consciousness exists as a negative power. It is not merely a positive reality, a *Dasein* that disappears and dies absolutely, crushed by what exceeds it and remains external to it; it also is that which at the heart of this positive reality negates itself and maintains itself in that negation. Concretely, this is the very existence of man, "who never is what he is," who always exceeds himself and is always beyond himself, who has a future, and who rejects all permanence except the permanence of his desire aware of itself as desire.

> To be sure, the discrete figure which is merely alive also suppresses its own independence in the very process of life, but when its difference ends, it ceases to be what it is. The object of self-consciousness, on the contrary, is equally independent in this negativity of itself, and is thus for itself genus, universal fluidity in the particularity of its own differentiation: this object is a living self-consciousness. (*PE*, I, 154; *PG*, 140; *PM*, 226)

Let us repeat, for this is the simple meaning of this entire dialectic: human desire occurs only when it contemplates another desire, or, to put it in a better way, only when it bears on another desire and becomes the desire to be recognized and hence itself to recognize. The vocation of man—to find himself in being, to make himself be—is realized only in the relation between self-consciousnesses. This being. . .is not the being of nature but the being of desire, the disquiet of the self, and that, consequently, what we are to rediscover in being—or make actual in it— is the mode of being proper to self-consciousness. Hegel even doubts that the word "being" is appropriate to this form of existence: "To present oneself as pure abstaction of self-consciousness consists in showing oneself as pure negation of its objective mode of being or in showing that one is attached neither to any determinate *Dasein* nor to he universal singularity of *Dasein* in general—in showing that one is not attached to life" (*PE*, I, 159; *PG*, 144; *PM*, 232). To say that spirit is, is to say that it is a thing: "If we ordinarily say of spirit that it is, that it has a being, that it is a thing, a specific entity, we do not thereby mean that we can see it or hold it or stumble against it. But we do make such statements" (*PE*, I, 284; *PG*, 252; *PM*, 369). Self-consciousness thus is what exists through refusing to be. Yet this essential refusal must appear in being; it must manifest itself in some way. This is the meaning of the struggle for mutual recognition.

The whole dialectic about opposed self-consciousnesses, about domination and servitude, presupposes the conception of two terms: "other" and "self." The other is universal life as self-consciousness discovers it, different from itself; it is the element of difference and of the substantiveness of differences. The self that faces this positivity is reflected unity that has become pure negativity. The self now discovers itself in the other; it emerges as a particular living figure, another man for man. This split and reproduction of self-consciousness is essential to the concept of spirit, but we must not neglect the duality on the pretext of grasping the unity. The element of duality, of otherness, is precisely the *Dasein* of life, the absolutely other, and, as we have seen, this other is essential to desire. To be sure, the other is a self, and as a result I see myself in the other. From this two things follow: that I have gotten lost, since I find myself as an other—I am for-an-other, and an other is for-me; and that I have lost the other, for I do not see the other as essence but see myself in the other. This has, in Hegel's phrase, a double consequence. The other appears as the same, as the self, but the self also appears as the other. Similarly, the negation of the other, which corresponds to the movement of desire, becomes self-negation as well. Finally—as in the case of stoicism—the complete return into the self, while claiming to suppress all otherness, in fact merely leaves the other free of the self and thus leads back to absolute otherness. Being is then other but no longer self. One point is essential in this dialectic, a dialectic easy enough to grasp in the subtle interplay that it presents: otherness does not disappear. We can say that three terms are present,

two self-consciousnesses and the element of otherness, that is, life as
the being of life, being-for-an-other that is not yet being-for-itself. It is
useful to distinguish these three terms, for as we shall see in the case
of the master-slave relation, there can be a master and a slave only because there is animal life, an existence according to the specific mode
of life. What sense would desire or work or enjoyment have if this third
term did not exist? But in fact, if we look more closely, we see that there
are only two terms, for the duality of the I, the fact of speaking of two
self-consciousnesses, of a master and of a slave, is the result of this
moment of nature, the result of the otherness of life. It is because this
moment of life is given that self-consciousness opposes itself. Thus, we
were right to begin with the self and the other, noting that the other
now appears as a self, or—and this comes to the same thing—that
mediation is essential to the *positing* of the I, though that need is
generally not noticed by the consciousness engaged in experience.

> In this experience (Hegel writes somewhat further on), self-
> consciousness learns that life is as essential to it as pure self-
> consiousness is. In immediate self-consciousness (with which
> the *Phenomenology* starts) the simple I is the absolute object
> which, for us or in-itself, however (for the philosopher who
> apprehends this immediate self-consciousness according to its
> phenomenological genesis), is absolute mediation and has as
> its essential moment subsisting independence (the positivity
> of vital being). (*PE*, I, 160; *PG*, 145; *PM*, 234)

THE STRUGGLE FOR RECOGNITION:
THE FIGHT FOR LIFE AND DEATH

"Life," Hegel writes, "is the natural position of consciousness, independence (*Selbständigkeit*) without absolute negativity" (*PE*, I, 160; *PG*, 145;
PM, 233). At the beginning, self-consciousness—which emerges as a
particular form in the midst of universal life—is only a living *thing*. But
we know that the essence of self-consciousness is *being-for-itself* in its
purity), the negation of all otherness. In its positivity, self-consciousness
is a living thing, but it is directed precisely against that positivity and
it must manifest itself thus. As we have seen, this manifestation requires
a plurality of self-consciousnesses. To begin with, the plurality lies in
the vital element of difference. Each self-consciousness sees in the other
only a particular figure of life and consequently does not truly know
itself in the other, and, similarly, is an alien living thing for the other.
Thus, "each is quite certain of itself but not of the other" (*PE*, I, 158;

PG, 143; *PM*, 232). Its certainty remains subjective; it fails to attain its truth. For certainty to become truth, the other, too, must present itself as pure self-certainty. These two concrete I's, which confront each other, must recognize each other as being not merely living things. And that recognition must not initially be a merely formal recognition: "The individual who has not risked his life can of course be recognized as a person, but he does not attain the truth of this recognition of an independent self-consciousness" (*PE*, I, 159; *PG*, 144; *PM*, 233). All spiritual life rests on these experiences, experiences that human history has superseded but that remain its underpinning. Unlike animals, men desire not only to persevere in their being, to exist the way things exist; they also imperiously desire to be recognized as self-consciousnesses, as something raised above purely animal life. And this passion to be recognized requires, in turn, the recognition of the other self-consciousness. *Consciousness of life rises above life.* Idealism is not only a certainty; it also proves itself, or rather establishes itself, in the risk of animal life. That men are wolves, in Hobbes' phrase, does not mean that, like animal species, they fight to survive or to extend their power. Insofar as they are animals, they differ: some are stronger, others weaker; some more clever, others less so. But these differences are merely within the sphere of life, and they are, therefore, inessential. The fight of each against all is a fight not only for life but also for recognition. It is a fight—in which the spiritual vocation of man is manifested—to prove to others as well as to oneself that one is an autonomous self-consciousness. But one can prove that to oneself only by proving it to others and by obtaining that proof from them. To be sure, historians can cite many causes for the struggle against others, but those causes are not the genuine motives of what is essentially a conflict for recognition. The human world begins here:

> One can preserve one's liberty only through the risk of one's life—and through the risk one proves that the essence of self-consciousness is not existence, is not the immediate mode in which self-consciousness initially arises, immersion in the expanse of life; that there is nothing present in self-consciousness which, for it, is not a disappearing moment; that self-consciousness is only a pure being-for-itself. (*PE*, I 159; *PG*, 144; *PM*, 233)

Human existence, the existence of the being who is continually desire and desire for desire, breaks loose from the *Dasein* of life. Human life appears as of a different order, and the necessary conditions of a history are thereby posed. Man rises above life, which is nevertheless the positive condition of his emergence; he is capable of risking his life and thereby freeing himself from the only slavery possible: enslavement to life.

The struggle for recognition is a category of historical life, not a specific, datable moment in human history, or rather prehistory. It is a condition of human experience, which Hegel discovered through his study of the conditions of the development of self-consciousness. Self-consciousness, then, experiences the struggle for recognition, but the truth of that experience gives rise to another experience: that of relations of inequality in recognition—the experience of mastery and servitude. Indeed, if life is the natural position of consciousness, then death is merely its natural negation. For that reason, "the supreme test by means of death suppresses precisely that truth which ought to have emerged through it and simultaneously suppresses the certainty of oneself in general" (*PE*, I, 160; *PG*, 145; *PM*, 233). Though self-consciousness appears as pure negativity and hence manifests itself as negation of life, the positivity of life is essential to it. By offering its life, the I indeed poses itself as raised above life, but at the same time it vanishes from the scene. For death appears only as a natural fact, not as a spiritual negation. Therefore, another experience is necessary, an experience in which negation would be spiritual negation, that is, an *Aufhebung*, which preserves while it negates. That experience will present itself in the labor of the slave and in the lengthy elaboration of his liberation.

Through risking life, consciousness experiences it to be as essential to it as pure self-consciousness is. For that reason, the two moments which at first are immediately united separate. One of the self-consciousnesses rises above animal life; able to confront death and not fearing the loss of its vital substance, it poses abstract being-for-itself as its essence and seems thereby to escape the enslavement to life. This is the noble consciousness, that of the master, and it is recogized in fact. The other self-consciousness prefers life to self-consciousness: it chooses slavery. Spared by the master, it is preserved as a thing is preserved. It recognizes the master, but it is not recognized by him. The two moments, self and other, are here dissociated. The self is the master who negates life in its positivity; the other is the slave, a consciousness too, but only the consciousness of life as positivity, a consciousness in the element of being, in the form of thingness. We see a new category of historical life here (that of the master and the slave) which plays a no less important role than the former category. It constitutes the essence of many historical forms, but it constitutes only a particular experience in the development of self-consciousness. Just as opposition among men leads to domination and servitude, so, by a dialectical reversal, domination and servitude lead to the liberation of the slave. Historically, genuine mastery belongs to the laboring slave and not to the noble who has merely risked his life and thrust aside the mediation of the *Dasein* of life. The master expresses the tautology I = I, immediate abstract self-consciousness. The slave expresses the mediation essential to self-consciousness (but which the master fails to notice) and frees himself by consciously carrying out that mediation.

In this new experience, the life element, the medium of life, becomes a new self-consciousness (the specific figure of the slave) and immediate self-consciousness (that of the master) poses itself facing it. Whereas in the prior experience the life element was only the form of the emergence of differentiated self-consciousnesses, it is now integated to a type of self-consciousness. The two moments of self-consciousness, self and life, confront each other now as two unique figures of consciousness. This is the case throughout the *Phenomenology*. Just as master and slave oppose each other as two figures of consciousness, so noble consciousness and base consciousness, and sinning consciousness and judging consciousness, oppose each other until finally the two essential moments of every dialectic are simultaneously disunguished and united as universal consciousness and individual consciousness.

DOMINATION AND SERVITUDE

The dialectic of domination and servitude has often been expounded. It is, perhaps, the best-known section of the *Phenomenology*, as much for the graphic beauty of its development as for the influence it has had on the political and social philosophy of Hegel's successors, especially Marx. It consists essentially in showing that the truth of the master reveals that he is the slave of the slave, and that the slave is revealed to be the master of the master. The inequality present in the unilateral form of recognition is thereby overcome, and equality reestablished. Self-consciousness is recognized, legitimized, in-itself—in the element of life—as well as for-itself: it becomes the stoic consciousness of liberty. It is noteworthy that Hegel is interested here only in the individual development of self-consciousness; he will show the social consequences of the recognition he discusses here only in the part of the *Phenomenology* that deals with spirit. There, the juridical world of persons, the world of Roman law, corresponds to stoicism. For the moment, however, we are not concerned with that extension of the dialectic. We need only consider the education of self-consciousness under slavery, and the truth of that education in stoicism. Hegel's argument draws on all the ancient moralists (and we can find a similar treatment of the categories of domination and servitude in Rousseau). Let us also note that this historical category not only plays an essential role in social relations, in relations between peoples, but also serves to translate a certain conception of the relations between God and man. In his early works, Hegel used this dialectic in his discussion of the Jewish people and of man living enslaved to the law, and even in his discussion of Kant's philosophy. He dealt with it in a special way in his *System der Sittlichkeit*, but it was in the *Realphilosophie* of Jena that he elaborated it in the precise way in which it is later developed in the *Phenomenology*.[5]

The relation between master and slave results from the struggle for recognition. Let us first consider the master: he is no longer merely the concept of consciousness for-itself, but its actual realization, that is, he is recognized as what he is. "It is a consciousness existing for-itself that now relates to itself through the mediation of *another* consciousness, of a consciousness whose essence is to be synthesized with independent being, or with thingness in general" (*PE*, I, 161; *PG*, 146; *PM*, 234–35). This passage already contains the contadiction inherent in the state of domination. The master is master only because he is recognized by the slave; his autonomy depends on the mediation of another self-consciousness, that of the slave. Thus, his independence is completely relative. Moreover, in relating to the slave who recognizes him, the master also relates through that intermediary to the being of life, to thingness. He relates in a mediated way both to the slave and to the thing. Let us consider this mediation that constitutes domination. The master relates to the slave through the intermediary of life (of independent being). In fact, the slave is, properly speaking, the slave not of the master, but of life; he is a slave because he has retreated in the face of death, preferring servitude to liberty in death. He is, therefore, less the slave of the master than of life: "That is the yoke from which he has been unable to free himself through struggle, and that is why he has shown himself to be dependent, having his independence in thingness" (*PE*, I, 162; *PG*, 146; *PM*, 235). The being of the slave is life. Hence, he is not autonomous; his independence is external to him—in life and not in self-consciousness. The master, however, has shown himself raised above that being; he has considered life as a phenomenon, as a negative datum, which is

---

5. In the *Early Theological Writings* Hegel envisions the relations between God and men among certain peoples as a relation between master and slave. He speaks of man's enslavement to law in Jewish legalism as well as in Kantian moralism. In these conceptions there is no possible reconciliation between the *universal* and the *particular*. It is important to note this if we are to understand the transition from the concrete master-slave relation to unhappy consciousness, which contraposes the universal and the particular within consciousness.

why he is the master of the slave by means of thingness. The master also relates to the thing through the intermediary of the slave; he can enjoy things, negate them completely, and thus affirm himself completely. For him, the independence of the being of life and the resistance of the world to desire do not exist. The slave, on the contrary, knows only the resistance of that being to desire and cannot, therefore, attain the complete negation of this world. His desire encounters the resistance of the real, and he is able only to elaborate things, to work on them. Servile labor is the lot of the slave, who in that way arranges the world so that the master can negate it purely and simply, that is, enjoy it. The master consumes the essence of the world; the slave elaborates it. The master values negation, which grants him immediate self-certainty; the slave values production, that is, the transformation of the world—which is "a delayed enjoyment" (*PE*, I, 165; *PG*, 146; *PM*, 238). But the master's self-certainty in his dominance and his enjoyment is in fact mediated by the being of life, or by the slave. Mediation has been made real in another consciousness, but, it does not thereby become less essential to self-consciousness. Besides, recognition is unilateral and partial. The slave acts on himself as the master acts on him: he recognizes himself as a slave. His actions are those of the master; they do not carry their own meaning, but depend on the essential action of the master. But the slave does not act on the master as he acts on himself, and the master does not act on himself as he acts on the slave. The truth of the master's consciousness thus lies in the inessential consciousness of the slave. But how can slave-consciousness be the truth of self-consciousness when it is alien to itself and when its being lies outside it? Yet in its development, in its conscious mediation, it genuinely makes independence real. It does so in three moments: *fear, service,* and *labor.*[6]

SERVILE CONSCIOUSNESS

When the slave first appears, his being lies outside his consciousness; he is a prisoner of life, submerged in animal existence. His substance is not being-for-itself but the being-of-life, which for a self-consciousness is always being-other. Nonetheless, the development of the notion of servitude will show us that in fact slave-consciousness brings about the

---

6. Hegel characterizes the condition of domination very sketchily, for if the master genuinely existed he would be God. In fact, the master believes that he is immediately for-itself, although mediation, which is essential to the movement of self-consciousness, dwells not in him but in the slave.

synthesis of being-in-itself and being-for-itself; it carries out the mediation implicit in the concept of self-consciousness.[7]
   In the first place, the slave regards the master outside him as his
own essence, his own ideal. For insofar as the slave recognizes himself
as a slave, he humiliates himself. The master is the self-consciousness
that the slave himself is not; and liberation is presented to the slave as
a form that is outside him. This humiliation (the slave's recognition of
his own dependence) and the slave's positing outside himself of an ideal
of liberty that he does not find within himself constitute a dialectic that
will reappear at the heart of unhappy consciousness when man, as consciousness of nothingness and of the vanity of his life, will stand opposed
to divine consciousness. In Hegelian language, the master appears to the
slave as *truth*, but as a truth that is eternal to him. Yet this truth is also
in him, for the slave has known fear, has feared death—the absolute
master—and all that was stable within him has been shaken. In the
fundamental anguish, all the moments of nature to which he adhered
as a consciousness immersed in animal existence dissolved. "This
consciousness experienced anguish not concerning this or that thing,
not at this or that instant, but concerning the entirety of its essence,
for it has felt the fear of death, the absolute master" (*PE*, I, 164; *PG*, 148;
PM, 237). The master did not fear death, and he raised himself immediately above all the vicissitudes of existence; the slave trembled before
it, and in that primordial anguish he perceived his essence as a whole.
The whole of life appeared before him, and all the specificities of *Dasein*
were dissolved in that essence. For that reason, the slave's consciousness
developed as pure being-for-itself, "but such a pure and universal movement, such an absolute dissolution of all subsistence, is the simple
essence of self-consciousness, pure negativity, pure being-for-itself, which
is in that consciousness itself" (*PE*, I, 164; *PG*, 148; *PM*, 237). Human
consciousness can take shape only through this anguish throughout the
whole of its being. At that point, specific attachments, the dispersion
of life in more or less stable forms, disappear, and in that fear man
becomes cognizant of the totality of his being, a totality never given as
such in organic life. "In pure life, in life which is not spirit, nothingness
does not exist as such." Moreover, the slave's consciousness is not only
the dissolution in him of all subsistence; it is also the gradual elimination
of all adherence to a determinate *Dasein*. For in service—in the particular
service of the master—that consciousness disciplines itself and detaches
itself from natural *Dasein*.

---

7. The path of mastery is a dead end in human experience; the path of servitude
is the true path of human liberation.

Fear and service cannot by themselves raise the slave's self-consciousness to genuine independence; it is labor that transforms servitude into mastery. The master is able to satisfy his desire completely; through enjoyment, he completely negates the thing. The slave, on the other hand, comes up against the independence of being. He can only transform the world and in that way render it adequate to human desire. But it is precisely in that apparently inessential action that the slave becomes able to give to his own being-for-itself the subsistence and the permanence of being-in-itself. Not only does the slave shape himself by shaping things; he also imprints the form of self-consciousness on being. Thus, in the product of his work, he finds himself. The master attains only a transitory enjoyment, but the slave attains, through his labor, contemplation of independent being as well as of himself. "This being-for-itself externalizes itself in labor and passes into the element of permanence; laboring consciousness thus comes to the intuition of independent being as an intuition of itself" (*PE*, I, 165; *PG*, 149; *PM*, 238). The labor of the slave thus attains the authentic realization of beings for-itself in being-in-itself. The thingness before which the slave trembled is eliminated, and what appears in that element of thingness is the pure being-for-itself of consciousness. Being-in-itself, the being of life, is no longer separate from the being-for-itself of consciousness; through labor, self-consciousness rises to its self-intuition in being. Stoicism will manifest to us the truth of this intuition of self in being-in-itself. In every case, for such a liberation to come about, all the elements we have distinguished must be present: primordial fear, service, labor. In the absence of that primordial fear, labor does not imprint the true form of consciousness on things. The I remains immersed in determinate being, and its proper meaning remains only an empty meaning: it is stubbornness, not liberty.

> When the entire content of natural consciousness has not been shaken, that consciousness remains in-itself part of determinate being; then, meaning itself is simply stubbornness [*der eigne Sinn ist Eigensinn*], a liberty still in the midst of servitude. As little, in this case, as pure form can become its own essence, can that form, considered as extending beyond the specific, be universal formation, absolute concept. It is merely a specific skill that dominates something specific but does not dominate universal power for objective essence in its totality. (*PE*, I, 166; *PG*, 150; *PM*, 240)

This universal power, this objective essence—the being of life—is now dominated by a consciousness that is not content to negate it but discovers itself within it, and puts itself on stage within it as a spectacle for itself. Self-consciousness has thus become self-consciousness in universal being: it has become *thought*. But this thought, of which labor was the first sketch, is still an abstract thought. The freedom of the stoic will be a freedom only in thought, not an actual and living freedom. Many more developments are needed before self-consciousness can realize itself completely.

CHAPTER 5

The Existence of Others

Jean-Paul Sartre

Formerly I believed that I could escape solipsism by refuting Husserl's concept of the existence of the transcendental "ego."[1] At that time I thought that since I had emptied my consciousness of its subject, nothing remained there that was privileged as compared to the other. But actually although I am still persuaded that the hypothesis of a transcendental subject is useless and disastrous, abandoning it does not help one bit to solve the question of the existence of others. Even if outside the empirical ego there is *nothing other* than the consciousness of that ego—that is, a transcendental field without a subject—the fact remains that my affirmation of the other demands and requires the existence beyond the world of a similar transcendental field. Consequently, the only way to escape solipsism would be here again to prove that my transcendental consciousness is in its very being affected by the extramundane existence of other consciousnesses of the same type. Because Husserl has reduced being to a series of meanings, the only connection that he has been able to establish between my being and that of the other is a connection of *knowledge.* Therefore, Husserl cannot escape solipsism any more than Kant could.

If now instead of observing the rules of chronological succession, we are guided by those of a sort of nontemporal dialectic, we shall find that in the solution that Hegel gives to the problem in the first volume of the *Phenomenology of Mind,* he has made significant progress over Husserl. Here the appearance of the other is indispensable not to the constitution of the world and of my empirical "ego" but to the very

---

1. "La transcendence de l'ego: Esquise d'une description phénoménologique." *Recherches philosophiques* VI (Paris: Boivin, 1936).

existence of my consciousness as self-consciousness. In fact, as self-consciousness the self itself apprehends itself. The equation "myself = myself" or "I am I" is precisely the expression of this fact. At first this self-consciousness is pure self-identity, pure existence for itself. It has certitude of itself, but this certitude still lacks truth. In fact, this certitude would be true only to the extent that its own existence for itself appeared to it as an independent object. Thus, self-consciousness is first a syncretic relation without truth between a subject and an object, an object that is not yet objectified and that is this subject himself. Since the impulse of this consciousness is to realize its concept by becoming conscious of itself in all respects, it tends to make itself valid externally by giving itself objectivity and manifest existence. It is concerned with making the "I am I" explicit and producing itself as an object in order to attain the ultimate stage of development. This state in another sense is naturally the prime mover for the becoming of consciousness; it is self-consciousness in general, which is recognized in other self-consciousnesses and which is identical with them and with itself. The mediator is the other. The other appears along with myself since self-consciousness is identical with itself by means of the exclusion of every other. Thus, the primary fact is the plurality of consciousnesses, and this plurality is realized in the form of a double, reciprocal relation of exclusion. Here we are then in the presence of that connection by means of an internal negation that was demanded earlier. No external nothingness in-itself separates my consciousness from the other's consciousness; it is by the very fact of being me that I exclude the other. The other is the one who excludes me by being himself, the one whom I exclude by being myself. Consciousnesses are directly supported by one another in a reciprocal imbrication of their being.

This position allows us at the same time to define the way in which the other appears to me: he is the one who is other than I; therefore, he is given as a nonessential object with a character of negativity. But this other is also a self-consciousness. As such he appears to me as an ordinary object immersed in the being of life. Similarly, it is thus that I appear to the other: as a concrete, sensible, immediate existence. Here Hegel takes his stand on the ground not of a univocal relation that goes from me (apprehended by the *cogito*) to the other, but of the reciprocal relation that he defines as "the self-apprehension of the one in the other." In fact, it is only in so far as each man is opposed to the other that he is absolutely for himself. Opposite the other and confronting the other, each one asserts his right of being individual. Thus, the *cogito* itself cannot be a point of departure for philosophy; in fact, it can be born only in consequence of my appearance for myself as an individual, and this appearance is conditioned by the recognition of the other. The problem of the other should not be posited in terms of the *cogito*; on the contrary, the existence of the other renders the *cogito* possible as the abstract moment when the self is apprehended as an object. Thus, the "moment" that Hegel calls *being-for-the-other* is a necessary stage of the development of self-consciousness; the road of interiority passes through the other. But the other is of interest to me only to the extent that he is another me, a me-object for me, and conversely to the extent that he reflects my me—that is, in so far as I am an object for him. Due to the fact that I must necessarily be an object for myself only over there in the other, I must obtain from the other the *recognition* of my being. But if another consciousness must mediate between my consciousness *for itself* and itself, then the being-for-itself of my consciousness—and consequently its being in general—depends on the other. As I appear to the other, so I am. Moreover, since the other is such as he appears to me and since my being depends upon the other, the way in which I appear—that is, the moment of the development of my self-consciousness—depends on the way in which the other appears to me. The value of the other's recognition of me depends on the value of my recognition of the other. In this sense to the extent that the other apprehends me as bound to a body and immersed in *life*, I am myself only *an other*. In order to make myself recognized by other, I must risk my own life. To risk one's life, in fact, is to reveal oneself as not-bound to the objective form or to any determined existence—as not-bound to life.

But at the same time I pursue the *death* of the other. This means that I wish to cause myself to be mediated by an other who is only other—that is, by a dependent consciousness whose essential characteristic is to exist only for another. This will be accomplished at the very moment when I risk my life, for in the struggle against the other I have made an abstraction of my sensible being by *risking* it. On the other hand, the other prefers life and freedom even while showing that he has not been able to posit himself as not-bound to the objective form. Therefore, he remains bound to external things in general; he appears to me and he appears to himself as *nonessential*. He is the slave, I am the master; for him it is I who am essence. Thus, there appears the famous "master-slave" relation that so profoundly influenced Marx. We need not here enter into its details. It is sufficient to observe that the slave is the truth of the master. But this unilateral recognition is unequal and insufficient, for the truth of his self-certitude for the master is a nonessential consciousness; therefore, the master is not certain of *being for himself* as truth. In order to attain this truth there is necessary "a moment in which the master does for himself what he does as regards the other and when the slave does as regards the other what he does for himself."² At this moment there will appear a self-consciousness in general that is recognized in other self-consciousnesses and that is identical with them and with itself.

Thus, Hegel's brilliant intuition is to make me depend on the other *in my being*. I am, he said, a being for-itself that is for-itself only through another. Therefore, the other penetrates me to the heart. I cannot doubt him without doubting myself since "self-consciousness is real only in so far as it recognizes its echo (and its reflection) in another."³ Since the very doubt implies a consciousness that exists for itself, the other's existence conditions my attempt to doubt it just as in the work of Descartes my existence conditions systematic doubt. Thus, solipsism seems to be put out of the picture once and for all. By proceeding from Husserl to Hegel, we have realized immense progress: first, the negation that constitutes the other is direct, internal, and reciprocal; second, it calls each consciousness to account and pierces it to the deepest part of its being the problem is posited on the level of inner being, of the universal and transcendental 'I'; finally in my essential being I depend on the essential being of the other, and instead of holding that my being-for-myself is opposed to my being-for-others, I find that being-for-others appears as a necessary condition for my being-for-myself.

Yet in spite of the wide scope of this solution, in spite of the richness and profundity of the detailed insights with which the theory of the master and the slave is filed to overflowing, can we be satisfied with it?

To be sure, Hegel has posed the question of the being of consciousnesses. It is being-for-itself and being-for-others that he is studying, and he holds that each consciousness includes the *reality* of the other. Nevertheless, it is certain that this ontological problem remains everywhere formulated in terms of knowledge. The mainspring of the conflict of consciousnesses is the effort of each one to transform his self-certitude into truth. And we know that this truth can be attained only in so far as my consciousness becomes an *object* for the other at the same time as the other becomes an *object* for my consciousness. Thus, when idealism asks, "How can the Other be an object for me?" Hegel while remaining on the same ground as idealism replies: if there is in truth a me for whom the other is an object, this is because there is an other for whom the me is object. Knowledge here is still the measure of being, and Hegel does not even conceive of the possibility of a being-for-others

---

2. *Phénoménologie de l'Esprit*, 148. Edition Cosson.
3. *Propedeutik, Sämtliche Werke*, XXI, 20.

that is not finally reducible to a "being-as-object." Thus, universal self-consciousness that seeks to disengage itself through all these dialectical phases is by its own admission reducible to a purely empty formula— the "I am I." Yet Hegel writes, "This proposition regarding self-consciousness is void of all content."[4] And in another place he says, "[It is] the process of absolute abstraction that consists in surpassing all immediate existence and that results in the purely negative being of consciousness identical with itself." The limiting term of this dialectical conflict, universal self-consciousness, is not enriched in the midst of its avatars; it is on the contrary entirely denudcd. It is no more than the "I know that another knows as me." Of course, this is because for idealism absolute being and knowledge are identical. But what does this identification involve?

To begin with, this "I am I," a pure, universal form of identity, has nothing in common with the concrete consciousness. The being of self-consciousness cannot be defined in terms of knowledge. Knowledge begins with *reflection* (reflexion), but the game of "the-reflection (reflet)-reflecting" is not a subject-object dyad, not even implicitly. Its being does not depend on any transcendent consciousness; rather, its mode of being is precisely to be in question for itself. The relation of the reflection to the reflecting is in no way a relation of identity and cannot be reduced to the "me = me" or to the "I am I" of Hegel. The reflection does not make itself be the reflecting; we are dealing here with a being that nihilates itself in its being and that seeks in vain to dissolve into itself as a *self*. If it is true that this description is the only one that allows us to understand the original fact of consciousness, then we must judge that Hegel has not succeeded in accounting for this abstract doubling of the me that he gives as equivalent to self-consciousness. . . . Selfness, the foundation of personal existence, is altogether different from an ego or from a reference of the ego to itself. There can be, therefore, no question of defining consciousness in terms of a transcendental ego-ology. In short, consciousness is a concrete being sui generis, not an abstract, unjustifiable relation of identity. It is selfness and not the seat of an opaque, useless ego. Its being is capable of being reached by a transcendental reflection, and there is a *truth* of consciousness that does not depend on the other; rather, the very *being* of consciousness, since it is independent of knowledge, preexists its truth. On this plane as for naive realism, being measures truth; for the truth of a reflective intuition is measured by its conformity to being: consciousness *was there* before

---

4. Ibid.

it was known. Therefore, if consciousness is affirmed in the face of the other, it is because it lays claim to a recognition of its being and not of an abstract truth. In fact, it would be ill conceived to think that the ardent and perilous conflict between master and slave had for its sole stake the recognition of a formula as barren and abstract as the "I am I." Moreover, there would be a deception in this very conflict since the end finally attained would be universal self-consciousness, "the intuition of the existing self by the self." Here as everywhere we ought to oppose to Hegel Kierkegaard, who represents the claims of the individual as such. The individual claims his achievement as an individual, the recognition of his concrete being, and of the objective specification of a universal structure. Of course, the *rights* that I demand from the other posit the universality of *self*; respect of persons demands the recognition of my person as universal. But it is my concrete and individual being that flows into this universal and fills it; it is for that *being-there* that I demand rights. The particular is hae the support and foundation of the universal; the universal in this case could have no meaning if it did not exist for the *purpose* of the individual.

This identification of being and knowledge results in a large number of errors or impossibilities. We shall consider them here under two headings; that is, we shall marshal against Hegel a twofold charge of optimism.

In the first place Hegel appears to us to be guilty of an epistemological optimism. It seems to him that the truth of self-consciousness can appear; that is, that an objective agreement can be realized between consciousnesses—by authority of the other's recognition of me and my recognition of the other. This recognition can be simultaneous and reciprocal: "I know that the other knows me as himself." It produces actually and in truth the universality of self-consciousness. But the correct statement of the problem of others renders this passage to the universal impossible. If the other can in fact refer my "self" to me, then at least at the end of the dialectical evolution there must be a common measure among what I am for him, what he is for me, what I am for myself, what he is for himself. Of course, this homogeneity does not exist at the start; Hegel agrees to this. The relation "master-slave" is not reciprocal. But Hegel affirms that the reciprocity must be capable of being established. Here at the outset he is creating a confusion—so easy that it seems voluntary—between *being-an-object* and *life*. The other, he says, appears to me as an object. Now the object is myself in the other. When Hegel wants to define this object-state more exactly, he distinguishes in it three elements: "This self-apprehension by one in the other is: (1) The abstract moment of self-identity. (2) Each one, however, has also this particularity, that he manifests himself to the other as an external object, as an immediately concrete and sensible existence. (3) Each one is absolutely for himself and individual as opposed to the other."[5]

We see that the abstract moment of self-identity is given in the knowledge of the other. It is given with two other moments of the total structure. But—a curious thing in a philosopher of synthesis—Hegel did not ask if these three elements did not react on one another in such a way as to constitute a new form resistant to analysis. He defines his point of view in the *Phenomenology of Mind* when he declares that the other appears first as nonessential (this is the sense of the third moment cited above) and as a "consciousness immersed in the being of life." But here we are dealing with a pure coexistence of the abstract moment and of *life*. It is sufficient, therefore, that I or the other risk our life in order that in the very act of offering oneself to danger, we realize the analytical separation of life and consciousness: "What the other is for each consciousness, each consciousness is for the other; each consciousness in turn accomplishes in itself by means of its own activity and by means of the activity of the other, that pure abstraction of being for itself. . . . To present oneself as a pure abstraction of self-consciousness is to reveal oneself as a pure negation of one's objective form, to reveal oneself as not-bound to any determined existence; . . . it is to reveal oneself as not-bound to life."[6] Of course, Hegel will say later that by the experience of risk and of the danger self-consciousness learns that life is as essential to it as pure self-consciousness; but this is from a totally different point of view, and the fact still remains that I can always separate, in the other, the pure *truth* of self-consciousness from his *life*. Thus, the slave apprehends the self-consciousness of the master; he is its truth although . . . this truth is still not adequate.[7]

But is it the same thing to say that the other on principle appears to me as an object and to say that he appears to me as bound to a particular existence, as immersed in *life*? If we remain on the level of pure, logical hypotheses, we shall note first that the other can in fact be given to a consciousness in the form of an object without that object's being precisely bound to that contingent object that we call a living body. *In fact* our experience presents us only with conscious, living individuals, but *in theory* it must be remarked that the other is an object for me because he is the other and not because he appears on the occasion of

---

5. Ibid., p. 18.
6. *Phenomenology of Mind*, 148.
7. Idem.

a body-object; otherwise we should fall back into the illusion of space. Thus, what is essential to the other *qua* other is objectivity and not life. Moreover, Hegel took this logical affirmation as his point of departure.

But if it is true that the connection between a consciousness and life does not distort the nature of the "abstract moment of self-consciousness" that remains there, immersed, always capable of being discovered, is the case the same for objectivity? In other words, since we know that a consciousness *is* before being known, then is not a known consciousness wholly modified by the very fact that it is known? Is "to appear as an object for a consciousness" still "to be consciousness"? It is easy to reply to this question: the very being of self-consciousness is such that in its being, its being is in question; this means that it is pure interiority. It is perpetually a reference to a self that it has to be. Its being is defined by this: that it *is* this being in the mode of being what it is not and of no being what it is. Its being, therefore, is the radical exclusion of all objectivity. I am the one who cannot be an object for myself, the one who cannot even conceive for myself of existent in the form of an object (save on the plane of the reflective dissociation). . . . This is not because of the lack of detachment or because of an intellectual prejudice or of a limit imposed on my knowledge, but because objectivity demands an explicit negation: the object is what I make myself not-be whereas I myself am what I make myself be. I pursue myself everywhere, I cannot escape myself, I reapprehend myself from behind. Even if I could attempt to make myself an object, I would already be myself at the heart of that object that I am; and at the very center of that object I should have to be the subject who is looking at it. Moreover, this is what Hegel hinted at when he said that the other's existence is necessary in order for me to be an object for myself. But by holding that self-consciousness is expressed by "I am I"—that is, by identifying it with self-knowledge— he failed to derive the consequences of his first affirmations; for he introduced into consciousness something like an object existing potentially to be disengaged without change by the other. But if to be an object is precisely not-to-be-me, then the fact of being an object for a consciousness radically modifies consciousness not in what it is for itself but in its appearance to the other. The other's consciousness is what I can simply contemplate and what because of this fact appears to me as being a pure given instead of being what has to be me. It is what is released to me in universal time (that is, in the original dispersion of moments) instead of appearing to me within the unity of its own temporalization. For the only consciousness that can appear to me in its own temporalization is *mine*, and it can do so only by renouncing all objectivity. In short, the *for-itself* as for-itself cannot be known by the other. The object that

I apprehend under the name of the other appears to me in a radically *other* form. The other is not a *for-itself* as he appears to me; I do not appear to myself as I am *for-the-other*. I am incapable of apprehending for myself the self that I am for the other, just as I am incapable of apprehending on the basis of the *other-as-object* that appears to me, what the other is for himself. How then could we establish a universal concept subsuming under the name of self-consciousness, my *consciousness* for myself and (of) myself and my *knowledge* of the other? But this is not all.

According to Hegel the other is an object, and I apprehend myself as an object in the other. But the one of these affirmations destroys the other. In order for me to be able to appear to myself as an object in the other, I would have to apprehend the other as subject that is, to apprehend him in his interiority. But in so far as the other appears to me as object, my objectivity for him cannot appear to me. Of course, I apprehend that the other-as-object *refers to me* by means of intentions and acts, but due to the very fact that he is an object, the other-as-a-mirror is clouded and no longer reflects anything. These intentions and these acts are things in the world and are apprehended in the time of the world; they are established and contemplated, their meaning is an object for me. Thus, I can only appear to myself as a transcendent quality to which the other's acts and intentions refer; but since the other's objectivity destroys my objectivity for him, it is as an internal subject that I apprehend myself as being that to which those intentions and those acts refer. It must be understood that this apprehension of myself by myself is in pure terms of consciousness, not of knowledge; by having to be what I am in form of an ekstatic self-consciousness, I apprehend the other as an object pointing to me. Thus, Hegel's optimism results in failure: between the other-as-object and me-as-subject there is no common measure, no more than between self-consciousness and consciousness of the other. I cannot know myself in the other if the other is first an object for me; neither can I apprehend the other in his true being—that is, in his subjectivity. No universal knowledge can be derived from the relation of consciousnesses. This is what we shall call their ontological separation.

But there is in Hegel another and more fundamental form of optimism. This may be called an ontological optimism. For Hegel indeed truth is truth of the whole. And he places himself at the vantage point of truth—that is, of the whole—to consider the problem of the other. Thus, when Hegelian monism considers the relation of consciousness, it does not put itself in any particular consciousness. Although the whole is to be realized, it is already there as the truth of all which is true. Thus, when Hegel writes that every consciousness, since it is identical with itself, is other than the other, he has established himself in the whole, outside consciousnesses, and he considers them from the point of view of the absolute. For individual consciousnesses are moments in the whole, moments which by themselves are *unselbständig*, and the whole is a mediator between consciousnesses. Hence is derived an ontological optimism parallel to the epistemological optimism: plurality can and must be surpassed toward the totality. But if Hegel can assert the reality of this surpassing, it is because he has already given it to himself at the outset. In fact, he has forgotten his own consciousness; he *is* the whole, and consequently if he so easily resolves the problem of particular consciousnesses it is because for him there never has been any real problem in this connection. Actually he does not raise the question of the relation between his own consciousness and that of the other. By effecting completely the abstraction of his own, he studies purely and simpiy the relation between the consciousnesses of others—that is, the relation of consciousnesses that are already for him objects whose nature according to him, is precisely that of being a particular type of object—the subject-object. These consciousnesses from the totalitarian point of view that he has adopted are strictly equivalent to each other although each of them is separated from the rest by a particular privilege.

But if Hegel has forgotten himself, we cannot forget Hegel. This means that we are referred back to the *cogito*. In fact, if, as we have established, the being of my consciousness is strictly irreducible to knowledge, then I cannot transcend my being toward a reciprocal and universal relation in which I could see my being and that of others as equivalent. On the contrary, I must establish myself *in my being* and posit the problem of the other in terms of my being. In a word, the sole point of departure is the interiority of the *cogito*. We must understand by this that each one must be able by starting out from his own interiority, to rediscover the other's being as a transcendence that conditions the very being of that interiority. This of necessity implies that the multiplicity of consciousnesses is on principle unsurpassable, for I can undoubtedly transcend myself *toward* a whole, but I cannot establish myself in this whole so as to contemplate myself and to contemplate the other. No logical or epistemological optimism can cover the scandal of the plurality of consciousnesses. If Hegel believed that it could, this is because he never grasped the nature of that particular dimension of being that is self-consciousness. The task that an ontology can lay down for itself is to describe this scandal and to found it in the very nature of being, but ontology is powerless to overcome it. It is possible . . . that we may be able to refute solipsism and show that the other's existence is both evident and certain for us. But even if we could succeed in making the other's existence share in the apodictic certainty of the *cogito*—that is, of my own existence—we should not thereby "surpass" the other toward any intermonad totality. So long as consciousnesses exist, the separation any conflict of consciousesses will remain; we shall simply have discovered their foundation and their true terrain.

What has this long criticism accomplished for us? Simply this: if we are to refute solipsism, then my relation to the other is first and fundamentally a relation of being to being, not of knowledge to knowledge. We have seen Husserl's failure when on this particular level he measures being by knowledge, and Hegel's when he identies knowledge and being. But we have equally recognized that Hegel, although his vision is obscured by the postulate of absolute idealism, has been able to put the discussion on its true plane.

In *Sein und Zeit* Heidegger seems to have profited by study of his predecessors and to have been deeply impressed with this twofold necessity: (1) the relation between "human-realities" must be a relation of being; (2) this relation must cause "human-realities" to depend on one another in their essential being. At least his theory fulfills these two requirements. In his abrupt, rather barbaric fashion of cutting knots rather than trying to untie them, he gives in answer to the question posited a pure and simple definition. He has discovered several moments—inseparable except by abstraction—in "being-in-the-world," which characterizes human reality. These moments are "world," "being-in," and "being." He has described the world as "that by which human reality makes known to itself what it is"; "being-in" he has defined as *Befindlichkeit* and *Verstand*.[8] We have still to speak of being; that is, the mode in which human reality is its being-in-the world. Being, Heidegger tells us, is the *Mit-Sein*—that is, "being-with." Thus, human-reality the characteristic of being is that human-reality is its being with others. This does not come about by chance. I do not exist first in order that subsequently a contingency should make me encounter the other. The question here is of an essential structure of my being. But this structure is not established from outside and from a totalitarian point of view as it was with Hegel. To be sure, Heidegger does not take his departure from the *cogito* in the Cartesian sense of the discovery of consciousness by itself; but the human-reality that is revealed to him and for which he seeks to fix the structures in concepts is his own. "Dasein ist je meines," he writes. It is by making explicit the preontological comprehension that I have of myself that I apprehend being-with-others as an essential characteristic of my being. In short, I discover the transcendental relation to the other

---

8. Roughly, *Befindlichkeit* is "finitude" and *Verstand* "comprehension."

as constituting my own being, just as I have discovered that being-in-the-world measures my human-reality. Henceforth the problem of the other is a false problem. The other is no longer first a particular existence that I encounter in the world—and which could not be indispensable to my own existence since I existed before encountering it. The other is the ex-centric limit that contributes to the constitution of my being. He is the test of my being inasmuch as he throws me outside of myself toward structures that at once both escape me and define me; it is this test that originally reveals the other to me.

PART III

Alienation and Recognition

CHAPTER 6

Hegel's Economics During the Jena Period

Georg Lukács

The *Economic and Philosophic Manuscripts* contain a crucial criticism of the *Phenomenology of Mind* in the course of which Marx gives a precise account of the achievement and the failing of Hegel's views on economics: "Hegel's standpoint is that of modern political economy. He grasps *labour* as the *essence* of man—as man's essence in the act of proving itself: he sees only the positive, not the negative side of labour. Labour is man's *coming to be for himself* within *alienation*, or as *alienated man*."[1] The present analysis of Hegel's economic views will confirm the accuracy of Marx's observations, both in their positive and in their negative aspects. Hegel did not produce a system of economics within his general philosophy; his ideas were always an integral part of his general social philosophy. This is in fact their merit. He was not concerned to produce original research within economics itself (for this was not possible in Germany at the time), but instead he concentrated on how to integrate the discoveries of the most advanced system of economics into a science of social problems in general. Moreover—and this is where we find the specifically Hegelian approach—he was concerned to discover the general dialectical categories conceded in those social problems.

Needless to say. Hegel was not the first to attempt a synthesis of economics, sociology, history, and philosophy. The isolation of economics from other areas of the social sciences is a feature of the bourgeoisie in its decline. The leading thinkers of the seventeenth and eighteenth

---

1. Marx, *Economic and Philosophic Manuscripts of 1844*, 177.

centuries ranged through the whole territory of the social sciences, and even the works of the outstanding economists such as Petty, Steuart, and Smith constantly ventured forth beyond the frontiers ot economics in the narrower sense. The real originality of Hegel's exploitation of economic discoveries would only be determinable in the context of a history that sets out to explore the interplay between philosophy and economics in modern ttmes (and even in Plato and Aristotle). Unfortunately Marxist historiography has entirely failed to make such a study, so that almost all the necessary groundwork sttll remains to be done. The pointers to such work in the writings of the classics of Marxism-Leninism have been largely ignored.

Nevertheless, something can be said about Hegel's originality here with relative accuracy. For the philosophy of the Renaissance and the Enlightenment, mathematics, geometry, and the burgeoning natural sciences and especially physics were the decisive models. The outstanding thinkers of the day consciously based their method on that of the natural sciences, even when their own subject-matter was drawn from the social sciences. (Of course, for that very reason, it would be interesting and important to discover whether and to what extent the study of economics had had any influence on their general methodology.) Not until the advent of classical German idealism can any other methodological model be found. Naturally, this model also had its antecedents; I need refer only to Vico, whose great achievement in this area has likewise been consigned to oblivion by the scholars of subsequent ages.

The shift in methodology is a product of the new emphasis on the "active side" in philosophy, an emphasis to be found more clearly in Fichte than in Kant. But subjective idealism necessarily held a far too constricted and abstract view of human praxis. In subjective idealism all interest is concentrated on that aspect of human praxis that can be included under the heading of "morality." For this reason the economic views of Kant and Fichte had little bearing on their general method. Since Fichte viewed society, as well as nature, as a merely abstract back drop for the activities of moral man, for *homo noumenon*, and since that backdrop confronted morality as an abstract negative, rigidly indifferent to the moral activity of man, it naturally did not occur to him to investigate the particular laws governing it. His *Closed Commercial State* shows that he had made a study of the Physiocrats. However, the main ideas of the work are not influenced by the knowledge he had acquired. It is a dogmatic attempt to apply the moral principles of his philosophy to the various spheres of society and represents a Jacobin dictatorship of morality over the whole of human society.

Kant's thought is in some respects more flexible and less narrow than Fichte's but he too does not get beyond the point of applying general abstract principles to society. Kant had indeed read the works of Adam Smith and gleaned from them an insight into the nature of modern bourgeois society. But when he attempts to put this knowledge in the service of a philosophy of history he arrives at quite abstract formula. This is what happens in his interesting little essay *Idea for a Universal History with a Cosmopolitan Purpose*, where he attempts to make a philosophical study of the principles of progress in the development of society. He comes to the conclusion that nature has furnished man with an "unsocial sociability" as a result of which man is propelled through the various passions toward progress: "Man desires harmony; but Nature understands better what will profit his species; it desires conflicts."[2] The influence of English thinkers is clear enough. All that has happened is that the discussions have become more abstract without gaining any philosophical substance. For the end-product is nothing but the bad infinity of the concept of infinite progress.

In Hegel's critique of the ethics of subjective idealism, he was unremittingly hostile to this moralistic narrow-mindedness, this unyielding contrast between the subjective and objective sides of social activity. We may infer from this that his view of economics differed fundamentally from that of Kant and Fichte. It was for him the most immediate, primitive, and palpable manifestation of man's social activity. The study of economics should be the easiest and most direct way to distill the fundamental categories of that acavity. . . . Hegel was decisively influenced by Adam Smith's conception of labor as the central category of political economy. Hegel's extension of the idea and systematic exposition of the principles underlying it in The *Phenomenology of Mind* have been fully defined by Marx:

> The outstanding achievement of Hegel's *Phenomenology*. . . is thus first that Hegel conceives the self-creation of man as a process, conceives objectification as loss of the object, as alienation and as transcendence of this alienation; that he thus grasps the essence of *labour* and comprehends objective man—true, because real man—as the outcome of man's *own labour*. The *real*, active orientation of man to himself as a species being, or his manifestation as a real species being (i.e., as a human being), is only possible by the utilization of all the *powers* he

---

2. Kant, *Kleinere Schriften zur Ethik und Religionsphilosophie* (Leipzig 1870), 7 and 8.

has in himself and which are his as belonging to the *species*—
something which in turn is only possible through the coopera-
tive action of all mankind, as the result of history—is only
possible by man's treating these generic powers as objects: and
this, to begin with, is again only possible in the form of estrangement.[3]

Hegel...was, guided in his ideas by an image of modern bourgeois
society, but this image was not simply a reproduction of the retrograde
conditions of Germany in his age (even though this did sometimes color
his view of the world much against his will). What he had in mind was
rather a picture of bourgeois society in its most developed form as the
product of the French Revolution and the Industrial Revolution in
England. With this image in his mind and with his insight into the role
of human activity in society, Hegel attempted to overcome the Kantian
and Fichtean dualism of subjectivity and objectivity, inner and outer,
morality and legality. His aim was to comprehend socialized man whole
and undivided as he really is within the concrete totality of his activity
in society.

His efforts were directed at the ultimate questions of philosophy.
Kant had greatly advanced the "active side" of philosophy, but the price
he had paid was to tear philosophy into two parts, a theoretical and a
practical philosophy, which were only tenuously connected. In particular,
Kant's idealist sublimation of morality barred the way to an explanation
of the concrete interplay between man's knowledge and his praxis.
Fichte's radicalism only deepened the gulf still further. Schelling's objectivity did indeed take a step toward reconciling the two extremes but
he was not sufficiently interested in the social sciences and his knowledge of them was too slight to make any real difference here. Moreover,
he was far too uncritical of the premises of Kant and Fichte.

It was left to Hegel to introduce the decisive change here and what
enabled him to do so was the possibility of exploiting the conception
of labor derived from Adam Smith.... Given his own philosophical
premises, it was not possible for Hegel to explore the economic, social,
and philosophical implications of this idea to their fullest extent.
But...the important thing is to emphasize that his approach to the
problem was determined by his complete awareness of its crucial significance for the whole system.

To clarify the interrelations between knowledge and praxis it is
essential to make the concept of praxis as broad in thought as it is in

---

3. Marx, *Economic and Philosophic Manuscripts,* 177.

reality, that is, it is vital to go beyond the narrow confines of the subjective and moralistic approach of Kant and Fichte. . . . Hegel thinks of human labor, economic activity as the starting point of practical philosophy. In the *System of Ethics* Hegel introduces his discussion of economics with these words: "In the potency of this sphere. . .we find the very beginning of a thorough-going ideality, and the true powers of practical intelligence."[4] In the lectures of 1805–6 this idea has gained in profundity. In a discussion of tools Hegel remarks: "Man makes tools because he is rational and this is the first expression of his *will*. This will is still abstract will—the pride people take in their tools."[5] As is well known the "pure will" is the central category of the ethics of Kant and Fichte. If Hegel now sees tools as the first expression of the human will it is evident that he is employing the term in a way directly opposed to theirs: for him it implies a conception of the concrete totality of man's activity in the actual world. And if he describes this will as abstract this just means that he intends to proceed from there to the more complex and comprehensive problems of society, to the division of labor and so on, that is, that one can only talk concretely of these human activities by talking of them as a whole.

In economics Hegel was an adherent of Adam Smith. This is not to say that his understanding of all the important problems of economics was an profound as that of Smith. It is quite clear that he did not have the sort of insight into the complex dialectic of the "esoteric" economic issues that Marx reveals in the *Theories of Surplus Value*. The contradictions in the basic categories of capitalist economics that Marx unveils there never became apparent to Hegel. But what Hegel does succeed in doing is to clarify a number of categories objectively implied by Smith's economics to a degree that goes far beyond Smith himself.

Hegel's views on economics are put forward first in the *System of Ethics*. This work represents the high point of his experiments with Schelling's conceptual system. In consequence the whole argument in this work is tortuous, over complicated and over elaborate. Moreover, the static mode of presentation often impedes the dialectical movement implicit in the ideas themselves. Much more mature and characteristic of Hegel himself are the essays on *Natural Law* and the economic arguments contained in the lectures of 1803–4 and especially those of 1805–6. The latter contain most developed statement of his economic views in Jena before the *Phenomenology* and embody an attempt to trace

---

4. Lasson, *Schriften zur Politik und Rechtsphilosophie Hegels*, SW, VII, 436.
5. *Realphilosophie*, II, 197.

a systematic dialectical progression from the simplest categories of labor right up to the problems of religion and philosophy. Wherever possible we shall refer to this larest stage of his development. It goes without saving that the *Phenomenology* is a much more advanced stage even than this. But the particular method used in that work has such profound implications for his general approach that it is very hard to select extracts from it for discussion for our present purposes....

Since the literature on Hegel has with very few exceptions simply ignored his preoccupation with economics, and since even those bourgeois writers who were not unaware that it did form an important part of his work were nevertheless quite unable to assess its significance, it is absolutely essential in our view to begin by stating just what his views were. Marx has shown both the importance and the limitations of Hegel's ideas in the passages we have quoted. But he presupposes a knowledge of those ideas; it is obvious, then, that we must begin with exposition if we wish to be able to appreciate the rightness of Marx's assessment. We can reserve our own criticisms for a later stage.

It is very striking that even in his earliest attempts to systematize economic categories Hegel not only uses the triadic form but also that the various categories are grouped together by means of Hegel's very characteristic mode of deduction. Thus, in the *System of Ethics* he begins his discussion with the triad need, labor, and enjoyment and he advances from there to the other, higher triad: appropriation, the activity of labor itself, and possesion of the product.[6] In the lectures of 1805–6 we find the whole matter of labor treated clearly, both the content (the relations of man to the object in the work-process) and the form (the dialectics of deduction as the dialects of reality itself). Hegel writes:

> Determination [dialectic] of the object. It is, therefore, content, distinction—distinction of the deductive process, of the syllogism, moreover: singularity, universality and their mediations. But (a) it is *existent*, immediate: its mean is thinghood, dead universality, *otherness*, and (b) its *extremes* are *particularity, determinacy* and individuality. In so far as it is other, its activity is the self's—since it has none of its own; that extreme is beyond it. As thinghood it is passivity, communication of [the self's] activity, but as something fluid, it contains that activity within itself as an alien thing. Its other extreme is the antithesis (the particularity) of this its existence and of activity. It is *passive;*

---

6. Lasson, *Schriften zur Politik und Rechtsphilosophie Hegels*, SW, VII, 418f. and 421.

it is for another, it [merely] touches that other—it exits only to be dissolved (like an acid). This is its being, but at the same time, active shape *against* it, communication *of the other.*

Conversely, [dialectic of the subject]: in one sense, activity is only something communicated and it [the object] is in fact the communication; activity is then pure recipient. In another sense, activity is activity vis-à-vis an other.

(The gratified impulse is the *annulled labour* of the self; this is the object that labours in its stead. Labour means to make oneself immanently [*diesseitig*] into a *thing.* The division of the impulsive self is this very process of making oneself into an object. ((Desire [by contrast] must always start again from the beginning, it does not reach the point of separating labour from itself.)) The impulse, however, is the unity of the self as made into a thing.)

Mere activity is *pure* mediation, movement; the mere gratification of desire is the pure annihilation of the object.[7]

The dialectical movement that Hegel attempts to demonstrate here has two aspects. On the one hand, the object of labor, which only becomes a real object for man in and through labor, retains the character that it possesses in itself. In the Hegelian view of labor one of the crucial dialectical moments is that the active principle (in German idealism: the idea, concept) must learn to respect reality just as it is. In the object of labor immutable laws are at work, labor can only be fruitful if these are known and recognized. On the other hand, the object becomes another through labor. In Hegel's terminology the form of its thinghood is annihilated and labor furnishes it with a new one. This formal transformation is the result of labor acting on material alien to it yet existing by its own laws. At the same time this transformation can only take place if it corresponds to the laws immanent in the object.

A dialectic of the subject corresponds to this dialectic in the object. In labor man alienates himself. As Hegel says, "he makes himself into a thing." This gives expression to the objective laws of labor that is independent of the wishes and inclination of the individual. Through labor something universal arises in man. At the same time, labor signifies the departure from immediacy, a break with the merely natural, instinctual life of man. The *immediate* gratification of one's needs signifies, on the one hand, the simple annihilation of the object and not its transformation. On the other hand, thanks to its immediacy it always starts up again

7. *Realphilosophie*, II, 197.

in the same place: it does not develope. Only if man places labor between his desire and its fulfillment, only if he breaks with instinctual immediacy of natural man will he *become* fully human.

The humanization of man is a theme treated at length in the lectures of 1805–6. Hegel's idealist prejudices make themselves felt in his belief that man s spiritual awakening, his transition from the world of dream, from the "night" of nature to the first act of conceptualization of naming, his first use of language, can take place independently of labor. In tune with this he puts labor on a higher plane altogether, one where man's powers are already developed. However, isolated remarks indicate that he did have some glimpses of the dialectic at work here. Thus, in his discussion of the origins of language he shows how in the process both object and the self come into being. In a marginal note, however, he observes:

> How does this necessity or stability *come about* so that the self becomes its *existence*, or rather, that the self, that is its *essence*, becomes its existence? For existence is *stable*, thing-like; the self is the form of pure unrest, movement or the night in which all is devoured. Or: the self is *present*, (*universally*) immediate in the name; now through mediation it must become itself through itself. Its unrest must become stabilization: the movement which annuls it as unrest, as pure movement. This [movement] is *labour*. Its *unrest* becomes *object*, stabilized plurality, order. Unrest becomes *order* by becoming object.[8]

The decisive importance of labor in the process of humanization is shown most vividly when Hegel writes his "Robinsonade": his story of the transition to civilization proper. His attitude to the so-called state of nature is quite free of the value judgment, whether positive or negative, which the state of nature so frequently invited in the literature of the Enlightenment. His view is closest to that of Hobbes and is expressed most trenchantly in a paradoxical thesis that he defended at his doctoral examination: "The state of nature is not unjust, and for that very reason we must leave it behind us."[9]

The development of this idea leads Hegel as early as *The System of Ethics* to formulate his "Robinsonade" of "master and servant." This theme is taken up again in the *Phenomenology of Mind* and remains an integral part of his philosophy ever after.[10]

---

8. Ibid., 185.
9. *Erste Druckschriften*, 405.
10. Lasson, *Schriften zur Politik und Rechtsphilosophie Hegels*, SW, VII, 442ff. Works, II, 140ff. *Encyclopaedia*, § 433f.

Let us now consider this, Hegel's most mature statement of the transition from a state of nature of civilization, as we find it set out in the *Phenomenology of Mind*. The starting point is Hobbes' *bellum omnium contra omnes*, the internecine wars of man in his natural condition that Hegel describes as annihilation without preservation. The subjugation of some people by others gives rise to the condition of mastery and servitude. There is nothing novel or interesting in this. What is important is Hegel's analysis of thc relations between master and servant and between them and the world of things:

> The master, however, is the power controlling this state of existence, for he has shown in the struggle that he holds it to be merely something negative. Since he is the power dominating existence, while this existence again is the power controlling the other (the servant), the master holds, *par conséquence*, this other in subordination. In the same way the master relates himself to the thing mediately through the servant. The servant being a self-consciousness in the broad sense, also takes up a negative attitude to things and annuls them; but the thing is, at the same time, independent for him, and, in consequence, he cannot, with all his negating get so far as to annihilate it outright and be done with it; that is to say, he merely works on it. To the master, on the other hand, by means of this mediating process, belongs the immediate relation, in the sense of the pure negation of it, in other words he gets the enjoyment. What mere desire did not attain, he now succeeds in attaining, viz. to have done with the thing, and find satisfaction in enjoyment. Desire alone did not get the length of this because of the independence of the thing. The master, however, who has interposed the servant between it and himself, thereby relates himself merely to the dependence of the thing, and enjoys it without reserve. The aspect of its independence he leaves to the servant, who labours upon it.[11]

It is just this unconfined dominion, this wholly one-sided and unequal relationship that precipitates its own reversal and makes of the master a purely ephemeral episode in history of the spirit while the seminal moments in the development of man spring from the consciousness of the servant.

> The truth of the independent consciousness is accordingly the *consciousness of the servant* . . . . Through work this conscious-

---

11. *The Phenomenology of Mind*, 235–6.

ness comes to itself. In the moment which corresponds to desire in the case of the master's consciousness, the aspect of the non-essential relation to the thing seemed to fall to the lot of the servant, since the thing there retained its independence. Desire has reserved to itself the pure negating of the object and thereby unalloyed feeling of self. This satisfaction, however, is purely ephemeral, for it lacks *objectivity* or *subsistence*. Labour, on the other hand, is desire restrained and checked, it is the ephemeral postponed; in other words labour shapes and fashions the thing. The negative relation to the object passes into the *form* of the object, into something that is permanent and remains; because it is just for the labourer that the object has independence. This negative mediating agency, this activity giving shape and form, is at the same time the individual ex-istence, the pure self-existence of that consciousness, which now in the work it does is externalized and passes into the condition of permanence. The consciousness that toils and serves accordingly attains bv this means the direct apprehension of that independent being as its self.[12]

We know from Hegel's philosophy of history that individuality is the principle that elevates the modern world to a higher plane than that reached by antiquity. In his youth Hegel had completely overlooked the presence of slavery in Greek civilization and directed his attention exclusively toward the nonlaboring freeman of the city-states. Here, how-ever, the dialectics of work leads him to the realization that the high-road of human development, the humanization of man, the socialization of nature can only be traversed through work. Man becomes human only through work, only through the activity in which the independent laws governing objects become manifest, forcing men to acknowledge them, that is, to extend the organs of their own knowledge, if they would ward off destruction. Unalloyed enjoyment condemns to sterility the master who interposes the labor of the servant between himself and the objects and it raises the consciousness of the servant above that of the master in the dialects of world history. In the *Phenomenology* Hegel sees quite clearly that the labor of man is sheer drudgery with all the drawbacks that slavery entails for the development of consciousness. But despite all that the advance of consciousness goes through the mind of the servant and not that of his master. In the dialectics of labor real self-consciousness is brought into being, the phenomenological agent that

---

12. Ibid., 237–8.

dissolves antiquity. The "configurations of consciousness" that arise in the course of the dissolution: septicism, stoicism, and the unhappy consciousness (primitive Christianity) are without exception the products of the dialectics of servile consciousness.

Hegel's discussion of work has already shown that the mere fact of work indicates that man has exchanged the immediacy of nature for a universal mode of existence. As he investigates the determinations of work he uncovers a dialectic in which technology and society interact to the benefit of both. On the one hand, Hegel shows how tools arise out of the dialectcs of labor. Starting with the man, who by using tools, exploits the laws of nature operative in work, he passes through various transitions until he reaches the nodal point where the concept of the machine emerges. On the other hand, though inseparably from the first process, Hegel shows how the universal, that is, the socially determined aspects of work lead to the increasing specialization of particular types of labor, to a widening gulf between the labor of the individual and the satisfaction of the needs of the individual. As we have emphasized, these two processes are intimately connected. As a disciple of Adam Smith Hegel knows perfectly well that a high degree of technical competence presupposes a highly advanced division of labor. By the same token he is no less aware that the perfection of tools and the development of machinery itself contribute to the extension of the division of labor.

Descriptions of this process can be found in all of Hegel's writings on economics. We shall quote his most mature statement of the theme in the lectures of 1905–6:

> The existence and scope of natural wants is, in the context of existence as a whole, vast in number; the things that serve to satisfy them are processed, their *universal inner* possibility is posited as something external, as *form*. This processing is itself manifold; it is *consciousness transforming itself into things*. But since it is universal it becomes abstract labour. The wants are many; to absorb this quantity into the self, to work, involves the *abstraction* of the *universal* images, but it is also a self-propelling formative process. The self that *exists for self is abstract*; it does indeed labour, but its labour too is abstract. Needs are broken down into their various aspects; what is abstract in them is their self-existence, activity, labour. *Because work is only performed for an abstract self-existing need the work performed is also abstract*. This is the concept, the truth of the desire we have here. And the work matches the concept.

There is no satisfaction of all the desires of the individual as
he becomes an object for himself in the life he has brought forth.
Universal labour, then, is *division* of labour, saving of labour.
Ten men can make as many pins as a hundred. Each individual,
because he is an individual labours for *one* need. The content
of his labour goes beyond *his own* need; he labours for the needs
of many, and so does everyone. Each person, then satisfies the
needs of many and the satisfaction of his many particular needs
is the labour of many others.[13]

Hegel also deduced technical progress from this dialectic of the
increasing universality of labor. Naturally, his arguments relating to tools
and machines were determined down to the very last detail by Adam
Smith. Germany as it then was, and especially those parts known personally to Hegel, could not provide him with the direct experience of
the sort of economic realities that might yield such knowledge. On such
matters he had to rely almost exclusively on what he had read about
England and the English economy. His own contribution was to raise
the dialectic immanent in economic processes to a conscious philosophical level.

The double movement that takes place in man and in the objects
and instruments of work is on the one hand the increasing division of
labor with its consequent abstraction. On the other hand, there is a
growing understanding of the laws of nature, of how to induce nature
to work for man. Hegel always emphasizes the connection between the
division of labor (together with the human labor transformed by it) and
technical progress. For example, he demonstrates the necessity for machines in the following passage:

His [i.e., man's] labour itself becomes quite mechanical or
belongs to a quite simple order of things. But the more abstract
it is, the more he becomes pure abstract activity, and this enables him to withdraw from the work-process altogether and
to replace his own labour with the activity of external nature.
He requires only movement and this he finds in external nature,
or in other words, pure movement is just a relationship of the
abstract forms of space and time—abstract external activity,
machines.[15]

13. *Realphilosophie*, II, 214f. Cf. also Lasson, *Schriften zur Politik und
Rechtsphilosophie Hegels*, SW, VII, 433f. and *Realphilosophie*, I, 236ff.
14. Ibid., 215.

But Hegel is the disciple of Adam Smith (and *his* teacher Ferguson) not only as an economist, but also as a critical humanist. That is to say, he is concerned to describe a process, to explain its subjective and objective dialectic as fully as possible and to show that it is not just an abstract necessity but also the necessary mode of human progress. But he does not close his eyes to the destructive effects of the capitalist division of labor and of the introduction of machinery into human labor. And unlike the romantic economists he does not present these features as the unfortunate side of capitalism that has to be improved or eliminated so as to achieve a capitalism without blemish. On the contrary, he can clearly discern the necessary dialectical connections between these aspects of capitalism and its progressive implications for both economics and society.

In the lectures of 1803–4, too, Hegel speaks of the movement toward universality as a result of the division of labor and the use of tools and machinery. He begins by illustrating the dialectical process, by showing how the inventiveness of an individual may lead to a general improvement, a higher level of universality: "Faced with the general level of skill the *individual sets himself up as a particular*, sets himself off from the generality and makes himself even more skilful than others, invents more efficient tools. But the really universal element in his particular skill is his *invention* of something universal; and the *others acquire it from him* thereby annulling his particularity and it becomes the common immediate possession of all." Thus, through the use of tools the activity of man becomes formal and universal, but it remains "his activity." Not until the arrival of the machine is there any qualitative change. He goes on to describe the impact of machinery on human labor:

> With the advent of *machines* man himself annuls his own formal activity and makes the machine perform all his work for him. But this deception which he practises against nature and with the aid of which he remains fixed within the particularity of nature, does not go unavenged. For the more he profits from the machine, the more he subjugates nature, then the more degraded he himself becomes. He does not eliminate the need to work himself by causing nature to be worked on by machines, he only postpones that necessity and detaches his labour from nature. His labour is no longer that of a living being directed at living things, but evades this negative living activity. Whatever remains becomes more *mechanical*. Man only *reduces* labour for society as a whole, not for the individual; on the contrary, he increases it since the more mechanical the work

is the less valuable it is and so the more labour he must perform
to make good the deficiency.[15]

When one considers the time when these remarks were written, and
especially the fact that they were written in Germany they clearly
represent a quite remarkable insight into the nature of capitalism. Hegel
cannot be reproached for thinking of capitalism as the only possible form
of society and for regarding the function of machines in capitalism as
their only possible function. On the contrary, it must be emphasized
that Hegel displays the same refreshing lack of prejudice and narrow-
mindedness that we find in the classical economists Smith and Ricardo:
he can see the general progress in the development of the forces of
production thanks to capitalism and the capitalist division of labor while
at the same time he is anything but blind to the dehumanization of the
workers that this progress entails. He regards this as inevitable and wastes
no time in romantic lamentations about it. At the same time he is much
too serious and honest a thinker to suppress or gloss over unpalatable
truths.

This can be seen particularly clearly when he proceeds to argue that
the division of labor in capitalism and the increase in the forces of production lead necessarily to the pauperization of great masses of people.
The economic causes of this have already been indicated in the remarks
just quoted. In the lectures of 1805–6 he describes the process even more
vividly:

> But by the same token the abstraction of labour makes man
> more mechanical and dulls his mind and his senses. Mental
> vitality, a fully aware, fulfilled life degenerates into empty ac-
> tivity. The strength of the self manifests itself in a rich, compre-
> hensive grasp of life; this is now lost. He can hand over some
> work to the machine; but his own actions become correspond-
> ingly more formal. His dull labour limits him to a single point
> and the work becomes more and more perfect as it becomes
> more and more one-sided . . . . No less incessant is the frenetic
> search for new methods of simplifying work, new machines etc.
> The individual's skill is his method of preserving his own ex-
> istence. The latter is subject to the web of chance which en-
> meshes the whole. Thus a vast number of people are condemned
> to utterly brutalizing, unhealthy and unreliable labour in work-
> shops, factories and mines, labour which narrows and reduces

---

15. Ibid., 237.

their skill. Whole branches of industry which maintain a large class of people can suddenly wither away at the dictates of fashion, or a fall in prices following new inventions in other countries, etc. And this entire class is thrown into the depths of poverty where it can no longer help itself. We see the emergence of great wealth and great poverty, poverty which finds it impossible to produce anything for itself.[16]

Hegel elsewhere presents this insight in summary, almost epigrammatic, form: "Manufacturers and workshops found their existence on the misery of a class."[17]

Hegel here describes social realities with the same ruthless integrity and the same habit of plain speaking that we find in the great classical economists. The insight is almost incredible by German standards of the time and it is not in the least diminished by certain misconceptions that make their appearance from time to time, such as the illusion that the ills he describes could be rememdied by the intervention of the state or the government. For such idealistic illusions are always accompanied by a sober assessment of the limits imposed on state intervention. Moreover, as we know, he consistently opposes all theories that advocate what he regards as excessive government control of economics and society. He does indeed cherish the belief that the state and the government have it in their power to reduce the glaring contrast of wealth and poverty, and above all the notion that bourgeois society as a whole can be kept in a state of "health" despite the gulf between rich and poor. We can obtain a clear picture of Hegel's illusions in this respect if we quote one of his remarks from the *System of Ethics*:

> The government should do all in its power to combat this inequality and the destruction it brings in its wake. It may achieve this immediely by making it harder to make great profits. If it does indeed sacrifice a part of a class to mechanical and factory labour, abandoning it to a condition of brutalization, it must nevertheless preserve the whole in as healthy a state as is possible. The necssary or rather immediate way to achieve this is through a proper constitution of the class concerned.[18]

This amalgam of profound insight into the contradictions of capitalism and naive illusions about the possible panaceas to be applied by the

16. *Realphilosophie* II, 232. Cf. also Lasson, 491f.
17. *Realphilosophie*, II, 257.
18. Lasson, 492.

state marks the whole of Hegel's thought from this time on. In *The Philosophy of Right* Hegel formulates his view in essentially the same terms but on a higher level of abstraction. And we see that his illusions are largely unchanged except that he now regards emigration and colonization as possible methods of ensuring the continued health of capitalist society. He says there: "It hence becomes apparent that despite an excess of wealth civil society is not rich enough, i.e. its own resources are insufficient to check excessive poverty and the creation of a penurious rabble."[19]

Thus, in Hegel's eyes capitalism becomes an objective totality moving in accoraance with its own immanent laws. In the *System of Ethics* he gives the following description of the nature of its economic system (or, as he calls it the system of needs):

> In this system the ruling factor appears to be the unconscious, blind totality of needs and the methods of satisfying them. . . .
> It is not the case that this totality lies beyond the frontiers of knowledge in great mass complexes. . . . Nature itself ensures that a correct balance is maintained, partly by insignificant regulating movements, partly by greater movements when external factors threaten to disrupt the whole.[20]

Thus, like Adam Smith, Hegel sees the capitalist economy as an autonomous self-regulating system. It is self-evident that in 1801 he could only think of disruptions as caused by external factors and not as crises brought about by contradictions within the system itself.

In the context of this self-propelling system of human activities, of objects that generate this activity and are activated by it, Hegel's concept of alienation receives a new, more concrete definition. In the lectures of 1803–4 Hegel describes this system as follows:

> *These manifold* exertions of needs as things must realize their concept, their abstraction. Their general concept must be a thing like them, but one which as an abstraction can represent them all. *Money* is that material existing concept, the unitary form or the possibility of all objects of need. By elevating need and work to this level of generality a vast system of common interest and mutual dependence is formed among a great people, a self-propelling life of the dead, which moves hither and thither, blind

---

19. *Philosophy of Right*, trans. Knox, Oxford 1942, § 245, p. 150.
20. Lasson, *Schriften zur Politik und Rechtsphilosophie Hegels*, SW, VII, 489.

and elemental and, like a wild animal, it stands in constant need of being tamed and kept under control.[21]

This "self-propelling life of the dead" is the new form that "positivity" asumes in Hegel's thought: "externalization." Work not only makes men human according to Hegel, it not only causes the vast and complex array of social processes to come into being, it also makes the world of man into an "alienated," "externalized" world. Here, where we can see the concept embedded in its original, economic context, its dual character becomes particularly obvious. The old concept of positivity had placed a one-sided emphasis on the dead, alien aspect of social institutions. In the concept externalization however, we find enshrined Hegel's conviction that the world of economics that dominates man and that utterly controls the life of the individual. is nevertheless the product of man himself. It is in this duality that the truly seminal nature of externalization is to be found. Thanks to it the concept could become the foundation and the central pillar of the highest form of dialectics developed by bourgeois thought.

At the same time this duality points to the limitations of Hegel's thought, the dangers implicit in his idealism. His great sense of reality leads him to emphasize this duality in his analysis of bourgeois society and its development, erecting its contradictions into a conscious dialectic. Despite the sporadic appearance of illusions he is much too realistic even to play with the idea that externalization could be overcome within capitalist society itself. But, for that very reason. . .will show, he extends the concept of externalization to the point where it can be annulled and reintegrated in the subject. Socially, Hegel cannot see beyond the horizon of capitalism, Accordingly, his theory of society is not utopian. But the idealist dialectic transforms the entire history of man into a great philosophical utopia: into the philosophical dream that externalization can be overcome in the subject, that substance can be transformed into subject.

In the lectures of 1805–6 Hegel gives a very simple and succinct definition of the process of externalization: "(a) In the course of work I make myself into a thing, to a form which *exists*. (b) I thus externalize this my existence, make it into *something alien* and *maintain* myself in it."[22] These latter remarks refer to exchange. The previous quotation alluded to money. Thus, in the course of our discussion of Hegel's view

---

21. *Realphilosophie*, I, 239f.
22. *Realphilosophie*, II, 217.

of capitalist society we have advanced to the higher categories of political economy: exchange, commodity, value, price, and money.

Here too, in all essentials, Hegel's remarks do not diverge from their basis in Adam Smith. But we know from Marx's criticism that this is where the contradictions in Smith's work appear, rather than in what he has to say about work and the division of labor. An naturally enough Hegel's dependence on Smith shows to much greater disadvantage here than in his discussion of work. There was no economic reality in Germany at the time that might have given Hegel the opportunity to test these categories himself and perhaps arrive at his own critique of Smith. Hegel's achievement is that he was not confined to the contemporary economic state of Germany; his philosophical examination of economic ideas does not reflect the backwardness of Germany, but is an attempt to analyze what his reading had taught him about the English economy. Given the greater complexity of economic categories and the fact that they inevitably contained contradictions, the effect on Hegel was that partly he just accepted those contradictions without comment and without recognizing them for what they were and partly he was forced to seek analogies in German conditions and to explain advanced theories in terms of the backward German economy.

This situation is apparent at many points in Hegel's discussions of economics, most of all in the fact that despite his fine dialectical appraisal of the philosophical implications of the Industrial Revolution in England he comes to the conclusion that the central figure in the whole development of capitalism was that of the merchant. Even where Hegel speaks with perfect justice about the concentration of capital and where he shows his understanding that this concentration is absolutely indispensable in capitalism he thinks of it in terms of merchants' capital:

> Like every mass wealth becomes a force. The increase of wealth takes place partly by chance, partly through its universality, through distribution. It is a focus of attraction which casts its net widely and collects everything in its vicinity, just as a great mass attracts a lesser. To him that hath, more is given. Commerce becomes a *complex* system which brings in money from all sides, a system which a *small business could not make use of.*[23]

Hegel talks here in very general terms. But. . .other statements, especially those concerned with the class structure of society, indicate

---

23. Ibid., 232f.

that when Hegel thinks of concentration of capital on a large scale, he always has merchants' capital in mind. For example, in the *System of Ethics* he refers to commerce as the "highest point of universality" in economic life. This cannot be a matter for astonishment if we reject that the most developed form of manufacturing in Germany at that time was linen weaving, which was still organized as a cottage industry.

For these reasons we can see all sorts of uncertainties and confusions in Hegel's definition of economic categories, especially in his notion of value. Hegel never understood the crucial development in the classical theory of value, namely, the exploitation of the worker in industrial production. It is in this light above all that we may interpret Marx's criticism of Hegel, quoted above, that Hegel only took the positive ideas about labor from classical economics, and not the negative sides. We have seen that he clearly sees and frankly describes the facts about the division of society into rich and poor. However, many progressive French and English writers saw and proclaimed this before him without coming any closer than he to a labor theory of value.

Hegel's confusion here is reflected also in his definition of value. He constantly hesitated between subjective and objective definitions, without ever coming down on one side or the other. Thus, in the later lectures we find such subjective definitions as: "Value is *my opinion* of the matter."[24] And this despite earlier statements, both in the same lectures and elsewhere, from which it is quite clear that he wishes to think of value as an objective economic reality. Thus, in the *System of Ethics* he says that the essence of value lies in the equality of one thing with another: "The abstraction of this equality of one thing with another, its concrete unity and legal status is *value*; or rather value is itself equality as an abstraction, the ideal measure; whereas the real, empirical measure is the price."[25]

However, all these unclarities and hesitations, and the confusion of economic and legal categories such as we find in this quotation. . .do not prevent Hegel from pursuing the dialectics of objective and subjective, universal and particular right into the heart of the categories of economics. In the process he brings a mobility into economic thought that was only objectively present in the works of the classical economists, or to put it in Hegelian terms, a mobility that was only present in itself, implicitly, and not explicitly, for us. Not until forty years later in the brilliant essay of the young Engels in the *Deutsch-Französische Jahr-*

---

24. Ibid., 217.
25. Lasson, *Schriften zur Politik und Rechtsphilosophie Hegels*, SW, VII, 437.

bücher do the dialectical structure and the interplay of the various categories of economics come to the surface once again, and this time, of course, at quite a different theoretical level, both economically and philosophically.

For example, in his analysis of exchange Hegel writes as follows:

> The concept [of exchange] is mobile, it is destroyed in its antithesis, it absorbs the other thing opposed to it, replacing that which it previously possessed; and it does so in such a way that that which existed before as an idea, now enters as a reality. . . an ideal which by its nature was at first a practical ideal, existing prior to enjoyment. Externally, exchange is two-fold, or rather a repetition of itself; for the universal object, superfluity, and then the particular, viz. need, is in substance a single object, but its two forms are necessarily repetitions of the same thing. But the concept, the essence of the matter is transformation. . . and its absolute nature is the identity of opposites.[26]

The dialectic of the categories of economics is much more striking in Hegel's discussion of money, where the reader can see even more clearly how in his view the structure of capitalism culminates in trade. Writing about the role of money he says:

> All needs are comprehended in this single need. Need which had been a need for a thing, now becomes merely an *idea*, unenjoyable in itself. The object here is valid only because it *means* something, and no longer *in itself*, i.e. to satisfy a need. It is something utterly *inward*. The ruling principle of the merchant class then is the realization of the identity of the *essence* and the *thing*: a man is as real as the money he owns. Imagination vanishes, the meaning has immediate existence; the essence of the matter is the matter itself: value is hard cash. The formal principle of reason is present here. (But this money which bears the *meaning* of all needs is itself only an *immediate thing*)—it is the abstraction from all particularity, character, etc., individual skill. The outlook of the merchant is this hardheadedness in which the particular is wholly estranged and no longer counts; only the strict letter of the *law* has value. The bill must be honoured whatever happens—even if family, wealth, position, life are sacrificed. No quarter is given. . . . Thus in this abstraction spirit has become object as *selfless* inwardness.

---

26. Ibid., 437f.

But that which is within is the Ego itself, and this Ego is its existence. The internal constellation is not the lifeless thing— *money*, but likewise the Ego.[27]

For all the obscurity of parts of this argument two highly progressive and extremely profound ideas emerge from these passages. First, Hegel has a much greater understanding of the nature of money than many eighteenth-century English writers on economics (such as Hume), who failed to recognize the objectivity of money, its reality as a thing, in Hegel's term, and who saw money as no sore than a relation. Second, here and in a number of other places it is evident that Hegel had at least a glimmering of the problem that Marx was later to describe as "fetishism." He stresses the objectivity of money, its thinghood, but sees no less clearly that in the last resort it is a social relation between men. This social relation appears here in the form of an idealist mystification (The Ego), but this does not detract in the least from the brilliance of Hegel's insight; it merely shows us once again the intimate connections between his achievements and his fallings.

---

27. *Realphilosophie*, II, 256f.

CHAPTER 7

Labor and Interaction

REMARKS ON HEGEL'S JENA *PHILOSOPHY OF MIND*

Jürgen Habermas

During 1803–4 and 1805–6 Hegel held lectures on the philosophy of nature and of mind at Jena. The *Philosophy of Mind* is linked to the *System of Morality*, which was only worked out in a fragmentary manner. These works of Hegel[1] still are under the influence of the study of political economy that Hegel was pursuing at the time. Marxist studies of Hegel always have pointed to this fact.[2] In spite of this, the distinctive position of the Jena *Philosophy of Mind* within the Hegelian system has not until now received adequate consideration. The conception that Lasson set forth in the preface to his edition of the Jena lectures continues to predominate: these works are regarded as a preparatory stage for the *Phenomenology* and the parallels to the later system are emphasized. In contrast to this, I would like to present the thesis that in the two Jena lecture courses, Hegel offered a distinctive, systematic basis for the formative process of the spirit, which he later abandoned.

The categories language, tools, and family designated three equally significant patterns of dialectical relation: symbolic representation, the labor process, and interaction on the basis of reciprocity; each mediates subject and object in its own way. The dialectics of languge, of labor,

---

1. *Das System der Sittlichkeit* is quoted from Lasson's edition of *Hegels Schriften zur Politik und Rechtsphilosophie, Sämtliche Werke*, vol. 7 (Leipzig, 1923), 415–99; the two versions of the Jena *Philosophie des Geistes* were also edited by Lasson: *Jenenser Realphilosophie I, Sämtlich Werke*, vol. 19, 195ff., and *Jenenser Realphilosophie II, Sämtliche Werke*, vol. 20, 177ff.

2. G. Lukács, *Der junge Hegel* (Berlin, 1954).

and of moral relations are each developed as a specific configuration of mediation; what is involved are not stages constructed according to the same logical form, but diverse forms of construction itself. A radicalization of my thesis would read: it is not the spirit in the absolute movement of reflecting on itself that manifests itself in, among other things, language, labor, and moral relationships, but rather, it is the dialectical interconnections among linguistic symbolization, labor, and interaction that determine the concept of spirit. The locus within the Hegelian system of the categories named would speak against this: they do not appear in the logic but in the _Realphilosophie_. On the other hand, at that time, the dialectical relations still adhere so sensuously (_anschaulich_) to the basic patterns of heterogeneous experience, that the logical forms diverge according to the material context from which they are drawn: externalization (_Entäusserung_) and alienation (_Entfremdung_), appropriation and reconciliation are not yet integrated. In any case, the tendency of the Jena lectures is that only the aggregate of the three dialectical patterns of existing consciousness can render spirit transparent in its structure.[3]

---

3. The structure of the lectures also speaks in favor of this thesis. The categories of language, tools, and family possession (_Familiengut_) extend into the dimension of external existence and therefore belong, according to the later cogent divisions of the system, to the configuration (_Gestalten_) of the objective spirit. Still, in spite of this, they do not appear in the Jena version under the corresponding title of "real" for "actual") "spirit," but instead appear in the first part of the _Philosophy of Spirit_, for which the editor has chosen the designation, within the system, of "subjective spirit." Now, according to the usage of the _Enzyklopädie_, subjective spirit consists of only those determinations that characterize the relationship of the cognitive and active subject to itself. The objectivations of language (transmitted symbols), of labor (productive forces), and of action in reciprocity (social roles) do not belong to this sphere. In terms of them, however, Hegel demonstrates the essence of spirit as an organization of middles (or middle ground). The Jena presentation obviously does not as yet obey the later system structure. The "real spirit" is not set as preceding the level of subjective spirit, but represents a division that more appropriately might have borne the title "abstract spirit." In it Hegel specifies the abstract determinations of spirit in the sense of representing a unity of intelligence and will produced in fundamental connection with symbolic representation, labor, and interaction— and not in the sense of those abstractions that remain as subjective spirit when we separate from the formative process of spirit all the objectification in which it has its external existence.

THE "I"

In the introduction to the *Subjective Logic*, Hegel recalls to mind that concept of the "I" in which his fundamental experience of the dialectic is contained:

> "I". . . is that initially pure unity relating to itself, and this it is not immediately, but in that it abstracts from all determinateness and content and, in the freedom of unlimited self-equality, passes back into itself. Thus it is universality; unity which is unity with itself only due to that negative comportment, which appears as abstraction, and which therefore contains all the determinateness, dissolved within itself. Secondly, "I" is singularity just as immediately as it is the negativity which relates to itself; it is absolute being-determinate which confronts the other and excludes it; individual personality. The nature of both the "I" and the concept consists both of this absolute universality, which is just as immediately absolute singular individuation [*Vereinzelung*], as well as a being-in-and-for-itself, which is simply being-posited, and which is this being-in-and-for-itself only through its unity with being-posited. Neither the "I" nor the concept can be comprehended if the two above-mentioned moments are not conceived simultaneously in their abstraction and in their perfect unity.[4]

Hegel takes as his point of departure that concept of the I Kant had developed under the title of the original synthetic unity of apperception. There the I is represented as the "pure unity relating to itself," as the "I think," which must be capable of accompanying all of my inner representations. This concept articulates the fundamental experience of the philosophy of reflection: namely, the experience of ego-identity in self-reflection, thus the experience of self of the knowing subject, which abstracts from all possible objects in the world, and refers back to itself as the sole object. The subjectivity of the I is determined as reflection—it is the relation of the knowing subject to itself. In it the unity of the subject as self-consciousness constitutes itself. At the same time, Kant interprets this experience of self-reflection in terms of the presuppositions of his theory of knowledge: he purifies the original apperception, which is to guarantee the unity of transcendental consciousness, of all empirical contents.

---

4. For another translation of this passage, see *Hegel's Science of Logic*, trans. W. H. Johnston and L. G. Struthers, (London: 1951) II, 217f.

Fichte furthers the reflection of self-reflection, *prior* to its distribution among the spheres, as the foundation of which it is, after all, to
serve, father, and encounters the problem of the foundation (*Begründung*)
indeed of the ultimate foundation—of the I. In this he pursues the
dialectic of the relation between the I and the other within the subjectivity of self-knowing.[5] Hegel, on the other hand, confines himself to
the dialectic of the I and the other within the framework of the intersubjectivity of spirit, in which the I communicates not with itself as
its other, but instead with another I as its other.

The dialectic of Fichte's *Wissenschaftslehre* of 1794, which is expressed in that the I simply posits itself, remains confined within the
condition of solitary reflection. As a *theory of self-consciousness*, it
resolves the aporias of that relation in which the I constitutes itself by
knowing itself in terms of (*bei*) an other identified as itself. Hegel's
dialectic of self-consciousness passes over the relation of solitary reflection in favor of the complementary relationship between individuals who
know each other. The experience of self-consciousness is no longer considered the original one. Rather, for Hegel it results from the experience
of interaction, in which I learn to see myself through the eyes of other
subjects. The consciousness of myself is the derivation of the intersection
(*Berschränkung*) of perspectives. Self-consciousness is formed only on
the basis of mutual recognition; it must be tied to my being mirrored
in the consciousness of another subject. That is why Hegel, cannot
answer the question of the origin of the identity of the I as Fichte does,
with a foundation of self-consciousness returning into itself, bnt solely
with a *theory of spirit*. Then spirit is not the fundament underlying the
subjectivity of the self in self-consciousness, but rather, the medium
within which one I communicates with another I, and *from* which, as
an absolute mediation, the two mutually form each other into subjects.
Consciousness exists as the middle ground on which the subjects encounter each other, so that without encountering each other they cannot
exist as subjects.

Fichte only deepens Kant's transcendental unity of self-consciousness; the abstract unity of synthesis is resolved into the original action
that produces the unity of the opposition of the I and the other, by which
the I knows itself. Hegel, on the other hand, retains Kant's empty identity
of the I; but he reduces this I to a moment, by comprehending it under
the category of the universal. I as self-consciousness is universal, because

---

5. See D. Henrich, *Fichtes ursprüngliche Einsicht* (Frankfurt, 1967).

it is an abstract I, that is, it has arisen from the abstraction of all contents given to a subject that knows or has mental representations. In the same way as it abstracts from the manifold of external objects, an I retains itself as identical must abstract from the succession of inner states and experiences. The universality of the abstract I is displayed in that, by means of this category, *all possible* subjects, thus *everyone* who says "I" to himself, are determined as individuals. But on the other hand, the same category "I" is also an instruction in each case to think a specific subject, which, as it says "I" to itself, asserts itself as an inalienably individual and singular subject. Thus, the identity of the I does not mean only that abstract universality of self-consciousness as such, but at the same time the category of singularity. "I" is individuality not only in the sense of a repeatable identification of a "this-there" (*Diesda*) within specifiable coordinates, but in the sense of a proper name, which signifies that which is simply individuated. "I" as category of singularity excludes the reduction to a finite number of elements, for example, to the currently known number of elementary components constituting the genetic substance.

While Fichte comprehends the concept of "I" as the identity of "I" and "not-I," Hegel from the outset comprehends it as the identtty of the universal and the singular. "I" is the universal and the singular in one. Spirit is the dialectical unfolding of this unity, namely, moral totality. Hegel does not select this term arbitrarily, for "spirit," with which we are familiar in ordinary language as in the spirit of a nation, of an epoch, or team spirit, always extends beyond the solitary self-consciousness. The I as the identity of the universal and the singular can only be comprehended in terms of the unity of a spirit that embraces the identity of an I with an other not identical with it. Spirit is the communication of individuals (*Einzelner*) in the medium of the universal, which is related to the speaking individuals as the grammar of a language is, and to the acting individuals as is a system of recognized norms. It does not place the moment of universality before that of singularity, but instead permits the distinctive links between these singularities. Within the medium of this universal—which Hegel therefore called a concrete universal—the single beings can identify with each other and still at the same time maintain themselves as nonidentical. The original insight of Hegel consists in that the I as self-consciousness can only be conceived if it is spirit, that means, if it goes over from subjectivity to the objectivity of a universal in which the subjects who know themselves as nonidentical are united on the basis of reciprocity. Because "I" in this precisely explicated sense is the identity of the universal and the singular, the individuation of a neonate, which within the womb of the mother has been an exemplar of the species as a prelinguistic living being, and thus could be explained biologically in terms of a combination of a finite number of elements quite adequately, once born can only be conceived as a process of socialization. To be sure, here socialization cannot be conceived as the adaptation to society of an already given individuality, but as that which itself produces an individuated being.[6]

THE OTHER

The *moral relationship* was clarified by the young Hegel in terms of the relationship between lovers: "In love the separated entities (*das Getrennte*) still exist, but no longer as separated—as united (*Einiges*) and the living feels the living."[7] In the second Jena lectures Hegel explains love as the knowing (*Erkennen*) that recognizes itself in the other. From the union of distinct entities (*Unterschiedener*) results a knowledge that is characterized by "double meaning": "Each is like the other in that wherein it has opposed itself to the other. By distinguishing itself from the other it thereby becomes identical (*Gleichsetzen*) with it; this is a cognitive process precisely in that . . . for the being itself the opposition is transformed into sameness, or that the one, as it looks at itself in the other, knows itself."[8] To be sure, Hegel does not explicate the relation of recognizing oneself in the other, on which in turn the concept of the I as an identity of the universal and the singular depends, directly from the relations of intersubjectivity, through which the complementary agreement of subjects confronting each other is secured. Rather, he presents love as the result of a movement, love as the reconciliation of a preceding conflict. The distinctive sense of an ego-identity based on reciprocal recognition can be understood only if it is seen that the dialogic relation of the complementary unification of opposing subjects signifies at the same time a relation of logic *and* of the praxis of life. That is shown in the dialectic of the moral relationship, which Hegel develops under the title of the *struggle for recognition*. It reconstructs the suppression and reconstitution of the dialogue situation as the moral relationship. In this movement, which alone may be called dialectical, the logical

---

6. From this viewpoint, that the process of individuation can only be conceived as socialization, and the latter in turn can only be conceived as individuation, Émile Durkheim, in his first great work, *De la division du travail social* (1893), developed the basis of a sociological theory of action.

7. Hegel, *Jugendschriften*, ed. Nohl, 379.

8. *Realphilosophie II*, 201.

relation of a communication distorted by force itself exercizes practical force. Only the result of this movement eradicates the force and establishes the noncompulsory character of the dialogic recognition of oneself in the other: love as reconciliation. What is dialectical is not unconstrained intersubjectivity itself, but the history of its suppression and reconstitution. The distortion of the dialogic relationship is subject to the causality of split-off symbols and reified logical relations—that is, relations that have been taken out of the context of communication and thus are valid and operative only behind the backs of the subjects. The young Hegel speaks of a causality of destiny.

In the fragment on the *Spirit of Christianity* he demonstrates this causality by the example of the punishment that strikes the one who destroys a moral totality. The "criminal" who revokes (*aufhebt*) the moral basis, namely, the complementary interchange of noncompulsory communication and the mutual satisfaction of interests, by putting himself as individual in the place of the totality, sets in motion the process of a destiny that strikes back at him. The struggle that is ignited between the contending parties and the hostility toward the injured and oppressed other makes the lost complementary interchange and the bygone friendliness palpable. The criminal is confronted by the power of deficient life. Thus, he experiences his guilt. The guilty one must suffer under the power of the repressed and departed life, which he himself has provoked, until he has experienced the deficiency of his own life in the repression of others' lives, and, in his turning away from the lives of others, his own alienation from himself. In the causality of destiny the power of suppressed life is at work, which can only be reconciled, when, out of the experiente of the negativity of a sundered life, the longing for that which has been lost arises and necessitates identifying one's own denied identity in the alien existence one fights against. Then both parties recognize the hardened positions taken against each other to be the result of the separation, the abstraction from the common interconnection of their lives—and within this, in the dialogic relationship of recognizing oneself in the other, they experience the common basis of their existence.

In the Jena lectures the dialectics of the struggle for recognition is removed from the context of "crime"; here the point of departure is the sensitive relationship between subjects who attach their whole being to each detail of a possession they have labored to gain. The struggle for recognition they conduct as a life-and-death struggle. The abstract self-assertion of parties contemptuous of each other is resolved by the combatants risking their lives and thus overcoming resolving and revoking (sublating) the singularity they have inflated into a totality: "Our knowledge that the acknowledged total consciousness only exists by sublating itself, now is known by this consciousness itself: it itself performs this reflection of itself within itself, that the single totality, in which it [the reflection] wants to preserve itself as such, absolutely sacrifices itself, sublates itself, and thereby does the opposite of what it sets out to do. The totality itself can only exist as a sublated one: it cannot preserve itself as an existing one, but only as one that is posited as sublated."[9] Destiny avenges itself on the combatants, not, to be sure, as destiny did in the case of the criminal, as punishment, but still in the same manner, as destruction of the self-assertion that severs itself from the moral totality. The result is not the immediate recognition of oneself in the other, thus not reconciliation, but a position of the subjects with respect to each other on the basis of mutual recognition—namely, on the basis of the knowledge that the identity of the I is possible solely by means of the identity of the other, who in turn depends on my recognition, and who recognizes me.[10] This Hegel calls the absolute salvation of singularity, namely, its existence as "I" in the identity of universality and singularity: "This being of consciousness, that exists as single totality, as one which has renounced itself, perceives itself [*schaut sich an*] precisely on that account in another consciousness. . . . In every other consciousness it is what it is immediately for itself, by being in another—a sublated totality; by this singularity has been saved absolutely.[11]

Hegel's concept of the I as the identity of the universal and the singular is directed against that abstract unity of pure consciousness relating solely to itself, the abstract consciousness of original apperception, to which Kant had attached the identity of consciousness as such. The fundamental experience of the dialectic, however, which Hegel develops in the concept of the I, derives. . .not from the experiential domain of theoretical consciousness, but from that of the practical. The consequences of the new departure for the critique of Kant were therefore first drawn by the young Hegel in a critique of moral doctrine.

Because Hegel conceives self-consciousness in terms of the interactional structure of complementary action, namely, as the result of a struggle for recognition, he sees through the concept of autonomous will that appears to constitute the essential value of Kant's moral philosophy.

---

9. *Realphilosophie I*, 230.
10. In his posthumously published work, *Mind, Self and Society* (1934), G. H. Mead repeats Hegel's insight—though under the naturalistic presuppositions of pragmatism—that the identity of the I can only constitute itself in the acquisition by practice of social roles, namely, in the complementary character of behavioral expectations on the basis of mutual recognition.
11. *Realphilosophie I*, 230.

He realizes that this concept is a peculiar abstraction from the moral relationships of communicating individuals. By *presupposing* autonomy—
and that means the will's property of being a law unto itself—in practical
philosophy in the same way as he does the unassailable and simple identity of self-consciousness in theoretical philosophy. Kant expels moral
action from the very domain of morality itself. Kant assumes the limiting
case of a preestablished coordination of the acting subjects. The prior
synchronization of those engaged in action within the framework of
unbroken intersubjectivity banishes the problem of morality from the
domain of moral doctrine—namely, the interplay of an intersubjectivity
that has been mediated by overidentification and loss of communication.[12]
Kant defines moral action according to the principle, "to act according
to no other maxims than that which can have itself as universal law as
its object."[13] Universality of moral law here not only means intersubjective obligation as such, but *the* abstract form of universal validity that
is bound a priori to general agreement. Every single subject must *attribute* its maxims for action to every other subject as equally obligating
maxims of action, doing so as it examines their suitability as principles
of a universal legislation: "It is not enough that. . .we attribute freedom
to our will when we have not sufficient reason to attribute just this same
freedom to all rational beings. Morality can only serve as a law for us
as rational beings, and thus it must be valid for all rational beings."[14]
The moral laws are abstractly universal in the sense that, as they are
valid as universal for me, *eo ipso* they must also be considered as valid
for all rational beings. Therefore, under such laws interaction is dissolved
into the actions of solitary and self-sufficient subjects, each of which
must act as though it were the sole existing consciousness; at the same
time, each subject can still have the certainty that all its actions under
moral laws will necessarily and from the outset be in harmony with the
moral actions of all possible other subjects.

The intersubjectivity of the recognition of moral laws accounted
for a priori by practical reason permits the reduction of moral action to
the monologic domain. The positive relation of the will to the will of
others is withdrawn from possible communication, and a transcen-
dentally necessary correspondence of isolated goal-directed activities
under abstract universal laws is substituted. To this extent moral action
in Kant's sense is presented, *mutatis mutandis*, as a special case of what
we today call strategic action.

---

12. See K. Heinrich, *Von der Schwierigkeit Nein zu sagen* (Frankfurt, 1965).
13. Kant, *Grundlegung zur Metaphysik der Sitten*, BA 98.
14. Ibid., 100f.

Strategic action is distinguished from *communicative actions* under
common traditions by the characteristic that deciding between possible
alternative choices can in principle be made monologically—that means,
ad hoc without reaching agreement, and indeed must be made so, because the rules of preference and the maxims binding on each individual
partner have been brought into prior harmony. The completely intersubjective validity of the rules of the game is part of the denition of the
situation within which the game is played, in the same way as the a
priori validity of the moral law is guaranteed by practical reason on the
transcendental level in Kant's moral doctrine. Both cases eliminate
problems of morality, which arise solely in the context of an intervening
communication and the intersubjectivity that emerges among actors on
the always precarious basis of mutual recognition. From the moral
viewpoint we must disregard the moral relationship in Hegel's sense,
and not take into consideration that the subjects are involved in a
complex of interactions as their *formative process*. We must disregard
what enters into the dialectical course of violent communication and
what results from it; thus, we must first abstract from the concrete
consequences and ramifications of action guided by moral intentions;
furthermore we must abstract from the specic inclinations and interests,
from the "welfare" (*Wohl*) by which the moral action is motivated and
which it can serve objectively; and finally, we must abstract from the
content (*Materie*) of duty, which is only determined within a specific
situation.[15] This threefold abstraction had been criticized by the young
Hegel in the statement: "As long as laws are the highest [instance]. . .the
individual must be sacrificed to the universal, i.e., it must be killed."[16]

INTERACTION

Because Hegel does not link the constitution of the I to the reflection
of the solitary I on itself, but instead understands it in terms of formative
processes, namely the communicative agreement (*Einigung*) of opposing
subjects, it is not reflection as such that is decisive, but rather the
medium in which the identity of the universal and the individual is
formed. And Hegel speaks of the "middle," or medium, by passing
through which consciousness attains existence. After our considerations
up to this point, we can expect that Hegel will introduce communicative
action as the medium for the formative process of the self-conscious

---

15. Hegel, *Enzyklopädie*, §504ff.
16. Hegel, *Jugendschriften*, ed. Nohl, 278.

spirit. And in fact in his Jena lectures he uses the example of the shared existence of a primary group, namely, family interaction, to construct the "family possession" (or welfare—*Familiengut*) as the existing middle of reciprocal modes of contact. However, besides the "family" two further categories are to be found, which Hegel develops in the same manner as media of the self-formative process: language and labor. Spirit is an organization of equally original media: "That first dependent existence— consciousness as middle—is the spirit's existence as language, as tool and as the (family) possession, or as the simple unity (*Einssein*): memory, labor, and family."[17] These three fundamental dialectical patterns are heterogeneous; as media of the spirit, language and labor cannot be traced back to the experiences of interaction and of mutual recognition.

Language does not already embrace the communication of subjects living together and acting; rather here it means only the employment of symbols by the solitary individual who confronts nature and gives names to things. In immediate perception (*Anschauung*) the spirit is still animalistic. Hegel speaks of the nighttime production of the representational faculty of imagination, of the fluid and not yet organized realm of images. Only with the appearance of language, and within language, do consciousness and the being of nature begin to separate for consciousness. The dreaming spirit, as it were, awakens when the realm of images is translated into the realm of names. The awakened spirit has memory; it is capable of making distinctions and at the same time of recognizing that which it has distinguished. Following the conceptions of Herder's prize essay,[18] Hegel sees the essential achievement of the symbols to be representation: synthesis of the manifold is bound to the representational function of features that permit the identification of objects. Naming and memory are but two sides of the same thing: "The idea of this existence of consciousness is memory, and its existence itself, language."[19]

As the name of things, the symbol has a double function. On the one hand, the power of representation consists in making present something that is not immediately given through something else that is immediately given, but which stands for something other than itself.

17. *Realphilosophie I*, 205.
18. Herder's prize essay, "*Über den Ursprung der Sprache*," in *Sämtliche Werke*, ed. Suphan, vol. 5 (Berlin, 1891)—translated by Alexander Gode in *On the Origin of Language: Two Essays by Jean-Jacques Rousseau and Johann Gottfried Herder*, ed. John H, Moran and Alexander Gode (New York, 1966). Only the first part of Herder's essay has been translated by Gode.
19. *Realphilosophie I*, 211; on this, see K. Löwith, "Hegel und die Sprache," in *Zur Kritik her christlichen Überlieferung*, 1966, 97ff.

The representational symbol indicates an object or a state of affairs as something else (*ein Anderes*), and designates it in the meaning that it has for us. On the other hand, we ourselves have produced the symbols. By means of them speaking consciousness becomes objective for itself and in them experiences itself as a subject. This relation, too, of the reflexive perception of the subject in language had already been characterized by Herder. In order that nature can constitute itself into the world of an I, language must thus achieve a twofold mediation: on the one hand, of resolving and preserving the perceived (*angeschaut*) thing in a symbol, which represents it, and on the other, a distancing of consciousness from its objects, in which the I, by means of symbols it has produced itself, is simultaneously with the thing and with itself. Thus, language is the first category in which spirit is not conceived as something internal, but as a medium that is neither internal nor external. In this, spirit is the *logos* of a world and not a solitary self-consciousness.

Labor Hegel calls that specific mode of satisfying drives that distinguishes existing spirit from nature. Just as language breaks the dictates of immediate perception and orders the chaos of the manifold impressions into identifiable things, so labor breaks the dictates of immediate desires and, as it were, arrests the process of drive satisfaction. Like symbols in language, here the instruments, in which the laborer's experience of his objects is deposited, form the existing middle. The name is that which has permanence (*das Bleibende*) as against the ephemeral moments of the perceptions; in the same way, the tool is that which is general as against the ephemeral moments of desire and enjoyment: "It is that wherein working has its permanence, that alone which remains of the laborer and the substances worked upon, and in which its contingency is eternalized; it is inherited in the traditions, while that which desires, as well as that which is desired, only subsist as individuals and as individuals pass away."[20] The symbols permit recognizing again the identical (*des Selben*), the instruments retain the rules according to which the domination of natural processes can be repeated at will: "In the tool the subjectivity of labor has been elevated to something universal; everyone can imitate it and work in precisely the same manner; thus it is the constant rule [*Regel*] of labor."[21]

Of course, the *dialectic of labor* does not mediate between subject and object in the same manner as the *dialectic of representation*. It begins not with the subjection of nature to self-generated symbols, but,

---

20. *Realphilosophie I*, 221.
21. Hegel, *System der Sittlichkeit*, in Lasson, *Schriften zur Politik*, 428.

on the contrary, with the subjection of the subject to the power of external nature. Labor demands the suspension of immediate drive satisfaction; it transmits the energies of human effort (*Leistungsenergien*) to the object worked on under the laws imposed by nature on the I. In this twofold respect Hegel speaks of the subject making itself into a thing—reifying itself—in labor: "Labor is the this-wordly [*diesseitige*] making oneself into a thing. The splitting up of the I existing in its drives (namely), into the reality-testing ego and into the repressed instinctual demands—J.H.) is precisely this making oneself into an object."[22] By way of my subjection to the causality of nature, the results of my experience come into being for me in the tools, by means of which I can in turn let nature work for me. As consciousness gains the unintended fruit of its labor through technical rules, it returns back to itself from its reification, and, indeed, it returns as the cunning (or artful) consciousness which, in its instrumental action, turns its experience of natural processes against these processes themselves: "Here the drive withdraws entirely from labor. It lets nature wear itself down, quietly watches it do so, and only with a slight effort controls the whole: cunning. The broad flank of brute force is attacked by the sharp point of cunning."[23]

Just like language, the tool is a category of the middle, by means of which spirit attains existence. But the two movements pursue opposing courses. The *name-giving consciousness* achieves a different position with respect to the objectivity of the spirit than does the *cunning consciousness* that arises from the process of labor. Only in the limiting case of conventionalization can the speaker have a similar relation to his symbols as the worker to his tools; the symbols of ordinary language penetrate and dominate the perceiving and thinking consciousness, while the artful consciousness controls the processes of nature by means of its tools. The objectivity of language retains power over the subjective spirit, while the cunning that outwits nature extends subjective freedom over the power of objective spirit—for in the end the labor process, too, terminates in mediated satisfaction, the satisfaction in the commodities produced for consumption, and in the retroactively changed interpretation of the needs themselves.[24]

Against Kant's abstract "I," the three patterns developed in the Jena lectures, of a dialectical relation between subject and object, bring out

---

22. *Realphilosophie II*, 197.
23. Ibid., 199.
24. For this relation, which by no means corresponds to the teleology of spirit realizing itself, Hegel's *Logic* offers no appropriate category.

the self-formative processes of the developed identity of the naming, the cunning, and recognizing consciousness. Corresponding to the critique of morality, there is also a critique of culture. In the methodological doctrine of the teleological capacity of judgment,[25] Kant treats culture as the ultimate aim of nature, insofar as we can understand it as a teleological system. Culture, Kant calls the bringing forth of the fitness (*Tauglichkeit*) of a rational being for any purposes whatsoever. Subjectively, this means skill in the purposive-rational choice of suitable means; objectively, culture is the epitome of the technical control over nature. Just as morality is conceived as a purposive activity according to pure maxims, which disregards the embeddedness of the moral subjects in an emergent intersubjectivity, so Kant also conceives culture as a purposive activity according to technical rules (that is, conditional imperatives) which abstracts in the same manner from the subject's involvement in the labor process. The *cultivated I* to which Kant attributes the fitness for instrumental action is conceived by Hegel, in contrast, as a result of social labor, and in fact, as a result that, changes world-historically. Thus, in the Jena elaboration of of the *Philosophy of Spirit* he never misses the opportunity to point to the development that cunning consciousness, arising from the employment of tools, undergoes, as soon as labor becomes mechanized.[26]

---

25. *Kant's Critique of Teleological Judgment*, trans. James Creed Meredith (Oxford, 1928), §22 (83), 92.
26. "The tool as such thus wards off from man his material destruction; but in this it still remains...his activity.... In the machine man abolishes [sublates] even this formal activity of his, and lets the machine do all the work for him. But this deception which he carries out against nature...is avenged on him; by what he gains from nature, and the more he subjugates her, the lower he becomes himself. By letting a variety of machines work on nature, he does not abolish the necessity of his own working, but only defers it, makes it remote from nature, and is no longer oriented as a being toward it as living nature: instead this negative living character takes flight, and the labor that remains for man itself becomes more machine-like" (*Realphilosophie I*, 237). Meanwhile, technical progress has gone far beyond that primitive stage represented by the mechanical loom; the stage that confronts us is characterized by the self-regulating control over system of goal-directed rational action; and it is uncertain whether the cunning consciousness of machines that stimulate the achievements of consciousness will not one day be itself outwitted (*überlistet*), even if the worker then would no longer—because control has slipped from his hands—have to pay the price for the growing power of technological control that he has had to pay up to now in the currency of alienated labor—for then labor itself would become obsolete.

What is valid for the moral and the technical consciousness, is valid, by analogy, for theoretical consciousness. The dialectic of representation by means of linguistic symbols is directed against Kant's concept of the synthetic achievements of a transcendental consciousness, conceived apart from all formative processes. For the abstract critique of knowledge conceives the relation of the categories and the forms of intuition to the material of experience according to the model of the artisan's activity, already introduced by Aristotle in which the working subject forms material; the terms employed themselves show this. If, however, the synthesis is not achieved by means of the superimposition of the categorial forms, but is bound initially to the representational function of self-generated symbols, then the identity of the I can just as little be supposed to be prior to the process of knowledge as to the processes of labor and interaction, from which the cunning and the recognizing consciousness first arise. The identity of the knowing subject is one that has first to be formed, to the same degree as the objectivity of the recognized objects first arises with language, within which alone the synthesis of the divergent elements, of the I and of nature, is possible as a world of the I.

LANGUAGE AND LABOR

Kant proceeds from the identity of the I as an original unity of transcendental consciousness. In contrast to this, Hegel's fundamental experience of the I as an identity of the universal and the singular has led him to the insight that the identity of self-consciousness is not an original one, but can only be conceived as one that has developed (*geworden*). In the Jena lectures, Hegel works out the threefold identity of the naming, the cunning, and the recognizing consciousness. These identities are formed in the dialectic of representation, of labor, and of the struggle for recognition, and thus contradict that abstract unity of the practical will, of the technical will, and of intelligence, with which both Kant's *Critique of Practical Reason* and of *Pure Reason* begin. From this viewpoint we can actually see the Jena *Philosophy of Spirit* as a preparatory study for the *Phenomenology*. For the radicalization of the critique of knowledge carried out as a science of appearing (*erscheinende* = phenomenal) consciousness consists precisely in relinquishing the viewpoint of a "ready-made" or "completed" subject of knowledge. Above all, the skepticism of critique, which is doubting that is not impervious to despair, and the skepticism of reflection, which is the penetration of illusion until consciousness itself is reversed, requires a radical beginning in a new sense. For we must drop even the fundamental distinction between theoretical and practical reason, between descriptively true statements and normatively correct decisions, and begin without any presupposition of standards at all—although just this beginning without theoretical presuppositions cannot be an absolute beginning, but must depart from natural consciousness. If we look back from this point to the Jena *Philosophy of Spirit*, then indeed the question of the *unity of the self-formative process* forces itself upon us, as this is initially determined by *three heterogeneous patterns of formation*. The question of the coherence of that organization of media is posed with special urgency once we recall the historical effects of Hegelian philosophy and call to mind the divergent interpretations that elevate each of the three fundamental dialectical patterns to the chief interpretative principle of the whole. Ernst Cassirer takes the dialectic of representation and makes it the guiding principle (*Leitfaden*) of a Hegelianized Kant interpretation, which at the same time is the foundation of a philosophy of symbolic forms. Georg Lukács interprets the movement of intellectual development from Kant to Hegel along the guideline presented by the dialectic of labor, which at the same time guarantees the materialistic unity of subject and object in the world-historical formative process of the human species; finally, the Neo-Hegelianism of a thinker such as Theodor Litt leads to a conception of the stepwise self-development of spirit that follows the pattern of the struggle for recognition. The three positions have in common the method, employed by the Young Hegelians, of appropriating Hegel at the cost of surrendering the identity of spirit and nature claimed by absolute knowledge. However, for the rest, they have so little in common that they only give evidence of the divergence of the three approaches, and that means of the conception of the dialectic underlying them. How, therefore, is the unity of a formative process to be conceived, which, according to the Jena lectures, goes through the dialectic of language, of labor, and of interaction?

Under the title *language* Hegel rightly introduces the employment of representational symbols as the first determination of abstract spirit. For the two subsequent determinations necessarily presuppose this. In the dimension of actual spirit, language attains existence as the system of a specific cultural tradition:

> Language only exists as the language of a people [*Volkes*]. . . .
> It is something universal, something granted recognition in itself, something that resounds in the same manner in the consciousness of all; within it every speaking consciousness immediately becomes another consciousness. Language, in the same way, only becomes true language, as to its contents, in

a people, it becomes the enunciation of that which everyone means.[27]

As cultural tradition, language enters into communicative action; for only the intersubjectively valid and constant meanings that are drawn from tradition permit the orientation toward reciprocity, that is, complementary expectations of behavior. Thus, interaction is dependent on language communication that has established itself as part of life. However, instrumental action, as soon as it comes under the category of actual spirit, as social labor, is also embedded within a network of interactions, and therefore dependent on the communicative boundary conditions that underlie every possible cooperation. Even disregarding social labor, the solitary act of using tools is also dependent on the employment of symbols, for the immediacy of animalistic drive satisfaction cannot be moderated without the creation of distance from identifiable objects, provided by naming consciousness. Instrumental action, at least when solitary, is monologic action.

More interesting and by no means as obvious as the relation of the employment of symbols to interaction and to labor, however, is the *interrelation of labor and interaction*. On the one hand, the norms under which complementary action within the framework of a cultural tradition is first institutionalized and made to endure are independent of instrumental action. Technical rules, to be sure, are first elaborated under the conditions of language communication, but they have nothing in common with the communicative rules of interaction. Into the conditional imperatives that instrumental action follows, enters in solely the causality of nature and not the causality of destiny. A reduction of interaction to labor or derivation of labor from interaction is not possible. On the other hand, Hegel does indeed establish an interconnection between the *legel norms*, in which social intercourse based on mutual recognition is first formally stabilized, and *proccesses of labor*.

Under the category of actual spirit, interactions based on reciprocity appear in the form of an intercourse, controlled by legal norms, between persons whose status as legal persons is defined precisely by the institutionalization of mutual recognition. However, this recognition does not refer directly to the identity of the other, but to the things that are subject to his powers of disposition. The institutional reality of the ego-identity consists in the individuals' recognizing each other as proprietors in the possessions produced by their labor or acquired by trade. "Not only my possession [*Habe*] or my property is posited here, but my person,

---

27. *Realphilosophie I*, 235.

because in my existence lies my all [*mein Ganzes*]: my honor and my life."[28] Honor and life are recognized, however, solely in the inviolability of property. Possession as the substrate of legal recognition arises from the labor process. Thus, instrumental action and interaction are linked in the recognized product of labor.

In the Jena lectures Hegel constructs this interconnection quite simply. In the system of social labor, the division of the labor process and the exchange of the products of labor are posited. From this arises a generalization of labor as well as of needs. For with respect to its content, the labor of each is general labor for the needs of all. Abstract labor produces goods for abstract needs. Thereby the produced goods receive their abstract value as exchange value. Of the latter, money is the concept brought to existence. The exchange of equivalents is the model for reciprocal behavior. The institutional form of exchange is the contract; the contract therefore is the formal establishment of a prototypical action in reciprocity. The contract "is the same thing as an exchange, but an ideal exchange. It is an exchange of declarations, not of things, but it has the same validity as the thing. For both the will of the Other as such has validity."[29] The institutionalization of the reciprocity actualized in exchange is accomplished by virtue of the spoken word being accorded normative force; complementary action is mediated by symbols, which fix the expectations of obligatory behavior:

> My word must have validity, not for moral reasons—so that inwardly I can remain the same for myself and may, not change my moral attitudes, convictions, and so forth—no, indeed I can change this; but my will only exists insofar as it is recognized. I contradict not only myself, but the fact that my will is recognized. . . . The person, the pure being-for-oneself, thus is not respected as single and solitary, as will separating itself from the common will, but only as the common will.[30]

Thus, the relation of reciprocal recognition, on which interaction is based, is brought under norms by way of the institutionalization of the reciprocity established as such in the exchange of the products of labor.

The institutionalization of ego-identity, the legally sanctioned self-consciousness, is understood as a result of *both* processes: that of *labor* and that of the *struggle for recognition*. The labor process, by means of

---

28. *Realphilosophie II*, 221.
29. Ibid., 218.
30. Ibid., 219.

which we free ourselves from the immediate dictates of natural forces, thus enters into the struggle for recognition in such a manner that the result of this struggle, the legally recognized self-consciousness, retains the moment of liberation through labor. Hegel links together labor and interaction, under the viewpoint of emancipation from the forces of external as well as internal nature. He does not reduce interaction to labor, nor does he elevate labor to resolve it in interaction; still, he keeps the interconnection of the two in view, insofar as the dialectics of love and conflict cannot be separated from the successes of instrumental action and from the constitution of a cunning consciousness. The result of emancipation by means of labor enters into the norms under which we act complementarily.

It is true that Hegel developed the dialectical interconnection between labor and interaction, taking his departure from a consideration presented in his *System of Morality*,[31] only one more time extensively, namely, in a chapter of the *Phenomenology of Mind*: the relationship of the one-sided recognition of the master by the servant (*Knecht*) is overturned by the servant's power of disposition over nature, just as one-sidedly acquired by labor. The independent self-consciousness, in which both parties recognize that they recognize each other, is constituted by way of a reaction, which the *technical* success of an emancipation by means of labor exerts on the relationship of *political* dependency between master and servant. To be sure, the relationship of dominance and servitude also gained admittance into the philosophy of subjective spirit after, and by way of, the *Phenomenology*. In the *Enzyklopädie*[32] it designates the transition to universal self-consciousness and thus the step from "consciousness" to "spirit." However, already in the *Phenomenology* the distinctive dialectic of labor and interaction has been deprived of the specific role that was still attributed to it within the system in the Jena lectures.

This can be explained by the fact that Hegel soon abandoned the systematics of these lectures and replaced it by the subdivisions of the *Enzyklopädie*, into subjective, objective, and absolute spirit. While in the Jena lectures, language, labor, and action in reciprocity were not only stages in the formative process of spirit, but also principles of its formation itself, in the *Enzyklopädie*, language and labor, once models of construction for dialectical movement, are now themselves constructed as subordinate real conditions (*Realverhältnisse*). Language is mentioned

---

31. *System der Sittlichkeit*, 442.
32. Hegel, *Enzyklopädie*, §433ff.

in a lengthy passage (§459) in the philosophy of subjective spirit at the point of transition from the faculty of imagination to that of memory, while labor, as instrumental action as such, is deleted entirely and instead, as social labor, under the title of the system of needs, designates an important stage in the development of objective spirit (§§524ff.). However, the dialectic of moral relationships has retained its specific role for the construction of spirit as such in the *Enzyklopädie*, just as it did in the Jena lectures. Yet when we look at this more closely, we will recognize in it not the dialectic of love and conflict, but rather that dialectic which Hegel developed in his essay on *Natual Law* as the movement of absolute morality.

RECOGNITION

We have sought the unity of the formative process of spirit in an interconnection of the three fundamental dialectical patterns, thus in the relation among symbolic representation, labor, and interaction. This distinctive interconnection, which, limited to one stage, is taken up again in the relationship between domination and servitude, does not reappear later. It is tied to a systematics that Hegel appears to have tried out only in the Jena period. To be sure, the Jena lectures incorporate a tendency that makes understandable why the specific interconnection of labor with interaction loses its significance. For in the Jena lectures Hegel proceeded from that absolute identity of the spirit with nature, which prejudices the unity of the spirit's formative process in a particular manner. In these lectures Hegel constructs the transition from the philosophy of nature to the philosophy of spirit no differently than he does in the *Enzyklopädie*: in nature, spirit has its complete external objectivity, and it therefore finds its identity in the sublation of this externalization. Spirit thus is the absolute presupposition (*absolut Erste*) of nature: "The *manifesting* [*Offenbaren*] which . . . is the *becoming* of nature, as the manifesting of spirit, which is free [in history], is the *positing* of nature as the *spirit's* [*seiner*] world; a positing which as reflection is at the same time *presupposing* [*Voraussetzen* = prepositing] of the world as independent nature."[33]

Under the presupposition of this thesis of identity Hegel has always interpreted the dialectics of representation and of labor idealistically: together with the name we enunciate the being of objects, and, in the same manner, that which nature is in truth is incorporated in the tool.

---

33. Ibid., §384.

The innermost part of nature (*das Innere*) is itself spirit, because nature only becomes comprehensible in its essence and "comes to itself" in man's confrontation with it: the interior of nature is expressed only in the realm of its names and in the rules for working upon it. If, however, hidden subjectivity can always be found in what has been objectivized, if behind the masks of objects, nature can always be revealed as the concealed partner (*Gegenspieler*), then the basic dialectical patterns of representation and of labor can also be reduced to one common denominator with the dialectics of moral action. For then the relationship of the name-giving and the working subject to nature can also be brought within the conflguration of reciprocal recognition. The intersubjectivity in which an I can identify with another I without relinquishing the nonidentity between itself and the other, is also established in language and in labor when the object confronting the speaking and the working subject is from the outset conceived idealistically as an opposite (*Gegenüber*) with which interaction in the mode of that between subjects is possible: when it is an *adversary* (*Gegenspierler*) and not an *object* (*Gegenstand*). As long as we consider each of these determinations of abstract spirit by itself, a specific difference remains. The dialectic of representation and of labor develops as a relation between a knowing or an acting subject on the one hand, and an object as the epitome of what does not belong to the subject on the other. The mediation between the two, passing through the medium of symbols or of tools is conceived as a process of externalization of the subject—a process of externalization (objectification) and appropriation. In contrast to this, the dialectic of love and conflict is a movement on the level of intersubjectivity. The place of the model of externalization is therefore taken by that of *separation* (or division—*Entzweiung*) and alienation, and the result of the movement is not the *appropriation* of what has been objectified, but instead the *reconciliation*, the restoration of the friendliness that has been destroyed. The idealistic sublation of the distinction between objects as objects (*Gegenstände*) and as adversaries (*Gegenspieler*) makes possible the assimilation of these heterogeneous models: if interaction is with nature as a hidden subject in the role of the other, possible then the processes of externalization and appropriation formally match those of alienation and reconciliation. The unity of the self-formative process, that operates through the medium of language, the tool, and moral relations, then does not have to be tied first to the interconnections of labor and interaction, still central for the Jena *Philosophy of Spirit*. For the unity of this process already subsists in the dialectic of recognizing oneself in the other, in which the dialectics of language and of labor can now converge with that of morality: under the presuppositions of the philosophy of identity they are only apparently heterogeneous.

To be sure, the dialectic of recognizing oneself in the other is bound to the relationship of interaction between antagonists who are in principle equal. As soon as nature in its totality is elevated to an antagonist of the united subjects, however, this relation of parity no longer holds; there cannot be a dialogue between spirit and nature, the suppression of the dialogic situation between the two, and a struggle for recognition that results in a constituted moral relationship—absolute spirit is solitary. The unity of absolute spirit with itself and with a nature, from which it differentiates itself as its other, in the end cannot be conceived in terms of the pattern of the intersubjectivity of acting and of speaking subjects, by which Hegel initially attained the concept of the I as the identity of the universal and the singular. The dialectical unity of spirit and nature, in which spirit does not recognize itself in nature as an antagonist, but only finds itself again as in a mirror image (*Gegenbild*), this unity can more readily be constructed from the experience of the self-reflection of consciousness. Therefore, Hegel conceives of the movement of absolute spirit in terms of the model of self-reflection, but in such a way that the dialectic of the moral relationship, from which the identity of the universal with the singular originates, enters into it: *absolute spirit is absolute morality.* The dialectic of the moral relationship that accomplishes itself on the criminal with the causality of destiny in the same way as on those who struggle for recognition, now proves to be the same movement as that in which the absolute spirit reflects itself.

The process of destiny, which in the theological works of Hegel's youth was conceived from the viewpoint of the members of a moral totality, as a reaction evoked by the subjects themselves through the suppression of the dialogic relationship, can subsequently be reinterpreted all the more readily within the framework of self-reflection as a self-movement of the totality, because Hegel can link it to the *dialectic of the sacrifice* (*Opfer*) which is already developed in the earliest fragments: "For the power of the sacrifice consists in the perceiving [*Anschauen*] and objectivating of the involvement with the inorganic; by which perception this involvement is dissolved, the inorganic is separated out and recognized as such, and thereby is itself incorporated into the indifferent [*Indifferenz*]: the living, however, by placing what it knows to be a part of itself within the same [the inorganic] and offering it up to death in sacrifice, at the same time has recognized the rights of the inorganic and separated itself from it."[34] The division of the moral totality now represents no more than the destiny of the absolute, which sacrifices

---

34. *Über die wissenschaftlichen Behandlungsarten des Naturrechts,* Jubiläumsausgabe, vol. 1, 500.

itself. According to this model of absolute morality, which Hegel first developed in the essay on *Natural Law* as the accomplishment of tragedy in the moral realm, spirit is conceived as identical with nature as its other, and the dialectic of self-consciousness is united with dialectic of moral relationships. The logic merely presents the grammar of the language in which the tragedy is written, which the absolute acts out with itself eternally: "that it eternally gives birth to itself into objectivity, and in this its character of objectivity thereby surrenders itself to suffering and death, and from its ashes ascends to glory. The divine in its shape [*Gestalt*] and objectivity has an immediately dual nature and its life is the absolutely united being of these two natures."[35]

But the essay on *Natural Law* and the *Logic* (*Grosse Logik*) are not linked by a continuous development. In the three parts of the Jena *Philosophy of Spirit* that we have discussed, Hegel's study of contemporary economics is reflected in such a manner that the movement of the actual spirit does not mirror the triumphal sacrificial march of the absolute, but develops the structures of spirit anew, as interconnections of symbolically mediated labor and interaction. The dialectic of labor does not readily fit into the movement of such a spirit conceived as absolute morality, and therefore forces a reconstruction. This Hegel relinquished again after Jena, but not without it leaving its traces. The position that abstract right occupies within the system does not flow directly from the conception of moral spirit. Rather, elements of the Jena *Philosophy of Spirit* are retained in it. Other elements of the concept developed in Jena are not, to be sure, incorporated in the later constructions of right.

Up to the essay on *Natural Law*, Hegel had conceived the domain of formal legal relations as the result of the decay of free morality, basing himself in this on Gibbon's depiction of the Roman Empire; this free morality the young Hegel had seen as realized in the idealized constitution of the Greek polis. In 1802 he still asserts that, historically, private law first evolved in the form of Roman law, within a condition of the citizen's depoliticization, of "decadence and universal degradation": the intercourse of privatized individuals, subject to legal norms, compares unfavorably with the destroyed moral relation. In the movement of absolute morality, law belongs to that phase in which the moral becomes involved with the inorganic and sacrifices itself to the "subterranean powers."

In contrast to this, in the Jena *Philosophy of Spirit*, the state of legality (*Rechtszustand*), which now is also characterized in terms of modern bourgeois private law, no longer appears as a product of the decay

35. Ibid.

of absolute morality, but, on the contrary, as the first configuration (*Gestalt*) of constituted moral relationships. Only the intercourse of individuals acting complementarily and subject to legal norms, makes an institution of ego-identity, namely, the self-consciousness that recognizes itself in another self-consciousness. Action on the basis of mutual recognition is only guaranteed by the formal relationship between legal persons. Hegel can replace the negative definition of abstract right by a positive one because meanwhile he has come to know the economic interrelation of private law with modern bourgeois society and has seen that these legal categories also incorporate the result of *liberation through social labor*. Abstract right places its seal on a liberation that literally has been worked for.

Finally, in the *Enzyklopädie* and the *Philosophy of Right*, abstract right once again changes its role within the system. It retains its positive determinations, for only within the system of these universal norms can free will attain the objectivity of external existence. The self-conscious and free will—the subjective spirit on its highest level—as a legal person becomes subject to the more rigorous determinations of objective spirit. However, the interrelationship between labor and interaction to which abstract right owes its true dignity is dissolved; the Jena construction is given up, and abstract right is integrated into the self-reflection of spirit, conceived as absolute morality. Now bourgeois morality is considered to be the sphere of disintegrated morality. In the fragmented system of needs, the categories of social labor, the division of labor and of commerce based on exchange, which make possible abstract labor for abstract needs under the condition of an abstract intercourse of isolated individual competitors, all have their place. But although abstract right determines the form of social intercourse, it is introduced from the *outside* under the title of jurisprudence. It constitutes itself independently of the categories of social labor, and only *after the fact* enters into its relationship with the processes to which, in the Jena lectures, it still owed the moment of freedom, as a result of liberation through social labor. It is solely the dialectic of morality that guarantees the "transition" (*Übergehen*) of the as yet internal will to the objectivity of law. The dialectic of labor has been deprived of its central role within the system.

LIBERATION

Karl Löwith, to whom we owe the most penetrating analysis of the intellectual break between Hegel and the first generation of his pupils,[36]

36. K. Löwith, *Von Hegel zu Nietzsche*, 1961; see also Löwith's introduction to the collection of texts, *Die Hegelsche Linke* (Stuttgart, 1962).

has also pointed to the subterranean affinity between the positions of the Young Hegelians and themes in the thought of the young Hegel. Thus, without any knowledge of the Jena manuscripts, Marx had rediscovered that interconnection between labor and interaction in the dialectic of the forces of production and the relations of production, which for several years had claimed Hegel's philosophical interest, stimulated by his study of economics. In a critique of the last chapter of the *Phenomenology of Mind*, Marx maintained that Hegel had taken the viewpoint of modern political economy, for he had comprehended labor as the essence of man, in which man has confirmed himself. It is in this passage of the Paris Manuscripts that the famous dictum is to be found:

> What is great in Hegel's *Phenomenology* and its final results is that Hegel comprehends the self-generation of man as a process, the objectification as the process of confronting objects [*Entgegenständlichung*], as externalization and as sublation of this externalization, that he thus comprehends the essence of labor and conceives objective man, the true because the actual man, as the result of his own labor.

From this point of view Marx himself attempted to reconstruct the world-historical process by which the human species forms itself in terms of the laws of the reproduction of social life. The mechanism of change of the system of social labor he finds in the contradiction between the power over natural processes, accumulated by means of social labor, and the institutional framework of interactions, which are regulated in a "natural" (*naturwüchsig*), that is, primitive and prerational, way. However, a precise analysis of the first part of the *German Ideology* reveals that Marx does not actually explicate the interrelationship of interaction and labor, but instead, under the unspecific title of social praxis, reduces the one to the other, namely, communicative action to instrumental action. Just as in the Jena *Philosophy of Spirit* the use of tools mediates between the laboring subject and the natural objects, so for Marx instrumental action, the productive activity that regulates the material interchange of the human species with its natural environment, becomes the paradigm for the generation of all the categories; everything is resolved into the self-movement of production.[37] Because of this, Marx's brilliant insight into the dialectical relationship between the forces of production and the relations of production could very quickly be misinterpreted in a mechanistic manner.

---

37. See my *Knowledge and Human Interest* (Boston, 1971), esp. chap. 3.

Today, when the attempt is being undertaken to reorganize the communicative nexus of interactions, no matter how much they have hardened into quasi-natural forms, according to the model of technically progressive systems of rational goal-directed action, we have reason enough to keep these two dimensions more vigorously separated. A mass of wishful historical conceptions adheres to the idea of a progressive rationalization of labor. Although hunger still holds sway over two-thirds of the earth's population, the abolition of hunger is not a utopia in the negative sense. But to set free the technical forces of production, including the construction of cybernetic and learning machines that can simulate the complete sphere of the functions of rational, goal-directed action far beyond the capacity of natural consciousness, and thus substitute for human effort, is not identical with the development of norms that could fulfill the dialectic of moral relationships in an interaction free of domination, on the basis of a reciprocity allowed to have its full and noncoercive scope. *Liberation from hunger and misery* does not necessarily converge with *liberation from servitude and degradation*, for there is no automatic developmental relation between labor and interaction. Still, there is a connection between the two dimensions. Neither the Jena *Realphilosophie* nor the *German Ideology* has clarified it adequately, but in any case they can persuade us of its relevance: the self-formative process of spirit as well as of our species essentially depends on that relation between labor and interaction.

CHAPTER 8

Hegel's Dialectic of Self-Consciousness

Hans-Georg Gadamer

The following essay treats one of the most famous chapters in Hegel's philosophy.[1] Paradoxically, the passionate dedication to freedom that characterized the era of revolutions in Europe and that was Hegel's passion too seems to be responsible for the fact that this chapter's true value in showing the nature and reality of freedom has not been comprehended. It is necessary, therefore, that in attempting to critically clarify its meaning, we guard against the effect of the excessively resounding slogan, "freedom." To this end it is wise to carefully consider the importance of this chapter's position in the chain of demonstration in Hegel's science of appearing spirit. I shall begin, accordingly, by showing that Hegel knows full well what he is after when he refuses to introduce transcendental idealism in the manner of Fichte, who, for his part, claims to think Kant to his conclusion.

What does it mean when Hegel asserts "that not merely is consciousness of a thing only possible for self-consciousness, but that the latter alone is the truth of such forms" (Ph 128)? A different problem is posed here from the one Kant poses and solves in his transcendental deduction of the pure concepts of the understanding. To be sure, the transcendental synthesis of apperception is a function of self-consciousness, but only insofar as it always makes the consciousness of something else, an object, possible. And even that consciousness of the self-deter-

---

1. Hegel, *Phenomenology of Mind*, chap. 4: "Self-consciousness": "The Truth and Certainty of Itself," and "The Independence and Dependence of Self-Consciousness: Mastery and Servitude" (Ph 133–50).

mination of reason that Fichte's "Doctrine of Science" develops out of the primacy of practical reason has a transcendental function and serves as a basis for knowledge of the "not-I." Opposed to this stands Hegel's emphatic declaration that in self-consciousness the concept of spirit has been reached and, thus, the turning point where consciousness "steps out of the varicolored appearance of the sensuous 'here' and the empty night of the supersensible 'beyond' into the spiritual daylight of the present" (Ph 140). In the overtones of Hegel's baroque formulation one detects that in the concept of spirit a reality has been reached which, like the light of day, embraces everything visible and includes all there is. That gives the chapter on "self consciousness" a central position within the whole of the path traversed in the *Phenomenology*. To be sure, self-consciousness is an immediate certainty, but that this certainty of self-consciousness is at the same time the truth of all certainty is at this point not yet contained in its immediate certainty as such. Hegel expressly points to the fact that even that idealism that calls itself transcendental philosophy and that asserts its certainty of being all reality, in fact recognizes another certainty: in Kant, the "thing itself," in Fichte, the "impetus" (*Anstoss*). Thus, Hegel can say that "the idealism which begins with this assertion is a form of pure assurance, which neither comprehends itself nor can make itself comprehensible to others" (177). I wish to shed some light on the difference it makes when, following Hegel, one conceives of the way of true idealism as the way from consciousness to self-consciousness. How is the certainty of consciousness that it is all reality thereby demonstrated? And does this certainty surpass not only Kant's transcendental deduction, but also Fichte's absolute idealism of freedom?

One should keep in mind that Schelling, too, thought that the standpoint of idealism lacked a substantial proof and considered the I of intellectual intuition and of self-consciousness to be the higher potency, the potentiated subject-object of nature. Of course, Hegel, here in his *Phenomenology of Spirit*, criticizes Schelling's concept of the absolute because of what the former considered the lack of mediation in its absoluteness. Yet the way in which Hegel derives the idealism of reason here and opposes it to transcendental or formal idealism reaffirms Schelling's concern and not merely in the way Hegel had done when he had previously attempted to mediate and surpass Fichte's and Schelling's systems in his essay on their "difference."[2] As a matter of fact, in Hegel's

---

2. Hegel, *Differenz des Fichte'schen und Schelling'schen Systems der Philosophie* (Hamburg, 1962).

subsequent system of philosophic sciences as well, he develops nature as the real foundation of spirit's actualization of itself. And in the later systematic ordering, the "phenomenology" is a part of this philosophy of reality insofar as it is the science of appearing and therefore real spirit. Thus, the merely formal principle of idealism has no place at all in the science of real spirit or, more to the point, that formal principle is made actual in that science insofar as self-consciousness is not merely the individual point of consciousness's certainty of itself, but rather reason. That means that thought is certain that it is experiencing the whole world "as its own truth and presence." In this way Hegel transforms Kant's problem of the transcendental deduction of the concepts of the under-standing and "proves" the idealism of reason via the certainty of self-consciousness.

For reason is not only in thought. Hegel defines reason as the unity of thought and reality. Thus, implied in the concept of reason is that reality is not the other of thought and, hence, that the opposition of appearance and understanding is not a valid one. Reason is certain of all that: "To it (self-consciousness), in that it so conceives of itself, it seems as if the world only now had come into being for it. Before this, it does not understand the world. It desires and works on it, withdraws from it and draws back into itself" (176). Thus, Hegel is describing the path on which "empty" idealism elevates itself to the idealism of reason. That everything is "mine" as the content of my consciousness is not yet the truth of this consciousness. As Hegel expresses it, "Self-conscious-ness has only come into existence for itself, and does not yet exist as unity with consciousness in general" (128). We can also say that in the individuals point of its self-certain self, its true essence as spirit and reason is not yet recognized.

It is determined in subsequent stages of appearing spirit that self-consciousness does not yet exist in its truth as long as it is the mere individual point of certainty of itself, that is, that it is the whole of reality only in unity with consciousness. . . . The *chorismos* and the Platonic hypostasizing of ideas needs to be dispensed with just as does the claim that nature can be explained by *principia mathematica*. Ontologically, the difference between idea and appearance is as invalid as that between the understanding and what it explains. It is a serious mistake to see this doctrine of the "inverted-perverted world" as a critique, or worse, a caricature of the sciences, for it is not at all inappropriate to assert that when it is "explaining," consciousness is in "immediate discussion with itself" (127). In contrast, the truth of positivism is precisely that it replaces the concept of explanation with that of description—as Kirchhoff's famous formulation expresses it.[3] In essence, Hegel has grasped this correctly. The dichotomization of reality into universal and particular, idea and appearance, the law and its instances, needs just as much to be eliminated as does the division of consciousness into consciousness on the one side and its object on the other. What is then thought of in the new way is termed the "inner difference" or "infinitude" by Hegel. Specifically, insofar as that which differentiates itself within itself is not limited from the outside by the boundary of something else from which it differentiates itself, it is infinite in itself. And I have shown that it is the concept of a self that possesses this infinitude, a concept just as much essential to life, the being of organic things that behave and enter into relationships, as it is to the consciousness of itself had by the I that understands itself, that is, this form of "repulsion of what has the same name, taken as what has the same name, from itself."

It has become clear "for us" that this other is not another: "I who am of the same name, repel myself from myself" (128). The repulsion of what has the same name and the attraction of who is named differently is not only the structure of self-consciousness, but also of the physical tension of electromagnetic phenomena and of the Platonic differentiation of idea from the appearance that participates in the idea as that of the same name. Hegel uses the concept of the homonymous abstractly here, so that it embraces both Plato's doctrine of ideas (homōnumon) as well as the modern concept of law and the electromagnetic equation. The self-referentiality characterizing self-consciousness is thus a truth for the understanding, but as an event in which it does not recognize itself. As soon as consciousness acquires a concept of this infinitude, it is no longer understanding, but rather appears in the form of self-consciousness. That point is reached at the level of life and knowledge of it. He who grasps the behavior of what is alive, that is, grasps it as differentiation of the undifferentiated, must first already know himself, that is, be self-conxiousness; but beyond this, he will ultimately come to the insight that his own forms of consciousness, whose truth had been a thing other than these forms themselves, are not different at all from their other (which is consciousness too) but undifferentiatedly one with it. Thus, these forms are self-consciousness. The truth does not, as the understanding presumed, lie beyond in the supersensible, in the inner; rather, consciousness is itself this inner, which is to say it is self-consciousness.

It is clear then that what appears as this differentiation of the undifferentiated has life's structure of splitting in two and becoming identical

---

3. Cf. G. R. Kirchhoff, *Vorlesungen über mathematische Physik und Mechanik* (Leipzig, 1874), preface.

with itself. That, Hegel worked out in those pages preserved through fortunate coincidence from his Frankfurt years. Life is the identity of identity and difference. Everything alive is bound to its other, the world around it, in the constant exchange of assimilation and secretion. And beyond this, the individual living thing does not exist as an individual, but rather only as the mode in which the species preserves itself. Thus, it bespeaks neither a lack of clarity nor arbitrariness on Hegel's part when, in the *Phenomenology*, the universal structure of life as inner difference or infinity is developed both at the end of the chapter on consciousness and the beginning of the chapter on self-consciousness: on the one hand, as the final development in the way the understanding thinks and, on the other, under the title, "Determination of Life," as an adumbration of the structure of self-consciousness. That is not a mere anthropomorphism that modern behavioral research would point out as such to man's humiliation. Rather, there is a methodologically compelling state of affairs here. Self-consciousness governs necessarily whenever any attempt at all is made to think what behavior is. Furthermore, in proceeding from the other side of this parallelism, we see that the structural identity between the life processes of what lives and self-consciousness demonstrates that self-consciousness is not at all the individualized point of "I = I," but rather, as Hegel says, "the I which is we and the we which is I" (Ph 140), which is to say, spirit. To be sure, Hegel first makes that assertion in the introduction to the dialectic of self-consciousness. For it is only clear "for us," for reflecting or observing consciousness, that life, the unity of the different, will also prove to be the truth of self-consciousness, namely, that it is all reality and hence reason. Hegel is seeking a kind of reconciliation here between the *anciens* and the *modernes*. For Hegel there is no opposition between existing reason, existing spirit, *logos, nous,* and *pneuma,* on the one hand, and the *cogito,* the truth of self-consciousness, on the other. The course of appearing spirit is the course that Hegel follows in teaching us to recognize the standpoint of the *anciens* in the standpoint of the *modernes.*

When Hegel says that in reaching self-consciousness we have now entered the homeland of truth, he means that truth is no longer like the foreign country of otherness into which consciousness seeks to penetrate. It had only seemed so from the standpoint of consciousness. Now, in contrast, consciousness as self-consciousness is a native of the land of truth and is at home in it. For one thing, it finds all truth in itself. For another, however, it knows that it embraces the entire profusion of life within itself.

At this point there is no longer need for an exact analysis of the sides of the dialectic constituting the cycle of life—the dialectic between the single exemplar and the species, the single creature and the whole. To know its result is sufficient for us, namely, the "reflected unity." What, on the one hand, is the "immediate continuity and homogeneity of its being" ("universal blood"), and on the other, has "the form of that which exists for itself discretely," and is also the pure process of both of these—in short, the "entirety which maintains itself simply in this movement"—is determined as the unitary species itself (138). What is alive is the species and not the individual. In other words, as life, it is a reflected unity for which the differences of the exemplars are no differences.

It is easy to see that the I has the same structure as this. For the I as well, thie differences are no differences—all that exists are the I's representations. Yet more than this structural identity is manifest here. That which is a self-consciousness is itself necessarily life. Thus, Hegel speaks specifically of this "other life." But, as self-consciousness, this other life is a special kind of life, namely, one that has consciousness and for which, accordingly, the species character of all that lives is given. It itself is not only a species in structure, that is, as "I," it is not only in fact the simple universal unifying in itself everything different; rather, it knows "for itself" that all other life is just species, while as self-consciousness it alone is "species-for-itself." The first immediate evidence of this is that it knows nothing other than itself. The "nullity of the other" fills it completely—quite like it fills life, incidentally, which knows nothing other than itself and maintains itself as individual by dissolving everything else, that is, inorganic substance, in itself and which maintains itself as species in careless profligacy and sacrifice of the individual. As self-consciousness it is conscious of this nullity of the other and proves this nullity to itself by destroying the other. That is its first mediation, through which self-consciousness "produces" itself as "true" certainty, as desire—a self-consciousness that Hegel refers to on occasion as the "unadulterated feeling of self" (148). For in fact, in its immediacy it is the vital certainty of being alive; in other words, it has the confirmation of itself that it gains through the satisfaction of desire.

At this point a "however" is required that qualifies the truth of this self-consciousness. It is all too clear that the self-consciousness of desire or of satisfaction of desire, respectively, provides no lasting certainty, for "in pleasure I thirst for desire."[5] Faust's unhappy odyssey through the world provides him with no fulfillment at all. That in which desire finds its satisfaction is, as long as desire is nothing other than desire, neces-

---

4. Goethe, *Faust*, 3250.

sarily something to be destroyed and rendered nothing, and thus it is nothing at all. For that reason the self-consciousness that desires does not find anything in this way in which it could feel confirmed. On the contrary, it needs to experience that the object can stand on its own (135). For us that is quite evident. We who have followed the course of the *Phenomenology of Spirit* to this point know, of course, that the self-consciousness of being alive is not a true, substantial self-consciousness. All it "knows" is that as something alive its identity consists only in constant annulment of the other and dissolution of self in the other, that is, in participation in the infinity of the cycle of life.

Consequently, the object of desire is itself "life"—precisely because the object for the consciousness of desire is "everything else" besides that consciousness, the latter being the self. That is pointed out in Hegel's dialectic when he raises the question of how the self-consciousness of desire comes to learn of the independence of its object. Hegel's meaning is not only that this other that desires annihilates exists independently of it in the sense that the object of desire is always brought into existence again whenever desire reignites. Beyond this, he is asserting that the object of desire as such, that is, as it is, not only for us, but for desire itself, has the structure of life. The exact sense of this must be understood. Plainly, the point is that it is not this or that specific thing, but rather something relatively indifferent, which on any given occasion, in being the object of desire and by providing satisfaction for the latter, gives one certainty of oneself. Desire is as little interested in the differences that various "objects" might have as the species is in the life of the individual, or the organism in the particular foodstuffs that it assimilates. He who is hungry wants "something to eat"—it does not matter what. Still, the self-consciousness of desire remains tied to this other: "for there to be this cancellation, this other must exist" (139). To this extent, the object stands on its own: "it is indeed something different from self-consciousness, the essence desire." One must take this statement at full value. It means that the feeling of self in desire, the latter igniting and going out as it does, is not at all the truth of self-consciousness that it appeared to be. On the contrary, the self-consciousness of desire knows itself to be dependent on the object of desire as something other than itself. "The certainty of self reached in its satisfaction" is conditioned by the object. It is indeed an "other" that desire wants. Only if this other exists can self-consciousness find satisfaction in negating it. Of course, the particular object of desire being annihilated no longer has self-sufficiency, for that is precisely what it loses. That which satiates our hunger and thirst is a mere other, of which we are the negation. But for just that reason this sensuous feeling of self is not true self-consciousness.

The condition of animal desire, for example, that of extreme hunger or thirst, consists, to be sure, in knowing nothing other than oneself. But it is not a coincidence that we speak in this regard of being as hungry as a bear or wolf—hunger predominates here to the extent that nothing fills us other than what fills an animal absorbed in the single dimension of its instinctual drives. And for that reason the animal does not, properly speaking, possess a consciousness of itself. That is evidenced by the fact that the satisfaction of desire cancels itself as self-consciousness. In order that desire might attain true self-consciousness, the object of desire must, in all of its "nothingness of the other," still not cease to exist. It must be living self-consciousness in the "particularity of its distinctness" (140). To be sure, as desire, the desire seeking real self-consciousness also knows only itself and seeks nothing but itself in the other. But such desire is only able to find itself in the other if this other is independent and grants that it does not exist in its own right, but rather that, in disregard of itself, it "is for another" (139). Only consciousness is able to be the other of itself in this way and to cancel itself in such a fashion that it does not cease to exist. It is in this sense that self-consciousness "must" get its satisfaction and the object "must" of itself carry out the negation of itself. The "must" here is the classical *ex hypotheseōs anagkaion* found in Aristotle: if self-consciousness is to become true self-consciousness, then it must stand on its own and find another self-consciousness that is willing to be "for it." Thus, the doubling of self-consciousness is a necessary consequence: self-consciousness is only possible as double. It also learns that fact from its experience. Only something that in spite of being negated is still there, in other words, only what negates itself, can by its existence confirm for the I what the latter strives for in its desiring, namely, that it needs to acknowledge no thing other than itself. But the experience that the self-consciousness of desire inevitably has is, after all, that that alone which by self-negation can give it self-consciousness, has to be self-consciousness itself. That means, however, that the second self-consciousness is not only free to voluntarily confirm the self-consciousness of the first, but also to deny recognition of it.[5]

---

5. Kojève (in the German edition of his lectures, *Hegel*, ed. I. Fetscher [Stuttgart, 1958], 12ff.) and, following him, Hyppolite (*Etudes sur Marx et Hegel* [Paris, 1955], 181ff.) even interprets the transition from desire (*Begierde*) to recognized self-consciousness using the concept of desire as a basis. True desire, they say, is the desire of the desire of another (*désir du désir d'un autre*), that is, love. Hegel himself, however, does not call that *Begierde* any longer, and in point of fact this French description of the transition from *Begierde* to recognized self-consciousness sounds wrong in German. If only Hegel had at least said *Verlangen*

One might well expect, then, that in the process of assuring itself of the recognition that self-consciousness needs, self-consciousness comes to direct its desire to another self-consciousness and seeks to deprive the latter of its independence. And, as a matter of fact, that is the case: in the self-consciousness of the master this new experience begins—an experience that leads, it must be added, to a higher form of free self-consciousness through the experience of the servant, not that of the master. But, before treating that experience, this famous chapter with the caption, "Independence and Dependence of Self-Consciousness: Mastery and Servitude," opens, as do all the others with an introduction in which Hegel analyzes the concept of the self-consciousness that has now been reached—a self--consciousness for which another self-consciousness is necessary. Here the dialectic of the concept of recognition is developed, that is for us, for the philosophical analysis that we are applying to this concept.

For us, namely, it is clear that if self-consciousness exists only when recognized as such, it will necessarily get caught up in the dialectic implied in the nature of recognition. Hegel describes the dialectic resulting from the doubling of self-consciousness as that of the "spiritual unity." The word "spiritual" is carefully chosen here. For we know that there is something like spirit, which is not self-consciousness as an individual point, but rather a "world," which because it is social, lives by reciprocal recognition. Hence at the start, Hegel is considering the dialectic of self-consciousness taken as the movement of recognition as the latter appears to us. We have, in other words, a reflection per se, which is not that of the consciousness in question, but rather that of the concept. Clearly, the concern here is not just with one sort of doubling of consciousness, that is, with the fact that there is another self-consciousness for self-consciousness. Besides that there is the duplication of self-consciousness within itself, for as self-consciousness that in itself is split and united, it itself says "I" to itself: and in this way it is the inner

---

(yearning, desire). Still the French sense of *désir* can be detected in certain German expressions, for instance, in the word *Ehrbegierde* (desire for honor), which does include the element of désir. On the other hand, there is no sense of désir in tne German *Liebesbegierde* (desire to be loved), which expresses something beyond the carnal human sense that *Begierde* often has. Far that reason Kojève's quite nice illustration of the esence of human *Begierde*—that it desires an object, even if it be intrinsically worthless, for the sole reason that somebody else desires it—is not yet apropos at the stage here. That illustration is used too early, for it has its true value as an illustration of later stages along Hegel's way, above all, the world of alienated spirit.

difference or infinitude which, as self-consciousness, it shares with life. But at this new stage we are concerned with the actualization of this infinitude, with the concept of "infinitude which is being realized in self-consciousness." The inner difference between "I" and "I" lying in self-consciousness now appears, now becomes the real difference of the "we" which is "I" and "you," real "I" and real other "I." That occurs in the movement of recognition.[6] It is a complicated movement, for it does not suffice to say that self-consciousness has lost itself *in* the other or *to* the other, that is, that it only has its self-consciousness in the other. If this were so, then it would no longer see the other as a self at all, but rather, only "itself" in the other. That would in fact be the case if it were so obsessed with honor that it sought to find its own self-consciousness in the other. And what it would see here is not at all the being of the other, but rather only its own being in otherness, its own being another, in which it believes itself to be confirmed. That, however, will not suffice. To be sure, as was the case for desire, self-consciousness must cancel "the other being standing on its own" in order to be certain of itself. But it must also hold itself back out of respect to the other, for this other is itself and it is essential for self-consciousness that the other continue to exist. Its own self-consciousness depends on the other, but the dependence here is unlike that of desire on its object—an object that is simply to be eliminated. Here self-consciousness depends in a more spiritual sense on the other as self. Only if the other is not merely the other of the first self-consciousness, "his other," but rather free precisely in opposition to a self, can it provide confirmation of the first's self-consciousness. That a person demands recognition from another implies, to be sure, that the other is canceled, but on the other hand, what is demanded of the other implies to an equal extent that the other is recognized as free and hence implies just as much the return of the other to itself, to its free existence, as it implies the return of the first self-consciousness to itself. There is not only the confirmation of one's own self here, but also confirmation of the self of the other.

And now it is clear that this whole process is only valid if it is completely reciprocal. Take, for instance trivial form of recognition, the greeting. "Each sees the other doing the same thing it is doing. Each does itself what it demands of the other. And for that reason it does what it does only insofar as the other does the same. One-sided action would

---

6. Gadamer deals extensively with the I-Thou relationship and the phenomenon of recognition within the framework of his hermeneutic theory. Cf. *Wahrheit und Methode* (Tübingen: Mohr, 1965), 340ff. (trans.).

serve no purpose" (142). As a matter of fact, it would not only be without purpose: it would be fatal for one's own consciousness of self. Think of the feeling of humiliation when a greeting is not returned, be it because the other refuses to take cognizance of you—a devastating defeat for your own consciousness or self—or because he is not the person you thought he was but someone else and hence does not recognize you—not a very nice feeling either. Reciprocity is that essential here. "They recognize each other as recognizing reciprocally," indeed, "a qualification of many facets and many connotations."

This illustration of the dialectic of recognition using the custom of the greeting is not merely a convincing example for the dialectic on the conceptual level. It is a convincing anticipation of the real social background that lies behind Hegel's description of the experience of self-consciousness and that explains the decisive role he assigns to death in his system. Hegel relies here on a very concrete experience. The dialectic of recognition is experienced in a process, that is, in the life-and-death conflict, and in the determination of self-consciousness to prove its truth, its being recognized, even at the risk of its life. That there is a genuine connection of this sort is confirmed in the institution of the duel—two people fighting it out to restore honor that has been offended. He who is ready to fight with the other, he who does another the honor of being willing to fight with him, demonstrates thereby that he did not intend to place the latter beneath him. And, conversely, he who demands satisfaction, demonstrates for his part that he cannot bear the humiliation he has suffered unless the other, by declaring himself ready to fight, nullifies it. As is well known, in a matter of honor, no other form of nullification will suffice, and the one offended may therefore refuse any form of reconciliation. The code of honor admits only the full reciprocity of the life-and-death conflict, for it alone restores the mutual recognition in which self-consciousness finds its social confirmation. That one would give one's all for one's honor bears witness to the significance of honor. And when Hegel demonstrates in what follows that the confirmation of self-consciousness achieved in being a master cannot be that of true self-consciousness and that the self-consciousness of ability in the slave who works is higher than that of the master who only enjoys, that too is not without confirmation in social practice. The bourgeoisie, which ascends by virtue of its work, takes over the nobility's code of honor, but once it loses its new sense of belonging to the ruling classes, it no longer understands that code. Its imitation of nobility's code of honor as instanced in the "academic" duels for satisfaction fought by "ruling class" students and graduates becomes meaningless. Thus, it is historically correct to say that the existence of such a code of honor is the symbolic representation of the result of the life-and-death conflict in which mastery and servitude split apart. Still, what Hegel provides is an ideal-type construction of the relationship of mastery and servitude, which is merely illustrated by the historical background of the emergence of mastery.[7] When Hegel derives free self-consciousness from the essential connection between the absoluteness of freedom and the absoluteness of death, he is not giving us an early history of the development of mastery. Nor is he giving us a history of the liberation from mastery. Rather, he provides an ideal genealogy of the relationship between master and servant.[8]

A self-consciousness that as living self-consciousness merely finds itself together with other self-consciousness, that is, "independent forms, consciousnesses submerged . . . in the being of life" (143), does not yet have validity. As pure being for itself, that is, as *self*-consciousness, it must present itself in and stand the test of the life-and-death conflict. The reciprocity of the code of honor that we described above is perfectly suited to make clear that this "presentation" cannot consist solely in self-consciousness's endeavor to annihilate the other existence, but rather that it must consist also in the elevation of its being above its own particular existence, its "being attached to life" (144). Thus, the reason why it must put its own life on the line is not that it is unable to become certain of itself without annihilation of the other and accordingly without a conflict with the other, but rather that it is unable to achieve true being-for-self without overcoming its attachment to life, that is, without annihilation of itself as mere "life." Only in this annihilation

---

7. Accordingly, the historical question of the origin of mastery as it is explained in contemporary ethnology—as an outgrowth of the conquest of peasant peoples by invading horsemen—can be held in abeyance. That theory is intended to explain how the master-slave structure of the state comes into being. Here, however, where we are still moving completely within the sphere of self-consciousness, that question is not thematic.

8. Kojève, as his epoch-making introduction to Hegel's thought (*Introduction à la Lecture de Hegel* [Paris, 1947]) demonstrates, sees this quite clearly. His own way to Hegel, is determined by the bloodletting of the Russian October Revolution and by the ensuing wish to acquire a better understanding of Marx, led him to apply Hegel historically in ways that are not entirely convincing. This is not the place to refute either the Marxists or Heidegger, even if it remains true that every revolution is bloody, just as is every war. Kojève's work, however, retains its value today, in particular, because it was he who first revealed the philosophic significance of the Jena manuscripts for understanding Hegel's conception of death.

can it become certain of itself. Of course, a further insight contradicting this one will come, namely, that the mutual risk of life cannot bring about what it is supposed to: certainty of self. The point of this dialectic is evidenced in the fact that the one who survives is no closer to his goal than the one who succumbs. That which is able to give self-consciousness certainty of itself must be a cancellation of the other self-consciousness different from outright annihilation of the latter. Thus, life is not only "as essential as pure self-consciousness" to the one who subjugates himself, but also to the other as well: the latter specifically needs the life of the first, but as a consciousness that is not for itself but for another. Because it has no true being for itself, the consciousness that submits is, like the slave of antiquity, thingness, object, *res*. Thus, the result of the experience of the life-and-death struggle for recognition is indeed that self-consciousness can only be when it finds itself confirmed in the other. That means, however, that it is double and that it divides into master and servant.

The dialectic of the master and servant is now worked out in two courses of experience: that of the master and that of the servant (148).[9] This exposition presents no special difficulties as far as the master is concerned. It is easy to see that the master achieves satisfaction of his desire with the help and service of the servant. The independence of the things on which the self-consciousness of desire remained dependent is now canceled. The servant delivers the thing, which he has worked on, to the master for the "pure" pleasure of the latter. As Kojève puts it, the servant sets the master's table. Why does the consciousness of the master nevertheless remain a faulty (*verkehrtes* self-consciousness? One might expect that here Hegel would play upon the master's dependency on the servant. This dependency is well known to us, not only from the Marxist slogan of the "general strike," but also from the dialectic of the will to power as Nietzsche develops it, and as it is confirmed in the everyday experience of serving. There is a dependency of the master on the servant and it demonstrates the falsity of the master's self-consciousness or, so to speak, the latter's actual servitude. Certainly, it stands as a matter of fact that the master becomes dependent on the servant and that the consciousness of being a master finds itself thereby limited. Hegel's dialectical analysis is far more rigorous. It seeks out the dialectical reversal within the self-consciousness of the master and is not content with a limitation that is externally imposed on mastery. As regards the mere fact of the master's dependency, could one not ask, is

---

9. Cf. Ph 148: "We only saw what servitude is in relationship to mastery."

it not too bad for the facts that they do not allow the master his full mastery? The master who knows himself to be dependent on his servant no longer has the genuine self-consciousness of a master but that of a servant—a phenomenon that includes, we know, the most comical forms of anxious obedience to the servant. For us it is clear that such a master is no master. But is it clear for the master? Is he not comical precisely because he feels himself to be a master, yet in truth is afraid? We who recognize the dependency of the master know as well that his dependency is actually that of desire and does not come from his failure to be recognized. But a new level of falsity in the self-consciousness of the master that would cause it to collapse would be reached only then when as self-consciousness it knew itself to be inferior to another sort of self-consciousness. The essential point in Hegel's argument seems to me to be that it is aimed precisely at the master's coming to realize his inferiority and that it rejects the more obvious dialectic of dependency. Hegel's argument deals with the consciousness of a master who is and remains a master. He has achieved everything he should—specifically, that another self-consciousness cancels itself as being-for-self and does to itself what the first self-consciousness does to it. Indeed, the servant is not only treated as an object, but also treats himself as an object, that is, he is absorbed in service and thus has his "self-consciousness" only in the master. In everything he does, the servant faithful to his master has the master in mind and not himself. He makes sure that the thing is nothing to the master and that the master is pure being-for-self, which sees itself confirmed in the services rendered to it. To this extent recognition ought to be achieved here.

Of what value to the master, to his self-consciousness, is the existence of such a servant? Here is Hegel's argument. The most august master, whom the servant never allows to have even the slightest sense of dependency—precisely this "master-only"—must recognize that he is thereby not certain of his being-for-self as the truth. What he is certain of in the servant is, after all, the dependency and inessentiality of the servile consciousness. That alone is his "truth" and it is a "faulty truth." Thus, Hegel is able to find the dialectical reversal within self-consciousness itself—in its claim, and not in its factual vulnerability. The truth of self-consciousness will have to be sought, not in the consciousness of the master, but in the servile consciousness—even if "to begin with," this consciousness is "outside of itself," that is, knows itself in the master and does not know itself as the truth of self-consciousness, or, does not know that the master is not the "independent consciousness" at all, but rather it itself.

Thus, the reversal follows in which servile consciousness as consciousness pushed back into itself, that is, as consciousness having returned to itself from having been outside itself, withdraws into itself. And, like someone who withdraws into himself, it begins to think differently. Or, to put this point in context, it now thinks with new awareness of self. Per se, servitude is the very antithesis of genuine self-consciousness. "For servitude the master is at first the essence." There is implied in the consciousness of serving the complete surrendering of self to the master and his needs. That means the complete subordination of all one's own needs to the sole important thing, service, service to the master who alone is important. Thus, for the consciousness of service "independent consciousness which is for itself is. . .the truth," but obviously it is not entirely aware of this. This consciousness does not yet have a self-consciousness or being-for-self of its own. Since servitude is entirely "for the other," the truth of independent consciousness, that is, that it is itself independent consciousness, exists "for it," but not yet "in it."

And here Hegel once again bases his argument on the role that the life-and-death conflict played for self-consciousness. He calls death the absolute master, meaning that there is yet a greater master than that into the service of which the servant delivers himself and to which he forfeits his independence. When one accepts the self-surrender of service, the human master too brings one to "dissolve" the ties with one's own natural existence and to deny the exigencies of it. That is implied in the servant's complete self-subordination. Nothing is as important to the consciousness that serves as the contentment of the master. But how much more in the fear of death, that total dissolution, does one in giving up everything outside oneself want to cling to oneself "the simple self-consciousness, pure being-for-self"! The absolute master, death, which demands absolute subjugation, throws the trembling individual entirely upon himself alone.

At this point, precisely because nothing else that one could hang onto withstands the fear of death, pure being-for-self is raised to the level of consciousness, which is to say that consciousness's actual concern is now for it.[10] And that is the reason why servitude now acquires a self-

---

10. If Gadamer is correct in his interpretation, death has the same role in Hegel's understanding of the transition from consciousness to self-consciousness as it has in Heidegger's understanding of the transition from inauthenticity to authenticity. The higher stage for both Hegel and Heidegger would be *Sein zum Tode*, being for it is only death that can put the individual in authentic relationship with himself. Cf. *Sein und Zeit* (Tübingen: Niemeyer, 1960), 46–53 (trans.).

consciousness of service: the servant proves his own being-for-self to himself in a new way, one different from the self-sacrifice of service: "it [servile consciousness] thereby cancels in each single aspect [i.e., not only in the universal dissolution in the fear of death] its attachment to natural existence and works this off." "Working off natural existence"—a key phrase has been reached here, one that indicates how knowledge of pure being-for-self, which the serving consciousness is now aware of for itself, is realized. Through work. Work is "inhibited desire": instead of immediately satisfying its desire, consciousness keeps to itself and does not annihilate the object ("delayed disappearance"). Rather, by "shaping" it, imprinting its form upon it, it converts it into something that remains. In producing the object, consciousness that works comes to "view independent being as itself." The meaning is clear. We have here the self-consciousness of ability, which sees itself continually and lastingly confirmed in that which it "shapes" and has shaped. Through work, self-consciousness that is for-itself settles in the "element of permanency." That, indeed, is the positive significance of forming: it yields a self-consciousness that even the slave can have. In essence, we have reached the *eph hēmin* of stoic consciousness.

Hegel, with ample justification, supplements this line of thought with a second. For there is a negative side of "forming" that goes deeper, in that it makes it possible to transcend fear.[11] Only now does it become completely clear that we are concerned with a phase in the genealogy of freedom, indeed, the decisive phase. The freedom of self-consciousness consists not only in the confirmation of self given in existent things (*seiendes*), but also in successful self-assertion in opposition to dependency on existent things. In bringing forth the product of its work, consciousness emerges for itself not as an existent thing, but rather as "being-for-self for itself." Here again Hegel finds self-consciousness's "trembling before the strange reality" to be of decisive importance for it. And, as a matter of fact, the mere anxiety of servile existence is by itself not the beginning of freedom. That someone in the anxiety of conflict places life before honor certainly does not yet indicate that he has suffered that trembling in the very innermost fibers of himself, a trembling in which alone one becomes certain of one's pure "being-for-

---

11. It is only in response to a typical misunderstanding (H. Popitz, *Der entfremdete Mensch* [Basel, 1953], 131ff.) that I would emphasize that the "negative" concept of work in Hegel, if taken to be evaluative, is actually a positive concept, no matter what one's point of view is. For the most part, Hegel tends to use Hegelian concepts like "negative" here in a Hegelian sense.

self." He who in disregarding an offense to honor, that is, who in spite of the fact that recognition has been refused him, clings to life, is in reality a slave held by the chain of natural existence. Hegel goes so far as to say that someone could "be recognized as a person even though he himself does not attain the truth of being recognized as an independent self-consciousness"—a remarkable statement. Evidently, Hegel is referring to the fact that the law, which treats no one as a thing (*res*), but rather always requires that the individual be recognized as a person, does not insure real self-consciousness precisely because it pronounces judgment "without regard to the person," that is, in recognition of all persons as equal. The elimination of slavery, then, does not yet end man's sense of being a servant. Work that one no longer performs for a master does not for that reason imply that the individual doing it is made free for true self-consciousness. In fact, not even one's "dexterity" put to free use would mean that. It, too, can represent a freedom that remains at the level of servitude, for such dexterity can be successful at all sorts of things without being independent, consciousness, that is, as true ability, a self-consciousness of "vocation." Similarly, obstinacy is only thought to confirm freedom and is, in fact, a form of rebellious dependency.

In contrast, if work is to be the basis of true self-consciousness, it must derive from what I have termed "consciousness of ability," something that is able to deal with the "universal might [death] and objective reality" (150). Hegel further develops this idea of freedom of ability by emphasizing that the formative activity cancels opposed, existent form. "But this objective, negative reality is precisely the alien reality before which it trembled." That is a daring thesis, and it remains for us to explicate it. Unquestionably, the experience of death is the experience of an ultimate dependency in our existence, which the latter in its being-for-self immediately resists. This alien master, who is master over everything, thus stands for everything alien on which our own self-consciousness is dependent. In this sense every cancellation of such an alien reality—and even if it be only a skilled cancellation of the existent form of things—is a liberation of our own self-consciousness. Only in this is there contained the confirmation proper to the self-consciousness of ability, namely, that it comes to be "for it as its own," this not only in the single existent that produces, but beyond this, in its own being-for-self as ability. "It posits itself"; it establishes itself as being-for-self in the element of permanency and is no longer mere dissolution in natural existence that "works off" its trembling with the feeling of self characteristic of anxiety and service. Although in work for the master it seemed to have no mind of its own (and as service did indeed have none), consciousness that serves, in surrendering itself to work as work—and not simply to the master—becomes conscious of itself. When it "puts out" the form as its own (when it produces), it recognizes itself. And thus precisely in work it has a mind of its own: "That, I can do!" To be sure, this is not yet the full encounter with self which, for instance, the work of art affords and which allows us to recognize, "That's me!" Hegel is not worried about the specific form that working consciousness has given the thing and that would allow consciousness to recognize itself in it. Indeed, his concern is not at all with the "thing," but rather only with form *qua* form. The sole thing that confirms self-consciousness here is the fact that the form is one that it itself gives to the thing and that it is one and the same each time. Thus, self-confirmation is not achieved in viewing any particular existent as such, but only in the form that is one's own and that precisely for this reason brings out the pure being-for-self contained in the freedom of one's ability. Therefore, strictly speaking, it is not at all the ability as such, this "dexterity," which withstands total dissolution—annihilation by the "not" of otherness—and provides the basis for true self-consciousness, but rather the consciousness of one's ability.

The history of freedom has by no means come to an end here, but in the history of the consciousness of freedom the decisive step has been taken. That is demonstrated by what follows: as the "total dissolution" of self-consciousness, this being-for-self has become "a new form of self-consciousness, a consciousness which *thinks*, i.e., a consciousness which is free self-consciousness" (151). What we have here is something truly universal in which you and I are the same. It will be developed as the self-consciousness of reason. Indeed, having reason or exhibiting reason-ableness means being able, in disregard of oneself, to accept as valid that in which no single self can consider himself superior to another. That two times two equals four is not my truth, not your truth and not a truth in need of mutual recognition by each of us. It is reason as certainty of being all reality. Since now the other cannot be other than reason, a firm basis is established here far experience, for the standpoint of observing reason. But beyond this, it is particularly true for all actualization or realization of self-consciousness, that is, for all active reason, that the objective, real world "has lost every sense of being alien" (314).[12] Here we have reached spirit, that is, spirit in the form of genuine universality such as ethicality and custom, which in being taken for granted, unite

---

12. Observing reason (*Beobachtende Vernunft*) and the realization of self-consciousness (*Verwirklichung des Selbstbewusstseins*) are two consecutive stages in Hegel's *Phenomenology of Mind*. Cf. Ph 183ff. and Ph 255ff. (trans.).

one and all. Self-consciousness is not lost in this universality. Rather it finds itself there and to its satisfaction, it knows its singleness was wrong.

It has not helped in understanding this chapter that Karl Marx made use of its master-servant dialectic in a very different context. . . . Marx does not simply misunderstand and misuse Hegel, for it is true that through work the servant reaches a higher self-consciousness than the master who enjoys; and that, indeed, is the presupposition of the former's liberation from servitude in the external realm of his social existence—as it was for the bourgeois citizen before him.

However, Hegel, in his dialectic, does not describe the wage worker, but principally the farmer and handworker in bondage. The emancipation of the cities and then of the farmers as it occurs in the revolutionary ascent of the *tiers état* to a position of political responsibility, is only similar in structure to the liberation of capitalism's wage-slave. In point of fact, for self-consciousness the actual purpose of work is fulfilled in the nonalienated work world. In the "phenomenology of spirit" that Hegel describes, the inner freedom of self-consciousness that results from the dialectic of mastery and servitude is by no means the last word. Accordingly, the critical approach that seeks, and then fails to find the liberation of the wage-slave from the mastery of capital in the result of Hegel's dialectic, is quite superficial. As an argument against the man who taught the unity of the "real" and the "reasonable"—and that, incidentally, can most certainly not mean the approbation of things as they stand—one cannot propose, as an updated critical insight, that self-consciousness, as free, must work itself into the whole of objective reality, that it must reach the self-evident truth of the solidarity of ethical spirit and the community of ethical customs, that it must complete the actualization of reason as a human and social task. Marx, to be sure, found the point at which to apply his criticism of Hegel not here, but rather, as seemed more appropriate, in Hegel's philosophy of right. But the dogmatic conception of consciousness and of idealism that the shared with his contemporaries kept him from recognizing that Hegel would never have dreamt for a moment that work is only the work of thought and that what is reasonable would be realized solely through thought. Thus, the work of which Hegel speaks is material work too, and the experience consciousness has is that all handwork is a matter of the spirit. Now let us assume that it is true that the mode of production in modern industry and the form of human commerce in the industrial society do not permit the worker to find a significance for himself in his work, which alone would make self-consciousness possible. Then, in view of the comprehensive character of this mode of work, the question necessarily arises who could be really free in the industrial society of today with its ubiquitous coercion of things and pressure to consume. Precisely in regard to this question Hegel's dialectic of master and servant seems to delineate a valid truth: if there is to be freedom, then first of all the chin attaching us to things must he broken. The path of mankind to universal prosperity is not as such the path to the freedom of all. Just as easily, it could be a path to the unfreedom of all.

PART IV

Dialectics of Desire
and Recognition

Of Human Bondage

LABOR AND FREEDOM IN THE *PHENOMENOLOGY*

Howard Adelman

INTRODUCTION

> *The easiest thing of all is to pass judgements on what has a solid substantial content: it is more difficult to grasp it, and most of all difficult to do both together and produce the systematic exposition of it.*[1]

It is easy to become absorbed in judging Hegel and his interpreters. It is harder to grasp the development of nonrational self-consciousness. This essay concentrates on "grasping" that development rather than the even harder task of providing a systematic exposition of it. The latter is facilitated by translating the language of religious myth into thought. In order to grasp that thought in the fullness of living, in the specific acts of individuals, it is appropriate in dealing with the middle section of the *Phenomenology* to translate thought back into myth. This is particularly true since the nonrational development discussed is, for Hegel, archetypically Jewish and Hegel realized how little of that "Jewish" spirit could be rendered by an intellectual analysis.[2]

These three aspects—classifying and judging, grasping the material at hand and expressing it, and producing a systematic exposition—are also ways of differentiating the three different aspects of the spirit depicted in the most basic divisions of the *Phenomenology of Mind*: consciousness

---

1. *Phenomenology of Mind* trans. J. B. Baille (London, 1931), 69–70. Hereinafter cited as *P.M.*
2. Cf. H. S. Harris, *Hegel's Development: Toward the Sunlight 1770–1781* (Oxford: Clarendon, 1972), 278.

(naming, classifying, and subsuming under general laws), self-consciousness (which leaves the lifeless universals for the fullness of experience), and the third section of rational self-consciousness, including reason, spirit, religion, and absolute knowledge. Since our subject matter falls within the middle section in the fullness of living experience and not its abstract corpse, it is appropriate to plunge directly in and dwell within the section.

But before we dive note the lifeless corpse that is our diving board. What began as a world full of sensations of which consciousness was certain, a dynamic world of flux and change in which one sought stability, ends up in understanding as a stable sysrem of mechanical forces in equilibrium in which, instead of certainty, everarhing is the opposite of what it appears and things are defined by what they lack. Life has been reduced to a system of forces in equilibrium within a self-moving world system. Life has become lifeless without movement and development.[3] Man has become master of the knowledge of nature, subsuming everything under his laws and categories, but he has not grasped life in the living of it for he has not faced the fact that life ends in the experience of death. The world is a projection of man's categories and laws and thereby his self has become other; man cannot find himself in that otherness. He cannot say who he is in what is projected. He is a lonely, empty "I." Adam in the Garden of Eden with all his powers of naming everything in nature is alone and needs a helpmeet.

THE TRUTH OF SELF-CERTAINTY

Desire

To be conscious of himself as a self, there must be another self-consciousness. This is generally agreed. It is also generally believed that the other self-consciousness does not appear in Hegel until the Lordship and Bondage section. What Hegel says, however, is that an independent self-consciousness does not appear as a *fact* for self-consciousness until then. But it does appear before this as an object that is not yet recognized as an independent self-consciousness. A helpmeet appears as a *physical* projection of myself, as "bone of my bone and flesh of my flesh." The other self-consciousness at this stage is not an intellectual projection. It has the physical shape of an independent self-consciousness but it has

---

3. Piaget has noted in child development as well that "the elimination of life leads to a mechanization of force (*The Child's Conception of Physical Causality* [Totawa, N.J.: Littlefield, Adams], 246).

not yet expressed the essential independent spirit. As Hegel says, " When for self-consciousness the distinction does not also have the shape of *being*, it is *not* self-consciousness" (*P.M.*, 219). Of course, everything is the opposite of what it appears, as has been learned from consciousness, and this fantasy is in reality the fact that I am born as a projection of another body into the world and project this in my isolated dream world as if everything out there were merely a projection of my own body.

If the infant thinks he is the center of the world, he feels he is nothing, that he is merely an extension of the mother. But he does not yet recognize that feeling. The consciousness of that feeling as first stage of *self*-consciousness, of consciousness as an inward state, emerges in an inverted way distorted by the prism of consciousness that experiences the world as a projection of self. The mother is an extension of self, but not merely any extension. The mother is a physical extension with whom one desires to be physically reunited.

The three moments of desire remain an abstraction. Desire has not yet become a vital experience. Adam is conscious of himself as the center of the universe. His consciousness tells him that he is not allowed to eat of the Tree of Knowledge of Good and Evil, that is, to eat of that which will destroy that consciousness of himself as the center of the world, and his consciousness as the essence of that self. Knowledge of his bodily self will destroy both the illusion that the self is the center of a self-moving cosmic system and the illusion that the essence of that system is simply thought. At this stage, however, Adam merely knows himself as one who names objects in nature and does not know his own body or govern its conduct. Adam is defined by what he lacks *in knowledge*, the knowledge of his body. Further, Adam is alone; he has no body in the world with whom he can be. It is a duality in which Adam has a body that he cannot know and has no body with whom he can be.

In the second moment, unknown to Adam's conscious experience, while Adam is sleeping another body appears that in consciousness must necessarily be a projection of his own body. Eve is made as a projection of Adam's flesh. Further, there is something in the ego, which is other than thought, which is rooted in the body, and which, when raised into thought, is interpreted as a projection of the body. One might say that, for Hegel, the superego is conscious thought when it addresses itself toward the body; responsibility for the body is reciprocally projected onto the thought of the world. The unconscious is in turn the body as a thing that makes other things; when raised into consciousness the responsibility for making things is projected onto the world as a unity of thought.

If consciousness is this refusal to take responsibility for the body while at the same time insisting that the self is the center of a self-moving world, then it is imperative for consciousness that the self rein-corporate that physical projection of itself as part of itself, even if again the responsibility for this instruction is also projected into the thought of the world as a whole. In the third moment desire, God *tells* Adam and Eve that they shall be one flesh. What was actualized without re-flection in the second moment is now posited as a unity in consciousness without actualization. What was a mere abstraction without realization becomes in the third moment a recognition of a duality, internal and external, with an imperative to achieve unity.

Life

Nevertheless, desire, as the first moment of learning the truth about oneself, is still an absraction. It has not yet been experienced in life. In the first moment of self-recognition, the meaning that the self is not-other has been given substantive meaning, but only in thought. The meaning of the self as that which identifies objects has not yet been dealt with. Since that self already exists in consciousness, what it needs is actualization in life.

If desire is the inversion of consciousness of self as a nonother, a bare ego, so that one becomes conscious that one is ignorant of one's own identity at the same time as the other is experienced, although only in the abstract, life is the inversion of the other aspect of consciousness, the consciousness of the object that receives its identity from the I. In the inversion, the object becomes an object for experience rather than for consciousness and thereby loses *its* identity. The only unity is the unity of the self in contrast to desire in general in which a duality exits in the ego between one's ignorance of who the self is and one's self as a concrete other; from an infantile perspective, we feel the mother is our self as other while we are curious about our own body as if it were another of which we are ignorant.

In the first moment of life, the self is experienced as extension. Thus, there is a negation in experience, as it appears to the self, of the negativity of the first moment as we reach out to make the other part of the self. There are objects independent of the self but the subject does not regard objects as having any continuity independent of the self. When an infant watches an adult come in one door and leave through another, it looks back to the first door to see that adult reappear. There is no extension except as a projection from the subject; there is no continuity in time except as a continuity within that spatial extension. The existence of *independent* objects in experience is not yet recognized: "The essential element (*Wesen*) is infinite as the supersession of all distinctions, the pure rotation on its own axis, itself at rest while being absolutely restless infinitude, the very self-dependence in which the differences brought out in the process are all dissolved, the simple reality of time, which in this self-identity has the solid form and shape of space" (*P.M.*, 221).

This is, of course, life as the self-moving world system described at the end of consciousness, but the solar system is no longer an object for consciousness here; rarher, I experience myself as a solar system. Life, which, in general, is the *experience* of unity of the self, in its first moment is a duality in the unity, for though independence of all objects is sublated in the existence of the self, the objects are still sublated as independent objects. The independence of objects is itself broken up in the second moment of life when there are no object as such, but only an infinitude of distinctions in experience. For the first moment is but an abstraction; its actualization in experience results in the immediate grabbing for the infinite number of objects presented among which no distinctions can be made. The mother's breast and the corner of the child's blanket are sucked as if they were the same.

In the third moment of life, the self posits itself by separating out objects as extensions of the self and then denying the separateness of the object by consuming it. In the process, stability is consumed. At the same time the self experiences objects as food for the body; the self is posited as a body to consume objects, as the continuity of the self in relationship to an undifferentiated continuity.

Life as living has become the process of defining oneself as the eater of fruit in a Garden of Eden in which no distinctions are made. There is no evaluation of what is good or bad for the body. Life, the reunion of the object world and the subject, is no longer a mere idea. Nor is it a natural instinct to guide us to the breast that provides sustenance. It has become universalized.

In life as spirit, *all* things are seen to exist for consumption by man's body. Man lives obsessed with the Tree of Life in the Garden of Eden. In the first moment of life, objects exist for man but are not yet in man. In the second moment, the existence of objects themselves is negated in favor of undifferentiated experience. In the final moment, the mother, Eve, is opposed to the self since she is not simply an object that exists only for consumption by the self; the individual, Adam, in turn exists, but only lives to feed his body. "Life as such is partly the Means of Spirit, and as such opposed to it; and partly it is the Living Individual, and Life is its Body."[4] Note that it is Eve who is the means of spirit. Adam has

---

4. Hegel's *Science of Logic*, vol. 2 (London, 1929), 403.

become his body, has become the solar system and ignores his body as other.

Desire in Life

The third stage following desire and life is the experience of desire in lile. It is not an abstraction of which we learn. Nor is it experience without consciousness. It is desire directed toward the consciousness for which we hunger, the lack of knowledge of our own bodies both in ourselves and as other.

In desire in general one is torn between the feeling of one's body projecting into the world as an object and the consciousness of ignorance of one's body. In desire in life, an inversion takes place. The self wants to "make" an object in the world, that body which is already projected in the world as ourselves, while at the same time being an independent life, a self that exists in its own right, which experiences all the fruit of the Garden as objects to be consumed. The self wants both to consume that object and to be consumed by it.

However, Eve wants to be one flesh with Adam, not just as an idea but as a concrete reality. It is Eve, the second moment in human creation, consciousness that maintains itself as an immediate unity who gives substance and acts out her will through her feelings as a concrete individual. Adam is hung up on his own duality—as the one given dominion over all of nature but who has no dominion or command over his own body, as the one who knows that he shall be one flesh with Eve but who knows he must not eat of the Tree of Knowledge of Good and Evil. His thoughts and feelings are internally torn apart.

> Thus one sex is mind in its self-diremption into explicit personal self-subsistence and the knowledge and volition of free universality, i.e. the self-consciousness of conceptual thought and the volition of the objective final end. The other sex is mind maintaining itself in unity as knowledge and volition of the substantive, but knowledge and volition in the form of concrete individuality and feeling. In relation to externality, the former is powerful and active, the latter passive and subjective.[5]

Adam and Eve ate of the Tree of Knowledge of Good and Evil and Adam knew Eve and Eve knew Adam.

---

5. Hegel's *Philosophy of Right*, trans. T. M. Knox (Oxford, 1942), 114.

And self-consciousness is thus only assured of itself through sublating this other, which us presented to self-consciousness as an independent life; self-consciousness is *Desire*. Convinced of the nothingness of this other, it definitely affirms this nothingness to be for itself the truth of this other, negates the independent object, and thereby acquires the certainty of its own self, as *true* certainty, a certainty which it has become aware of un objective form.

In this state of satisfaction, however, it has experience of the independence of its object. Desire and the certainty of its self obtained in the gratification of desire, are conditioned by the object: for the certainty exists through cancelling this other; in order that this cancelling may be effected, there must be this other. Self-consciousness is thus unable by its negative relation to the object to abolish it; because of that relation it rather produces it again, as well as the desire. (*P.M.*, 225)

But, of course, this whole section leading to desire in life is itself an abstraction *in feeling*, a fantasy that is not yet recognized as such by the self-conscious individual. Because these feelings are filtered through the prism of consciousness, where the child is the self-moving center of a world he controls, and since the child does not yet know who he himself is and cannot yet make distinctions among feelings, thoughts, and actions, he thinks that what he feels is real. In experience the other is an independent self-consciousness that is not sublated into the self. They do not become one flesh. The child comes to the shocking recognition of a truth, that the other is an *independent* object.

But if the self only knows and recognizes itself as the center of the *whole* world excluding nothing, then it experiences frustration. The self finds new satisfaction only when it projects onto the other the desire to negate itself, to become one with the first self; this is seen as the essence of the other. It is Eve who seduces Adam, who negates herself as other, who is seduced by "force" of desire that Adam *"controls"*: "On account of the independence of the object, therefore, it can only attain satisfaction when this object itself effectually brings about negation within itself. The object must *per se* effect this negation of itself, for it is inherently (*an sich*) something negative, and must be for the other what it is" (*P.M.*, 225–26). To ensure *satisfaction*, self-consciousness has had to come to recognize another self-consciousness who is not merely oneself objectified, while retaining the illusion that it is oneself "subjectified," as it were, oneself out there but as an independent source of action.

When God discovers that Adam and Eve have eaten of the fruit of the Tree of Knowledge of Good and Evil and have become conscious of their mortality, consciousness, which saw the world out there as the objectification of self, now must take account of the self as an actor. Man has set out on the path of history; thought operates through that which is acted out by passion. Emotions and thoughts are sundered so that feeling ignores thought and thought distorts feeling.

LORDSHIP AND BONDAGE

> Self-consciousness exists in itself and for itself, in that, and by the fact that it exists for another self-consciousness; that is to say that it is only by bang acknowledged or "recognized." (P.M., 229)

This is how the section "Lordship and Bondage" begins. And Hegel warns us immediately after making this assertion that in the distinction of the moments of self-consciousness, these moments must be taken as *not* distinguished. They must always be understood and accepted in their *opposite* sense. To interpret the above to mean that a self-consciousness is truly other takes Hegel's meaning in the introduction not in its *opposite* sense but in its literal sense. The latter self-consciousness is not a self-consciousness that also is said to exist in and for itself.

Hegel is *not* simply talking about two self-conscious beings in relationship to one another. He is talking about the *nature* of self-consciousness itself where double meaning is rooted; it is the nature of self-consciousness to see double meaning even when reflecting on its own nature. Self-consciousness at this stage is still narcissistic, seeing the other as the extension of self at the same time as it experiences the self as other than itself, and, as such, wanting the same reunion with itself as it wants with the other.

Seeking recognition by another self-consciousness is *acting out* the process of self-recognition. How does narcissistic thought, which considers the world as an extension of itself, come to recognize the self, which experiences the world as alien and other?

Self-Consciousness Doubled

To understand this question we must clarify the sense in which one self-consciousness appears to itself as another self-consciousness outside itself. Hegel says that self-consciousness has "outered itself," has come outside itself when self-consciousness has before it another self-consciousness. To see this simply as a depiction of two selves in relationship makes no sense of how one self-consciousness is outered. At the end of "Truth of Self-Certainty" we were left with a self that had not abandoned thought, which had taken the other self as an extension of its own body; feeling, however, reveals the self as other, as a subject with an independent source of will. The development is now carried forward but on the level of the immediacy of feeling, and, since we are dealing with the phenomenology of experience, we are concerned with feelings as they first appear in development. And when they first appear they are still accompanied by thought. The rest of the middle section of the *Phenomenology* has as one of its themes the increasing effort of feeling to jettison thought.

The first moment (of lordship and bondage) is concerned with sexual feelings as an experience (not the experience of sex), and the first moment of that moment is concerned with the thoughts that accompany these sexual feelings. In the negative moment (particularly if masculine imagery is utilized) the self experiences itself as split. The self is *not* itself but is lost in the other. On the other hand, the self is not other, since that self was projected into the other. This moment of negation is itself negated; in the immediacy of feeling, the self experiences itself as a unity (since the self experiences itself by sublating the other, an other that is itself, and therefore the self sublates itself). Sublating itself and sublating the other are then one and the same experience. But, upon reflection on this experience, the self recognizes itself as only one with itself by cancelling itself as other and cancelling being in the other. The other goes free; the pair split.

The second moment of the development of sexual feeling negates the consciousness, negates thought, and considers the relationship strictly as an *act*. As consciousness, one self-consciousness is active and the other merely passive, continuing the subject-object dichotomy. But as an action, it is mutual. Therefore, the consciousness of the first moment is reflected in the mutual immediate feelings of the partners in the second moment.

As a result, in the third moment, when recognition comes, one begins with a double consciousness both in relationship to oneself and to the other. One is conscious of restrictions at the same time as one has risked oneself by projection outward toward the other. One also assumes that, in one sense, one is the other; but one is also not the other. No wonder lovers are all mixed up. Unity can only be experienced by repetition, by cancelling itself as existing for itself, which is identical with experiencing one's self-existence only in the self-existence of the other. Upon reflection, "they recognize themselves as mutually recognizing one another" (*P.M.*, 231). "And the eyes of them both were opened, and they knew that they were naked" (Genesis 3:7). Each recognizes his own body and the body of the other; each also recognizes that the other recognizes both his own body and the body of the other.

The Battle

In the first moment of lordship and bondage, the sexual appetite, the desire to be one flesh, is acted out in fantasy, and thereby experienced, but only in consciousness as the enactment of living desire. In the second moment lordship and bondage, two bodies, self-conscious of themselves as bodies, experience the body itself *in actuality.*

Each individual now experiences himself as the unity of his own body: "Self-consciousness is primarily simple existence for self, self-identity by exclusion of every other from itself. It takes its essential nature and absolute object to be Ego; and in this immediacy, in this bare fact of its self-existence, it is individual" (*P.M.,* 231).

The second moment of the lordship and bondage is the antithesis of two individuals as bodies and not spirits; for each the other is only an unessential object. Each is *not* thought and *not* other. Each tries to be only his or her body. This is the battle.

Each experiences itself as a body and not as other. Then each acts out that experience. For Eve, in the immediate unity of feeling, Adam becomes unessential, although she is servant to him and he is her master. Her essence is the experience of her body as a mode of reproduction. In the bringing forth of children, she suffers in pain and *labor.* Eve is enslaved within her body; she is as an object over which her husband has mastery; she is a slave to natural reproduction. Both are experienced as one and the same. Sex is experienced merely as reproduction. Adam at this time *names* her Eve for she no longer lives in herself but is the mother of all that lives.

Adam experiences his body in his labor on the soil and becomes a slave to that soil. Eve experiences her body in the labor to bring forth future life and, therefore, as the means for life's continuity. But Adam experiences the unity of his body as a duality. For the body not only performs, but Adam recognizes that it will cease performing. Adam becomes conscious that he will die.

In this, each achieves an *abstraction* of existence, Eve as the mother of all living, and Adam as the bare struggle for survival, knowing that he will die. This is the first moment of the struggle (which is the second moment in the development of lordship and bondage). Lordship has appeared in Adam's mastery over Eve, and in death's mastery over Adam and bondage is experienced in Eve's labor pains and Adam's labor and toil, but neither lordship nor bondage has been brought into reflection, into *self*-consciousness.

In the second moment of the struggle the battle is acted out. For Adam and Eve experience their submission only in consciousness that has not yet become actualized (the precondition of its becoming self-conscious). And it is acted out by that which embodies the first moment as a unity of feeling. Their unity is embodied in their children—Cain and Abel.

Adam and Eve are conscious of their individuality as a body, but their bodies are fettered to one another, and to life, Eve as the mother of all living and Adam as the one who earns a living and knows he will die. The acting out of the independence of the body is left to their children.

Cain, as the firstborn, is akin to his father and tills the ground. Abel, as the secondborn, is akin to his mother and is a keeper of sheep just as his mother tended her babes. They express their independence from the objects produced by their labor by the "pure negation of its objective form"—Cain sacrifices some of his produce and Abel one of his lambs. Action entailed the death of the objects of their own labor, thereby risking that which is their own life objectified. They are prepared to alienate the products of their labor, for their bodies as laboring devices are still felt to be alien. The immediacy of feeling follows this split in consciousness. Only the animal offering receives recognition as a sacrifice. Cain becomes *angry* and *crestfallen*, for he had *not* been *recognized* as an individual independent of the objects of his labor. Cain kills Abel.

In the second moment of the struggle (Cain and Abel) a *second* action is involved in the attempt to bring to recognition the body as individual and independent of that on which it labors. In the action of the other, Abel, the shepherd, gains recognition from God (the world as thought), and not Cain. Yet, in fact, shepherding becomes obsolete and is succecded by agriculture. Only one economic form of life can survive as primary; one must die. Though each economic form of life aspires to primacy and the death of the other, the one that dies both projects responsibility for its death onto the subsequent form and views the succeeding form as living everafter, but as empty meaningless existence. There is thus a double action and death involved—the death of one's body in an objective form as the sacrifice of the products of one's labor, and the death of a competing form of economic life: "The process of bringing all this out involves a twofold action—action on the part of the other and action on the part of itself. Insofar as it is the other's action, each aims at the destruction and death of the other. But in this there is implicated also the second kind of action, self-activity; for the former implies that it risks its own life" (*P.M.*, 232).

The life-and-death struggle involved is *not* one between two warriors but between two embodiments of different forms of economic life. The struggle is to gain recognition for their bodily independence. In so doing, they "risk life," their own life objectified into otherness through labor, though this has not yet come into consciousness. They literally "stake their life"; one sacrifices his agricultural produce and the other an animal. Each takes the risk in order to be recognized as unfettered to themselves as other: "The individual who has not staked his life, may, no doubt, be recognized as a Person; but he has not attained the truth of this recognition as an independent self-consciousness. In the same way each must aim at the death of the other as it risks its own life thereby" (*P.M.*, 233).

In the second moment of the struggle (which is the second moment in the development of lordship and bondage), Cain, who fails to gain recognition for his independence, slays Abel. The truth of the independence of the self as a body is cancelled. "Death is the natural, 'negation' of consciousness, negation without independence which thus remains without the requisite significance of actual recognition" (*P.M.*, 233).

The lack of independence is itself negated as a fact; the negation is negated. Abel is dead. Cain is evicted from the soil and loses his source of sustenance. He becomes a fugitive and wanderer, one of the living dead who cannot even be put to death. In the second moment of the struggle, unity and independence of the self is realized but as a "lifeless existence," "merely existent and not opposed."

And the meaning must be taken in its opposite sense, for it is Abel's feeling projected into Cain. This is how consciousness translates the feelings engendered by the experience of being suckled as an infant and shepherded about. The self projects itself as the shepherd, but in order to grow into independence the shepherd must be killed off. But, of course, there is a double inversion. Since in consciousness the other is a projection of the self, the thought of killing the other is also projected onto otherness. It is the other that wants to snuff out the life of the self. The mother becomes the monster of the crib who wants to devour her own children.

But after destroying itself in fantasy, the self feels itself as not only alone but cut off from its own body as well. For feeling projected into fantasy through the prism of consciousness, which insists that the self exist in and for itself, reveals again that in the struggle between feeling and thought thought is victorious and cuts feeling off from the body and the reality of death. If the first stage in the acceptance of death is total denial (Eve), the second stage involves denying that consciousness will die while accepting the death of the body. But *I* don't die; the real I lives on. But in being cut off from the body and feelings, its living is lifeless.

Independence and Dependence of Self-Consciousness

In the first moment of lordship and bondage, the moment of immediate self-consciousness, the self becomes conscious of itself as having substantial bodily independence. In the experience of the second moment, the consciousness of oneself as an independent body seems to dissolve, for survival seems to depend on thought in general. In the third moment the negation of the negation is inverted and self-consciousness is posited as existing not only for itself but for another, which at this stage is regarded as a thing. The third moment entails the inversion of lifeless existence in the recognition that life is essential to existence and is not to be sacrificed.

In the first moment of this third moment, self-consciousness for itself and for another exists as a duality without unity, but for the first time they exist *in consciousness* as master or lord, thought in general, which is independent, and the essential nature of which is to be for itself, and as bondsman, as a body that is dependent for its *existence* on another and whose essence is life for another.

Noah is an artisan, unlike Cain the agriculturalist, or Abel the shepherd.[6] He designs a boat. Noah is the descendant of Seth, the third-born son of Adam and Eve, through whom the third moment could be realized. And it is only when Seth's son is born that man began "to call upon the name of the Lord" (Genesis 4:26). The lordship of God emerges only at this stage. God is the only one who is independent and whose *essential* nature is to be for itself. Noah is dependent for his existence on the soil that the Lord hath cursed. Further, the essence of Noah's existence is to live for another; his name means comforter, from the Hebrew *na hen*, "to comfort."

Now God as the Lord exists for itself in *consciousness* but not in actuality. Actualization is mediated through another, man as a body— or Noah in particular—whose existence is bound up with the existence of all things. For it is upon Noah's shoulders that his own salvation and salvation of everything else depends. Further, Noah's existence is to live for an other—God; Noah walks with God. Feeling for another is ultimately in the service of thought that is for itself.

---

6. Cf. Harris, *Hegel's Development*, 273–79, for a clear discussion of Hegel's earlier explicit references to Noah.

In the description following the introduction of the master or lord and the bondsman, what is depicted is not primarily the relationship of the master to the slave but of the master (a) to self-existence, to existing in and for himself, and (b) to the fact that the realization of self existence requires that the master's existence be experienced through that which is other, to an existence that is an object in the world. As a projection in the physical world the master is related to his self-existence only through mediation in a twofold sense. The master has a relationship to an independent self-existing being only because he controls the life of the bondsman and has power over that self-existence; that is, it is the self-existence as other over which the master has control. Second, the master has a relationship to his self-existence only because the bondsman obeys the master, believing that what he too wants, independent self-existence, is possessed by the master. The body feeling as filtered through the prism of consciousness comes to think that only the mind or thought possesses independence.

If the master is related to his self-existence mediately in a twofold sense, in the bondsman (a) seen as an existence independent of the master, and (b) seen as cognizing the master as possessing an independent self-existence, there is also a twofold sense in which the master is related to himself as other, as a thing in the world. Insofar as it is through the bondsman's work on the things in the world that the master relates to otherness, his immediate relationship to the external world is mediated by the bondsman. Insofar as he alone has the pure enjoyment of the thing, he is immediately related to self-existence as other, and mediation is negated. The master, since he does not work on the world, is indifferent to the independence of the object.

The relationship must now be considered from the point of view of the bondsman. Noah does not work in forced labor for the Lord. He freely gives himself in the service of the Lord. Slaves and bondsmen have a common characteristic in that both give service without pay, but only the servant of the Lord gives it freely. As opposed to forced slavery, the bondsman is also one who is bound, in the sense that he gives security for the other. Noah is the archetypal bondsman freely giving himself in the service of the Lord, doing all that God commands.[7] "We have thus

---

7. Lawrence of Arabia captures the essence of the experience of giving oneself freely into bondage in service of an idea: "Willy-nilly it [the ideal] became a faith. We had sold ourselves into its slavery, manacled ourselves together in its chain-gang, bowed ourselves to serve its holiness with all our good and ill content. The mentality of ordinary human slaves is terrible—they have lost the world—

here the moment of recognition, viz. that the other consciousness cancels itself as self-existent, and, *ipso facto*, itself does what the first does to it" (*P.M.*, 236). In a second sense of bondsman, Noah is the one who builds the ark and provides security for *all* that is other. But giving security to the world is properly God's role:

> In the same way we have the other moment, that this action on the part of the second is the action proper of the first; for what is done by the bondsman is properly an action on the part of the master. The latter exists only for himself, that is his essential nature; he is the negative power without qualification, a power to which the thing is naught. And he is thus the absolutely essential act in the situation, while the bondsman is not so, he is an unessential activity. But for recognition proper there is needed the moment that what the master does to the other he should also do to himself, and what the bondsman does to himself, he should do to the other also. On that account a form of recognition has arisen that is one sided and unequal. (*P.M.*, 236)

What does the lord do to the other that he should also do to himself? He commands the other who is good but does not command himself. He destroys that which he considers evil but does not yet self-destruct. What does the bondsman do to himself that he should do to the other as well? He gives himself freely but he should get others (including his lord) to give freely without *quid pro quo*. The bondsman must bind the other to give security for himself.

God as master is again Lord and Master of all he surveys and returns to Noah the dominion that he took any from Adam, a dominion over the birds and the beasts and all life on earth; but Noah does not have dominion over man. Noah does not appear to have the power to do to others what he does to himself. God as Lord and Master does have the power to do to himself what he does to others. The Lord commands himself neither to curse the ground anymore nor to smite everything living, and in so doing voluntarily begins to self-destruct, to destroy his own power.

Noah not only lacks the power to do to others what he does to himself, he is also, even though made in the image of God, not a very good

---

and we had surrendered, not body alone, but soul to the overmastering greed of victory. By our own act we were drained of morality, of volition, of responsibility, like dead leaves in the wind" (T. E. Lawrence, *Seven Pillars of Wisdom* [New York: Doubleday, 1926, 1962], 28).

representation of the Lord. This is true in a double sense. For considered from the "thought-side," from the point of view of consciousness, the bondsman is totally dependent on the Lord to tell him what to do. He is dependent on the Lord for his consciousness as practical reason, as conscience. The truth of God is found only in an unessential consciousness that needs to reveal itself as an independent self-consciousness.

The external, however, is only the acting out of the internal, and the inner side of Noah as the archetypal bondsman is the reflection of the external bondage to the Lord and must be unveiled. God as Master and Lord is taken to be an independent consciousness, but this is an illusion of thought, for the Lord depends on man for his realization. The mind depends on the body for expression. But if this is an illusion of feeling reflected in thought, the truth exists in feeling itself. For Noah felt the fear of death, of total destruction, fear for the entire being of the world, and as such knew in his gut that death was the sovereign master, that the lord and master was absolute negativity. The illusory thought that takes the Lord to be the embodiment of all independent self-consciousness and the feeling that the Lord is absolute negativity come together *in* Noah, in his work. For, in work, self-sacrifice rather than sacrifice of the other, he cancels out his dependence and attachment to natural existence, thereby establishing himself as an independent consciousness, and at the same time negates that existence through work. But they have, not yet come together in his self-consciousness.

Thus, labor makes man free but man has still to come to the recognition of this. For it is the worker who experiences natural existence and his body as essential and does not suffer the illusion of consciousness desiring to be freed from external existence. Instead of the world existing as objects that are projections of the self, the self projects itself into the world with its labor to create a world of objects. The desire negate the object and assert the independence of the self becomes the negation of the self as consciousness detached from feelings to create and fabricate a world of independent objects. In giving form to objects, the freedom is made substantive and given permanence. It is when the self works in voluntary bondage in labor that the self first externalizes itself as an objectified individual self-consciousness. And it must be work impelled by the fear of death, not simply of the death of one's own self, for that would only mean working in the anxiety of loss of contingent existence, but in the fear of the death of existence in general. Further, that work must express itself not merely in contingent forms but in forms that are permanent and therefore resist death, forms in which the sacrifice of the body expresses the spirit in a true objective immortality.

CHAPTER 10

Labor, Alienation, and Social Classes in Hegel's *Realphilosophie*

Shlomo Avineri

The two sets of lectures given by Hegel during his period at Jena generally known as *Realphilosophie* I and *Realphilosophie* II occupy a unique place in the development of his system.[1] *Realphilosophie* II, which is far more extensive in its section dealing with *Geistesphilosophie,* is the more important for any attempt to reconstruct the stages of Hegel's philosophy of society and state. Rosenzweig saw in it Hegel's first detailed attempt to describe the middle zone between the state and prepolitical man, the zone Hegel would later call "civil society."[2] Marcuse sees here Hegel's first discussion of the historical realization of the free subject and the various spheres of integration through which consciousness has to pass.[3] And to Lukács the *Jenenser Realphilosophie* signifies Hegel's construction of man's own self-creation by himself, *die Menschenwerdung des Menschen.*[4]

---

1. For the proolems of the status of the texts, see the editor's remarks to the reedition of *Realphilosophie II,* in G. W. F. Hegel, *Jenaer Realphilosophie* (Hamburg, 1967), v–vi. Though the editor denies that the text known as *Realphilosophie I* is an earlier version of an attempt at a comprehensive system, we shall, for convenience's sake, continue to refer to the two texts as *Realphilosophie I* and *II.* For the complex problem of dating Hegel's manuscripts of the Jena period, see H. Kimmerle, "Zur Chronologie von Hegels Jenaer Schriften," *Hegel-Studien* 4 (Bonn, 1967), 125–76. See also Kroner's Introduction to Hegel's *Early Theological Writings* (Chicago, 1948), esp. 28–43.
2. F. Rosenzweig, *Hegel und der Staat* (München/Berlin, 1920) I, 178.
3. H. Marcuse, *Reason and Revolution,* new ed. (Boston, 1960), 73.
4. G. Lukás, *Der junge hegel* (Zürich/Wien, 1948), 415. See also J. Hyppolite, *Studies on Marx and Hegel,* trans. J. O'Neill (London, 1969), 70–92.

187

It is indeed a remarkable set of texts. The theme first propounded a few years earlier in the *System der Sittlichkeit*, the self's struggle for recognition through the other, leading to the emergence of objective spirit in the form of social and political institutions, is here developed in detail. It has thus become accepted that the *Realphilosophie*, together with the preceding *Jenenser Logik und Metaphysik*, set the scene for the *Phenomenology*.

But beyond this, there arises the question of the relationship between the *Realphilosophie* and Hegel's *Philosophy of Right*. In a way, Hegel tried all his life to write one book, and the *System der Sittlichkeit*, the *Realphilosophie*, the *Phenomenology*, and the *Philosophy of Right* are different versions and drafts of the same opus. It is this aspect of the *Realphilosophie* that I would like to bring out in this essay. It will be my intention to show both the rare achievement of Hegel's understanding of modern society as well as some serious flaws in his claim to integrate the inherent tensions of this society into a comprehensive social philosophy.

Various writers, notably Lukács, juxtapose Hegel's radicalism in the *Realphilosophie* to the quietism of the *Philosophy of Right*, and thus oppose a young, radical, and critical Hegel to the later author of the *Rechtsphilosophie*, who limits himself to *Nach-denken* at the falling of dusk. It will be my argument that the *Realphilosophie* combines a radical analysis of modern society with a spirit of resignation and acquiesence, and that Hegel's political and social solutions in the *Realphilosophie* do not differ fundamentally from those proposed in the *Philosophy of Right*. The dialectical continuity of Hegel's thought seems to me to be vindicated by such a critical reacting of the *Realphilosophie*: since his earliest writings Hegel was always haunted by what he calls "positivity" in his Bern manuscripts and "destiny" in some of the Frankfurt fragments: the dialectical necessity of the combination between the process of man's creation of his own world and his alienation is the main theme of the *Realphilosophie*. Yet when Hegel has to face the extremities of alienation—poverty—he is at a loss: poverty in these texts is as much insoluble as it is in the *Philosophy of Right*, where Hegel bluntly admits that "the important question of how poverty is to be abolished is one of the most disturbing problems which agitate modern society"[5]—and leaves it at that. But despite the fact that Hegel is as reluctant in the *Realphilosophie* to give instruction as to what the world

---

5. G. W. F. Hegel, *Philosophy of Right*, trans. T. M. Knox (Oxford, 1958), Addition to Para, 244.

ought to be as he will later turn out to be in the preface to the *Philosophy of Right*, the *Realphilosophie* manages to raise a number of crucial questions that continued to agitate nineteenth-century thought: the text abounds in motifs anticipating Feuerbach's religious criticism and Marx's social critique—though neither Feuerbach nor Marx was ever that acquainted with these texts. Yet it is the same motifs that later appear in the *Philosophy of Right* that thus serve as a link between the young Hegel and the young Marx.

The *Realphilosophie* deals with the philosophy of nature as well as with the philosophy of man: but since the themes of social and political criticism figure so prominently in any contemporary discussion of Hegel's legacy, it seems to me appropriate to discuss at some length those texts of Hegel where these issues are treated by him most extensively. Hegel does come back to these problems in the *Philosophy of Right*, but in a much more cryptic way. He sometimes uses what looks like a code or a cipher to refer to issues settled by his earlier analysis of the subject. Without knowing what he is referring to one sometimes cannot fully grasp his intention.

For the purpose of this essay, a general acquaintance with the *Philosophy of Right* will be assumed, and I shall limit references to it. It should, however, be understood that at the background of the argument the relationship to the *Philosophy of Right* will always be present, though the discussion will generally limit itself to the analysis of the *Realphilosophie*, and particularly to Part B (*Geistesphilosophie*) of *Realphilosophie* II. The parallel section in *Realphilosophie* I is much shorter and more condensed, and since its main argument is far better brought out in the later version, the references to this earlier version will be necessarily limited.

The struggle for recognition through the other, after finding its initial articulation in speech, comes up against the world of material objects. In his earlier *System der Sittlichkeit* Hegel had already shown how need is the feeling of being separated from the objective world and how through desire one achieves in satisfaction the transcendence of this separation on the immediate level.[6]

This need to assert oneself in the other is expressed very clearly at the outset of the section of the *Realphilosophie* dealing with the objective world. Through recognition by the other, the subject attains universality, his existence has a meaning for subjects outside himself:

---

6. G. W. F. Hegel, *Schriften zur Politik und Rechtsphilosophie*, ed. G. Lasson (Leipzig, 1913), 422.

hence the transition to objective spirit, *wirklicher Geist.*[7] Intersubjective relations attain this universality also through the device of contract, which elevates individual will to a universal object: "The universal is the substance of the contract."[8] In breaking a contract, one is injuring not only the immediate incidental subject who happens to be the other party to it, but a universal, objective, and social arrangement. Society, not the individual, is hurt, and punishment thus expresses the general will and not merely the injured party.

The same universality appears in property. Hegel makes an initial distinction between possession and property; this distinction follows the traditional line, but then Hegel adds to it another aspect that brings out the centrality of the aspect of recognition in the constitution of property. While possession pertains to my relation to the *object*, property signifies my relation to other *subjects* who recognize my possession of that object: "The right of possession relates immediately to things, not to a third party. Man has a right to take into possession as much as he can as an individual. He has this right, it is implied in the concept of being himself: through this he asserts himself over all things. But his taking into possession implies also that he excludes a third. What is it which from this aspect binds the other? What may I take into my possession without doing injury to a third party?"[9] It is from these considerations that Hegel derives the transsubjective, nonindividual nature of property: *property pertains to the person as recognized by others;* it can never be an intrinsic quality of the, individual prior to his recognition by others. While possession relates to the individual, property relates to society: since possession becomes property through the others' recognition of it as such, property is a social attribute. Thus, not an individualistic but a social premise is at the root of Hegel's concept of property, and property will never be able to achieve in his system an independent stature. This is significant because Hegel's description of the economic process is taken from classical political economy, yet on the basic nature of property he holds a totally different view. Property always remains premised on social consensus, on consciousness, not on the mere fact of possession.

---

7. *Realphilosophie II*, 210: "Everyone wants to count for the other; it is everyone's purpose to perceive himself in the other. Everyone is outside himself."
8. Ibid., 219.
9. Ibid., 207. Cf. *Realphilosophie I*, 240, on the transition from possession to property: "The security of my possession (becomes) the security of the possessions of all; in my property, all have their property. My possession has achieved the form of consciousness."

Yet there still remains an element of accidentality in possession, even when turned into property, since the objects of possession relate to this or that individual in a wholly arbitrary way. It is only through labor that "the accidentality of coming into possession is being *aufgehoben*," maintains Hegel.[10] By thus appearing central to Hegel's views on property, labor becomes also a focus to Hegel's conception of the self. It has already been pointed out by several writers that Hegel owes many of his views on labor to his early acquaintance with the writings of Adam Smith and Steuart.[11] Lukács has, however, remarked that the way labor appears in Hegel's system integrates it most profoundly into speculative philosophy, for it is here "that the active principle (in German idealism, Thought, the Concept) must learn to respect actuality as it is."[12] It is through the instrumentality of labor that Hegel constructs his paradigm of a society differentiated according to types of labor, and it is on this stratification, based on a division of labor, which he later on builds his political edifice. It is in this discussion on labor that Hegel comes closest to motifs to be found later in Marx, and it is these motifs that appear again in the *Philosophy of Right* in those paragraphs (# 241–46) which seem to pose a question mark to the fundamental conservatism of the whole book.

Labor first appears in the *Realphilosophie* as an indication of man's growing awareness of his confrontation with and differentiation from nature.... The establishment of property institutionalizes man's relations to other human beings through its integration and incorporation of the objective world into consciousness: nature becomes part of the natural history of man. In a parallel way labor is the transformation of the appetites from their initial annihilative to a constructive attitude toward the objective world; whereas primitive man, like the animals, consumes nature and destroys the object, labor holds up to man an object to be desired not through negation but through creation.[13]

Hegel's achievement in describing the movement of labor has a double edge: on one hand, Hegel shows how labor is necessarily connected with alienation. Alienation to Hegel is not a marginal aspect of

---

10. *Realphilosophie*, II, 217.
11. See esp. P. Chamley, *Economie, politique et philosophie chez Steuart et Hegel* (Paris, 1963), as well as his article "Les origines de la pensée économique de Hegel," *Hegel-Studien* 3 (1965): 225–61. Also Lukács, *Der junge Hegel*, 410–20; Marcuse, *Reason and Revolution* 76ff; Rosenzweig, *Hegel und der Staat*, I, 159.
12. Lukács, *Der Junge Hegel*, 414.
13. *Realphilosophie* I, 220, Cf. "System der Sittlichkeit," *Schriften zur Politik*, etc., 422f.

labor that can be rectified or reformed: it is fundamental and immanent to the structure of society; it cannot be dispensed with and the conditions of alienation and misery cannot be abolished within the existing society. While thus closing the door on any rosy belief in easy reforming solutions, Hegel's radical criticism of labor in society does not result in any radical call for activism or rebellion: his insights into modern society call for an integration of this experience through political mediation, not through radical upheaval and disuption.

This vision of the working of modern society comes to Hegel not through any empirical study of social and economic conditions in his contemporary Germany: these conditions he had analyzed in *The German Constitution*, and his description certainly does not bring forth a vital, active, and productive society. Hegel's views on modern society are far more a distillation of the Smithian model, raised to the level of a philosophical paradigm.[14] Labor to Hegel is the positive outcome of man's confrontation with the natural, external, objective world. The process of labor is an objectification of man's subjective powers, and it is through the instrumentality of work on an object that man, a subject, becomes an objective actuality: "I have done something, I have externalized myself; this negation is positive; externalization (*Entäusserung*) is appropriation."[15]

Hegel had earlier perceived a similar externalization in exchange, where the alienation of one's claims to an object makes one's relation to it actual.[16] Yet in exchange, consciousness still accepts the external world as given, whereas in labor it is creating this world while simultaneously relating to other human beings: "Only here has appetite the right to appear, since it is actual (*wirklich*), i.e. it has itself general, spiritual being. Labor of all for all and the satisfaction of all. Everyone serves the other and sustains him, only here has the individual for the first time an individuated being; before that it has been only abstract and untrue."[17] Labor is thus by necessity *social* labor; contrary to the

---

14. This aspect of Hegel has been realized very early on by Marx in his *Economic-Philosophical Manuscripts*, where he says: "Hegel's standpoint is that of modern political economy. He conceives labor as the *essence*, the self-confirming essence of man." Yet because Marx bases his résumé of Hegel on the *Phenomenology*, and the *Realphilosophie* remained unknown to him, he ends up with a faulty conclusion: "He (Hegel) observes only the positive side of labor, not its negative side." See K. Marx, *Early Writings*, trans. T. B. Bottomore (London, 1963), 203.
15. *Realphilosophie*, II, 218.
16. Ibid., 217.
17. Ibid., 213.

atomistic, individualistic view of labor, which sees labor as primary and exchange as secondary and derivative, based on a surplus, labor for Hegel is always premised on a reciprocal relationship, subsuming exchange under its cognitive aspects. No one produces for himself, and all production presupposes the other—hence a basic element of recognition is always immanent in labor.

While the goal of production is recognition through the other, its motive is need. Consciousness, by desiring an object, moves man to create it, to transform need from a subjective craving and appetite into an external object: labor is therefore always intentional, not instinctual; it represents man's power to create his own world.[18] Production is thus a vehicle in reason's actualization of itself in the world: in a passage that prefigures his later dictum about the rational and the actual, Hegel remarks that "Reason, after all, can exist only in its work; it comes into being only in its product, apprehends itself immediately as another as well as itself."[19]

There is, however, another link between needs and production, and this one is more problematic. Though every human need is concrete, the totality of needs for which the totality of production is undertaken is abstract and cannot be concretely expressed prior to the process of production and distribution having been completed. Production thus becomes abstract and the division of labor appears related to the needs of production and not to the needs of the producers. Man produces not the objects of his own specific needs, but a general product that he then can exchange for the concrete object or objects of his needs: he produces *commodities*, and the more refined his tastes become, the more objects he desires that he cannot produce himself but can achieve through the production of more objects that he then exchanges. There thus appears a universal dependence of each human being on the universality of the producers and the character of labor undergoes a basic change:

> Because work is being done for the need as an abstract being-for-itself, one also works in an abstract way.... General labor is thus division of labor.... Every individual, as an individual, works for *a* need. The content of his labor (however) transcends *his* need; he works for the satisfaction of many, and so (does) everyone. Everyone satisfies thus the needs of many, and the satisfaction of his many particular needs is the labor of many others. Since his labor is thus this abstraction, he behaves as

---

18. *Realphilosophie* I, 236; II, 214.
19. *Realphilosophie* I, 233.

an abstract self, or according to the way of thingness, not as a comprehensive, rich, all-encompassing spirit, who rules over a wide range and masters it. He has no concrete work: his power is in analysis, in abstraction, in the breaking up of the concrete into many abstract aspects.[20]

The dialectical nature of social labor is thus evident: on one hand, it creates sociability, a universal dependence of each on all, makes man into a universal being—the characteristic of civil society, as later described in the *Philosophy of Right* (# 182–83). On the other hand, this reciprocal satisfaction of needs creates a hiatus between the concrete individual and his particular and concrete needs. By working for all, the individual does not anymore work for himself; an element of distance and a need for mediation are thus thrust between his work and the satisfaction of his needs. Social labor thus necessarily entails alienation:

> Man thus satisfies his needs, but, not through the object which is being worked upon by him; by satisfying his needs, it becomes something else. Man does not produce anymore that which he needs, nor does he need anymore than which he produces. Instead of this, the actuality of the satisfaction of his needs becomes merely the possibility of this satisfaction. His work becomes a general, formal, abstract one, single; he limits himself to one of his needs exchanges this for his other necessities.[21]

The more labor becomes thus divided and specialized, the more commodities can be produced; the more labor becomes removed from the immediate satisfaction of the producer, the more productive it becomes; man thus achieves ever greater comfort at the price of ever greater abstraction and alienation in the process of production itself: "His labor and his possessions are not what they are for him, but what they are for all. The satisfaction of needs is a universal dependence of all on all; there disappears for everyone the security and the knowledge that his work is immediately adequate to his particular needs; *his* particular need becomes universal."[22] The process of labor—originally man's recognition through the other, intended to create for each his own objective world— becomes a process over which man loses all control and direction. Man is far from being integrated into the objective world through creative consciousness, that is, labor; the abstract nature of labor, together with

---

20. *Realphilosophie* II, 214–15.
21. *Realphilosophie* I, 237–38.
22. Ibid., 238.

the division of labor, make him totally alien to this objective world. Hence Hegel comes to be troubled by the real conditions of factory labor, and his general anthropology of labor becomes social analysis. Quoting Adam Smith, Hegel says:

> The particularization of labor multiplies the mass of production; in an English manufacture, 18 people work at the production of a needle; each has his particular and exclusive side of the work to perform; a single person could probably not produce 120 needles, even not one. . . . But the value of labor decreases in the same proportions as the productivity of labor increases. Work becomes thus absolutely more and more dead, it becomes machine labor, the individual's own skill becomes infinitely limited, and the consciousness of the factory worker is degraded to the utmost level of dullness. The connection between the particular sort of labor and the infinite mass of needs becomes wholly imperceptible, turns into a blind dependence. It thus happens that a far-away operation often affects a whole class of people who have hitherto satisfied their needs through it; all of a sudden it limits (their work), makes it redundant and useless.[23]

This analysis thus makes Hegel into one of the earliest radical critics of the modern industrial system. Hegel goes on to point out the necessary link between the emergence of machinery and the intensification of alienation and here again Hegel takes a middle position between the idealizers of the machine and the machine-smashers: while recognizing the alienation caused by the introduction of the machine, it is a necessary element in the anthropological determination of modern society based on ever-increasing production. Originally, Hegel contends, tools were nothing else than the mediation between man and his external world;[24] as such, they always remain a passive object in the hands of the producer. But,

> In the same way, (the worker) becomes through the work of the machine more and more machine-like, dull, spiritless. The spiritual element, the self-conscious plentitude of life, becomes an empty activity. The power of the self resides in rich comprehension: this is being lost. He can leave some work to the machine; his own doing thus becomes even more formal. His dull work

---

23. Ibid., 239.
24. *Realphilosophie* II, 197–98.

limits him to one point, and labor is the more perfect, the more onesided it is. . . . In the machine man abolishes his own formal activity and makes it work for him. But this deception, which he perpetrates upon nature. . .takes vengeance on him. The more he takes away from nature, the more he subjugates her, the baser he becomes himself. By processing nature through a multitude of machines, he does not abolish the necessity of his own labor; he only pushes it further on, removes it away from nature and ceases to relate to it in a live way. Instead, he flees from this negative livingness, and that work which is left to him becomes itself machine-like. The amount of labor decreases only for the whole, not for the individual: on the contrary, it is being increased, since the more mechanized labor becomes, the less value it possesses, and the more must the individual toil.[25]

We thus have here in one of the more speculative documents of German idealist philosophy one of the most acute insights into the working of modern, industrial society: from an a priori philosophical anthropology, Hegel moves on to incorporate the results of political economy into a philosophical system—an attempt almost identical in its systematic structure with Marx's program forty years later. How many of Marx's later concluions are already to be found, explicitly or implicitly in Hegel's earlier texts, requires however, a separate discussion.

Commodity-producing society needs, according to Hegel, also a universal, abstract criterion that can mediate between labor and the subject. This is money:

These multiple labors of the needs as things must also realize their concept, their abstraction: their universal concept must also be a thing just like them, but (it must be) a universal, which represents all. *Money* is this materially existing concept, the form of the unity or of the potentiality of all the things relating

---

25. *Realphilosophie* I, 232, 237. The parallels with Marx's description in the *Economic-Philosophical Manuscripts* are, of course, striking (*Early Writings*, 120–34). The major difference, however, has already been pointed out by Lukács: while to Hegel alienation is a necessary aspect of objectification, Marx believes that alienation resides not in the process of production, but in its concrete conditions. For Hegel, objectification and alienation are identical; for Marx, they are separable. Therefore, Marx believes in the possibility of ultimate redemption, whereas for Hegel one will never be able to dissociate the rose from the cross of the present. Philosophy can only interpret the world, not change it.

to needs. Need and labor are thus elevated into this universality, and this creates in a great nation an immense system of communality (*Gemeinschaftlichkeit*) and mutual dependence, a life of death moving within itself (*ein sich in sich bewegendes Leben des Toten*). This system moves hither and thither in a blind and elemental way, and like a wild animal calls for strong permanent control and curbing.[26]

But before Hegel constructs these agencies intended to limit the free play of the forces of the market, he goes into some detail regarding the sociological aspects of commodity-producing society. Aspects of class domination appear in a very prominent way in Hegel's description when he expresses his awareness of the fact that the wealth of nations can be built only at the expense of the poverty of whole classes: "Factories and manufacturers base their existence on the misery (*Elend*) of a class," he remarks.[27] And in another context his description is no less brutal in its candor: "(This power) condemns a multitude to a raw life and to dullness in labor and poverty, so that others could amass fortunes, so that these could be taken away from them."[28]

This sinking into poverty and barbarity is seen by Hegel as being caused by the rapid expansion of the market and of production: social labor not only satisfies needs, but it is constantly creating new needs, tastes, and fashions. Again, in a rare insight into the dialectics of ever-changing demand creating pressure for ever-increasing production, Hegel says "Needs are thus multiplied; each need is being subdivided into many; tastes becomes refined and differentiated. One demands a level of finish which carries the object ever nearer to its use."[29] Fashion becomes the determinant of production, and Hegel is thus one of the first thinkers to grasp the immanent logic of constantly changing fashions and fads and its function within the productive process. The constant disquiet of concrete life in industrial society is here described from the consumer's point of view as well:

---

26. *Realphilosophie* I, 239–40. Cf. II, 215–16. Again the parallel with Marx's fragment on "Money" (*Early Writings* 189–94) is very close.

27. *Realphilosophie* II, 257. Cf. ibid., 232: "A mass of the population is condemned to stupefying, unhealthy and precarious labor in factories, manufactures, mines, etc."

28. Ibid., 238. The last sentence refers already to Hegel's justification of property taxes, and he goes on to say that "the inequality of property causes it to be accepted on the condition that high taxes are imposed."

29. Ibid., 231–32. The slightly censorious tone evokes echoes of Rousseau.

But this plurality creates *fashion*, the versatility and freedom in the use of these things. The cut of clothes, the style of furnishing one's home, are nothing permanent. This constant change is essential and rational, far more rational than sticking to one fashion, imagining to find something permanent in such particular forms. The beautiful is not ordered by one fashion; but here we have to do not with free beauty, but with beauty that attracts. . . . Hence it has accidentality in it.[30]

These fluctuations in taste have a bearing on the basic lack of security that characterizes modern society: whole sectors of the population live by the whim of a changing mode, and Hegel's description of the conditions of life of these classes sinking into poverty is truly amazing when one reflects that he reaches his conclusions through an immanent development of the consequences of the theories of political economy:

Whole branches of industry which supported a large class of people suddenly fold up because of a change in fashion or because the value of their products fell due to new inventions in other countries. Whole masses are abandoned to poverty which cannot help itself. There appears the contrast between vast wealth and vast poverty—a poverty that cannot do anything for itself. . . .

Wealth, like any other mass, makes itself into a power. Accumulation of wealth takes place partly by chance, partly through the universal mode of production and distribution. Wealth is a point of attraction. . . . It collects everything around itself—just like a large mass attracts to itself the smaller one. To them that have, shall be given. Acquisitition becomes a many-sided system which develops into areas from which smaller businesses cannot profit. The highest abstraction of labor reaches into the most particular types of labor and thus receives an ever-widening scope. This inequality of wealth and poverty, this need and necessity, turn into the utmost tearing up (*Zerrissenheit*) of the will, an inner indignation (*Empörung*) and hatred.[31]

---

30. Ibid., 232.
31. Ibid., 232–33. It is extremely interesting to note that the term "inner indignation" (*Empörung*) used here by Hegel is the same he uses in the Addition to Para. 244 of the *Philosophy of Right* where he says that "Poverty in itself does not make man into a rabble; a rabble is created only when there is joined to poverty a disposition of mind, an inner indignation against the rich, against society, against the government, etc." Moreover, the only oblique reference in

It is precisely here that any possibility of a radical transformation of society presents itself to Hegel—only to be discarded: this possibility remains an "inner indignation," not an act that has to be externalized. At the height of Hegel's critical awareness of the horrors of industrial society, he remains quietistic and seeks a solution through integration, not through disruption—an aspect that Lukács tends to overlook.

For the passage that immediately follows this critical analysis of industrial society deals with the emergence of the state as regulating and integrating economic activity within a political framework, transcending the forces of the market. In the course of developing this idea, Hegel adds some further touches to his picture of industrial society when he sees in the state an instrument ensuring economic expansion overseas:

> Government comes onto the scene and has to see to it that every sphere be preserved. . . . [It has to look for] ways out, for channels to sell the product abroad, though this makes it more difficult, since it is to the detriment of the others. [But] freedom of commerce remains necessary, interference must be as inconspicuous as possible, for this is the sphere of arbitrariness (*Willkür*). The appearance of power must be prevented, and one should not try to save that which cannot be saved, but try to employ the remaining classes in another way. Government is the universal overseer; the individual is buried in the particular. The [particular] occupation will admittedly be abandoned by itself, but with the sacrifice of this generation and an increase in poverty. Poor taxes and institutions are required.[32]

The state thus appears at the moment at which society seems to be heading for disruption and chaos: it is the reintegration of the self into itself as a universal being after economic life has particularized, atomized it, and made its activity into an abstraction. The basic scenario of Hobbes is, in a way, being reenacted here within a context presenting a synthesis of speculative philosophy and political economy: the abstraction of *bellum omnium contra omnes* becomes concrete in terms of human activity and consciousness.

Marx to Hegel's discussion of poverty in the *Philosophy of Right* is a fleeting hint that *Empörung* is not enough; see K. Marx and F. Engels, *The Holy Family*, trans. R. Dixon (Moscow, 1956), 51.
32. *Realphilosophie* II, 233. Lukács misses the whole point about the complex place of the state in Hegel's system when he dismisses this minimalist view of governmental intervention in Hegel as one of his "illusions" (*Der junge Hegel*, 423).

Hence while stressing the minimalist function of the state in those of its activities impinging upon economic life ("freedom of commerce remains necessary, interference must be as inconspicuous as possible.... The appearance of power must be prevented"), Hegel can at the same time point to the immanence of political life: "The individual has his supposed right only in the universal. The state is the existence, the power of right, the keeping of contract and... the existing unity of the word."[33]

This ambivalent status of the state will later enable Hegel to construct the realms of art, religion, and philosophy as spheres transcending the state yet functoning within its context. The state, while incorporating the individual in a universal unity, does not subsume his activities under its existence. Because on one hand the individual uses the state as an instrument for his own particular ends while on the other the state is the individual's true being, the classical means/ends relationship between individual and state is being transcended: "This unity of individuality and universality exists then in a double way; in the extreme of the universal, which is itself an individuality—as government. This is not an abstraction of the state, but an individuality which has the universal as such as an end, while the other extreme has the individual person as an end."[34] The general will thus appears in Hegel's system in a radically different way than in Rousseau's: Hegel points out in several instances that any social contract theory is a *petitio principi*, because it takes consensus, the readiness to abide by the terms of the contract, for granted. In the same way, as there could be no right in the state of nature, the general will could not be perceived as the constitutive aspect of the body politic.[35] The general will for Hegel is not the premise on which the state is being founded, historically or logically, but the emergent outcome of the lengthy process of *Bildung*, which created through differentiation and opposition the political consciousness out of the diverce elements of man's struggle for recognition.[36] The general will is the will of the individuals made into an object within the institutions of the state: "The general will is the will of all and each.... It has first of all to constitute itself as general out of the will of the individuals so that it will appear as the principle and element, but on the other hand it is first and essential. The individuals have to make themselves into a universal

---

33. *Realphilosophie* II, 234.
34. Ibid., 248–49.
35. Ibid., 205, 245–47.
36. On *Bildung*, see George A. Kelly, *Idealism, Politics and History* (Cambridge, 1969), 341–48.

through negation of themselves, through externalization and education *(Entäusserung und Bildung)."*[37]

This objectification of the individual will as it appears in the general will, in the state, entails the recognition by the individual that what appears as something alien and external—political power—is nothing else than the externalization of his own will. The law is this objectification of the subjective will: "The rule of Law is not meant to be an act of legislating as if the others did not exist: they are there. The relation is the movement of the person educated to obey towards the commonwealth.... The second element is the trust that appears, i.e. that the individual knows himself to be in it as his own essence, that he finds himself preserved in it."[38] This need for external limitations of the individual's will is the essence of what Hegel calls *Polizei*. The possible misunderstandings connected with this term in the *Philosophy of Right*, emanating as it were from its present usage, can be at least partly cleared up when we recall that for Hegel *Polizei* comes "from Politeia, public life and rule, the action of the whole itself."[39] This public authority is needed since in caring for himself alone and enjoying the quiet bliss of his property rights, the individual may hurt another by simply disregarding the impact that his own actions may have on the life of another. An element of *List der Vernunft* comes into the picture when Hegel describes how the state is willed by the individuals for their own self-preservation and better protection while it also represents an actuality transcending this interest: "The general *form* is this turning of the individual into a universal and the becoming of the universal. But it is not a blind necessity, but one mediated through knowing. In other words, each is an end to himself, i.e. the end is the motive, each individual is immediately the cause. It is his interest that drives him (to the state), but it is likewise the universal which has validity is the middle, allies him with his particularity and actuality."[40] The state is the transcendence of the individual in the universality of the law; the externalization of the will makes the individual into a person because only in this way does he achieve actuality for the other. This universal power is the commonwealth, where the actions of the individual, because they can

---

37. *Realphilosphie* II, 244–45.
38. Ibid., 248. Cf. the definition of "Right" (p. 206): "Right is the relation of the person to another, the universal element of its free being or the determination and its empty freedom."
39. Ibid., 259.
40. Ibid., 243.

impinge on the lives of everyone else, achieve objective, universal substance.[41]

The fact that the state is both instrumental and immanent is being represented in the individual by his dual role as a particular being and a universal one. In one of the most pointed expressions that prefigures both his own mature thought as well as Marx's later argument against it, Hegel says that man is both a member of civil society and a citizen of the state and has to strike a balance between these two aspects of his existence: "Both individualities are the same. The same (individual) takes care of himself and his family, works, signs contracts, etc., and at the same time he also works for the universal and has it as an end. From the first viewpoint he is called *bourgeois*, from the second *citoyen*."[42]

These two aspects of human activity lead to Hegel's discussion of social classes: the crucial point is, of course, that Hegel does not see the antinomy between man as *bourgeois* and as *citoyen* as something to be overcome in a total, new unity: it is part of the dialectical progress of man toward his self-recognition. This should be kept in mind, since one of the common errors in discussing this problem in Hegel is to be carried away by the apparent similarity between Hegel's discussion of civil society and some aspects of Marx's analysis. The truth of the matter is that Hegel's point of departure is the exact opposite of Marx's. For Marx classes are aggregates formed by types of social labor, linked together by the common relationship of their members to the means of production, seeking a political articulation for their socioeconomic interests. The class nature of political power is to Marx a sin against the state's claim for expressing the universal as against the particularism and egotism of civil society. For Hegel, the institutionalization of class relationships into the political structure is the way through which the atomism of civil society is being integrated into a comprehensive totality. The different classes represent to Hegel not only modes of production, but modes of consciousness that are relevant to a society differentiated in its structure according to criteria taken from Hegel's general system. While for Marx classes represent a division of labor that has to be overcome, for Hegel they stand for the integration of this division, regrettable, yet necessary, into a meaningful whole. Classes reflect the various stages of consciousness, just as periods in history.[43] For Hegel,

---

41. *Realphilosophie*, I, 232–33; II, 237, 244.
42. *Realphilosophie* II, 249. The French terms appear in hegel's original German text. For Marx, of course, the splitting of man into *citoyen* and *bourgeois* is the measure of his alienation in modern, post-1789 society. Cf. "On the Jewish Question," *Early Writings*, 13–31.
43. *Realphilosophie*, ii, 253.

classes always remain *estates*, in the sense that they represent a legitimized differentiation (interestingly enough, Hegel uses the term "class"
only when referring to those directly involved in labor). Each estate stands
for a different mode of consciousness: the principle of immediate trust
and obedience is represented in the peasantry; the principle of law and
order the principle of universality in the bureaucracy, in the middle
classes; and the priciple of universality in the bureaucracy, the universal
class. Though the principle of classification is similar to that of the
Philosophy of Right, the internal division of each estate is more complex
and represents a slightly more sophisticated awareness of class differentiation than the neat divisions Hegel would adopt later. Furthermore,
in the *Realphilosophie* the form of labor performed by each class figures
more prominently, and thus the connection between class and the anthropology of labor is brought out much more clearly.

The peasantry is distinguished by being the class of immediate labor,
whose concrete work relates to a natural object (land) and not to a product. It thus represents a low level of consciousness, not yet differentiated
from substantiality. On a social level this reflects itself in the peasantry
accepting its work and role as they are without much questioning: the
peasantry is the class of immediate trust, unreflective consciousness:

> The estate of immediate trust and raw concrete labor is the
> peasantry.... The peasantry is thus this trust lacking in
> individuality, having its individuality in the unconscious in-
> dividual, the earth. As for labor, (the peasant's) work does not
> have the form of abstract labor: he takes care, more or less, of
> almost all his needs.... The inter-relationship between his
> purpose and its realization is unconscious, natural. He ploughs,
> sows, but it is God who orders that it will thrive; it is the season
> and his trust that (cause) that it will become by itself what he
> had put into the ground. The activity is underground. He pays
> taxes and tributes because that's how it is; these fields and
> cottages have been situated in such a way from time immemor-
> ial; *that's how it is*, and that's all....
>
> Concrete labor is elemental, substantial subsistence. In war,
> this estate makes up the raw mass.[44]

---

44. Ibid., 254–55. In the *Philosophy of Right* Hegel includes in the "agricultural
class" both the peasantry and the nobiiity and there thus emerges a slight
idealization of the virtues of agricultural life that is totally lacking here. Here
it is only the peasantry that is being described, and the similarity, to Marx's
judgment on the "idiocy of village life" and the basically individualistic, asocial
mode of production of the peasantry is again striking.

When Hegel goes on to the second class, he distinguishes between
the burghers (*Bürgerstand*) and the class of businessmen (*Kaufmannstand*). The *Bürgerstand* is made up mainly of artisans, its labor being
characterized by adaptation of nature; the business class, on the other
hand, is distinguished by its being engaged in exchange. Both the artisans
and the businessmen see in law and order the principle of their existence;
property, acquisitiveness, and social mobility are the pillars of their being.
In a striking description of the social ethos of the *Bürgerstand*, Hegel
gets at the root of so many of what are unmistakenly middle-class values:

> (The burgher) knows himself as a property owner, not only
> because he possesses it, but also because it is his right—so he
> assumes: he knows himself to be recognized by his particularity.
> Unlike the peasant, he does not enjoy his glass of beer or wine
> in a rough fashion, as a way of elevating himself out of his
> dullness. . . but because (he wants) to show by his suit and the
> finery of his wife and children that he is as good as the other
> man and that he has really made it. In this he enjoys himself,
> his value and his righteousness; for this did he toil and this has
> he achieved. He enjoys not the pleasures of enjoyment but the
> joy of his self-esteem.[45]

In the business class, on the other hand, a higher degree of abstraction is achieved: "The work of the businessman is pure exchange,
neither natural nor artificial production or formation. Exchange is the
movement, the spiritual, the means, liberated from utility and need as
well as from working, from immediacy."[46] The mode of existence of the
businessman calls forth the emergence of money as a commodity by
itself:

> The object itself is being divided into two: the particular thing,
> the object of commerce, and the abstract, money—a great
> invention. All needs are reduced to this unity. The object of need
> has become a mere image, unusable. The object is here some-
> thing that has meaning purely according to its value, not for
> itself, not in relation to the need. . . . A person is real to the
> extent that he has money. . . . The formal principle of reason
> is to be found here—it is abstraction from all particularity,
> character, historicity, etc. of the individual. The disposition (of
> the businessman) is this harshness of spirit, wherein the

---

45. *Realphilosophie* II, 256.
46. Ibid.

particular, now completely alienated, does not count anymore. (There exist)only strict rights. The bill of exchange must be honored—he himself may be distroyed—his family, welfare, life, etc. may go to pieces—total lack of mercy.[47]

Again, what stands out here is not only the striking similarity with Marx, but the fact that no radical call of action follows this harsh analysis: the nature of modern society is grasped with an amazing lucidity given the period in which these texts were written. But all is being incorporated within the integrative functions of the state. No rebellion, no deviation.

The integration is carried out through the mediation of the universal class: "The public estate works for the state. . . . Its disposition of mind is the fulfillment of its duty."[48] The business class expresses already a sort of universality—the universality of the market—but it is still abstract. Universality becomes concrete only in the class of public servants who represent "the intervention of the universal into all particularity"; the civil servant is likened to the arteries and the nerves that run through the body; they are not, of course, identical with it.[49]

The universal class is at the apex of the social pyramid not only because of its universal intentionality, but also because it is the only class of society whose objective is knowledge itself, not nature, artefact, or abstraction, as is the case with all other classes. The specific academic background of the German bureaucratic tradition is very much in evidence in this concept of the universal class as an educated estate, including not only civil servants in the narrow sense but also teachers, doctors, lawyers: "This pure knowledge has to be realized, has to give a content to itself out of itself, a free content, which it at the same time also an uninterested object. . . . This is science generally. Spirit has here an object with which it deals without relating to appetite and need. It is fulfilled thought, intelligence that knows itself."[50] This concept of science as noninstrumental knowledge, knowledge knowing itself, then enables Hegel to relate the state to the realms of art, religion, and philosophy, which are thus beyond objective spirit but need the state for their proper functioning. In the universal class, this is already hinted at, and thus Hegel can close his discussion of the estates and the state and move on to these spheres—exactly as he closes the *Philosophy of Right* moving in this direction.

---

47. Ibid., 256–57.
48. Ibid., 259.
49. Ibid., 257.
50. Ibid., 260.

The discussion of *Kunst, Religion,* and *Wissenschaft* is outside the scope of this essay. Suffice it to say that in the *Realphilosophie* just as well as in Hegel's later writings, the edifice of the state is nothing else than an infrastructure for absolute spirit—never an end-in-itself.

For the purpose of our discussion, however, a crucial point has to be raised, and this has to do with what appears as a gap between Hegel's discussion of the working of modern society and the kind of integrated solution he envisages for it through the system of estates. Pointing to the French Revolution, Hegel incorporates it here into his system in the same dialectical way in which he deals with it in the *Phenomenology* and elsewhere. It is the integrative side of the Revolution that he accepts, while rejecting what he calls its negativity and abstractedness. In a footnote Hegel remarks that the French Revolution did indeed abolish class privileges, but "the abolition of class differentiation is mere empty talk."[51]

This is significant, for the society Hegel describes in *Realphilosophie* is post-1789 society. The aristocracy is not mentioned—contrary to the *Rechtsphilosophie,* where it appears as the upper crust of "the agricultural class." While emphasizing that the privileges of the aristocracy as to taxation and the like have to be abolished,[52] Hegel sticks to the necessity to mete out different treatment to different classes. He even suggests, for example a different, more rough and immediate penal code for the peasantry as compared to the middle class; taxes should primarily rest on the burgher class, commercial law should apply in all its severity to the business class only, and even marriage laws should be modified when applied to different estates.[53]

Yet while Hegel thus tries to give to each estate its due place in the hierarchy of consciousness, the system of estates seems to exclude the class of people who are at the root of commodity production. Had Hegel not described the conditions of life of the worker in civil society, it would have been beside the point to ask him for a solution to his problem. But once Hegel did grasp, and with so much rare insight, the social implications of commodity production, the complete lack of this class of people in his integrated system of social estates is a serious defect: for

51. Ibid.

52. Ibid., 238: "An aristocracy that does not pay taxes runs the great risk of losing violently."

53. Ibid., 258. The reference to different marriage laws is probably intended to mean that the system of inheritance, which is part of marriage law, should he different when applied to landed property as against moveable property. In the *Philosophy of Right* Hegel similarly advocates primogeniture for the landed gentry.

Hegel's social system includes the peasants, the *Bürgerstand* and the *Kaufmannstand*, the civil service: nowhere does the worker appear as being integrated into the social system.

Lukács attributes to the limitations of Hegel's age the fact that he saw in the businesman, rather than the captain of industry, the central figure of commodity-producing society. For Lukács this proves that Hegel's views of civil society are yet crude and undeveloped.[54] This criticism seems to make sense, yet one wonders whether it is as cogent as it sounds: at least from our present vantage point we can perhaps see Hegel's description as having more relevance than Lukács credits him with. The captain of industry, the traditional entrepreneur, turned out, after all, to be a passing phenomenon of relatively short duration. With the extension of the market, the traditional industrialist is almost completely disappearing, while it is the businessman who remains at the center of the commodity-producing society, though it may be the corporate rather than the traditional private businessman. Here Hegel's insight, basing the nature of modern society on the organization of exchange far more than of pure production, is perhaps more profound than that of Marx (and Lukács).

But Hegel's failure to integrtate the worker—whom he had discovered earlier in the manufacture and factory—into his system of estates is a failure of far greater magnitude. It reappears again in the *Philosophy of Right*, where after discussing pauperization and the failure of civil society to integrate the poor into the industrial system, Hegel leaves poverty an open question, without suggesting any solution. Both in the *Realphilosophie* and the *Philosophy of Right*, the worker remains for Hegel in civil society, but not of civil society.

Thus, Hegel's imposing synthesis of a radical critique of modern society with a system of integration through consciousness is left with a serious flaw in its center. Hegel's political solution in the *Realphilosophie* is the same as in the *Philosophy of Right*: he sees in the monarch the focal point of subjective liberty and raises it to be the principle of the modern age: in the monarchy, subjectivity is represented and vindicated.[55] Again, there is no way to confront a later, monarchist Hegel with an earlier, radical one: in 1805, as in 1818, monarchy is the form of government integral to modern society according to Hegel.

This monarchy is to Hegel the expression of public opinion, and thus the middle between innovation and preservation. The dialectics of

54. Lukács, *Der junge Hegel*, 427.
55. *Realphilosophie* II, 250.

controlled change are never better expressed by Hegel than when he says, "Today, one rules and lives differently in states whose constitution has remained nonetheless the same—and this constitution changes according to the times. Government must not come forward on the side of the past and defend it obstinately; but similarly it should always be the last one to be convinced to introduce changes."[56] All the quietism of the preface to the *Philosophy of Right* appears here, and Hegel's inability to jump over Rhodes is, perhaps, after all, at the root of his failure to integrate his rare insights into modern society into a system within which every group or class will be able to find its fulfillment. In this way, Hegel's failure perhaps brings out in paradoxical way his own dictum that when it comes to giving instruction to the world as it ought to be, philosophy always comes on the scene too late. Hegel's great achievement in the *Realphilosophie*—later to be incorporated into the *Philosophy of Right*— was to hold up a mirror to a society in its infancy in which it could see its image as it would look in maturity.

Hegel's achievement has been truly impressive: he can, now, be said to be of the first modern thinkers to ariculate the specific difference of contemporary society, and his achievement calls for a reevaluation of the traditional view of Hegel as a philosopher lost in "abstract" speculations. But the society Hegel so well understood did not have and could not have at that time a solution to the structural problem of poverty, "one of the most disturbing problems which agitate modern society." The problem could be conceived, but not its solution. And if the greyness of the philosopher's mirror failed to show a solution that the greyness of life did not yet bring forth, surely Hegel would be the last one to blame the philosopher.

---

56. Ibid., 251.

CHAPTER 11

Master and Slave

THE BONDS OF LOVE

Jessica Benjamin

The balance *within* the self depends upon mutual recognition *between* self and other. And mutual recognition is perhaps the most vulnerable point in the process of differentiation. In Hegel's notion of recognition, the self requires the opportunity to act and have an effect on the other to affirm his existence. In order to exist for oneself, one has to exist for an other. It would seem there is no way out of this dependency. If I destroy the other, there is no one to recognize me, for if I allow him no independent consciousness, I become enmeshed with a dead, not-conscious being. If the other denies me recognition, my acts have no meaning; if he is so far above me that nothing I do can alter his attitude toward me, I can only submit. My desire and agency can find no outlet, except in the form of obedience.

We might call this the dialectic of control: if I completely control the other, then the other ceases to exist, and if the other completely controls me, then I cease to exist. A condition of our own independent existence is recognizing the other. True independence means sustaining the essential tension of these contradictory impulses—that is, both asserting the self and recognizing the other. Domination is the consequence of refusing this condition.

In mutual recognition the subject accepts the premise that others are separate but nonetheless share like feelings and intentions. The subject is compensated for his loss of sovereignty by the pleasure of sharing, the communion with another subject. But for Hegel, as for Freud, the breakdown of essential tension is inevitable. The hypothetical self presented by Hegel and Freud does not *want* to recognize the other, does not perceive him as a person just like himself. He gives up omnipotence only when he has no other choice. His need for the other—in Freud, physiological, in Hegel, existential—seems to place him in the other's power, as if dependency were the equivalent of surrender. When the subject abandons the project of absolute independence or control, he does so unwillingly, with a persistent, if unconscious, wish to fullfill the old omnipotence fantasy.[1] This is a far cry from actually appreciating the other as a being in his or her own right.

Since the subject cannot accept his dependency on someone he cannot control, the solution is to subjugate and enslave the other—to make him give that recognition without recognizing him in return. The primary consequence of the inability to reconcile dependence with independence, then, is the transformation of need for the other into domination of him.

For Freud and Hegel this is precisely what happens in the "state of nature." In Freud's terms, aggression and the desire for mastery—necessary derivatives of the death instinct—are part of our nature. Without the restraint of civilization, whoever is more powerful will subjugate the other. The wish to restore early omnipotence, or to realize the fantasy of control, never ceases to motivate the individual. In Hegel's terms, self-consciousness wants to be absolute. It wants to be recognized by the other in order to place itself in the world and make itself the whole world. The I wants to prove itself at the expense of the other; it wants to think itself the only one; it abjures dependency. Since each self raises the same claim, the two must struggle to the death for recognition. For Hegel this struggle does not culminate in the survival of each for the other, in mutual recognition. Rather, the stronger makes the other his slave.

But this viewpoint would imply that submission is simply the hard lot of the weak.[2] And indeed, the question of why the oppressed submit is never fully explained. Yet the question of submission is implicitly raised by Hegel and Freud, who see that the slave must grant power of recognition to the master. To understand this side of the relationship of domination, we must turn to an account written from the point of view of one who submits.

---

1. See Freud's remarks on omnipotence in "On Narcissism" (*SE* 14:67–102) and in *Civilization and Its Discontents* (*SE* 21:57–146).

2. De Beauvoir, following Hegel, begins *The Second Sex* (New York: Knopf, 1952) with the argument that the question is not why men want to dominate, but why they are able to do so. This approach, comparable in a way to Freud's assumption that man is a wolf to man unless restrained by civilization, might make submission seem unproblematic, but, in fact, de Beauvoir explores woman's psychology in detail.

THE FANTASY OF EROTIC DOMINATION

Sadomasochistic fantasy, the most common form of erotic domination, replicates quite faithfully the themes of the master-slave relationship. Here subjugation takes the form of transgressing against the other's body, violating his physical boundaries. The act of violation of the body becomes a way of representing the struggle to the death for recognition. Ritual violation is a form of risking the psychological, if not the physical, self.

I have based my analysis of sadomasochistic fantasy on a single, powerful study of the erotic imagination, Pauline Réage's *Story of O*. Réage's tale is a web in which the issues of dependency and domination are inextricably intertwined, in which the conflict between the desire for autonomy and the desire for recognition can only be resolved by total renunciation of self. It illustrates powerfully the principle that the root of domination lies in the breakdown of tension between self and other.

Perhaps the greatest objection to this work by feminists has been directed against its depiction of O's voluntary submission. For them, the account of O's masochism is not an allegory of the desire for recognition, but simply the story of a victimized woman, too weak or brainwashed or hopeless to resist her degradation.[3] Such a viewpoint cannot, of course, explain what satisfaction is sought and found in submission, what psychological motivations lead to oppression, humiliation, and subservience. It denies the unpleasant fact that people really do consent to relationships of domination, and that fantasies of domination play a vigorous part in the mental lives of many who do not actually do so.

Story of O confronts us boldly with the idea that people often submit not merely out of fear, but in complicity with their own deepest desires. Told from the point of view of the woman who submits, and representing, as it does, the fantasy life of a gifted woman writer,[4] the story compels the reader to accept the authenticity of the desire for submission. But

---

3. See Andrea Dworkin, "Woman as Victim: *Story of O*," *Feminist Studies* 2, no. 1 (1974): 107–11; and Susan Griffin, *Pornography and Silence: Culture's Revenge Against Nature* (New York: Harper and Row, 1981). Part of the failure of such analyses, which are endemic to the feminist movement against pornography, is the denial of the difference between voluntary, ritual acts of submission that are subjectively considered pleasurable and acts of battery or violation that are terrifying and involuntary although they may occur within a theoretically voluntary contract like marriage.

4. Regine Deforges, *Confessions of O: Conversations with Pauline Reage*, trans. S. d'Etree (New York: Viking, 1979).

the narrative also makes clear that the desire for submission represents a peculiar transposition of the desire for recognition. O's physical humiliation and abuse represent a search for an elusive spiritual or psychological satisfaction. Her masochism is a search for recognition through an other who is powerful enough to bestow this recognition. This other has the power for which the self longs, and through his recognition she gains it, though vicariously.

At the beginning of *Story of O*, the heroine is, without warning, brought by her lover to Roissy Castle, an establishment organized by men for the ritual violation and subjugation of women. There she is given specific instructions:

> You are here to serve your masters. . . . At the first word or sign from anyone you will drop whatever you are doing and ready yourself for what is really your one and only duty: to lend yourself. Your hands are not your own, nor are your breasts, nor most especially, any of your orifices, which we may explore or penetrate at will. . . . You have lost all right to privacy or concealment. . .you must never look any of us in the face. If the costume we wear. . .leaves our sex exposed, it is not for the sake of convenience. . .but for the sake of insolence, so your eyes will be directed there upon it and nowhere else so that you ay learn that there resides your master. . . . [Your] being whipped. . .is less for our pleasure than for your enlightenment. . . . Both this flogging and the chain attached to the ring of your collar. . .are intended less to make you suffer, scream or shed tears than to make you feel, through this suffering, that you are not free but fettered, and to teach you that you are totally, dedicated to something outside yourself.[5]

A great deal is contained in these several lines. First, O is to lose all subjectivity, all possibility of using her body for action; she is to be merely a thing. Second, she is to be continually violated, even when she is not actually being used. The main transgression of her boundaries consists of her having to be always available and open. Third, her masters are to be recognized by her in an indirect form. The penis represents their desire, and through this indirect representation they will maintain their sovereignty. By interposing it between her and them they establish a subjectivity that is distanced, independent of her recognition. Indeed, they claim that their abuse of her is more for her "enlightenment" than

5. Réage, *Story of O*, 15–17.

their pleasure, so that even in using her they do not appear to need her. Their acts are carefully controlled: each act has a goal that expresses their rational intentions. Their sadistic pleasure consists not in direct enjoyment of her pain, but in the knowledge of their power over her—the fact that their power is visible, that it is manifested by outward signs, that it leaves marks.

Why must they find enjoyment more in their command than in her service, and why must it be distanced, that is, symbolized by the penis? Because in order to maintain their separate subjectivity, they must scrupulously deny their dependency on her. Otherwise they would suffer the fate of Hegel's master, who, in becoming dependent on his slave, gradually loses subjectivity to him. A further danger for the master is that the subject always becomes the object he consumes. By negating her will, they turn her into an object. And when her objectification is complete, when she has no more will, they can no longer use her without becoming filled with her thing-like nature. Thus, they must perform their violation rationally and ritually in order to maintain their boundaries and to make her will—not only her body—the object of their will.

Finally, the symbolization of male mastery through the penis emphasizes the difference between them and her. It signifies the denial of commonality that gives them the right to violate her. Each act the master takes against O establishes his separateness, his difference from her. He continually places himself outside her by saying, in effect, "I am not you." The rational function (calculation, objectivity, and control) is linked to this distance. The penis symbolizes the master's resistance to being absorbed by the thing he is controlling: however interdependent the master and slave may become, the difference between them will be sustained. The story is driven forward by the dialectic of control. Since a slave who is completely dominated loses the quality of being able to give recognition, the struggle to possess her must be prolonged. O must be enslaved piece by piece; new levels of resistance must be found, so that she can be vanquished anew. She must acquiesce in ever deeper humiliation, pain, and bondage, and she must will her submission ever anew, each time her masters ask her, "O, do you consent?" The narrative moves through these ever deeper levels of submission, tracing the impact of each fresh negation of her will, each new defeat of her resistance.

The culmination of the dialectic, the point when O has submitted and René, her lover, has exhausted the possibilities of violating her, would, logically, present a narrative problem. But before the problem can arise, before René becomes bored with O's submission and she is used up and discarded, a new source of tension is introduced. One day René presents O to Sir Stephen, his older (and more powerful) stepbrother, to whom she is to be "given." Unlike René, Sir Stephen does not love O. He is described as having a "will of ice and iron, which would not be swayed by desire," and he demands that she obey him without loving him, and without his loving her.[6] Yet this more complete surrender of her person and acceptance of her object status further arouses O's desire, makes her wish to matter in some way, to exist for him." Sir Stephen finds new ways of intensifying O's bondage: he employs her to entice another woman; he sends her to another castle, Samois, where O will abuse and be abused by other women; and he makes her "more interesting" by having her branded and her anus enlarged. These measures make Sir Stephen's form of mastery even more rational, calculating, and self-controlled than René's—more fully independent of his slave.

Furthermore, the fact that René looks up to Sir Stephen as to a father suggests that he is the loved authority not only for O, but also for René. He is the person in whose eyes René wants to be recognized; giving Sir Stephen his lover is a form of "obeisance," and René is obviously "pleased that [Sir Stephen] deigned to take pleasure in something he had given him." Indeed, O realizes that the two men share something "mysterious. . . more acute, more intense than amorous communion" from which she is excluded, even though she is the medium for it. René's delivery of O to Sir Stephen is a way of surrendering himself sexually to the more powerful man. "What each of them would look for in her would be the other's mark, the trace of the other's passage." Indeed, for René, Sir Stephen's possession of O sanctifies her, leaving "the mark of a god."[7]

René's relationship with Sir Stephen calls for a reinterpretation of the story up to this point: we now see that the objectification of the woman is inspired both by the need to assert difference from her, and by the desire to gain prestige in the father's eyes. Thus, René begins to relinquish his love for O, the tender and compassionate identification that moved him when she first surrendered, for the sake of his identification and alliance with the father. We might say that the desire for recognition by the father wholly overtakes the love of the mother; it becomes another motive for domination. (This shift in allegiance shows how the roots of domination lie not only in the preoedipal drama of mother and child, but also in the oedipal triad. . . . O's unimportance to either man by comparison with their bond to each other becomes a further aspect of her humiliation and negation.

Despite the narrative's attempt to create more dramatic tension, the story eventually becomes heavy with O's inexorable loss of subjectivity.

---

6. Ibid., 82.
7. Ibid., 81.

Playing the complementary part to her masters, O relinquishes all sense of difference and separateness in order to remain—at all costs—connected to them. O's deepest fears of abandonment and separation emerge as her tie to René is gradually dissolved by her bondage to Sir Stephen. Briefly left alone, she begins to believe she has lost René's love; she feels that her life is absolutely void. She thinks, paraphrasing a Protestant text she had seen as a child, "It is a fearful thing to be cast out of the hands of the living God." O is the lost soul who can only be restored to grace by putting herself in the hands of the ideal, omnipotent other.

As the story continues, O's desire for connection increasingly assumes the symbolic and ritual character of a devotion: now it is her task to live according to her new lover's will, to serve him whether he is present or not. Her lover is like a god, and her need for him can only be satisfied by obedience, which allows her to transcend herself by becoming an instrument of his supreme will. In this way O's story, with its themes of devotion and transcendence, is suggestive of the surrender of the saints. The torture and outrage to which she submits is a kind of martyrdom, seeming "to her the very redemption of her sins."[8] O's great longing is to be *known*, and in this respect she is like any lover, for the secret of love is to be known as oneself. But her desire to be known is like that of the sinner who wants to be known by God. Sir Stephen thrills her because he knows her instantly; he knows her to be bad, wanton, reveling in her debasement. However, this knowing can only go so far, because there is progressively less of O the subject left to be known.

Story of O concludes with a note that proposes two possible endings to the story. In the first, Sir Stephen returns O to Roissy and abandons her there. In the second, O, "seeing that Sir Stephen was about to leave her, said she would prefer to die. Sir Stephen gave her his consent." This is her final gesture of heroism, her last opportunity to express her lover's will. The gesture is in keeping with O's paradoxical hope that in complete surrender she will find her elusive self. For this hope is the other side of O's devotional servitude: in performing the tasks her masters set her, O seeks affirmation of herself. O is actually willing to risk complete annihilation of her person in order to continue to be the object of her lover's desire—to be recognized.

O's fear of loss and abandonment points to an important aspect of the question of pain. The problem of masochism has been oversimplified ever since Freud's paradoxical assertion that the masochist takes pleasure

---

8. Ibid., 93.

in pain? But current psychoanalytic theory appreciates that pain is a route to pleasure only when it involves submission to an idealized figure. As O demonstrates, the masochist's pleasure cannot be understood as a direct, unmediated enjoyment of pain: "She liked the idea of torture, but when she was being tortured herself she would have betrayed the whole world to escape it, and yet when it was over she was happy to have gone through it."[10] The pain of violation serves to protect the self by substituting physical pain for the psychic pain of loss and abandonment. In being hurt by the other, O feels she is being reached, she is able to experience another living presence.[11] O's pleasure, so to speak, lies in her sense of her own survival and her connection to her powerful lover. Thus, as long as O can transpose her fear of loss into submission, as long as she remains the object and manifestation of his power, she is safe.

---

9. Freud, "The Economic Problem of Masochism" (*SE* 79:155–72). The idea of massochism as pleasure in pain was perhaps an overly influential condensation of Freud's thinking (in "Instincts and Their Vicissitudes" he distinguishes between the "pain itself" and "the accompanying sexual excitement"). It has been amended by many contemporary psychoanalysts, who interpret masochism in terms of the ego or the self and its object relations; they see masochism as a desire for submission to an idealized other in order to protect against overwhelming feelings of psychic pain, object loss, and fragmentation. See my review of the problem in "The Alienation of Desire"; see also Masud Khan, *Alienation in Perversions* (New York: International Universities Press, 1979); Robert Stoller, *Sexual Excitement* (New York: Simon and Schuster, 1980); and *Perversion* (New York Pantheon, 1975); Esther Menaker, *Masochism and the Emerging Ego* (New York; Human Sciences Press, 1973); and V. Smirnoff, "The Masochistic Contract," *International Journal of Psychoanalysis* 50 (1969): 665–71. These writings point to the underlying narcissistic dilemmas that are "solved" by the infliction of pain administered by an idealized authority. These explanations do have a precedent in Freud's original idea of "moral masochism" (see "The Economic Problem of Masochism") and which Karen Horney subsequently related to low self-esteem and difficulty in separation ("The Problem of Feminine Masochism," in *Feminine Psychology* [New York: Norton, 1967]).
10. Réage, *Story of O*, 152.
11. As Masud Khan (*Alienation in Perversion*) pointed out, Freud lacked a conception of psychic pain, since it is the property of the self, for which he also lacked a concept. Khan discusses the importance of finding a witness for ones psychic pain, a witnessing that allows the person to achieve a deep sense of self. He also describes the case of a woman for whom the immersion in a compelling sadomasochistic relationship seemed to be the alternative to psychic breakdown. This form of pain substituted for a deep depression based on very early abandonment and loss.

The experience of pain has yet another dimension. In Freud's terms, pain is the point at which stimuli become too intense for the body or ego to bear. Conversely, pleasure requires a certain control or mastery of stimuli. Thus, Freud suggested that the erotization of pain allows a sense of mastery by converting pain into pleasure.[12] But this is true only for the master: O's loss of self is *his* gain, O's pain is *his* pleasure. For the slave, intense pain causes the violent rupture of the self, a profound experience of fragmentation and chaos.[13] It's true that O now welcomes this loss of self-coherence, but only under a specific condition: that her sacrifice actually creates the master's power, produces his coherent self, in which she can take refuge. Thus, in losing her own self, she is gaining access, however circumscribed, to a more powerful one.

The relationship of domination is asymmetrical. It can be reversed, as when O takes on the role of torturer, but it can never become reciprocal or equal. Identifcation plays an important part in this reversible relationship, but always with the stipulation that the masochist gains her identity through the master's power, even as he actively negates his identity with her. Inflicting pain is the master's way of maintaining his separate identity. In her pain, O's body "moves" her masters, but chiefly because it displays the marks they have left. Of course, their "emotion" is always checked, and is finally diminished as she becomes increasingly a dehumanized object, as her thing-like nature makes her pain mute. Nonetheless, her submission to their will embodies the ultimate recognition of their power. Submission becomes the "pure" form of recognition, even as violation becomes the "pure" form of assertion. The assertion of one individual (the master) is transformed into domination; the other's (the slave's) recognition becomes submission. Thus, the basic tension of forces *within* the individual becomes a dynamic *between* individuals.

DOMINATION, DEATH, AND DISCONTENT

The relationship of domination is fueled by the same desire for recognition that we find in love—but why does it take this form? Even if we accept that O is seeking recognition, we still want to know why her search culminates in submission, instead of in a relationship of mutuality. Why this complementarity between the all-powerful and powerless instead of the equal power of two subjects?

---

12. Freud's point ("The Economic Problem of Masochism") is that eroticization allows unmanageable, nagative stimuli to be managed.
13. See Leo Bersani, *Baudelaire and Freud* (Berkeley: University of California Press, 1977).

We already have some sense of how Freud and Hegel have approached these questions. Their answers, as I have pointed out, assume the inevitable human aspiration to omnipotence and they begin and end in the same place, in the no-exit of domination, in the closed system of opposites: doer and done-to, master and slave. It is true that Hegel's discussion of recognition implies an ideal of mutuality in which both subjects partake of the contradictory elements of negation and recognition. But the polarization of these two "moments" is a necessary part of his dialectic, and therefore each subject winds up embodying only one side of the tension. In psychoanalytic terms, this breakdown of wholeness is understood as "splitting."[14] Wholeness can only exist by maintaining contradiction, but this is not easy. In splitting, the two sides are represented as opposite and distinct tendencies, so that they are

---

14. The psychoanalytic concept of splitting, like that of repression, has a narrow, technical use as well as a broader metapsychological and metaphoric meaning. Just as repression became a paradigm for a larger cultural process, so might splitting be suggestive not only for individual psychic processes but also for supraindividual ones. Technically, splitting refers to a defense against aggresion, an effort to protect the "good" object by splitting off its "bad" aspects that have incurred aggression. But in its broader sense, splitting means any breakdown of the whole, in which parts of self or other are split off and projected elsewhere. In both uses it indicates a polarization, in which opposites—especially good and bad—can no longer be integrated: in which one side is devalued, the other idealized, and each is projected onto different objects.

Freud not only used the term "repression" to refer to specific defense, but also as the fundamental pillar (*Grundpfeil*) of psychoanalysis (*An Outline of Psychoanalysis*, SE 23:139–208). Splitting was originally used by Freud in a narrower sense (see "The Splitting of the Ego," SE 23:271–78), but was made a key concept by Melanie Klein (see *Envy and Gratitude* [New York: Basic Books, 1957], 324–25) and those influenced by her. Here splitting refers variously to the process of separating the object into good and bad to keep the bad from contaminating the good, to the early division between love and hate, to the splitting off part of the self and projecting it onto the object, and related mechanisms. Freud did refer to the splitting of bad and good object in just this sense in a footnote to "The 'Uncanny'" (*SE* 17:217–52). Kernbert (*Borderline Conditions and Pathological Narcissism* [New York: Jason Aronson, 1975]) has claimed splitting (especially idealization and devaluation) is the crucial defense in borderline disorders, thus giving it a function parallel to that of repression in neurosis. I prefer Fairbairn's view (*Psychoanalytic Studies of the Personality* [London: Routledge and Kegan Paul, 1952]), which insists on the defensive character of splitting—however ubiquitous—to Klein's view, which makes it a developmental phase.

available to the subject only as alternatives. The subject can play only one side at a time, projecting the opposite side onto the other. In other words, in the subject's mind, self and other are represented not as equally balanced wholes, but as split into halves. But is the splitting assumed by Hegel inevitable? Is the breakdown of tension inescapable?

George Bataille has directly applied the Hegelian dialectic to erotic violation. His work enables us to look more closely at *Story of O*, to see how splitting and breakdown assume an erotic form. Individual existence for Bataille is a state of separation and isolation: we are as islands, connected yet separated by a sea of death. Eroticism is the perilous crossing of that sea. It opens the way out of isolation by exposing us to "death . . . the denial of our individual lives."[15] The body stands for boundaries: discontinuity, individuality, and life. Consequently the violation of the body is a transgression of the boundary between life and death, even as it breaks through our discontinuity from the other. This break, this crossing of boundaries, is for Bataille the secret of *all* eroticism; and it assumes its starkest expression in erotic violation. It should be noted, however, that the break must never *really* dissolve the boundaries—else death results. Excitement resides in the *risk* of death, not in death itself. And it is erotic complementarity that offers a way to simultaneously break through and preserve the boundaries: in the opposition between violator and violated, one person maintains his boundary and the other allows her boundary to be broken. One remains rational and in control, while the other loses her self. Put another way, complementarity protects the self. Were both partners to give up control, the dissolution of self would be total. The violated partner would have no controlling partner to identify with; she could not "safely" abandon herself. When both partners dissolve the boundary, both experience a fundamental sense of breakdown, a kind of primary, existential anxiety; instead of connection to a defined other, there is a terrifying void. Thus, the desire to inflict or receive pain, even as it seeks to break through boundaries, is also an effort to find them.[16]

As we have seen in *Story of O*, the control, order, and boundary that the master provides are essential to the erotic experience of submission. Indeed, it is the master's rational, calculating, even instrumentalizing

---

15. Georges Bataille, *Death and Sensuality* (New York: Walker, 1962), 11–25, esp. 24.
16. In the view of self psychology, it is the fear of losing the self, fragmenting, and falling apart that is the primary motive in masochism (see Robert Stolorow and Frank Lachmann, *Psychoanalysis of Developmental Arrests* [New York: International Universities Press, 1980]).

attitude that excites submission; it is the image of his exquisite control
that makes for his thrilling machismo. The pleasure, for both partners,
is in his mastery. His intentions, with their sacramental formality, take
on the purposefulness of a higher order. The sadist's disinterestedness,
the fact that he does it "less for [his] pleasure than for [the masochist's]
enlightenment," offers containment and protection. This protective power
constitutes the all-important aspect of authority, without which the
fantasy is not satisfying.[17] This authority is what inspires love and transforms violence into an opportunity for voluntary submission.

Although the elements of self-control, intentionality, and authority
are meant to uphold the difference between violator and violated, control,
as we have seen, tends to become self-defeating. The fact that each partner represents only one pole in a split unity creates the major difficulty
in sustaining tension. The continual problem in relations of domination,
says Bataille in his commentary on Hegel, is "that the slave by accepting
defeat. . .has lost the quality without which he is unable to *recognize*
the conqueror so as to satisfy him. The slave is unable to give the master
the *satisfaction* without which the master can no longer rest."[18] The
master's denial of the other's subjectivity leaves him faced with isolation
as the only alternative to being engulfed by the dehumanized other. In
either case, the master is actually alone, because the person he is with
is no person at all. And likewise, for her part, the slave fears that the
master will abandon her to aloneness when he tires of being with someone who is not a person.

Eventually the other's unreality becomes too powerful; the sadist
is in danger of becoming the will-less thing he consumes unless he separates himself completely. And the masochist increasingly feels that she

---

17. A woman who had once been involved in a sadomasochistic relationship
complained of her partner that "he was bumbling, he never hurt me where or
how I wanted to be hurt." Indeed, a good sadist is hard to find: he has to intuit
his victim's hidden desirs, protect the illusion of oneness and mastery that stem
from his knowing what she wants. Elizabeth Harris, "Sadomasochism: A Personal
Experience," in R. Linden, D. Pagano, D. Russell, and S. Star, eds., *Against Sadomasochism* (Palo Alto: Frog in the Well, 1982). The psychoanalytic interpretation
of masochism shows how the masochist is the hidden director of the experience,
as Stoller (*Sexual Excitement*) points out. Those who write about sadomasochism
from a personal experience concur. See Susan Farr, "The Art of Discipline," in
Coming to Power: Writings and Graphics on Lesbian S/M (Boston: Sanois, 1982).
18. Georges Bataille, "Hemingway in the Light of Hegel," *Semiotext(e)* 2, no. 2
(1976): 12–22. See also Richard Sennett, *Authority* (New York: Knopf, 1980), for
a reading of Hegel in terms of power and obedience.

does not exist, that she is without will or desire, that she has no life apart from the other. Indeed, once the tension between subjugation and resistance dissolves, death or abandonment is the inevitable end of the story, and, as we have seen, *Story of O* is deliberately left open to both conclusions. This ambiguity is appropriate because for the masochist the intolerable end is abandonment, while for the sadist it is the death (or murder) of the other, whom he destroys. A parallel dynamic, in which complementarity replaces reciprocity, is a frequent undertow in "ordinary" intimate relationships: one gives, the other refuses to accept; one pursues, the other loses interest; one criticizes, the other feels annihilated. For both partners, the sense of connection is lost: extreme self-sufficiency leads to detachment from the other; extreme dependency vitiates the separate reality of the other.

Metaphorically, then, and sometimes literally, the sadomasochistic relationship tends toward death, or, at any rate, toward deadness, numbness, the exhaustion of sensation. This end is ironic because such a relationship is initiated in order to reintroduce tension—to counteract numbness with pain, to break encasement through violation. Bataille implies that we need the split unity of master and slave in order to maintain the boundaries that erotic union—the "little death" of the self—threatens to dissolve. But, as we see, split unity culminates in disconnection. The exhaustion of satisfaction that occurs when all resistance is vanquished, all tension is lost, means that the relationship has come full circle, returned to the emptiness from which it was an effort to escape.

But why is loss of tension the beginning and inevitable end of this story? Freud's theory of the instincts offers us one interpretation. Indeed, his whole explanation of the discontents of civilization hinges on his interpretation of loss of tension.[19] Freud believed that only the idea of a death drive that impels us toward complete absence of tension could explain the prevalence of destruction and aggression in human life. Projecting the death dive outward in the form of aggression or mastery was our main protection against succumbing to it. Here, as I see it, is Freud's effort to explain domination, his parallel to the master-slave paradox.

Domination, for Freud, is inevitable since otherwise the death instinct, that primary drive toward nothingness (complete loss of tension), would turn inward and destroy life itself. But fortunately aggression must contend with its "immortal adversary," the life instinct, eros. Eros,

---

19. Freud, *Civilization and Its Discontents;* see also *Beyond the Pleasure Principle* (*SE* 18:7–64) on the death drive.

in general, and sexuality, in particular, neutralize or bind aggression. Freud writes that the life and death instincts almost never appear in isolation, but "are alloyed with each other. . .and become unrecognizable." The best place to observe and analyze this merger is erotic life: sadism and masochism are "manifestations of the destructive instinct. . . strongly alloyed with erotism."[20] Indeed, erotic domination, Freud continues, may be the prime place to apprehend the alliance of eros and the death instinct:

> It is in sadism, where the death instinct twists the erotic aim in its own sense, and yet at the same time fully satisfies the erotic urge, that we succeed in obtaining the clearest insight into its nature, and its relation to Eros. But even where it emerges without any sexual purpose, in the blindest fury of destructiveness, we cannot fail to recognize that the satisfaction of the [death] instinct. . .[presents] the ego with a fulfillment of the latter's old wishes for omnipotence.[21]

When aggression is projected outward and harnessed by civilization, it winds up doing *outside* what it would otherwise do *inside*: reducing the world, objectifying it, subjugating it. If we translate this process back into Hegel's terms, this means that the self refuses the claim of the outside world (the other) to limit his absoluteness. He asserts omnipotence. Omnipotence, we might then say, is the manifestation of Freud's death instinct. When the destructive instinct is projected outward, the problem of omnipotence is not solved, but merely relocated. Nor does the fusion of the death instinct with eros solve the problem. For even the alloy of destruction and eros, as the cycle of escape from and return to deadness in erotic domination illustrates, brings us back to the death drive's original aim: the reduction of all tension.

---

20. Freud, *Civilization and Its Discontents*, 119. Freud concludes this passage with his famous remark that aggression is "the greatest impediment to civilization," threatening us with the "hostility of each against all and of all against each"; that the evolution of civiliation depends upon "the struggle between Eros and Death" (p. 122).
21. Freud, *Civilization and Its Discontents*, 121. I am suggesting here that we see instinctual tension as a metaphor for the experience of the self, for the condition of stasis between self and other represented in the mind as a condition of the self. This representation has a real appearance—what began as something between subjects winds up being experienced as the fantasy life of the subject, appearing as instinctual or primary, as purely internal and self-generating.

CHAPTER 12

Hegel and Lacan

THE DIALECTIC OF DESIRE

Edward S. Casey and J. Melvin Woody

Lacan claims to be an orthodox Freudian, championing Freud's authentic meaning against the challenge of French phenomenology and the heretical ego psychology of the American Freudians. He attacks both the transparency of consciousness in Sartre's existential phenomenology and the primacy of the ego in American psychoanalytic theory, insisting that the ego is not the locus of truth and reality and autonomous control, but is rather a concretion of illusions, a source of *méconnaissances* or misrecognitions" that must be dissolved in the course of psychoanalysis in order to liberate the authentic self, the *je* or "I."

Lacan finds Hegel a natural ally in these quarrels because Hegel, too, is a critic of consciousness and of the ego—not of ego psychology, of course, but of the ego-centered philosophies that have dominated modern European thought. These include Descartes's rational *cogito*, the introspective consciousness of English empiricism, and the autonomous, transcendental ego of Kant and Fichte. All are misconceptions insofar as they are founded in the idea of a purely epistemological ego—or "thinking being." For they thereby abstract not only from human activity and labor but also from the social, cultural, and historical conditions of human mentality. Thus, Kojève describes the program of the *Phenomenology of Spirit* somewhat dramatically by depicting it as Hegel's attempt to understand himself—*not* as a disembodied ego or Cartesian *cogito*, but as he sits at a table in Jena in 1806, writing the *Phenomenology* and hearing, in the distance, the cannon shots on the eve of the Battle of Jena, in which Napoleon defeated Prussia. To understand himself, Hegel must understand what it is to philosophize at that historic moment, in a world in which Napoleon is about to end the Holy Roman Empire that Charlemagne had begun a thousand years before. But, Kojève asks,

> What is it to "understand" Napoleon?...Generally speaking, to understand Napoleon is to understand him in relation to the whole of anterior historical evolution, to understand the whole of universal history. Now, almost none of the philosophers contemporary with Hegel posed this problem for himself. And none of them, except Hegel, resolved it. For Hegel is the only one able to accept, and to justify, Napoleon's existence..... The others consider themselves obliged to condemn Napoleon, that is, to condemn the historical *reality*: and their philosophical systems—by that very fact—are all condemned by that reality. (*Introduction to the Reading of Hegel*, 34–35)

These philosophers condemn Napoleon—and thereby themselves— because the abstract purity of the epistemological ego has been translated into a moralizing "beautiful soul" so obsessed with the purity of its own intentions that it does not *act*, but only passes judgment upon those who do—and of course Napoleon is the preeminent historic agent of the era. These philosophers are all words and no deeds, and by their very opposition to historical reality they show that their words are empty abstractions. They fail to understand Napoleon, as they fail to understand themselves, because they do not recognize that their abstract conception of themselves and Napoleon are both products of the culture of the Enlightenment, and that their condemnation of history is merely the verbal counterpart of what the Revolution and Napoleon are actively realizing by the destruction of the old order and the Holy Roman Empire. To understand Napoleon they would have to acknowledge this underlying identity of self and other, give up their abstract moralistic purity, and accept their own historicity.

Hegel insists that the individual who fails to recognize his own historicity and sets himself up as a pure, autonomous ego, independent of the customs and culture of his society and era, is a stranger to himself. Much of the work of the *Phenomenology of Spirit* is intended to dissolve such an illusory conception of the self as an abstract ego and to bring the self-estranged consciousness to a full recognition of itself as both creature and creator of history. It is an enterprise that may well be compared with psychoanalysis and with Lacan's attack upon the ego as a source of misrecognition and the alienation of the authentic subject. The easiest way to exhibit the Hegelian background of Lacan's view is to explore the parallel between these two programs for rescuing the self from its estrangement, or its "captivation by the ego," in Lacan's phrase.

The point of departure for Hegel's critique of ego philosophies is his analysis of consciousness, which culminates in a critique of the sort of naive scientific thinker who seeks to contemplate an objective world uncontaminated by subjectivity. This thinker still does not recognize that the mind plays an active role in knowledge, that the scientific object is a reflection of the scientific subject. The account ends with a strange passage on "die verkehrte Welt," an inverted, mirror world in which all scientific polarities are reversed—rather like speculations about a universe of antimatter in recent physics. Hegel carries this out to comic lengths to emphasize that the scientific consciousness must recognize itself in this mirror in order to get beyond mere consciousness and reach the level of self-consciousness. But self-consciousness emerges only if it is not nature that is the object of consciousness, but rather another self. Hegel therefore turns to the origins of consciousness in the relation to an alter ego: "Self-consciousness is faced by another self-consciousness; it has come *out of itself*. This has a twofold significance: first, it has lost itself, for it finds itself as an other beings secondly, in doing so it has superseded the other, for it does not see the other as an essential being. but in the other sees its own self" (*PS*, 111).

This image of the emergence of self-consciousness from the recognition of the self in a mirror, or in another self, is familiar to readers of Lacan. The point of departure for Lacan's critique of ego psychology is his account of "the mirror stage"—the stage when the infant, still uncoordinated and relatively powerless, first achieves consciousness of itself by recognizing itself in an object outside itself, its image in a mirror. According to Lacan, this specular, mirror image of the self is "the matrix and first outline of what is to become the ego,"[1] and since it shows the body in reversed form, it presages the ego's role as a source of misrecognition and illusion.

What is not to be found in the looking glass, according to both Hegel and Lacan, is any awareness of self as subjective agency. The two agree that what the mirror does not reflect is the subject's *desire*, which is the motive source of all human activity and is the most primitive form of self-awareness. Kojève explains simplest, that

---

1. J. Laplanche and J.-B. Pontalis, *The Language of Psycholanalysis*, trans. D. Nicholson-Smith (New York: Norton, 1973), 250–52. For Lacan's own formulation, see J. Lacan, *Écrits: A Selection*, trans. Alan Sheridan (New York: Norton, 1977), 1–7.

the man who attentively contemplates a thing, who wants to
see it as it is without changing anything is "absorbed" so to
speak by this contemplation—that is, by this thing. He forgets
himself. . . . [But] when he experiences a desire, when he is
hungry, for example, and wants to eat . . . he necessarily becomes
aware of *himself.* Desire is always revealed as *my* desire. (37)

In contrast to the knowledge that keeps man in a passive
quietude, Desire disquiets him and moves him to action. (4)

Thus far, Lacan could concur on purely Freudian grounds—and
might defend his orthodoxy with references to Freud's discussions of Eros
and Thanatos and the economics of the libido. But what Lacan in fact
does is to take over Hegel's analysis of desire as interpreted and elaborated
by Kojève. Hegel's analysis focuses upon what distinguishes *human* desire
from merely vital, biological drives. If Lacan's version of Freudian theory
and practice offers an alternative to reductionism, it is as much the result
of this adoption of Hegel's analysis of desire as it is of the linguistic theory
of the unconscious. Indeed, the linguistic and Hegelian themes may be
regarded as necessary complements of one another. Paul Ricoeur objects
to Lacan's interpretation of Freud because it "eliminates energy concepts
in favor of linguistics" (367, no. 37). By insisting upon a linguistic or
semiotic theory of the unconscious, Ricoeur argues, Lacan and his
followers are led to neglect the energetic, biological dimension of Freud's
theory, the "economics" of the libido. But, Ricoeur insists, it is just this
natural, energetic ingredient that is required to explain the difference
between ordinary language and the symbolism of the unconscious.
Ricoeur regards this as the critical juncture for the philosophical interpretation of Freud:

> For a philosophical critique, the essential point concerns what
> I call the place of that energy discourse. Its place, it seems to
> me, lies at the intersection of desire and language. . . . The
> intersection of the "natural" and the "signifying" is the point
> at which the instinctual drives are "represented" by affects and
> ideas: consequently the coordination of the economic language
> and the intentional language is the main question of this epis-
> temology and one that cannot be avoided by reducing either
> language to the other. (395)

Ricoeur admits, the difficulty here centers in "the idea of an 'energy that
is transformed into meaning.' " And he concedes that in order to resolve
this difficulty, "it may be that the entire matter must be redone, perhaps
with the help of energy schemata quite different from Freud's" (395).

It is at just this point, "the intersection of the 'natural' and the 'signifying,' " that Lacan's adoption of Hegel's account of human desire plays such a decisive role. The linguistic interpretation of the unconscious seems to call for a complementary redefinition of desire in less naturalistic terms than those afforded by Freud's "energy discourse." Hegel's discussion of desire in the *Phenomenology of Spirit* supplies this complement by focusing upon how human desire transcends biological needs and organic drives. And if Ricoeur is correct in claiming that psychoanalysis is essentially a "hermeneutics of desire," then the adoption of the Hegelian theory of desire is bound to have important implications for both the theory and the practice of the interpretation of the "language" of the unconscious. Kojève's elaboration of Hegel's analysis of desire might almost have been designed to address this enigma of how "energy is transformed into meaning" in a way that pertains directly to the problem of interpretation as it appears within the interpersonal setting of analysis.

In his commentary upon Hegel's discussion of desire, Kojève explains that the very being of man implies and presupposes a biological reality, an animal life and animal desire. But,

> if animal Desire is the necessary condition of Self-Consciousness, it is not the sufficient condition. (4)

> The animal attains only Selbst-*gefühl, Sentiment* of self, but not Selbst-*bewusstsein*, Self-*Consciousness*—that is, it cannot *speak* of itself, it cannot *say* "I." . . . For Self-Consciousness to exist . . . there must be transcendence of self with respect to self as *given*. And this is possible, according to Hegel, only if desire is directed not toward a *given* being, but toward a *nonbeing* . . . that is, toward another Desire, another greedy emptiness, another I. . . . (Desire is human—or, more exactly, "humanizing," "anthropogenetic"—only provided that it is directed toward another *Desire* and an *other* Desire. (39–40)

> Thus, in the relationship between a man and a woman, for example, Desire is human only if the one desires, not the body, but the Desire of the other; if he wants "to possess" or "to assimilate" the Desire taken as Desire—that is to say, if he wants to be "desired" or "loved," or, rather, "recognized" in his human value, in his reality as a human individual. (6)

Lacan takes up this analysis and elaborates it into a three-way distinction among *desire*, merely natural or biological *need*, which is mute; and *demand*, which is that peculiarly human demand for love that transcends all mere objects of satisfaction and transmutes them into proofs of love. Lacan reserves the word "desire" to refer to that transcendent, unconditional ingredient in the demand for love, the peculiarly human emptiness that cannot be satisfied by any object or proof of love. As Lacan puts it, "for both partners in the relation, both the subject and the Other, it is not enough to be subjects of need, or objects of love.... They must stand for the cause of desire" (*Écrits*, 287). So, Lacan explains, "if the desire of the mother *is* the phallus, the child wishes to *be* the phallus in order to satisfy that desire" (289). And elsewhere he elaborates: "The child, in his relation to the mother, a relation constituted in analysis not by his vital dependence on her, but by his dependence on her love, that is to say, by the desire for her desire, identifies himself with the imaginary object of this desire in so far as the mother herself symbolizes it in the phallus" (*Écrits*, 198).

Lacan's understanding of the significance of the phallus is crucial here. The phallus is not the physical organ, the penis or clitoris, but the symbolic object whose unveiling culminated the ancient mysteries. Lacan insists upon this special symbolic status: "The phallus is the privileged signifier of that mark in which the role of the logos is joined with the advent of desire (287). The phallus thus stands at that "intersection of desire and language" that Ricoeur describes as the philosophically critical crossroads of psychoanalytic theory. For Lacan, it marks the transcendence of human desire beyond organic need—a transcendence that is owing to language. It also stands for *jouissance*, that unconditional fulfillment or perfection of being that is the aim of a human desire that cannot be satisfied by any object because "the being of language is the non-being of objects" (263). In effect, the phallus is the symbol of that movement whereby man surpasses the merely vital or biological toward a fulfillment that is forever wanted—and forever wanting—in human existence.

Hegel, too, had insisted that this distinctively human desire to be desired aims beyond every determinate need and seems even to defy any form of satisfaction. It is a desire to be desired as a desirer; *not* simply to satisfy a *need*, nor as an object of *love*, as Lacan says, but as a human subject who transcends every object or instinct or merely vital need. But an individual can only prove to the other that he *is* such a transcending subject by risking his life in conflict with another subject. Kojève explains:

> For man to be truly human, for him to be essentially and really different from an animal, his human Desire must actually win out over his animal Desire.... All the Desires of an animal

are in the final analysis a function of its desire to preserve its life. Human Desire, therefore, must win out over this desire for preservation. . . . (6–7)

In other words, Man will risk his biological *life* to satisfy his *nonbiological* desire. And Hegel says that the being that is incapable of putting its life in danger in order to attain ends that are not immediately vital—i.e., the being that cannot risk its life in a fight for *Recognition*, in a fight for pure *prestige*—is *not* a truly *human* being. (41)

But one cannot extract recognition from a corpse! A struggle to the death can only end in impasse. If the struggle is to have any positive result, one of the two adversaries must surrender, abnegate his own desire in order to save his life and become a slave who labors to satisfy the desire of the other, the master. But the master cannot be fully satisfied by the recognition of a mere slave who has sacrificed his human autonomy to save his life. *Self*-consciousness is achieved only through consciousness of another self, an alter ego, and the master cannot encounter a fully human self in the slave. It is only the slave who encounters in the master, as his alter ego, a fully autonomous human being. But this otherness must be overcome; the self must recognize itself in its other. The master must acknowledge his dependence upon the slave, and the slave must recognize his own mastery. In fact, it is the slave who, by means of his labor, may eventually achieve satisfaction and recognition. The slave alters and reshapes the world through his work and thereby realizes and embodies his own subjective agency in the world. He can therefore *recognize* himself in that world. By laboring to satisfy the desire of the other, then, the slave *works through* his natural fear of death and realizes his freedom by mastering the natural world, thereby achieving self-recognition.

Lacan applies this analysis of the struggle for recognition and the master-slave relation to the development of the child and to the psycho-analytic process. The child desires to be desired—desires, symbolically, to *be* the phallus that the mother desires. But he must repress this desire under the prohibition of the paternal "No," or as Lacan puts it "in the Name of the Father," which signifies the socialization of the child, the acquisition of language, law, and culture whereby the individual becomes human. This subordination of desire to law and language is the locus of primal repression. The threat of castration is simply the apt symbol for this abnegation of the desire to be desired, symbolized by the desire to be the phallus. Lacan also finds here the source of the necessity that led Freud to "link the appearance of the signifier of the Father, as author of the Law, with death, even to the murder of the Father" (*Écrits*, 199).

Thus, according to Lacan, there is a "life-and-death struggle" at the origin of individual acculturation much like that which Hegel saw as the precondition of all human history. In both cases, this struggle leaves the desire for recognition unsatisfied, and the subsequent development—whether of the career of the individual or the history of the species—is plagued by tensions that betray the unresolved conflict whence it springs. Lacan writes: "The concrete field of individual preservation. . . is structured in this dialectic of master and slave, in which we can recognize the symbolic emergence of the imaginary struggle to the death in which we earlier defined the essential structure of the ego" (*Écrits*, 142).

Lacan sees this same dialectic in psychoanalytic transference. He frequently characterizes the analytic relationship in just these Hegelian terms, describing it as a struggle for recognition or as a master-slave relation in which the analysand assumes the role of the slave, who agrees initially to undertake the "work" of analysis in order to satisfy the analyst-master. If the process is to be fruitful, however, the analyst must eventually eschew the role of master and help the analysand toward self-recognition through the labor of free association, thereby freeing an authentic "I" from captivation by the ego.

Of course, all of this must be taken metaphorically. In Lacan's case, nothing should be taken too literally—and Lacan himself remarks that Hegel's account describes "a mythical rather than a real genesis" (*Écrits*, 308). It is probably best to see Hegel's analysis of the struggle for recognition and the master-slave dialectic as his substitute for the Enlightenment's myth of the origin of human civilization in a social contract between autonomous, rationally self-interested egos. Kojève treats this dialectic as a metaphor for the whole of human history, in which the labor of the slave corresponds to the historical process of *Bildung*, or culture-building, wherein man both creates and alienates himself:

> The historical process, the historical becoming of the human being, is the product of the working Slave and not of the warlike Master. . . . Thanks to his work, *he* can become other: and thanks to his work, the *World* can become other. And this is what actually took place as universal history and, finally, the French Revolution and Napoleon show. (52–53)

And that brings us back to the beginning, to Hegel's effort to understand himself as he writes, hearing the sounds of Napoleon's cannon at Jena, and to his attempt to help the reader overcome his self-estrangement by appropriating his own historicity, recognizing himself as both creature and creator of history. It is, again, an undertaking that invites comparison with psychoanalysis, especially as Lacan describes it: "Analysis can have for its goal only the advent of a true speech and the realization by the subject of his history in his relation to a future" (*Écrits*, 88).

Yet for all the fertile parallels Lacan discovers between psychoanalysis and the program of Hegel's *Phenomenology*, the two enterprises are not the same, and he is well aware of how they differ. In Hegel's case, the task of reconciliation with his own historical reality requires an understanding of the whole of world history, or at least of how the history of the West has led to the confrontation between the German intellectual and the Napoleonic armies. Only the philosophical comprehension of the history that culminates in Napolean will yield such self-understanding and reconciliation. Self-knowledge is not to be attained through the simple transparency of the Cartesian *cogito* or Kant's transcendental unity of apperception, for man is not an enduring substance, knowable through the contemplation of some timeless essential attributes. Man is a free agent and he cannot know *what* he is until he acts, since he constitutes himself through acting upon and altering his world. Man's essence is defined by his history, by what he has done, and that means that he can only come to know himself by alienating or othering himself, by building himself a world and then recognizing himself in that world of culture and history, understood as the product of his human deeds.

But the individual who fully recognizes all this, and understands that history is a human creation, is himself no longer a mere creature of history. *That* individual, of course, is Hegel himself. By fully understanding his own historicity, Hegel claims to transcend it, not by ascending to a realm of Platonic Ideas, nor by escaping into a timeless mystic unity, but precisely by insisting that man's freedom makes him radically temporal and historical; and yet to understand this history is to transcend it in a knowledge that is absolute because it grasps the truth of all the antecedent forms of consciousness and culture, and knows itself to be the product of those forms. It thereby comprehends the whole of history within itself. So, Hegel concludes, "Spirit necessarily appears in Time, and it appears in Time just so long as it has not *grasped* its pure Notion, i.e., has not annulled Time. . . . Time, therefore, appears as the destiny and necessity of Spirit that is not yet complete within itself, the necessity to enrich the share which self-consciousness has in consciousness" (*Phenomenology*, 487).

Hegelian plenomenology and Lacanian psychoanalysis part company here. For Lacan would forswear such a claim to absolute knowledge, emphasizing that the analyst must abjure any comparable assertion of omniscience. And this is surely not because of any modesty on Lacan's part, but because of his conviction that there is no final insight or definitive version of truth to be had. If Lacan nevertheless acknowledges the radical historicity and temporality of human existence by insisting upon the roles of language, law, and culture in the constitution of the individual subject, he must avail himself of a different conception of human temporality, historicity, and culture than Hegel's. He found such an alternative conception in the philosophy of Martin Heidegger.

CHAPTER 13

The Concept of Recognition in Hegel's Jena Manuscripts

Henry S. Harris

The importance of the concept of recognition in the *Phänomenologie des Geistes* can scarcely be overestimated since it is the root element of the concept of *Geist* itself.[1] The great arc of spirit's appearing goes from the mutual recognition of absolute enmity to that of absolute charity. The application of these two extremes (recognition in death, and recognition in life, as we might call them) to the relation of man and God is what then produces the concept of absolute knowledge.

It is for this reason that the evolution of the concept of recognition in Hegel's earlier manuscripts interests me. Of course, all of Hegel's discussions of recognition are interesting for their own sake. The life-and-death struggle, and its resolution in the relation of lord and bondsman, has attracted so much attention that the role of mutual recognition in Hegel's earlier reflections about labor and politics could never pass unnoticed. At the opposite pole, any formulation of the romantic ideal of love by a major thinker is bound to find an audience. But if we are to understand Hegel properly we must try to see these polar opposites in their proper systematic context; and there is no question that, in the end, what unites them is the concept of recognition. Examination of the earlier texts in this light seems to me to confirm—as we might expect—that the concept itself evolved steadily along with all of the content that it eventually served to relate.

---

1. Compare the way *Geist* is defined upon its first appearance (*Phänomenologie des Geistes*, ed. Hoffmeister (Hamburg, 1952), 140.

Thus, I find it significant that Hegel's interest in the *experience* of mutual recognition was first aroused when he was seeking to explicate the "living" religion of Greek mythology as a step toward the establishment of a new mythology consonant with the highest insights of the Kantian *Aufklärung*: "To observe a stream, how according to the laws of gravity it must fall ot deeper regions...is to comprehend it—to give it a soul, to take part in it as in one's equal—is to make a god of it—,"[2]

The enlivening of objects into subjects is only possible in the experience of love; and because it is rigidly contrasted with the mastering relation established by means of concepts, Hegel quite naturally maintains at this stage that the religious experience cannot be conceptualized: "Religion is one with love. The beloved is not opposed to us, he is one with our essential being; we see only ourselves in him—and yet also he is still not we—a miracle that we cannot grasp."[3]

Hegel's insistence that our relation to God in religious experience is one of love involves the equality of the participants. How there can be equality between the worshipper and his God is certainly a mystery, once we have abandoned the nymphs and dryads to the storybooks. But equality itself is a conceptual problem at this stage, in any case, since Hegel has analyzed conceiving as a kind of mastery. There are thus two basic reasons why the transition from finite reflection to the experience of the absolute must take place by a kind of leap, and must have a practical rather than a theoretical character.

The only obvious way out of the difficulty was to found the theory of the absolute on a different kind of cognitive experience altogether. The model for this was provided by the aesthetic theory of Schiller; and Hegel was already using that to explicate his thesis that "Religion ist eins mit der Liebe." But Schelling's theory of the absolute identity showed how one could begin from the *Anschauung* that "a divinity is subject and object, both at once"[4] and develop speculative knowledge from the top downward, comprehending everything from God's point of view. Thus, the endless striving for conceptual mastery that is involved in finite experience can be avoided. One can *first* make the leap to the experience of the absolute, and then develop one's philosophical science from there.

What is lost if one does this, however, is precisely the experience of the striving. The struggle of man toward self-knowledge and the knowl-

---

2. *Positiv wird ein Glauben genannt, Theologische Jugendschriften*, ed. Nohl (Tübingen, 1907), 376.
3. Ibid., 377.
4. Ibid., 376.

edge of God is frozen into eternal stillness, once we have *achieved* union with God and can look at everything from the divine point of view. Having come to the conclusion that the leap was unavoidably necessary, Hegel was bound to make it. But no one who has studied his early manuscripts closely would expect him to remain comfortable for very long when he found himself safe on the other side of the gulf. It was precisely the experience of the leaping that had always interested him.

For this reasons there is a great tension between the published and the unpublished writing in Hegel's early years at Jena. In the essays that appeared in the *Critical Journal of Philosophy*, for which Schelling and Hegel took joint responsibility and in which *nothing* was signed by either of them (except for a footnote in which Hegel denied that he was acting as Schelling's mouthpiece in writing and publishing the *Differenz*-Schrift) the experience of recognition serves to formulate the relation between identity philosophy and other philosophies but it has no place in the structure or development of our cognition of the absolute identity itself.[5] Even in the essay *On Natural Law*, in which we might reasonably expect to find the concept of recognition, it does not appear. This is all the more surprising because the life-and-death struggle is presented both as the path to servitude and as the realization of identity with the *Volk*; and the transition from *Sittlichkeit* (life in the *Volk*) to legal personality is treated historically just as it is in the *Phenomenology*.[6] We could hardly ask for a clearer instance of the suppression of a mode of thought that was peculiar to Hegel himself in order to maintain a common front with Schelling.

There is just one context in which the concept of recognition occurs in the published essays. In the *Differenz*-Schrift, Hegel wrote of "the inward Light-Principle" as positing itself in the natural polarity of sex:

---

5. See the *Einleitung* of the *Kritisches Journal* (in *Gesammelte Werke*, Band 4: *Jenaer Kritische Schriften*, ed. H. Buchner and O. Pöggeler [Hamburg, 1968], 117–28). The relation between identity philosophy and other speculative philosophies is analyzed as essentially one of mutual recognition—the aim of criticism being to bring out the identity that is recognized, by overcoming the differences that arise from historical circumstance or individual weakness. The relation between identity philosophy and reflective philosophies, on the other hand, is a "struggle for recognition" that must end in the demonstration of the nullity of the reflective opponent. This all or nothing alternative is the incipient dialectic of the concept of recognition. As a rigorously exclusive alternative it is perfectly compatible with "Shelling's system"; but I think we can be certain that this formulation of the theory of criticism originated with Hegel.

6. See *Gesammelte Werke*, Band 4, 448–50, 455–57.

"it posits itself as both subjective and objective and objective at once, still more firmly in the animal [than in the plant] through the polarity of the sexes; the individual seeks and finds itself in another. In the animal the light abides more intensively in the inner [life], where it posits itself as more or less changeable voice—or in other words, it posits animal individuality as something subjective in universal communication, self-cognizing and to be recognized."[7]

It is worth remembering here that although Hegel professes to be discussing (and indeed illustrating) "*Schelling's* system," he has not yet gone into a formal partnership with Schelling, in which their individual personalities are to be submerged. Also the language of "*self*-discovery" and "*self*-assertion" is plainly metaphorical here, since the animal is not properly capable of *self*-consciousness. Thus, the whole passage can pass as a rhetorical flourish, and need not be taken as having any implications for the conceptual analysis of *human* relations.

If we look at it in the context of the Frankfurt fragments on one side, and of the *Phänomenologie* on the other, however, it plainly *does* have important implications. The "incomprehensible" miracle of human sexual love is here exposed as being merely a natural instinct. It is mysterious only because it is *below* the level of thought, not because it is above it. Thus, the rational observer can quite easily say what the rationale of the animal's instinctive behavior is. "Self-recognition in the other" has become a *concept* because Hegel has found in the continuum of Schelling's *Naturphilosophie* a way to "dominate" it, and to employ it as a tool.

On the other side, the results of this conceptualization of sexual polarity are taken over into the structure of the *Phänomenologie* without change. The extremely enigmatic dialectic of "Leben und Begierde"[8] begins to yield up its secrets when we read it as an account of *sexual* desire, an account of how the *genus* appears to the living consciousness that is not yet self-conscious, or as a phenomenology of *animal* awareness. The passage is difficult precisely because Hegel does not personify the animal consciousness in the *Phänomenologie* as he did in the *Differenz*-Schrift.

What we catch a single glimpse of here in the *Differenz*-Schrift, therefore, is a veritable revolution in Hegel's thinking, which his partnership with Schelling obliged him to keep to himself. The first important result of it (at least among the documents that have come

---

7. Ibid., 73.
8. *Phänomenologie* (1952), 134–39.

down to us) is in the *System der Sittlichkeit*. In this manuscript the main conceptual schemas, the vocabulary of *Potenz, Anschauung, Begriff, Subsumtion, Totalität* and so on, belongs to the joint enterprise. I think it is a mistake to speak of all this equipment as simply borrowed or taken over from Schelling, but that is a question that others must settle. What is certain is that Hegel's use of it is very much his own; and we can see many signs of the emerging dialectic of consciousness in which recognition plays such a crucial role.

Thus, the reduction of sexual love to a mystery of nature is here confirmed: "each intuits herself in the other, though as a stranger, and this is *love*. The inconceivability of this being of oneself in another belongs therefore to nature, and not to ethical life, for the latter, with respect to the different [poles], is the absolute equality of both"[9] and the mysterious sentence that Hegel cancelled in the first draft of the Frankfurt fragment on love (*welchem Zwecke denn...*)—"the child is the parents themselves"[10]—is now explained through Hegel's doctrine of the realization of feeling as sense-perception: "In this perfectly individualized and realized feeling, the parents contemplate their unity as a reality; they are this feeling itself and it is their visible identity and mediation born from themselves."[11]

But when we move from the level of feeling and perception to that of thought and conception, no dialectical *concept* of mutual recognition is allowed to intrude. The education of the child and even the condition of *Bildung*, the state of equal independence in which family ties are dissolved, is described objectively (from above, so to speak) not subjectively (from within). We are allowed to see the implicit structure of consciousness as *feeling*, but not to observe the living motion of its development into thought.

Similarly, we are allowed to see the implicit structure of thinking consciousness, but not to observe the process by which it becomes *Sittlichkeit*. Communal recognition is clearly shown to be the presupposition and medium of all contract and exchange. The concept of legal personality emerges hand in hand with the institution of money as the "indifference" of (i.e., the universal expression for) property. This world of formal recognition is then differentiated into masters and servants *by the extent of their possessions* (i.e., ultimately in terms of money). For although Hegel speaks at first of "unequal power of life" and "greater

---

9. *System der Sittlichkeit*, ed. Lasson (Hamburg, 1967), 17–18.
10. *Positiv wird*, 381.
11. *System der Sittlichkeit*, 19.

strength or weakness" so that this whole paragraph[12] could easily be taken as description of serfdom, he ends by insisting that the difference between Herr and Knecht is *not* an absolute one (with respect to the concept of personality"): "the lord is in possession of a surplus, of what is physically necessary; the servant lacks it."[13] The relation of *Knecht-schaft*, whether it be between lord and serf, master and servant, or employer and wage-laborer is a relation of person to person. That is all that matters to Hegel's argument here. How the relationship is first set up, and how it develops from one stage to the next is not his present concern. He is simply expounding the theory of the household, and showing how it can come to have subordinate members within it. The whole theory of personality here culminates in a demonstration that effective individuality belongs properly to the family as a household *unit*. The communal recognition, upon which all of these variant relationships depend is properly a function of the *Volk*; it is an aspect of the "true reality" which "cannot fall within this Potenz."[14]

Hegel does, however, answer the question of how the system of recognition is set up, incidentally and partially, in the course of making his transition through "the negative, or freedom, or transgression." His object here is to show how the family group maintains itself in a state of nature, against the arbitrary freedom of self-conscious life. He treats first the barbarian hordes as the pure Intuition of the Negative, which even a united *Volk* can withstand only by reverting to the same condition itself. But then he considers the occurrence of open injuries, between free families or tribes. Injury here sets up vendetta chain reactions that can be terminated by the acceptance of the outcome of a battle of designated champions as the "judgment of God." But where the conflict concerns something that is a matter of life and death for the group we get a full-scale war, and the outcome of that (in the event of a clear victory) is bondage for the vanquished.

None of this is described in the way that it will be in the *Philosphie of Spirit* of 1803–4. Even the *On Natural Law* essay is clearer about war because the existence of the *Volk* is there explicitly presupposed, while here it is the goal of the development. But the equalization of conscious-nesses in the *Zweikampf*,the way in which good and bad conscience alike are blotted out in the ideal of honor, is a crucial element in the life-and-death struggle of the *Phänomenology*; and the fact that the destiny of

---

12. Ibid., 33–34.
13. Ibid., 35.
14. Ibid., 32.

the whole tribe hangs on the outcome of the conflict, shows us why the dialectic of recognition in the *Phenomenology* moves from the life-and-death struggle to *Herrschaft und Knechtschaft* without troubling about the fact that the self-consciousness that *does* "go to the death" cannot be enslaved. When an independent consciousness is wiped out (no matter how), the consciousness that is naturally dependent upon it always remains for enslavement.[15]

In the *System of Ethical Life* there is *no* apparent transition to *Sittlichkeit* proper at all. The dialectic of the Negative culminates with War, which can end either in conquest and enslavement, or in a standoff. Either of these outcomes could be the moment of begetting for a genuine political life. Thus, Hegel's early hero Theseus reconciled the warring tribes of Athens without enslavement; while the invading Dorians everywhere brought the indigenous agricultural population of the Peloponnese into subjection. Hegel was certainly as much interested in the founding of cities as he was in the founding of religions. But the structure of his system will not allow him to deal with it directly here. The family whether in the context of marketplace equality or in that of tribal aristocracy, is one *Potenz* of the Absolute *Idee*; the *polis* is another *Potenz*, the next higher (organically complete and independent) one. They are connected by having the same negative in crime and warfare. This is their "indifference point as identity," or the consciousness of the absolute *Begriff* as the unity of opposites (life at the nature pole, and freedom at the ethical pole). Hegel explicitly calls the *Wut* in which barbaric havoc becomes indistinguishable from the civilized defensive reaction "der absolute Begriff."[16]

On the opposite sides of this indifference point, the dialectic moves in opposite directions. On the side of Relation (the family) the argument goes always *upward* from feeling to thought, from nature to ethical relation; on that of *Sittlichkeit* (the *polis*) the dialectic moves downward

---

15. Some points in the *System der Sittlichkeit* that are relevant for the *Phänomenologie* become much clearer when we study it in connection with the "Philosophie des Geistes" of 1803–4. Thus, the way that all finite relationships are *equalized* (or made indifferent) in the family in "Die absolute Sittlichkeit nach dem Verhältnis," prepares us for the doctrine of the family as the "Selbständigkeit des Bewußtseins" in 1803–4; and this is what the expression still refers to in the *Phänomenologie*. And what the natural relation—or the resting concept—of dependent and independent consciousness is, is only half stated in the *System der Sittlichkeit*. The other side is explicitly stated for the first time in the "Philosophie des Geistes" of 1803–4.

16. *System der Sittlichkeit*, 43.

from ethical freedom to natural feeling. There is thus a mirror relation, a parallelism between the two main, *Potenzen*. At the same time, we know that there is a subsumptive order here too, that the later *Potenz* in the series is also higher. So we must look for the principle according to which the ascending sequence is articulated. We could fairly say that *this*, rather than the *Potenzbegriff* is the architectonic principle of the whole.

"Ethical life must be the absolute identity of intelligence, with complete annihilation of the particularity and relative identity which is all that the natural relation is capable of. . . an imperfect self-objectification and intuition of the individual in the alien [individual]," says Hegel.[17] If we ask where an experience of this kind is to be found in the lower *Potenz*, the answer is not far to seek. The objectification of the intelligence itself is *language. Bildung*, as the cultural interaction of free rational agents, is the medium in which the intuition of the *Volk* can exist. But in spoken language the objectification is essentially transient. It is more permanently realized in all the market relations of property-exchange and contract. Thus, *recognition*—subjective in *Bildung*, objective in commerce—is the element or medium of political existence. The connection is equally clear on the negative side, as soon as we look for it. The family experiences the negative might of the *Begriff* in theft and murder; the negation of that negation is the positive might of recognized custom, the communal *Sitten* that make transgression against any member into a *public* offense. Recognition is thus the absolute *Begriff* on its positive side, the concept as life rather than death, or as intelligence rather than nature.

But how can the incomplete objectification and self-intuition of the individual in the other that takes place in *Bildung* and in everyday commerce be accompanied, as Hegel says it is, by "völlige Indifferenz des Selbstgenusses"? For two of the three social classes the answer is obvious. The military nobility is the class of absolute *Sittlichkeit* (i.e., of "das absolute Leben im Vaterlande und für das Volk") because its primary calling is to defend the community on the battlefield. Thus, it experiences the cancellation of all other interests that are necessarily produced by the life-and-death struggle. At the other extreme (that of nature) the peasantry go through the same experience, supposedly without any clearly differentiated consciousness of private and public interests that needs to be wiped out. Thus, it is only in the class of relative *Sittlichkeit* that the problem becomes crucial. Here the sentiments of

---

17. Ibid., 52.

patriotism, "love for the fatherland, and the *Volk*, and its laws, which Hegel explicitly denies to be the true manifestation of absolute *Sittlichkeit*, must be maintained. The means for this is the religion of the *Volk*. All the justice of civil life, the habitual recognition of civic equality and personal rights, must be founded in a religious commitment to the maintenance of the communal life that is the real substance of which the private life of the citizen in all its specific circumstantial detail is a concrete mode: "and this universality which has strictly united the particular with itself is the divinity of the people, and this universal, intuited in the ideal form of particularity, is the God of the people. He is an ideal way of intuiting it."[18]

In the *System of Ethical Life* nothing finite is allowed to move. Hence all the developmental *activity* of consciousness is reduced as nearly as possible to the simple immediacy of feeling and perception, to *Anschauung*. Thought structures are examined only in formal abstaction, so that their phenomenological aspect vanishes from view—the different concrete shapes that they assume at different stages of social life are all lumped together or put side by side without comment. Nevertheless, what is here directly or abstractly presented includes everything necessary for a phenomenological display (of the Hegelian kind). The display is not carried out. But everything is prepared for it; and hence we can say that the bridge between human and divine self-consciousness is already in position.

As soon as his explicit partnership with Schelling came to an end, through the departure of Schelling from Jena, Hegel promptly set to work on an exposition of his system, which would make the bridge *visible*. His fidelity to the original common program of identity philosophy is shown by the fact that the system is still organized in *Potenzen*. But the "Begriff des Geistes" is declared at the outset to be consciousness;[19] and the development of *Bewußtsein* is analyzed as a process of "self-recognition in another." Much of the matter and argument of the *System of Ethical Life* is repeated in this new context, but the sequence of the stages is much easier to follow because the real connecting link is now explicit. I shall confine myself here mainly to the points where the discussion develops positions that we have already noted in the earlier manuscripts, and to the major anticipations of the way recognition

---

18. Ibid., 55.
19. The assertion is repeated in more than one draft—see *Gesammelte Werke*, Band 6, ed. K. Düsing and H. Kimmerle (Hamburg, 1975), 266 line 3, 269 lines 9–10, 280 lines 3–4.

appears in the *Phenomenology*. It would be impossible to deal, in a short essay, with all the ways in which this manuscript anticipates and throws light on the later work. Fragmentary and incomplete as it unfortunately is, and as I am inclined to suspect that it always was, this first attempt at a *Geistesphilosophie* within the triadic pattern that remained canonical for Hegel from henceforth, is by far the most important of his Jena manuscripts for the understanding of his first big book.

Let us begin, then, with the passage about Adam's naming of the animals: "the first act, by which Adam established his lordship over the animals, is this, that he gave them a name, i.e., he nullified them as beings (*Seyende*) and made them into ideal [entities] on their own."[20] Here we can see how much Hegel has preserved, in a modified form, of his original doctrine that "Begreifen ist beherrschen."[21] Consciousness is essentially a will to power. If man is to become self-conscious as a free being, this urge to control must itself be brought under a higher kind of control. Both the necessity and the futility, the self-frustrating character, of the life-and-death struggle can already be foreseen at this point, which is the crucial moment of the the firth *Potenz*, the birth of the spirit as language. For until we share the medium of language we are not spiritual beings at all: "in its sensing capacity the spirit itself is animal."[22] But the creation of language involves a dominating relation toward our world of experience; and our own initial access to the common language of the *Volk* involves *our* being dominated by those who already securely control it.

Language is the impersonal institution, the form of social consciousness, or of spirit, which is prerequisite to, and presupposed by, the dialectic of recognition in which *free* self-awareness is generated. Any language user is "self-conscious" is a sense (and he, or more particularly she, may be self-conscious in a highly sophisticated sense—as Ismene is, in Sophocles' *Antigone*, for example). But this linguistically mediated self-awareness is not yet "freedom," still less "rationality." So, whereas the *System of Ethical Life* began with the pratical *Potenz* of feeling, the new *Geistesphilosophie* begins with the theoretical *Potenz* of language. The *Phenomenology* will follow the path of the *Geistesphilosophie* (in a far more developed form). But the fact that the pattern is controlled and determined by the dialectical theory of recognition is much plainer in 1803–4 than it is in the mature work.

---

20. Ibid., 288 lines 4–6.
21. *Positiv wird*, 376.
22. *Gesammelte Werke*, Band 6, 293 lines 4–5.

Another sign of this controlling influence—of Hegel's determination to underline the necessity of the life-and-death struggle—is his emphasis on the "Freiheit des Eigensinns" that characterizes the "empty self."[23] This *Eigensinn*, the primitive determination of the immature human animal to have "its own way," is only explicitly referred to in the *Phenomenology* when the institution of servitude as already been established. In the *First Philosophy of the Spirit* it has to be referred to much earlier, because Hegel wants to examine the process of familial education (in which this *Eigensinn* is chastened and reformed into identification with the *Sitten*). In the *Phenomenology* education is only dealt with *explicitly* as a political process. There we watch rather the *rediscovery* of *Eigensinn* in reaction against a more external form of discipline.

Except for this early injection of *Eigensinn* (with an explicit glance forward to the "struggle for recognition")[24] the dialectic proceeds now through the same steps that are traversed in the exposition of the *Begriff* of self-certainty ("Gewißheit seiner selbst") in the *Phenomenology*.[25]

Thus, the first stage of this second *Potenz* of the *Philosophy of the Spirit* of 1803–4 is desire. This is a point of contact with the *Phenomenology* about which there will be little dispute. But the theory of "labor" that Hegel develops out of it here is only developed after the struggle-experience in the later work. The difference arises from the same cause as in the earlier case. Hegel introduces *Eigensinn* early because he wants to lay out the structure of family life as the "resting concept" of "independent consciousness"; and just as the domestic education of free men in childhood differs from the social discipline of the adult self, so the labor and skilled craftsmanship of an extended family or clan-group differs from that of a feudal manor.

This aspect of the dialectic of independent consciousness disappears from view in the *Phenomenology* because of Hegel's desire to focus our attention there on a logical sequence of singular *Gestalten*. But the next phase is one that we can still detect in the later work. For the highest development of *Begierde* is "love" which is the foundation for the institu-

---

23. Ibid., 296 line 8.
24. Ibid., 296 lines 11–13.
25. Or, at any rate, I want to *claim* that the same steps are traversed in that later discussion (*Phänomenologie*, 134–40). But, for reasons that we cannot here go into, they are present there only in an implicit form. My claim should therefore be treated strictly as a hypothesis for further investigation and testing. The way in which the present discussion leads to the same terminus in experience (the "Kampf um Anerkennung") is a solid enough reason for submitting the hypothesis to careful scrutiny.

tion of marriage. The crucial point at which "animal desire" becomes a *human* relationship is when "the woman comes to be a being on her own account for the man. She ceases to be [simply] an object of his desire."[26] The *Potenz* of the "tool" and of "labour" was taken up with the realization of Adam's lordship over the animals in the Garden that nature has bequeathed to him. But in the relation of Adam to Eve we reach the first dawning of the process of self-recognition. And it is *this* turning point that Hegel is referring to (if I am not mistaken) when he says in the *Phenomenology* that "the object of immediate desire is *something alive*."[27]

At this stage of the *Phenomenology* there is nothing explicit about the institution of marriage because the institution itself belongs to *Sittlichkeit*—the system of social recognition whose *real* evolution we (the philosophers) are there observing. We have still far to go in the *Phenomenology* before we can deal with institutional structures. But marriage as an experience, marriage in the sense of that "concord" that as the bachelor Hobbes rudely says, "dependeth upon natural lust,"[28] is the natural foundation of the *family*. The parents must recognize the relative permanence of their relationship (quite apart from any system of formal *public* recognition) if they are both to act as parents for the child—in whom as Hegel wrote in 1797 "the union itself has become undivided."[29] Each partner now exits in the consciousness of the other;[30] and both intend to exist in the consciousness of the child, by passing on to him all that they have learned about the world. The object of their labor of upbringing is to make it possible for them to step aside, and leave the child to carry on alone when they are gone. For this reason Hegel claims aphoristically "in that they bring its consciousness to life, they generate their own death."[31] This looks back to his concern about death as the dissolution of the bond of love in 1797. But the description of the educational process from the side of the child looks forward to the *Phenomenology*. For in Hegel's theory of education, the pupil is a *consciousness in subjection*. He must give up his *Eigensinn*, his own view and his own wishes, and accept the views and the goals of the grown-ups who are able to enforce their will upon him. In the "natural order," or the "ethics of relation," these grown-ups are his parents. Thus, the

---

26. *Gesammelte Werke*, Band 6, 301 lines 16–17.
27. *Phänomenologie*, 135.
28. *Leviathan*, chap. 13.
29. *welchem Zwecke denn*, 381.
30. See *Gesammelte Werke*, Band 6, 302 lines 7–8.
31. Ibid., 303 line 13.

or the "ethics of relation," these grown-ups are his parents. Thus, the relation between parent and child (and specifically of father and son) is the "Pure Begriff of Recognition" expounded at the beginning of the section the *Phenomenology* called "Selbständigkeit und Unselbständigkeit des Selbstbewußtseins; Herrschaft und Knechtschaft."[32] If we read what Hegel says there in the light of what he says about domestic education in the *System of Ethical Life* and the first *Geistesphilosophie* taken together, all is plain. Father and son as adults *do* recognize each other, and the son does go off into the world to do what the father has already done. He has suffered subjection in order that he may *come* to mastery. But as a true master he must demonstrate his independence, or else those who now are dependent on him in the natural order will suffer subjection in a new non-natural, way. The "independent consciousness" that is committed to the struggle in the *Phenomenology* is the same "totality of consciousness" that is committed to it in the first *Philosophy of the Spirit*. It is the "strong man keeping his goods" (which include his wife, children, servants, his ox, ass, and so forth).

Because of the mutilated state of the text we cannot be certain how Hegel made the transition from the *Potenz* of the family and its goods to the "struggle for recognition." To me the most plausible hypothesis is that the struggle functions as "the negative" in a transition from "formal existence" (the family) to "real existence" (the *Volk*). On this view, the basic pattern of the *System of Ethical Life* is preserved, while the adoption of the standpoint of *Bewußtsein* renders the sequence of the stages much more straightforward. But nothing important to my present argument hangs on the acceptance of this interpretation. The text is all that matters, and one could not ask for a clearer confirmation of my present thesis than the way the next fragment of the final draft begins: ". . . it is absolutely necessary that the totality which consciousness has reached in the family recognizes itself as the totality it is in another such totality of consciousness. . . This is reciprocal *recognition* in general, and we are to see how this recognition. . . can exist."[33] Just why the

---

32. *Phänomenologie*, 141. For the proper understanding of the argument in the *Phänomenologie*, it is (as I see it) vitally necessary to grasp that the first clause of this heading refers to the family (or tribal) relation *before* the struggle for recognition, while the second clause refers to the estranged social relation *after* the struggle. Otherwise we shall not comprehend what the struggle is really about, and we shall never be able to see how a struggle that logically *terminates* in the death of one or both of the contestants, can none the less *result* in the servitude of a dependent consciousness.

33. *Gesammelte Werke*, Band 6, 307 lines 3–5, 7–10.

securing of recognition must eventually bring on a mortal conflict is clearly stated in both drafts; but for that matter it was already clear enough in the *System of Ethical Life*. Before the establishment of a general system of universally recognized legal rights, the security of property can only rest on a sense of honor (like that of Achilles, for example) which sees itself as embodied in *all* of its goods, and hence as "touched" whenever those goods are touched against their master's will. Apart from this conception of the family personality the struggle for recognition cannot arise as a strictly *individual* phenomenon. Empirically it never *is* a strictly individual experience; for in the actual genesis of political society it is not the nuclear family or household, but the extended family or tribal household, that comes to be united with others like it in the *Volk*. Thus neither here, nor in the *Phenomenology*, is Hegel pretending to offer a historical account of the genesis of political society. The transition from the "state of nature" to "political society," which is what is expounded in both works, is an ideal construction designed to show us the function and significance of aggression and of the resulting fear of injury and death in the development of rational consciousness, and particularly in the formation of rational social institutions.

Thus, the fact that the outcome of the struggle in the first *Geistesphilosophie* is the establishment of *Sittlichkeit*, whereas in the *Phenomenology* it is the institution of servitude is not difficult to explain. The clear statement regarding the logically possible outcomes of war in the *System of Ethical Life* is the only key that we need. The struggle can end in a standoff, or a victory that is not decisive, and a long series of such struggles can terminate in the making of a political union by some Theseus, on the basis of the mutual respect created by the struggles. If one's object is to show how the *Sittlichkeit* of Sophoclean drama came into being, then this mutual respect is the *necessary* outcome of the struggle, since only a prepolitical experience of this sort can make the work of a Theseus *possible. Both* sides must abandon their *Eigensinn*.[34] This is Hegel's concern in 1803–4.

But the struggle can also end in the outright victory of one party. Sometimes, indeed, this outcome is the "necessary" (this is to say the *natural*) one: as, for instance, in the conflict between what Hegel calls in the *Phenomenology* "the animal and plant religions."[35] The inevitability of the outcome here is his way of justifying Aristotle's verdict that the Oriental peoples were all natural slaves, not properly capable of

---

34. Ibid., 315 line 18.
35. See *Phänomenologie*, 485.

political existence. But where the outcome is "necessary" in this sense, it is the struggle itself that is not really "necessary."

Where the struggle is really a struggle, and the outcome is definite or decisive, we have the situation analyzed in the *Phenomenology*. If the victory is decisive enough to result in the complete subjection of the vanquished, then the outcome was empirically necessary, that is, it was historically inevitable. But, at the same time, to say that the struggle was necessary is precisely to assert that this outcome was *spiritually* accidental, that it was the simple result of the balance of natural forces between the parties, and that victory could just as easily have gone the other way if circumstances had been different. The "necessary" outcome in this case (the real case of Sparta and Messenia, and—at a higher livel— of the free peoples conquered by the Romans) is a subjection that is not natural but spiritual. *Eigensinn* is not now surrendered, but it has to go underground, and it finds its satisfaction in quite novel shapes. And if one's object is not the comprehension of the *Sittlichkeit* of Sophocles, but the reintegration of modern *Moralität* into a new, rationally self-consciou *Sittlichkeit*, then *this* is the line of "necessary" development that one will eventually have to follow to its end.

In fact, *both* the Athenian line of development and the Spartan-Roman one are "necessary," but if we are going to follow the evolution of the *Gestalten* of *individual* consciousness beyond the point of the struggle, we *must* follow the Spartan-Roman line. In the *Geistesphilosophie* of 1803–4 the Athenian line is the one that Hegel follows. Consciousness therefore ceases at this point to be a *personal* function and becomes impersonal. Similarly, recognition becomes impersonal, that is to say, it becomes a function of public institutions. The dialectical concept of recognition[36] would eventually have emerged once more, when the discussion reached the level of absolute spirit, or religion; but the manuscript breaks off long before we get that far. What it offers us before

---

36. The dialectical concept of recognition is that which empresses the structure of a relation in which each side recognizes *itself* in the other, but in which the equality of the parties is not—or not yet—admitted. In the dialectic of social relations a *real* motion toward equality is necessarily set up by this kind of self-recognition. But it is important to realize that in the conceptual sphere there can equally well be an *ideal* motion from simple equality to dialectical inequality. Thus, the doctrine of "the one eternal Reason" in which spirit recognizes spirit (see, for instance, the *Differenz*-Schrift, *Gesammelte Werke*, Band 4, 10, 31; and compare n. 5) becomes in Hegel's mature conception of the history of philosophy a dialectical process in which the *inequality* of different speculative visions is what makes their historical sequence important.

it breaks off is Hegel's most detailed account of the economic evolution of modern society as an ever-deepening *breakdown* of self-recognition, of the growing barriers against the laborer's finding himself in his work, or his finding a reflection of his human nature in his actual life. This was a problem that Hegel became conscious of very early, and which he cannot be said ever to have solved. Since the *Weltgeist* appears not to have solved it yet, this is no great wonder.

When we move on from the first *Geistesphilosophie* to the second one, which Hegel wrote two years later, the change in the form of presentation is dramatic, even though the sequence of dialectical stages is not very different. But the most important difference is that this time the enterprise is carried through to a conclusion. Perhaps we do not have all that Hegel wrote about the *Volk* in 1803–4. But it seems to me certain that he did not finish the system to his own satisfaction; and his previous failure to complete the *System of Ethical Life* is beyond dispute.

The other important difference is that the principle of consciousness has been pushed into the background once more. Instead, we see here the first sketch of the mature articulation of objective spirit into the stages of family, civil society, and state. The dialectic of family consciousness and the transition to civil society (here called *Anerkanntseyn*) follows the pattern established two years before: beginning with the evolution of language we pass to the dialectic of desire, labor, and love. The family is summed up in the following moments:

''(a) [the moment] of love as natural, [the] begetting of children;
(b) self-conscious love, conscious feeling [*Empfindung*], awareness [*Gesinnung*];
(c) shared labour, and acquisition, reciprocal help and care;
(d) education.
No single [moment] can be made into the whole purpose,''[37]

Hegel—and in that single comment, the contrast with the point of view of 1803–4 can be seen, for the remark in the earlier manuscript about the parents "generating their own death" as they educate the child was meant to underline the sense in which education is the goal of the whole institution.[38]

---

37. *Gesammelte Werke*, Band 8, ed. R.-P. Horstmann, et al. (Hamburg, 1976), 213 lines 4–8.
38. The simplification of the dialectical chain in the *Phänomenologie* has a similar object. But the fact that in that simplification love, labor, and education are all alike pushed into the background in favor of independence and freedom brings out the essential relativity of any attempt to isolate one moment as the *Zweck* of the whole.

The struggle for recognition is now explicitly declared to be the ideal transition from the "state of nature." It is what takes the place in Hegel's theory of the "original contract" in the philosophy of the Enlightenment. This fact was already marginally noted in the manuscript of 1803–4.[39] But now it becomes the point of focal importance, since the transition is here made directly from the struggle to the world of "social contracts," the civil society of recognized status.[40]

By reverting to something like the procedure of the *System of Ethical Life*, and discussing civil society abstractly, before proceeding to discuss political existence proper, Hegel avoids the bad infinity of the historical dialectic of the economic system—which is where the manuscript of 1803–4 (as we have it) appears to founder. When he comes to deal with constitutional theory, he is similarly able to express the conceptual significance of either outcome of the life-and-death struggle, without having to bring the historical process itself within the scope of his systematic dialectic. He does this by showing that the conceptual justification of political tyranny is that it reduces all citizens to a state of common subjection that makes the rule of law, the condition of *Anerkanntseyn*, possible. Theseus, the great hero of Hegel's youth, is now put in the same class as the Peisistratidae, whose overthrow the Athenians celebrated in their songs of freedom.[41] In fact, his examples here range all the way from Theseus to Robespierre, by way of Machiavelli's *Prince*. But it is evident enough that there was a difference in Hegel's mind between the founding of Athens by Theseus, and the establishment of the French Republic, even though he mentions them both in the same breath. This coincidence, which is only the most striking example of the tension between naive *Sittlichkeit* on the one side, and properly self-possessed introreflected political consciousness on the other, which pervades the whole discussion, shows us the cost of Hegel's retreat from the more phenomenological experiment of two years earlier.

The *Philosophy of the Spirit* of 1805–6, does, however, contain one important new development in the use and application of the dialectic

---

39. *Gesammelte Werke*, Band 6, 315 lines 15–18.
40. How this transition is to be understood as "necessary" I have already explained. For this is the same transition from the familial "state of Nature" to the political community of the *Volk* that was presented in the manuscript of 1803–4. But now it is first viewed abstractly—that is, in terms of its significance for the normal relations of single households—whereas in 1803–4 it was viewed *concretely*—that is, as the consciousness (either direct or mediated) of a new social whole.
41. *Gesammelte Werke*, Band 8, 258 lines 10 and 27.

of recognition. Hegel's original problem in 1797, we should here recall, concerned the process of mutual recognition between man and God. Until 1806 none of his systematic manuscripts got to the point of dealing with this problem, though we know from Rosenkranz and Haym that Hegel dealt with it, sometimes at length, in his lectures. Haym complains that the lecture manuscript from which the *System of Ethical Life* was written up degenerated into "mere history."[42] He is, of course, a very dangerous and unreliable authority on this question, he could not begin to comprehend the systematic character of the *Phenomenology* itself.[43] All the same I think he was perhaps not far from expressing what Hegel himself felt when he first endeavored to reduce his lectures to a handbook for his students.[44] For although we know that he had earlier attempted (perhaps more than once) to deal with the evolution of religion historically—as a "history of God," in fact[45]—Hegel is satisfied in 1806 to present the absolute religion not in a historical context at all, but in the context of a contemporary theory of Church and State: "man lives in two worlds—in one he has *his own actuality, which vanishes,* . . . in the other his absolute preservation—he knows himself as absolute essence—He dies to actuality with [its] knowing and willing, in order to acquire the eternal—the *unactual, life* in the [realm of] thought— [*the*] *universal* self."[46]

And in his conclusion he briefly expounds this self-recognition of the *Volk* in its God as the speculative self-knowledge of the philosopher: "In philosophy it is the Ego as such, that is the knowing of the absolute

---

42. *Hegel und seine Zeit* (Berlin, 1857), 164.

43. He calls it "eine durch die Geschichte in Verwirrung und Unordnung gebrachte Psychologie, und eine durch die Psychologie in Zerrüttung gebrachte Geschichte" (*Hegel und serine Zeit*, 243).

44. I take the *System der Sittlichkeit* manuscript to be part of the textbook that Hegel planned to publish for his first "encyclopedic" course in the summer semester of 1803; see *Hegel-Studien* 4 (1967): 54. But, of course, I do not in any way dissent from the current interpretation of the reports of Rosenkranz and Haym, who associated it with the manuscripts of Hegel's lectures on *Naturrecht* that were still available to them.

45. See *K. Rosenkranz: Hegels Leben* (Berlin, 1844), 133–41, for the fullest account of how the lecture manuscript, from which the *System der Sittlichkeit* was written up, continued. The fragmentary manuscripts that have survived from the immediately following years tend to support the hypothesis that Hegel made more than one attempt to write the "history of God." (Compare *ist nur die Form. Gesammelte Werke*, Band 6, 330–31; and *seiner Form* (which will be published in Band 5).

46. *Gesammelte Werke*, Band 8, 284 lines 9–14.

spirit. . . Ego *is* here *cognizant* of the Absolute; cognizes it—comprehends it—it is nothing else—*immediately*, it is *this* self."⁴⁷ Surely the doubled emphasis on *erkennt* (i.e. cognizant) here is meant to remind us of the process of *Anerkennung* which provided the path to this final self-indentification of man and God.

Thus, this last systematic manuscript of the Jena period adds the coping stone to the great arc of recognition in the *Phänomenologie*. But at the same time it abandons the concrete method of approach, in which every step is viewed as a stage in the actual "experience of consciousness." Hegel seems to have discovered this approach when he was working out the transition from the family to the *Volk* in the *System of Ethical Life*. His first deliberate attempt to use it apparently came to grief over the difficulty of organizing the economic development of modern society into a "systematic" form that was not simply an analytical narrative of its actual history. Everyhting that we know about Hegel's philosophy of religion from *Faith and Knowledge* onward strongly suggests that he experienced the same difficulty in that area.

The system of 1805–6 represents a surrender on both the economic and the religious fronts. It illustrates graphically why we should not think of Schelling as Hegel's "evil genius," who *imposed* a suprahistorical systematic ideal upon his mind. For although the system of 1803–4 still uses much Schellingian conceptual equipment that has vanished from the system of 1805–6, the latter is much closer in spirit to the system described in the *Differenz*-Schrift than the former.

At the same time, the system of 1805–6 tells us that the surrender is temporary. It is the prelude to a new beginning. The "history of God" that is banished from within its own structure is the last thing that it refers to: "It [the Spirit] has to establish the unity for itself—and hence [ebenso] in the form of immediacy it is *world history*. In world history what is sublated is this: that nature and spirit are only *implicitly* [ansich] one *essence*—spirit comes to be the knowing of that same [nature]." And the final marginal addition is an explicit reference to the total system into which this characterization of the projected *Phenomenology* fits: ". . . Man does not become master over nature, till he has become it over himself—Nature is in itself the cecoming of man *to the spirit*; for this "in-itself" to *be there*, the Spirit must comprehend itself."⁴⁸

Thus, by the time he wrote out the system of 1805–6 Hegel had realized that the task of systematic philosophy is twofold. *First* there

---

47. Ibid., 286 lines 16–21.
48. Ibid., 287 lines 21–27.

is the conceptual struggle across the great gulf between man and God; *then* there is the conceptual presentation of the world from the divine point of view. He had seen from the first (i.e., from 1797) that the relation between man and God must be understood and expressed in terms of free mutual recognition, not in terms of domination; he had seen also that if the recognition of God is an intuitive "leap" the world of finite experience cannot be satisfactorily comprehended after the leap. This was his fundamental complaint against Spinoza, and it conditions his attitude towards Schelling's essentially Spinozist view of the absolute identity from the *Differenz*-Schrift onward. As a result of his struggles to overcome this weakness in identity philosophy he discovered how to conceptualize recognition; but he also came to see that the "system of recognition" must be clearly distinguished from the "system of philosophy" as such. It thus becomes the "first part" of the system, the essential prolegomenon. And finally—last but no means least!—he experienced and exemplified the inevitable weakness of a system that lacks this prolegomenon. Without it, we cannot successfully distinguish at the level of self-conscious spirit between the "form of immediacy" and the form of conceptual self-possession, between Paradise created, and Paradise lost and regained. We shall always be able to *see* the difference between the conqueror of the Minotaur and the "seagreen Incorruptible";[49] but the true philosophy should enable us to *say* what we see.

---

49. Robespierre. (*Thomas Carlyle's* phrase in *The French Revolution*, Part II, Book IV, chap. 4, last sentence, sums up the combination of high principles and coward's complexion that he ascribed to the lawyer from Arras.)

CHAPTER 14

Notes on Hegel's "Lordship and Bondage"

George Armstrong Kelly

What is living in Hegel? The mid-twentieth century is prone to answer: his sense of the collective, his notion of a politically structured people as the unit of historical meaning, his grounding of right in intersubjective purpose, his penetrating explorations of psychological and sociological conflict. Both admirers and hostile critics fasten onto these categories, because, as issues of debate, they are not only living in Hegel, but living in our time.

Thus, Hegel's philosophy did not, as it were, merely paint "gray on gray." Not surprisingly, however, contemporary interest in this "ultimate philosophy" is due chiefly to the suggestive expansion of its insights, rather than to any desire for systematic reconstruction. In a discretionary way, Hegelian problems and patterns have gained a new lease in the fields of social and religious thought and among those for whom classical political theory is not a dead exercise. One might say that Hegel remains vital because he continues to raise polemical questions. When a giant structure of human speculation is superseded—a fate that some feel, wrongly I think, that Hegel tacitly acknowledged for his own philosophy—but survives *in membris disjectis*, anthologies tend to be compiled for partisan purposes. Karl Löwith reminds us that this was the destiny of the fragile Hegelian balance in the hands of the philosopher's immediate disciples.[1] The last generation has seen a renewal of this *Kulturkampf*, but now on the far side of total war, Marxism, and

---

1. See Karl Löwith, *From Hegel to Nietzsche*, trans. David E. Green (New York, 1964), 65–135.

religious crisis. The opposition of "What did Hegel mean?" and "What does Hegel mean for us?" is posed and reposed. I personally feel—as a historian of ideas—that some intellectual mischief is caused by the failure to raise the two questions in mutual rapport.

An important case in point would be the characteristic modern treatment of Hegel's famous scenario of "Lordship and Bondage," the account of liberation through work that so deeply affected the young Karl Marx in his 1844 manuscripts.[2] This tableau is most fully developed in the *Phänomenologie des Geistes* of 1807, but is also covered more tersely in the *Propädeutik* (1808–45), and the *Enzyklopädie der philosophischen Wissenschaften* (editions 1817, 1827, 1830, and 1840–45), essayed in rudimentary form in both series of Jena lectures on the philosophy of spirit (1803–4 and 1805–6), alluded to in the *Grundlinien der Philosophie des Rechts* (1821), and, according to some interpreters, foreshadowed in the discussion of Hebrew religion in the so-called early theological essays.[3] As a form of consciousness, lordship and bondage was continuously indispensable to Hegel's dialectical deduction of the formation of subjective mind and had occupied him from his earliest attempts to construct a system. Since there can be no quarrel about the centrality of this philosophical "moment," it becomes essential to grasp its precise meaning and content.

A full précis of this much admired passage will be dispensed with here. I have no particular dispute with, for example, Hyppolite's treatment, as far as it goes.[4] However, many modern readings—inspired by Kojève's artful exegesis in his *Introduction à la lecture de Hegel*[5]—tend

---

2. Karl Marx, *The Economic and Philosophical Manuscripts of 1844*, ed. Dirk J. Struik (New York, 1964), esp. 170–93 ("Critique of the Hegelian Dialectic and Philosophy as a Whole"). Marx writes (p. 177): "The outstanding achievement of Hegel's *Phenomenology* and of its final outcome . . . is thus first that Hegel conceives the self-creation of man as a process, conceives objectification as loss of the object, as alienation and as tanscendence of this alienation; that he thus grasps the essence of labor and comprehends objective man . . . as the outcome of man's *own labor.*" It would be appropriate here to mention that, like Hegel, I assign no particular significance of nuance to the synonyms "slavery," "bondage," and "servitude." I have also chosen to avoid taxing the patience of the reader with unnecessary dialectical vocabulary.

3. Cf. Jean Hyppolite, *Genèse et Structure de la Phénoménologie de l'Esprit de Hegel* (Paris, 1946), I, 166; and T. M. Knox, trans., *Hegel's Early Theological Writings* (Chicago, 1948), into. by R. Kröner, 13.

4. Hyppolite, *Genèse et Structure*, I, 161–71.

5. This remarkable study is a compilation of Alexandre Kojève's courses on the *Phenomenology* (ed. Raymond Queneau [Paris, 1947]), given at the Sorbonne in the years 1933–39, which exerted a powerful influence on Sartre and French Hegelianism in general.

to distort lordship and bondge in the total Hegelian structure. Though every student of Hegel is deeply enriched by Kojève, this experience is not without its dangers. In the present case, the difficulty seems to me chiefly twofold: the subjectivity of the scenario is largely ignored, and the master-slave relationship is made an unqualified device for clarifying the progress of human history. The one tendency leads to a unilaterally "social" interpretation of the *Phenomenology*, particularly the section on *Selbstbewusstsein*;[6] the other easily gathers in anachronistic overtones of the Marxian class struggle.

The regulative idea of lordship and bondage runs like a golden thread through much of Kojève's analysis. His general introduction stresses the point: "The Slave alone is able to transcend the World as it is (in thrall to the Master) and not perish. The Slave alsone is able to transform the World that forms him and fixes him in bondage, and to create a World of his own making where he will be free."[7] In a later passage, Kojève asserts that he has given an "anthropological" reading of the *Phenomenology*, and that Hegel intends a "metaphysical" dimension as well, the two currents being necessarily syncretized in the final chapter on absolute knowledge.[8] A footnote here seems to clarify Kojève's resolve to treat equally of the interior and exterior relations of the consciousness (as was surely Hegel's purpose) under the anthropological notion. But, in fact, although both exterior (political) and interior (psychological) consequences are acknowledged, he sees the master-slave relationship purely as an external confrontation. For Kojève this *motif* persists in various ascending forms until the Hegelian end of time. Thus: Work and Struggle = Freedom = Time = History = Transience = Nothing = Man. In more humble language, the future belongs to the once-terrorized

---

6. "Awareness" is conceivably a better translation of *Bewusstsein* than is "consciousness," but there are problems with each. I have reluctantly chosen the traditional term because in Hegel's language *Bewusstsein* is an agent as well as a condition or capacity.

7. Kojève, 34.

8. Ibid., 308–9 and 308n. A comment on the perspective of the *Phenomenology* imposes itself at this point. I tend to agree with those who hold that the sequence and development of the *Phenomenology* are *sui generis* and related to the intention of the work, as juxtaposed, especially, to the *Encyclopedia*. Thus, these differences alone do not allow us to conclude that Hegel changed his philosophical viewpoint between 1807 and 1817. In cases of disagreement between a "philosophy of mind" and a "phenomenology of mind," caution of interpretation is advised. This reservation does not seem applicable to the case of "lordship and bondage."

producer, progressively liberated by the spiritualized quality of his own labor, not to the seemingly omnipotent consumer, who treats both the servant and his product as mere dead things. Effectively, the slave releases history from nature, and it is the slave's satisfaction that will bring history to a close. Thus, while retaining the Hegelian primacy of ideas over things, Kojève, like Marx, tends to regard forms of servitude as epiphenomena of the relations of production.

As students of the career of philosophical ideas know, Kojève's lectures on Hegel have had an enormous impact. To take a recent example, the British scholar, John Plamenatz, in his two volumes on European political thought, has, with full acknowledgment, provided a Kojève *cum* Hyppolite reading in his chapter on the *Phenomenology*. He casts lordship and bondage entirely at the interpersonal level, and his conclusion reflects the familiar line of argument: "the future is with the slave. It is his destiny to create the community in which everyone accords recognition to everyone else, the community in which Spirit attains its end and achieves satisfaction."[9] But where did Hegel ever say this? Plamenatz's criticisms of Hegel (via the French commentaries) are grounded in the same analysis. How, he inquires, can one explore the possibilities of community in terms of one master and one slave, as Hegel appears to do? How can one refuse to see that manual toil is not the exclusively dignified form of labor; is there not also managerial toil?[10] Although Hegel is sometimes no easier to vindicate than he is to understand, this type of question will not seem so pressing if lordship and bondage is given a more balanced, more "phenomenological" interpretation. By "phenomenological" I mean that Hegel's ego must be seen here as an ideal type, collective only in the sense of exemplary, subject to a genetic onslaught of existential moods (*Gestalten*), each of which will be cancelled but also retained as a moment of eternal significance.

I am not proposing some legerdemain that will take the "social" out of Hegel. Clearly he argues that the true ethical life (*Sittlichkeit*) of man is "concrete" and "objective," grounded in collective experience according to the immanent harmonics of a rational community where liberty and order coalesce. "The experience of what spirit is," according to the *Phenomenology*, is "the Ego that is 'we', a plurality of Ego, and 'we' that is a

---

9. John Plamenatz, *Man and Society*, 2 vols. (New York, 1963), II 155.
10. Ibid., II 190–92. However, neither Kojève nor, especially, Karl Marx would ask Plamenatz's second question. Cf. Marx, *Manuscripts of 1844*, 177: "The only labor which Hegel knows and recognizes is *abstractly mental labor.*"

single Ego."[11] Although the pages that introduce the discussion of self-consciousness announce this principle, collective mind does not become a reality until reason (*Vernunft*) achieves intersubjectivity and passes into spirit (*Geist*).[12] Lordship and bondage is a "moment" of *Selbstbewusstsein* that foreshadows society and has explicit historical ramiscations. However, the view that the scenario represents a purely social phenomenon is one-sided and needs correction.

What I am about to argue is that lordship and bondage is properly seen from three angles that are equally valid and interpenetrable. One of these angles is necessarily the social, of which Kojève has given such a dazzling reading. Another regards the shifting pattern of psychological domination and servitude within the individual ego. The third then becomes a fusion of the other two processes: the interior consequences wrought by the external confrontation of the self and the other, the other and the self, which has commenced in the struggle for recognition (*Kampf des Anerkennens*).[13] On the overtly social plane there are, at a given point in history, slaves and masters. In the interior of consciousness, each man possesses faculties of slavery and mastery in his own regard that he struggles to bring into harmony; the question arises whenever the will encounters a resistant "otherness" that goes beyond mere physical opposition to its activity. In turn, the social and personal oppositions are mediated by the fact that man has the capacity to enslave others and to be enslaved by them. Because of the omnipresence of spirit the continuum is not broken by the distinction between world and self.[14]

In brief, man remits the tensions of his being upon the world of fellow beings and is himself changed in the process. This relationship should be stressed, since it furnishes the bridge between psychology and history. Let it be added here also that Hegel's psychology is moral, not analytical: this is why experience continually causes it to shift its ground

---

11. G. W. F. Hegel, *Phänomenologie des Geistes*, ed. J. Homffmeister (Hamburg, 1952), 140; *Phenomenology of Mind*, trans. J. Baillie (London, 1927), 227. I have furnished Baillie's translation throughout.
12. Ibid., Hoffmeister, 313ff.; Baillie, 455ff.
13. Among the various classical and biblical resonances of this image (e.g., Eteocles and Polynices, Cain and Abel), one detects the motif of Jacob's struggle with the angel, secularized in Hegel's hands. Cf. Genesis 32:24–28: "Let me go and I will bless thee" becomes "Let me go and I will serve thee."
14. Here, one is tempted to believe that as in so many other sectors, Hegel begins with a characteristically Aristotelian image; cf. *Politics*, 1255b: "The part and the whole, like the body and the soul, have an identical interest; and the slave is part of the master, in the sense of being a living but separate part of his body.

and why it is, in the deepest sense, historical, a psychology of development, a *Bildungsroman*.

On the one hand, Hegel is showing that mere political mastery or subjection cannot inaugurate the long adventure of history and freedom unless faculties of the subjective mind, necessarily present in all men, create the possibility and condition the result. On the other hand, it is clear that none of this is conceivable in a solipsistic universe. "Es ist ein Selbstbwusstsein für ein Selbstbewusstsein"[15] is the abrupt and dramatic prelude to the struggle for recognition out of which mastery and slavery will arise. The possibility of philosophy, morality, and right depends on the postulation of a second finite ego and, ultimately, on the assumption of a plurality of egos. Much in the same way that Fichte produces a second ego in order to ground his doctrine of natural right,[16] Hegel posits society at the dawn of self-consciousness for a still more profound purpose: the analysis of the broken ego striving to restore itself. But if the self and the other are, to speak bluntly, men, they also dwell within each man. They are original principles of the ego, awakened to combat by the appearance of another ego in which they are reduplicated, and thenceforward transformed by history. Without this shock, there would be no history, only desire *(Begierde)*, man's link with the animal world, and the unproductive and repetitive cycles of biological nature.

Hegel is, to be sure, much less explicit about the internal aspects of lordship and bondage than he is about the interpersonal and historical dimensions. The most casual reading of the *Phenomenology* and other texts makes clear that Hegel intends the analysis of relations among men and a reflection on the rise of historical communities through conquest. But my elucidation in no way denies this obvious fact.

Certain other contingencies obscure the reading I am suggesting. In the first place, the "social" implications of the tableau are even more emphatic in the Jena sketches, to which a scholar will wisely refer if he wants to understand the evolution of Hegel's thought. In many passages of this early and experimental "philosophy of the spirit" Hegel is deeply concerned with the concrete formation of society, the nature of work and its elevation to spiritual substantiality, and the creation of

---

15. Hegel, *Enzyklopädie und Schriften aus der Heidelberger Zeit, Sämtliche Werke*, VI, ed. H. Glockner (Stuttgart, 1927), paragraph 352, 253: "It is a self-consciousness for a self-consciousness."
16. J. G. Fichte, *Grundlage des Naturrechts, Sämmelte Werke*, III (Berlin, 1845), 30ff.; *The Science of Right*, trans. A. E. Kroeger (Philadelphia, 1869), 48ff. "Natural right" demands a judge, a "third party," and this is precisely the facility that Hegel denies to the origin of civil society.

a scheme of dialectical development. Different sequences of unfolding and different terminologies—some derivative (mainly Schellingian) and some original—are essayed in these lectures. What will later have discrete places in the treatment of subjective and objective spirit—desire, labor, love, family, *Volksgeist*, and the like—are seen struggling for systematic deployment. And admittedly in the "recognition" scenario the emphasis is on the concrete and social. In the 1803–4 lectures, the deduction of the family precedes the struggle for recognition, indicating that Hegel is here concerned with anthropohistorical development rather than the presentation of "facts of consciousness."[17] But in the 1805–6 lectures, in a passage corresponding to what Hegel will later call "anthropology" (the forms of the human soul before the awakening of consciousness), the other is evoked as a Schellingian "dark principle": "The Other [is] Evil, a being-in-itself, the subterranean principle, the thing which knows what lies in daylight and witnesses how it purposively [brings about] its own decline, or is in such active opposition that, on the contrary, it substitutes negativity for its own being, for its own self-preservation."[18] The *Encyclopedia* will clarify for us how the preconscious being is bifurcated even before it gains awareness of its own selfhood, and how lordship and bondage will display an analogous autoalienation at the higher conscious level.

A second factor that might mislead is the characteristic Hegelian insistence, against Kant, that the properties of the mind are integral and not the derivations of separate faculties or principles, like theoretical and practical reason (cognition and will),[19] or like the Fichtean dichotomy of finite ego and pure ego resolved only by an *ought*.[20] Of course, this is the "standpoint of reason," the goal of the Hegelian philosophy. But one obviously cannot jump from here to the conclusion that lower forms of consciousness apprehend themselves monistically. In fact, the opposite is true, whether the other is felt as impulse, as a hostile stranger, or as a transcendent God. Since Hegelian philosophy is process, even though its apotheosis is unity, it has mostly to do with the logical, genetic, or historical oppositions that have come about in the progress of the spirit.

G. R. G. Mure, in his excellent study of Hegel's *Logic*, has called particular attention to the dualistic tread of "higher" and "lower" prin-

---

17. Hegel, *Jenenser Realphilosophie*, I, ed. J. Hoffmeister (Leipzig, 1932), 223ff.
18. *Jenenser Realphilosophie*, II, ed. J. Hoffmeister (Leipzig, 1931), 200.
19. See, for example, Hegel, *Philosophy of Right*, trans. and ed. T. M. Knox (Oxford, 1945), *Zusatz* to paragraph 4, 227.
20. *Enzyklopädie*, in Glockner, VI, paragraph 332, 246.

ciples in Hegel and has doubted their effective resolution.[21] I share this feeling. One cannot of course gather in the depths of the *Phenomenology* by looking at it through post-Enlightenment spectacles alone. In the background always and at the surface much of the time Hegel is wrestling with the problems of Greek antiquity and seeking both to overcome and to eternalize them in an alien climate. The Platonic parallel between the struggles in the state and the struggles in the soul is never far distant. I will permit myself the liberty of saying that the great figures of Aristotle, Plato, and Sophocles bestride, respectively, the sections on *Bewusstsein*, *Selbstbewusstsein*, and *Geist*. The problem of lordship and bondage is essentially Platonic in foundation, because the primal cleavage in both the history of society and the history of the ego is at stake. The two primordial egos in the struggle that will lead to mastery and slavery are also locked in battle with themselves.

A third deterrent to a balanced reading of lordship and bondage is the temptation to treat the *Phenomenology* as an enigmatic philosophy of history. Sometimes this is done so that its "progressive" implications can be favorably compared with the conclusions of Hegel's later lectures. But the schematic arrangement of Hegel's finished system, given by the *Encyclopedia*, should warn us away from this adventure: history belongs to objective spirit and phenomenology to subjective, even though the experience of objective spirit is a fact of consciousness. Although the *Phenomenology* must necessarily utilize history to illustrate forms of consciousness, it is not to be inferred the two genealogies are integrally parallel. Hegel's conscious avoidance of proper names is the best clue to his design.

This point can become confused, since Hegel in both instances is dealing with temporal process and since historical time is the condition for human thought. The evolution of mind runs along the same time scale as the fate of nations. Thus, philosophical analyses that are conceptually independent must be joined in communicative discourse and must plunder the same treasury of empirical materials. Mind as *Geist* is the integrative operator, just as temporality makes the operation possible. But the *Phenomenology* is not primarily a disquisition on political philosophy; it is the record of the spirit's efforts to attain peace in the knowledge that there is nothing outside itself.

One may question, as I do, the prestidigitatory feats of Hegel in keeping these two lines of philosophical inquiry discrete and correlative at the same time. There is more than animus in Haym's famous com-

---

21. G. R. G. Mure, *A Study of Hegel's Logic* (Oxford, 1950), 367–68.

plaint that "etwas Anderes ist die Geschichte, und etwas Anderes ist die Psychologie."[22] In fact, we all do read the *Phenomenology* as historical and political commentary quite legitimately, since it is concerned with the external relations of mind amid a plurality of egos. But the transformations of mind within itself are equally important. Both destinies, according to Hegel, will be identical in the last analysis.

Finally, if we hypothesize that mastery and slavery contains both developments, we shall not be greatly disturbed by Hegel's leaps between the social and the solitary in his deduction of *Selbstbewusstsein*, as he delineates the forms of "otherness" (*Anderssein*) in stoicism, septicism, and the "unhappy consciousness."

The clue to the whole matter is, I think, given in the following passage from the *Phenomenology*:

> The conception of this its [of self-consciousness] unity in its duplication, of infinitude realizing itself in self-consciousness, has many sides to it and encloses within it elements of varied significance. Thus its moments must on the one hand he strictly kept apart in detailed distinctiveness, and, on the other, in this distinction must, at the same time, also be taken as not distinguished, or must always be accepted and understood in their opposite sense.[23]

If Hegel means what I think, he is encouraging us to draw the plenitude of associations from the self-other confrontation. Thus, although Hegel can be only, imperfectly conveyed by static formulas: self = other; self = self + other; self (other) < > other (self); and self + other in self = self + other in other, and so one, I regard the final formulation as most complete. In the following discussion, Hegel expands this idea:

> This process of self-consciousness in relation to another self-consciousness has. . .been represented as the action of one alone. But this action on the part of the one has itself the double significance of being at once its own action and the action of that other as well. . . . The action has then a *double entente* not only in the sense that it is an act done to itself as well as to the other, but also in the sense that the act simpliciter is

---

22. Rudolf Haym, *Hegel und seine Zeit* (Orig. ed. 1857; photostatic reproduction, Heldesheim, 1962), 241: "History is quite different, and psychology is quite different."

23. Hoffmeister, 141; Baillie, 229.

the act of the one as well as of the other regardless of their distinction.[24]

A corresponding passage from the *Propädeutik*, being simpler (prepared for the instruction of preuniversity students), has perhaps greater clarity:

A self-consciousness which is for another self-consciousness is not only for it as a pure object, but *as its other self*. The ego is not an abstract universality which, as such, contains no distinction or determination. The ego being thus object for the ego, it is for it, in this view, like the same ego which it itself is. In the other, it intuits itself.[25]

One difficulty in following Hegel lies in the fact that he often tries to convey the experience of the consciousness both from its own point of view and from the high ground of the philosopher. Another is in the perpetual passage from inner to outer, which is the motor of the consciousness's experience that will be dissolved in ultimate knowledge. But the awakening of opposed faculties in the ego proposed by the fact of society is the principle on which self-consciousness would seem to depend. First, the spiritualization of desire will create the basis for selfhood. Then recognition will be demanded for its authentication. The faculties of the ego must contend in order to act, since a single comprehensive faculty, in however many egos, would render them either totally static or totally destructive (which amounts to the same thing).

Correspondingly, the pattern unfolds in social life. The mutual awareness of two persons, their reciprocal need for recognition, their struggle to obtain it, and the final subjection of the one to the other— these stages idealize the primitive sources seen this time from the angle of society but still rooted in the problem of the developing consciousness. Plamenatz should have no difficulty with the fact that there are only two protagonists. For, from this angle, when the struggle concludes in mastery and slavery, the master will perceive but a single slave-machine that does his bidding and the slave but a single source of oppression. Hegel's formulation here establishes the mediating link between consciousness and society, serving somewhat the same purpose as the analogous device of the *homo economicus*. Indeed, it is to the famous tale of Robinson and Friday that Hegel refers us in the *Propädeutik*.[26]

---

24. Hoffmeister, 142; Baillie, 230.
25. *Philosophische Propädeutik*, Glockner, III, paragraph 30, 108.
26. Ibid., paragraph 35, 110.

Just as the Hegelian analysis demands the postulation of two egos (one man as spirit would be God, or would possess no spirit),[27] so at each of its ascending stages the consciousness must apprehend itself as two estranged principles until its goal is reached. This is most clearly seen in the *Encyclopedia*, where we can delve behind the stirrings of subjective mind or "phenomenology" proper into "anthropology," which has as its focus the notion of the "natural soul." Here spirit has emerged out of nature but not yet awakened to consciousness. In this relatively little-studied part of Hegel's work, the soul corresponds roughly to what psychoanalysis will later label the "preconscious"; here are contained many perceptive insights into neurotic anxiety, undoubtedly based on the philosopher's personal experience and the tragic deterioration of his friend Hölderlin.[28]

In *Encyclopedia*, paragraphs 318–19 (1817),[29] Hegel makes it clear that the soul is life on the margin of consciousness, that it primitively feels its bifurcation, its antagonism with otherness. It is subjectively anchored to its future self-conscious career and yet mired in the blind universality of nature. On the other hand (paragraph 323),[30] the opposition is productive and necessary. Here is the primary internal opposition in the genesis of the human condition.

Consciousness arises when the natural soul, by setting its instinct against nature, can affirm itself as an ego (paragraph 327).[31] The relationship to otherness is now a dichotomy between self and natural soul (paragraph 329).[32] Self-consciousness, on the other hand, will require the affirmation by the ego of its own identity, taking the immediate form of desire (paragraphs 344–46).[33] Here the *"Selbstbewusstsein"* section of *Phenomenology* properly commences, with the inadequacy of repetitive desire, the application of desire to another ego, the struggle for recognition, and the dialectical resolution in lordship and bondage. The internal struggle that expressed itself first in the natural soul, then in the consciousness, has not been resolved or abandoned. Rather, personality can

---

27. Cf. *Phenomenology*, 226–27: "A self-consciousness has before it a self-consciousness. Only so and only then *is* it self-consciousness in actual fact; for here first of all it comes to have the unity of itself in its otherness."
28. See Johannes Hoffmeister, *Hölderlin und Hegel in Frankfurt* (Tübingen, 1931).
29. Glockner, VI, 236–37.
30. Ibid., 242.
31. Ibid., 244.
32. Ibid., 245.
33. Ibid., 251–52.

emerge only because of its need for set recognition, a consequence of ceasing to direct desire merely upon the objects of sheer natural appetition (paragraph 351).[34] A higher, resistant otherness has been encountered; it expresses itself externally as a second ego, internally as primitive reason or self-mastery, and reciprocally as the capacity for will and freedom. But, like the original assertion of self-consciousness through the ego's becoming aware of itself, this new stage of being must in turn be authenticated. This will happen in the struggle for recognition, where appetition and spiritual self-regard contend. They can no more destroy each other than can the social antagonists: the career of man is the proof. Thus, mastery and slavery ensue, both within the ego and, as Hegel makes abundantly clear (paragraph 355), in the history of society.[35]

The parallel explanations are necessary. For, taken from a purely social point of view, there is no good reason why two identical egos, locked in combat, should not struggle to a static stalemate. To say that Hegel's resolution is good dialectics answers nothing. Instead we should discern the idea that natural inequalities arise in consequence of internal imbalances, not through the absence or presence of pure principles in single individuals. I shall return to this point in connection with theories of history.

"Where did Hegel's ideas on the relation of lord and servant originate?" inquires Dirk J. Struik in his edition of Marx's 1844 manuscripts.[36] This interesting question has a considerable bearing on the subject at hand. We can help clarify the significance of Hegel's passage by referring to the intellectual milieu in which his philosophy took shape.

It is important to understand that this is still a world where normative psychology is seen as dominating the forms of society. Despite primitive stirrings of a social science, one still asks the question "what is man?" in order to understand the social order man has created. The strife within man's nature is a commonplace; as Montesquieu put it: "man . . . is composed of the two substances, each of which, in its flux and reflux, imposes and suffers domination [*empire*]."[37] On the psychological plane we should recall Hume's striking dictum that "reason is the slave of the passions" and the consequent attempts of German idealism to restore the primacy of reason by enlarging its content. We should

---

34. Glockner, VI, 253.
35. Ibid., 255.
36. Marx, *Economic and Philosophical Manuscripts*, 232.
37. Charles, Baron de Montesquieu et de la Brède, *Pensées, Œuvres Complètes* (Paris, 1949), I, 1015.

notice also that the reason-passion relationship gathers in a metaphorical content which is precisely that of mastery and servitude. In essence, Kant's philosophy, grounded in the ideal of personal autonomy, is a theorization both of how the individual can acquire mastery over his content-directed interests through the exercise of morality or "pure practical reason" and of the conditions by which a legitimate social order can make this possible. The famous aphorism "man needs a master"[38] carries both public and private overtones. In fact, according to Kant, man *ought* to be his own master. But, in the words of Richard Kroner, "because he ought to master himself, man is not really free but divided against himself, half-free and half-slave. At best, he is his own slave, enslaved by his master, reason."[39]

Behind this urgent question, which burst out of speculation and into history with the coming of the French Revolution, lies the dual pre-occupation of Rousseau: his assertion that there is no "right of conquest" in society, and his profound research into the warring sides of the human personality that the shock of social relations has induced. "A man thinks he is master of others, whereas he is actually more of a slave than they," writes Rousseau in *Contrat social* I, i;[40] in his eighth *Lettre de la Mon-tagne* he repeats: "He who is a master cannot be free."[41] As we know from the second discourse, *Émile*, and the autobiographical writings, a struggle of the human faculties underlies the social dilemma.[42]

Not only for Hegel, but for his great predecessors and his age as a whole, mastery and slavery was a multidimensional problem—and a paradoxical one. The paradox is this. Antiquity, which had sanctioned the institution of slavery, had nevertheless intensely researched the dilemma of man's enslavement of himself. The Enlightenment, by contrast, progressively attacked social bondage as abusive and immoral, while scratching only at the surface of its spiritual dimensions. And yet the Enlightenment, taken generally, viewed the social order from indi-vidualistic premises. Descartes had founded the ego and, from the time of Hobbes on, the empirical school had constructed a mechanistic

---

38. Immanuel Kant, "Idea for a Universal History from a Cosmopolitan Point of View," *Kant on History* ed. L. W. Beck (New York, 1963), 17.

39. Kroner, introduction to Knox (trans.), *Hegel's Early Theological Writings*, 11.

40. C. E. Vaughan, *The Political Writings of Jean-Jacques Rousseau*, 2 vols. (New York, 1962), II, 23.

41. Ibid., II, 234.

42. Cf. *Émile ou L'Éducation* (Paris, 1961), Book IV, 404; "O my friend, my protector, my master. . .prevent me from being the slave of my passions, and force me to be my own master by obeying my reason and not my senses."

psychology that purported to explain the nature of society by way of its members. The revival of antiquity, in substance as well as form, by Rousseau on the one hand and the German idealists on the other—even when the battle of ancients and moderns had been seemingly won by the latter—is in part a response to this perplexity. The Enlightenment had furnished a sense of progress; it had not restored the conviction of harmony. Both the mind and the social order were implicated. If society was in process, then the mind could not be explored statically as the rationalists had taught. With Hegel there is the recognition that both elements of explanation are necessary and that they must be mediated. This becomes possible only when mind is seen to have a history of its own. The tensions that propel social history are correspondingly translated to the development of the ego (a procedure in which the works of Rousseau and Kant are way-stations). Here the profundities of Greek thought find their place and their role. The problem of mastery and slavery lies along this axis. For Hegel, however, the resolution can be only tragic or unbearably smug (one takes his pick) because history, the carrier of *Geist* and freedom, is also the perfect warrant of man's fate.

A passage from Fichte's *Contributions to the Rectification of Public Opinion Concerning the French Revolution* (1793) further illustrates the currency of the lordship-bondage metaphor. Here the youthful Fichte employs the figure of the warring personality in a coinage borrowed from the French historian Marmontel.[43] Reason (i.e., the principle of the Revolution) rhetorizes against conventional self-interest (hereditary privilege):

> From our birth, he [reason] invited us to a long and terrible duel where liberty and slavery were at stake. If you are stronger, he told us, I will be your slave. I will be a very useful servant for you; but I will always be a restless servant, and as soon as there is some slack in my yoke, I will defeat my master and conqueror. And once I throw you down, I will insult you, dishonor you, trample you under. Since you can be of no use to me, I will profit by my right of conquest to seek your total destruction.[44]

We do not know whether Hegel read Fichte's incendiary tract against the German Burkeans, but it seems likely that he did, since it was, to

---

43. Jean-François Marmontel, contributor ot the *Encyclopédie*, replaced Duclos in 1771 as historiographer of France. He was elected to the *Conseil des anciens* in 1797, but was retired from public life by the *coup d'Etat* of 18 Fructidor. Fichte cites one of his poems.
44. J. G. Fichte, *Beiträge zur Berichtigung der Urteile des Publikums über die Französische Revolution*, ed. Stcker (Leipzig, 1922), 51.

say the least, hot copy among young intellectuals. In any case, the contemporary associations of lordship and bondage are not to be understood without the illustrations from across the Rhine.

However, when Hegel came to formulate his mature system, he was, as we know, not an unqualified admirer of the French Revolution or of the autocracy of abstract reason with its "bad infinity." The new "right of conquest" had no more appeal than the old. Like all stages of human struggle, the oppositions of the ego had to be reconciled, not concluded in a new unilateral domination.[45] In the primitive scenario of the *Phenomenology* the resolution of lordship and bondage is in "stoicism," and it is probably no accident that there are resemblances between this form of consciousness and Kant's transcendental idealism, the idea posed above the French Revolution.[46] Though I do not want to draw parallels out of context in Hegel's system, it may not be amiss to call attention to the climate of ideas in which his thoughts about lordship and bondage developed. Undoubtedly the split-personality view of contemporary European philosophy counts for much.

Another brief excursion into German intellectual history can provide a different illustration. When Hegel was developing the rudiments of the master-slave dialectic, he was associated, though not uncritically, with the philosophical ideas of his younger but more precocious friend Schelling. By the time he published the *Phenomenology* in 1807 he had struck his own highly original posture. In the meantime, the split between the philosophies of Schelling and Fichte (which Hegel himself attempted to mediate in his *Differenz des Fichte'schen und Schelling'schen Systems* of 1801) had become irreconcilable and had led to vituperative exchange. The same half-decade saw the rise of the romantic movement, under the aegis of Novalis and the Schlegels, and the efflorescence of interest in philosophy of history, which had been heralded by Lessing and Herder in the previous century.

---

45. See *Enzyklopädie*, Glockner, VI, paragraph 393, 276–78.
46. See esp. *Philosophy of Right, introduction*, paragraphs 19–21, 28–30. Cf. Hegel's early (1797) attack on Kant (re: *Religion Within the Limits of Mere Reason*, IV, 2, paragraph 3) in his essay "Der Geist des Christentums und sein Schicksal," *Hegels theologische Jugendschriften*, ed. Herman Nohl (Tübingen, 1907), 265–66: "between the Tungusian Shaman, the European prelate governing Church and State, or the Mogul or Puritan, and the man obedient to the commandment of duty [the Kantian], the distinction is not to be made that the one enslaves himself while the other is free, but that the one is dominated from without, while the other, having his master within, is by that token his own slave.

Schelling's philosophy, which began from the premise of the identity of the absolute, required a theory of history by which the descent of the absolute into the plurality of creation and the return of created things to the absolute could be explained. The key this movement was to be discovered in the principle of human freedom. Schelling traced the idea grandiosely and abstractly in the *System des transzendentalen Idealismus* (1800), in the *Vorlesungen über die Methode des akademischen Studiums* (1802), and in some later writings. In reply to Schelling and, more especially, the romantics, Fichte entered the lists with his public lectures, the *Grundzüge des gegenwärtigen Zeitalters*, delivered in 1804 and published in 1806. Fichte's scheme of philosophical history, built on purely deductive foundations and in some ways indebted to Kant, challenged his opponents on a variety of issues that do not concern this essay.[47] What is of interest is a fundamental assumption that Fichte and Schelling shared and which could scarcely have failed to draw Hegel's attention.[48]

The speculative histories of Fichte and Schelling were phased and developmental; both in effect sought to deduce the pattern whereby original man, innocent but instinctual in nature, mounted to his goal of rationality in freedom, or achieved what Schelling described as a "second nature." In order to do this, the principle of reason had to be explained at its origin. Schelling was the first to postulate that at the dawn of humanity there had been creatures of pure instinctual reason and simple barbarians. Fichte borrowed this explanation (which is not without its obvious indebtedness to mythology): "out of nothing, nothing can arise; and thus Unreason can never become Reason. Hence, in one point of its existence at least, the Human Race must have been purely Reasonable in its primitive form, without either constraint or freedom."[49]

---

47. For a full clarification of these issues, see Xavier Léon, *Fichte et son temps*, 3 vols. (Paris, 1924), II, 394–463.
48. We know that Hegel read Fichte's excursus on philosophical history and thought little of it, as well as of the "popular philosophy" in which Fichte indulged; see Hegel's letter to Schelling, dated Jena, Jaunary 3, 1807, No. 82, *Briefe von und an Hegel*, ed. J. Hoffmeister (Hamburg, 1952), I, 131. His knowledge of the *Grundzüge* was probably too late to affect the *Phenomenology*; however, he was perfectly familiar with all Schelling's ideas antecedent to 1804 because of their close collaboration at Jena.
49. J. G. Fichte, *Grundzüge des gegenwärtigen Zeitalters*, Lecture IX (Hamburg, 1956), 138; *Characteristics of the Present Age, The Popular Works of Johann Gottlieb Fichte*, trans. William Smith (London, 1884), II, 147. See also F. W. J. Schelling, *Vorlesungen, Sämmtliche Werke* (Stuttgart, 1854–60), V, 224–25.

However, this *malvolk* had no history; for them, one day was like the next, and "religion alone adorned their existence."[50] It was thus necessary to postulate a race of barbarians. The union of the two races was what made history and society possible. In the *Normalvolk* there was no tension to activate the spring of progress; on the other hand, they embodied the principle of human destiny. The savages, on their part, lacked this principle utterly, but they contained the force of historical propulsion. Consequently, after an interlude when Cartesian paradise and Darwinian brutishness presumably coexisted, society took form with the dispersion of the races, the subjection of the savages to *Normalvolk* kings, intermarriage, and the tortuous ascent of miscegenated man to freedom. Apparently, Asia was the historical location for this event; the Old Testament was a "myth of the normal people."[51]

The parallel between this historical hypothesis of Schelling and Fichte and Hegel's lordship and bondage is much more than coincidental. Either the idea was in the air, or there was direct cross-fertilization from Schelling. However, Hegel does not accept this solution.[52] He nowhere endorses any speculation concerning original "rational" men and original "savage" men. Reason is not a natural principle in his anthropology, any more than it is for Rousseau. In Hegel, . . . the appearance of self and self-awareness will succeed the primitive efforts of the preconscious soul to wrest its being from nature. Consequently, although a social event, mastery and slavery will result necessarily from struggles of awareness and recognition within the ego and not from the absolute opposition of racial principles embodied in discrete, historical individuals. Hegel is defending a doctrine of original equality that is curiously and dangerously denied by Fichte.[53]

Thus, I believe that the passage in the *Phenomenology* and in other works can be justifiably interpreted, inter alia, as an attempt to explain inequality at the foundation of society without resorting to the dual-nature hypothesis. The alternative is to explain it from within the ego. Here, precisely, is the "phenomenological" dimension that we lack in Kojève.

---

50. *Grundzüge*, 139; Smith, 148.
51. *Grundzüge*, 143; Smith, 152.
52. See Hegel, *Die Vernunft in der Geschichte* (Hamburg, 1955), 31.
53. Fichte is, of course, the German philosopher who, par excellence, stessed equality and was often attacked as a Jacobin. However, there is a nervous resemblance, across all human history, between the *Normalvolk* of the *Grundzüge* and the *Urvolk* of the *Addresses to the German Nation* (1808).

Let us attempt to restore this dimension. The "master" who emerges from the struggle for recognition can be identified with the primitive notion of control or decision. Hegel tells us specifically that this act of victory is the birth of freedom (*Encyclopedia*, paragraph 355).[54] Man is the only creature which, under certain "non-natural" pressures, is willing to stake its life. This is, so to speak, the first creative act of the human personality: the slave will invent history, but only after the master has made humanity possible. The master's solution, however, is without issue. Hegel has already (in *Encyclopedia*, paragraph 323 and elsewhere)[55] pointed out the danger of imbalance between higher and lower principles. One cannot abandon nature, nor should one drown himself in it. In the master-slave situation, there is neither education, nor progress, nor history—only the repetitive fulfilment of the master's wants.

In this impasse, the master-principle—courage, decisiveness, idealism—is seen to pass into its opposite, becoming, as Kojève points out,[56] a new form of *Begierde*. Higher development can come only from the slave-principle, which has itself been transformed through the experience of subjection and terror into the activities of labor, conservation, and memory—the conditions of human advance. Here are manifold historical overtones that it is not difficult to exploit. I think, though, that two points must be argued against Kojève: (1) the slave-master dialectic is appropriate only to a certain stage of consciousness for Hegel, even though it is still cancelled and retained (*aufgehoben*); succeeding history will be a record of more subtle and comprehensive forms of estrangement; (2) both principle are equally vital in the progress of the spirit toward its destiny: if Marx developed one side of this dichotomy, Nietzsche seized upon the other.[57]

This is decisively clarified by Hegel himself in the *Philosophy of Right*:

> The position of the free will, with which right and the science of right begin, is already in advance of the false position at which man, as a natural entity and only the concept implicit, is for that reason capable of being enslaved. This false, *comparatively*

54. Glockner, VI, 254.
55. Ibid., 242.
56. *Lecture de Hegel*, p. 52.
57. Though he doubted its persistency in Europe, Hegel was not loath to praise the masterly virtue (involved in a complex manner with his defense of war); cf. *Philosophy of Right*, paragraph 328A, 212: "To risk one's life is better than merely fearing death."

primitive [my italics], phenomenon of slavery is one which befalls mind when mind is only at the level of consciousness. The dialectic of the concept and of the purely immediate consciousness of freedom brings about at that point the fight for recognition and the relationship of master and slave.[58]

In a corresponding *Zusatz* Hegel adds: "if a man is a slave, his own will is responsible for his slavery, just as it is its will which is responsible if a people is subjugated. Hence the wrong of slavery lies at the door not simply of enslavers or conquerors but of the slaves and the conquered themselves."[59]

This should be sufficient to show that "the future belongs to the slave" is an unwarranted and romanticized refraction of Hegel's thought. Slavery cannot found the right of political communities any more than it can account for the free personality. But it is necessary for history as well as for the development of mind: both right and free personality appear in history and do not repose above it. In the *Encyclopedia* of 1845 (paragraph 435, *Zusatz*) Hegel describes the subjection of the servant as "a necessary moment in the education (*Bildung*) of every man."[60] "No man," he adds, "can, without this will-breaking discipline, become free and worthy to command." As for nations, "bondage and tyranny are necessary things in the history of peoples." This could be adapted to the Marxian view of the proletariat. But as we recall from the *Phenomenology*, the dialectical outcome is not a historical class struggle but the temporary refuge of stoicism, where emperor and slave see the world with the same eyes. Even though "only through the slave's becoming free can the master be completely free."[61] the Hegelian future will unfold out of their joint endeavors. They can no more be incessantly opposed than can the organic faculties of the ego itself.

My conclusion is foreshadowed. Although inner and outer, higher and lower, reason and passion are undoubtedly intended to be dissolved at the ultimate Hegelian apex, the internality of the ego cannot be disregarded in understanding the development of *Selbstbewusstsein*. The social reading, taken alone, can encourage sharp distortions. Nor is history for Hegel simply a record of the millennial efforts of the slave to overthrow the master, just as the development of spirit is not the continuous attempt of a single faculty to triumph in the ego. In both

---

58. Knox (trans.), paragraph 57, 48.
59. Ibid., 239.
60. Glockner, X (*System der Philosophie*, III), 288.
61. Ibid., *Zusatz* to paragraph 436, 290.

cases, the aspiration is harmony and self-knowing identity, the sense of "being at home" (*zuhause sein*) so frequently evoked in Hegel, the assimilation of freedom and fate. The failure to read Hegel's texts (especially those leading up to "lordship and bondage") with close attention to levels of discourse can beget social hypotheses that do not square with Hegel's known conclusions. We can further profit by exploring the philosophical and historical issues of Hegel's own time instead of superimposing those of an industrial epoch which he only narrowly, if shrewdly, glimpsed. That the character of the rational Hegelian society is much more Platonic than it is Marxian is already clear from the Jena lectures, which antedate the *Phenomenology*.[62] Kojève's original exegesis of Hegelian themes is a profound work for our own times. But from the standpoint of historical understanding a "Marxian" *Phenomenology* does not make very good sense. This view ignores the depth and passion of Hegel's Greek attachments; it ignores, too, the complicated range of his struggle with the Kantian split vision. These are the two combatants wrestling on the soil of Christian Europe for the possession of Hegel's own ego.[63] It is to be questioned whether he resolved this struggle of the old world and the new in his higher *Sittlichkeit* of the nation-state and in his "Christianity without pictures."

---

62. *Jenenser Realphilosophie*, II, 253–63. We must not ignore, however, that Hegel carefully draws the distinction between the Platonic (Lacedemonian) and the modern policy (p. 251).

63. The Greeks for Hegel, as for Schiller, Hölderlin, and others, have developed the perfect harmony and proportion of humanity; Kant's morality, on the other hand, represents the infinity of striving and is framed not for man but for "all rational beings." In one of his most electrifying and brilliant passages, Hegel describes the impact of the infinite and the finite, always in the same metaphor of struggle and comprehension: "I am the struggle [between the extremes of infinity and finitude], for this struggle is a conflict defined not by the indifference of the two sides in their distinction, but by their being bound together in one entity. I am not one of the fighters locked in battle, but both, and I am the struggle itself. I am fire and water" (*Volesungen über die Philosophie der Religion*, Glockner, XV, 80).

CHAPTER 15

The Struggle for Recognition

HEGEL'S DISPUTE WITH HOBBES
IN THE JENA WRITINGS

Ludwig Siep
Translated by Charles Dudas

In his well-known book *The Political Philosophy of Hobbes: Its Basis and Genesis* (1936),[1] Leo Strauss advanced the thesis that Hegel's concept of struggle for recognition as well as his analysis of lordship and bondage reflects a notable Hobbesian influence. In a footnote he adds: "The connection between Hegel and Hobbes especially evident in Hegel's *Theologische Jugendschriften* is the more particular area of research that Alexandre Kojève and myself will investigate" (63). As far as we are aware, there has been no substantial delivery on that promise to date. Ever since that time, both the Hobbesian and Hegelian literature alludes to research that would establish the Hegel-Hobbes connection, but never amounts to more than mere references.[2] Here, a thoroughgoing analysis of a certain aspect of the relation will be undertaken in which, following Strauss's

---

1. This English edition was published by Clarendon Press, Oxford, in 1936; the unrevised German edition, from which we quote in the following, Strauss had published (Neuwied: Luchterhand, 1964).

2. Raymond Polin, *Politique et philosophie chez Thomas Hobbes* (Paris: Presses Universitaires de France, 1953); Bernard Willms, *Die Antwort des Leviathan* (Neuwied/Berlin: Luchterhand, 1970); and *Revolution und Protest* (Stuttgart: Kohlhammer, 1969); Manfred Riedel, *Studien zu Hegels Rechtsphilosophie* (Frankfurt am Main: Suhrkamp, 1969); Karl-Heinz Ilting, "Hegels Auseinandersetzung mit der aristotelischen Politik," *Philosophisches Jahrbuch* 1971 (1963–64): 38–58.

initiative, a connection between the young (Jena) Hegel's concept of *struggle for recognition* and Hobbes' *war of each against all* will be the more specific focus. The goal therefore is not to analyze influence, but to probe the fundamental difference in the thematic relation between the first proposition of the rationale regarding the law of nature in modern times and that Hegel's philosophy of the spirit which claims to have sublated it. This difference, however, is easily eroded if we take Hobbes' state of nature to have a direct bearing on Hegel's philosophy. For Strauss's (et. al.) interpretation is by no means neutral with respect to Hegel's idea. In order to make Hobbes' state of nature the point of departure for our comparison, we will set out by attempting to provide a brief critique of Strauss's interpretation.[3]

It appears that Strauss sees Hobbes' war immediately in the light of the struggle for recognition, while he conceives of this struggle as a battle of two people for honor and interprets the connection among struggle, lordship and bondage, and the social contract in terms of the processes of experience to be described in what follows. According to Strauss, the state of nature leads to ambition and pride, to a blinding conceit for recognition of individual superiority, from which there follows a fundamental attack on honor so that he to whom recognition is denied will feel contempt toward the one who burdens him with this demand. The result of this injury is wrath (desire fueled by anger), which in turn leads to war (struggle/battle). The fear of death one lives through within the struggle gives rise to the first shape of experience, that is, the compelling drive for superiority is revealed as illusory in view of the fact that by nature men are equally in the position to threaten each other's lives. The fear of death then leads, on the one hand, to a certain moderation of wrath paired with a self-depreciation with regard to the goal of survival. Through this experience there is opened up the possibility for the other to see his honor maintained through the recognition allotted to him on the behalf of a living entity whom he consequently does not kill but subdues: "this is how the relation between Master and Slave will ensue" (30). Consequently, this relation can be overcome only when both parties sense the fear of death, a perspective from which they come to acknowledge death as their "common enemy." Unity can then follow on the basis of an equality or sameness, which in turn leads to the construction of the artifice of the *leviathan* state.

---

3. We have based our critique strictly on the aforementioned book and not on Strauss's later works on Hobbes where the thesis discussed here is not substantially revised.

This interpretation appears suspect to us in two ways. On the one hand, we doubt whether honor in fact comprises the obvious motive behind Hobbes' struggle. Second, we question whether Strauss oversimplifies Hobbes' struggle as a duel, that is, a battle solely between two people. With respect to the first point, one must remark that in *The Elements of Law* and *De Cive* Hobbes tends to attribute to honor the most significant motive behind the struggle. In both of these writings, Hobbes even notes that the men have a foretaste of death (*Elements* I XII, 11 and *De Cive* III, 12)[4] of which the fundamental basis, according to *De Cive*, is the intensity of the spiritual struggle[5] for honor and to which all spiritual desire [*Lust*] (*animi voluptas*, 160) can ultimately be traced. Nevertheless, it remains questionable whether Hobbes generally regards honor as the decisive motive for struggle.

Although the sublation of the principle of individuality in the struggle for family honor in the *System of Ethical Life* is of pivotal significance, further development of the theory of struggle in the Jena writings does not refer to the realm of the family but latches onto the development of the struggle for honor by the person. Both forms of struggle, therefore, seem to share little with Hobbes' theory of the war of each against all. Once the move to destroy through invalidation is set in motion, once law is negated and the risk to life consciously reckoned with, then the struggle in *System of Ethical Life* becomes more clearly a struggle between two people, entailing a noble concept of honor resembling Hobbes' struggle for self-preservation and power. It is in this sense that we find Hegel's theory of struggle in his *System of Ethical Life* hinging fundamentally on Hobbes' concept. In Hegel it becomes evident—as it does in Hobbes—that the struggle of the individual is aimed at a radical freedom from everything that binds him and which for him is represented in the institutions of natural ethics. This negation of natural ethics and its unification in the individual in law and in the family significantly demonstrates that the individual himself comprises a totality. In order to posit the development of the individual's consciousness of perfect freedom as being perfect, the freedom of the person in the struggle for honor must first be abstracted from all constraints. This means that in the second part of his *System of Ethical Life*, Hegel is

---

4. We cite Hobbes from the following edition: *Elements of Law*, ed. Ferdinand Toennies, 2d edition (London: Cass, 1969); *De Cive*, ed. Sir William Molesworth (London: J. Boh, 1839–45); *Leviathan*, ed. Michael Oakeshott (Oxford: Basil Blackwell, 1957).

5. "maximum certamen sit ingenium" (*De Cive* I, 5, 162).

not directly concerned with the Hobbesian war of each against all. He represents different aspects of the struggle, above all the struggle between two people for the honor of the other one, while at the same time he deals with Hobbes' state of nature argument in a dissenting thesis that the original freedom of the individual is revealed as the law of all over all in the course of the struggle itself.

However—as Hegel turns the thought of struggle against Hobbes and, above all, against the individualistic law of nature—the struggle simultaneously involves the overcoming of the principle of particularity, that is, of an ethics that founds itself on empirical consciousness. This turn against Hobbes already points to the meaning that Hegel bestows on honor, namely, that while Hobbes[6] sees honor placed in the service of self-preservation—even though this may actually endanger it—for Hegel it already stands in opposition to the ability of the individual to transgress both the dominion of the law and of self-preservation. The struggle for honor, therefore, fulfills a function for those who, within the parameters allowed for by the law of nature, are not yet fully endowed with the courage necessary for the individual to be brought to the consciousness or representation of his "pure particularity." This consciousness as well as the identity of particularity with universality, of oneness with the people, also gets disseminated in different forms of the struggle. In the struggle of the two, it is with respect to personal honor that the lifting into pure freedom occurs, while for family honor and ultimately for that of the people it is individuality itself that is overcome for the sake of all. In contrast with Hobbes' concept of the law of nature, the overcoming of the struggle for Hegel cannot take place through law or through the state that secures it. Rather, overcoming resides much more in the law-fixated consciousness of the individual than in his absolute particularity and raises the individual to the level of absolute ethics held in the realization of the people and the state. It is through the latter that the individual stands in a positive relation to the state—whereas in Hobbes, the stance is a negative one. Does this mean that in *System of Ethical Life* the state does not possess the function to secure the law at all?

Let us take another look at the relation among struggle, law, and state in the third chapter of *System of Ethical Life*, which, in addition, contains a standard doctrine with respect to the law of nature proposal that is very much in harmony with Plato's concept. Here law appears to be an organizational form, the working law, as expression of the second state's concept of possession and profit. Insofar as before the law the

---

6. At least from the time of the *Leviathan*.

particular has absolute worth, the law itself is merely a relation of understanding (61) and does not, in any sense, belong to absolute ethics. Only the first "absolute" state contains absolute ethics "as its own principle" (63). It manifests itself as courage in the struggle for the grounding and for the national honor (60) of the state, for the sake of which the and particular "surrenders to the danger of death" [i.e., "will jeopardize its life"] (58). Nevertheless, the sheltering of the particular and of his rights plays a role in the state. He belongs to absolute ethics only insofar as the particular counts as member of the people.

Hegel deals with the "prudence of law" in the second chapter of the third section, which takes as its object the government and its various authorities. While the "civil prudence of law" (89) carries a subordinate meaning for the government—with respect to which it could "entrust itself to the second and third state"—the "grievous prudence of law" certainly involves a significant effort. It is not freely exercised in the particular as such, but only through what is implicit in the negation of recognition, that is, the "negation of the universal" (89). However, the state's highest level of justice and injustice (the lawful and the unlawful) is again in war, inasmuch as the people turns itself into a "transgressor" by sacrificing the life and possessions of its members. Far from seeing the existence of the state as constituting itself in the protection of the lives of individuals, and consequently, as Hobbes saw it, in granting priority to the individual for self-preservation above and beyond the good of all the others, Hegel situates the highest form of ethics attainable by the particular in courage, which in war substantiates "the evidence of truthfulness of the particular"—at its highest in self-sacrifice.[7] The defense of honor and wrath comprising the struggle for honor between individuals simultaneously belonging to the people in a pre-State *state of nature* will be, according to Hegel, "assumed by the people itself" (67).

As opposed to Hobbes, the struggle is not over the revelation of an absolute *Unsittlichkeit* (an-ethics) in this situation. Rather it constitutes an important level of development of an immanent ethics, since what the individual experiences in the struggle is not his complete isolation and peril—an insight that might lead to a system of universal protection of life. It is experienced much more in the freedom *from* his own life, as he recognizes in himself the moment of absolute spirit. It is never-

---

7. Rosenkranz comments on how *System of Ethical Life* threads its way as Hegel suggests that philosophy comprises "supplement to war" for those who "are stuck with the ignominy of not being dead" (*Dokumente zu Hegel Entwicklung* [*Documents on Hegel's Development*] [Stuttgart, 1936], 314).

theless meaningful that, instead of a twofold sublation, one is spurned by the principle of individuality that rests on ethics in a process of deployment of consciousness in three instances, language, tool, and family, and to this end consciousness conceives of itself as spirit and recognizes its instances as "existing in a *people*" (235).[8] The point of the struggle in this process is to be found within the third instance—in it consciousness comprehends itself as a totality and, in its attempt to gain recognition from the other totality, sublates its individual self. The obvious difference in *System of Ethical Life* with respect to the struggles consists in Hegel's development of the struggle in the *Jena System of 1803–4*, where the different forms of struggle are no longer explicated as forms of "transgression" but are contained in one form that pertains to the struggle for life and death that from the very outset is a struggle for recognition. What follows from this is that here the struggle does not involve negation of various forms of natural ethics—law, recognition, family. The *Jena System of 1803–4* does not acknowledge either a "natural ethics" or a negative sublation in transgression. Institutions of law and the economic sphere—value, exchange, contract, and the like—find themselves, for the first time, at the highest[9] level of ethics as forms of the *spirit* of a *people.*

It is here that we can see the first signifcant change in Hegel's position with respect to the law of nature. In *System of Ethical Life*, following Plato and even Rousseau,[10] Hegel had attributed the domain of law and economics to the principle of individuality built on ethics and, through sublation, to its own negation. But under the influence of English national economy, especially Adam Smith (239), Hegel's concept of law of nature presents itself in the form of particularity sublated in the universal of a *people* and it already postulates the self-sublation of individuality in terms of the struggle for recognition. It is through this that the relation between struggle and recognition is reversed: struggle no longer negates recognition but, instead, makes it its goal. Struggle is part and parcel of the process of recognition itself, whether or not the contradictions involved in the struggle for recognition are sublated. Whether this points to an assimilation of or advance toward Hobbes will, for the moment,

---

8. The page numbers refer to J. Hoffmeister's 1932 edition, which carries the title *Jenenser Realphilosophie I*.

9. "The highest level," obviously, can only be spoken of with regard to the given texts that break away from the discussion of estate and government.

10. One can think of the significance of overcoming *amour propre*, which rules in the domain of possession and acquisition, and its move toward *amour pour la partie* und *vertu* (love for the party and virtue) in Rousseau.

be left aside as we focus on how constraint through positive law overcomes the freedom of endless struggle.

In spite of these difficulties, even the articulation of philosophy of the spirit in the 1803–4 manuscripts with respect to the raising of consciousness to the level of spirit must be understood in the sublation of the principle of individuality. In this text, Hegel freely starts from a comprehensive or all-encompassing, empirical, and absolute consciousness held within the concept of consciousness. Therefore, the concept of individual consciousness must be determined so as to embrace the development of theoretical consciousness itself. This demonstrates that theoretical consciousness at its highest level is understanding, that is, formal reason (217), or the ability "to abstract from all absolutes" and "to reflect itself absolutely in itself" (218, 216, respectively). It is in the manner of such "an absolutely simple point" (218) that consciousness is individual consciousness. It is revealed as "particular" in its contrast to every other thing or to the "totality of being" (216). This particularity, as it develops the instances of practical consciousness—that is, the "absolute oppositional reference"—must be sublated: the "spirit must endlessly prove itself by sublating particularity" (218). This then takes place in the potential of the tool, wherein individual consciousness sublates its opposition in respect of the "object." The tool is not only an external existence of consciousness, a unity of activity and passivity, a "to work and to be worked upon," but it is also already an "existing universality" in which "the working person endures" (221). The tool, however, is by no means a final sublation of individuality. Rather, inasmuch as the "opposition is sublated from without," so consciousness "breaks down in itself" (198) into a difference-conscious individual that is then revealed as a "difference in kind."

In the third potential of consciousness, namely, the family, the sublation of the difference of the individual is at the same time the sublation of individuality itself. In the *System of Ethical Life*, however, this sublation postulates that the individual raises himself to the "totality of particularity." Totality here certainly means not only indifference, but also implies the unity of itself and the other. Consequently, individual consciousness proving itself to be a totality in the family means that the individual becomes itself in the other. This takes place in upbringing: the parents perceive in the child their own consciousness as their "becoming" in an other (223). In this procedure, consciousness "itself has become an other" but in such a way that it does not lose itself in this being-an-other for it "perceives itself in the other" (225). The other consciousness is not known in opposition with itself; rather, to know oneself in the other means being a totality. However, this cannot yet come to consciousness within the family: "It is absolutely important that the totality to which consciousness attains in the family, should recognize itself in an other similar totality of consciousness." This is, in fact, the starting point of the struggle for recognition.

This perceiving-of-itself-in-an-other within the family has not, as yet, sublated the difference of consciousness, or the practical, that is, the oppositional relation of the particular: each one is "for the other immediately an absolute particular" (225). The process in which the totality of particularity perceives itself in the other can thus also only derive its movement from an oppositional, exclusive activity. The "exclusive point" has expanded itself into a totality, nevertheless it has remained exclusive. It matters, therefore, that the other be excluded from my totality and that this exclusion be perceived by him as such. This is precisely what happens in the struggle for honor. Should my consciousness in any "particularity of his possession or his being" be hurt or violated, it will show itself in that this externality "has lost its opposition against me" (227), and also in the way that I exclude the other from it. The hurt or injury is important here, too, in order to prove or demonstrate my totality by means of defense with respect to the counterattack.

But here Hegel also combines the struggle for honor with the loss of possession: "in his possession everyone must necessarily be unsettled" (227). The basis for this lies in the fact that for Hegel—and here is where he significantly rejoins state of nature to the law of nature—the possession of a particular who has not yet become universal through the being of recognition granted him by the people (240), is in itself contradictory—whereas in *System of Ethical Life* this counts as the form of a pre-State natural ethics. This foundation of the struggle through the contradictoriness of possessions in the state of nature remains open, of course, whether it be the loss of possession of honor, the proof of which requires the totality of particularity, or merely involves the struggle for honor. But does the claim for totality also mean a claim for the "totality of being" (217), which would also include the claim for the possession of the other? In my view, there is no support for such a proposition in the Hegelian text. The totality of the particular nevertheless is limitless in its demand upon the other; it has not yet come to respect this claim since the other still has not discerned the identity of its own consciousness. Freedom, in the way it attributes totality for me and thereby excludes the other, is just as limitless as is the negation of recognition in the *System of Ethical Life*. The externality taken up in the totality of consciousness is fully undetermined. So what needs to be demonstrated here is that this totality arises out of a practical oppositional relation toward, as well as of the exclusion of, the other.

It is to this end that it is important—and it is precisely this that is achieved in the loss of possession—that both invest the totality of their consciousness in the same object. The fact that for each this object is not external but essential—their relation to it being "immediately endless"—can only become evident when all the moments of its totality, which means its life as well, are equivalent. Insofar as each party makes his complete "existence" (229) dependent on this particularity, he will be excluded by the other from the loss of life. And because this exclusion on the part of both is significant as the proof of their totality, each party must stake his life "to go for the death of the other" (228). Only in the struggle for life and death can each bring the other to the realization whether this is "reasonable" (229). When neither of them relinquishes the proof of his rationality and thereby becomes "the slave of the other,"[11] the struggle for one party must end in the "annihilation unto death" (229). Since each perceives his totality in the consciousness of the other and insists on having his act of exclusion of the other recognized by him, the struggle for recognition in this encounter proves to be contradictory. The "absolute contradiction" constituted thereby lies in the fact that each of the parties, in order to validate the totality of his particularity vis-à-vis the consciousness of the other, must sublate either his own particularity or that of the consciousness of the other from whom recognition is demanded. In the "realization" of my totality as consisting in recognition by the other, "I sublate myself as the totality of particularity" (229). In spite of this contradiction, the struggle for the development of consciousness remains significant because it leads to a "reflection of itself in its self" (230)—in the course of which "reflection" here, but also later in the *Phenomenology*, makes progress by veering away from the earlier form of consciousness.

The consciousness of particularity realizes that particularity "accomplishes the opposite of what it was aiming at." Instead of its intended self-assertion, the totalizing particularity sublates itself. It can only perceive itself as a totality in the other consciousness, that is, know itself as recognized through the sublation of its particularity or as "universal consciousness." Without the intermittent level of the struggle for one

---

11. Here, however, Hegel sees the master-slave relationship as not yet containing the possibility for a one-sided recognition: the one who "sublates the struggle in the face of death" has "neither proven himself as a totality nor has he recognized the other as such" (p. 229).

of the superordinate particulars, the moment of a comprehensive whole, as in the *System of Ethical Life*, is achieved in the sublation of individual consciousness sketched in the *Jena System of 1803–4* as the struggle for life and death with its resulting "reflection" in absolute spirit: "The being of this sublated being of particular totality is the totality of absolute universality, or absolute Spirit." In absolute spirit the consciousness of particularity is actually sublated as recognized, and both are "immediately one and the same" (230). The particular consciousness no longer knows itself as an enduring particularity but as a "mere possibility" (231), that is, as one that has continually "renounced itself." Both as an individual and as a family, it has sacrificed itself for the sake of the whole, the people. The recognition of this renunciation, of this readiness for death for the sake of the people, at the same time sublates the particularity through the other and gives it a new "existence" in the "absolute consciousness" of a people. "Its eventual recognition is its existence and in this existence alone it is sublated" (232).[12]

Recognition is also possible when the parties are no longer intent upon striving for the honor of the particular in the struggle and instead recognize themselves as members of a people. Nevertheless, the struggle is now the first step on the way toward recognition and no longer the negation of it as in the *System of Ethical Life*. The idea of recognition, which Hegel had taken from Fichte, already meant in Fichte's *Grundlage des Naturrechts* (*The Science of Rights*) the formation of a collective consciousness by way of a mutually mediated individualization in the recognition of the other.[13] The fact that Hegel inserts the struggle into this process whereby the struggle for honor essentially becomes a struggle for recognition means two things. First of all, in order to illustrate in the manner of a shibboleth the movement of recognition in Fichte as well as in *System of Ethical Life*, Hegel sets out to treat the process of integration through dissolution by sharpening the radicalization of the moment of separation to allow for the realization of recognition through the sublation of an immanent contradiction. Second, the struggle becomes more meaningful as a way toward integration, that is, toward the preparation of a positive sublation of the principle of particularity in absolute ethics. Whereas in the *System of Ethical Life* the was merely a negative sublation of this principle and, in the case of natural ethics,

---

12. Even the moment of exclusion is reached in this higher existence, inasmuch as each party is conscious of the sublated being of the other (p. 231).
13. The concept of recognition in Fichte and in the early Hegel aimed at elaborating their writing in the larger context of work.

had to be "indifferentiated," it appears for the first time only in the third part of the system of absolute ethics where it presents itself as the positive sublating moment of the totality of particularity in the absolute consciousness of the process of recognition. The struggle thereby is actually a transition to absolute spirit insofar as it induces a reflection or a turnabout of consciousness. In order to contain the transition of the struggle itself, Hegel no longer needs what had been so important in the *System of Ethical Life*, namely, the intertext of family wrath. Having attained its new position within the development of consciousness, the struggle can no longer sublate itself in favor of the family; although it postulates the family, it can no longer remain subordinate to it.[14] The achievement of total consciousness on the family level (for example, its freedom from contradiction in the exclusive activity or struggle of the particular) now sublates itself definitively over and beyond the level of the family. This exclusive totality, however, is no longer a negative compliance of *ethics* within the family, which would somehow prove to be its contradiction, but retains the noncontradictoriness it has achieved within the family as its own moment. For in order to experience itself as a moment of the whole, the "totality of particularity" can only achieve its universally recognized existence if it sublates its being in the people.

Therefore, when the struggle reaches its final level in the notable development of individual consciousness and appears as a consequence of practical relationships between particulars outside the domain of the *Volkgeist* (spirit of the people), it becomes evident that Hegel has now assumed into his theory of ethics the thesis on the relationships of the individual in the state of nature that leads to the war of each against all. Moreover, the transformation of this thesis will certainly be more significant than it appears in the *System of Ethical Life*. For although both Hegel and Hobbes begin with the "nature" of consciousness wherein the individual's potential for endless freedom plays itself out in mutual harm as well as in driving the other "to death" (229), it is with respect to man's determinacy in nature that Hegel, unlike Hobbes, does not reduce the issue to drives and affects of bodily movements. Rather, consciousness has proven itself in its development of theoretical and practical potentials as "master over nature" (197) and "constructs itself as spirit

---

14. As far as we are concerned, we cannot see, as does H. Kimmerle (p. 233), a sort of "preformation" of the struggle within the family, if only because Hegel uses the metaphor "death" to describe the externalization of parental consciousness in regard to its *other*, namely, the child who, in turn, forms its own consciousness out of this "material" (pp. 223ff).

understanding nature for-itself." This being-for-itself expands itself into the family and into the struggle for totality and for the unity of all contradiction. Struggle thereby reveals consciousness as being "reason-able," but no longer in the sense of mere formal reason as at the end of theoretical development. Struggle as the manifestation of reason that is not dependent on nature stands in contrast to Hobbes' theory of struggle as conflict where the individual's own reason does not directly cater to the individual himself. The positive consequence of struggle, as we have seen earlier, is also expressed in the relation between struggle and the movement of recognition. It is through this that the struggle which, in the *System of Ethical Life* had merely been a "negative subla-tion" of itself as "the least. . .ethical" (52), now achieves an ethicalizing (*versittlichende*) function. Not only does it bring the total freedom of the individual into consciousness but, at the same time, it points out how important it is for the sake of consciousness that it should sublate the principle of individuality. Struggle opens up the way to a decisive reflection wherein the individual can experience himself as the element of a people.

While law is only possible after the struggle, that is, as the precondi-tion of recognition, it is through this that the struggle can now fully enter into the situation that the contract had taken on in the law of nature. That Hegel was aware of this reference to contract theory and of its confines upon individual freedom is illustrated by the following marginal comment he made: "No design, no contract. . . . The particular must not surrender merely a portion of his freedom but all of it. His particular freedom is only his narrow-mindedness—his death" (232). Moreover, the limitation on freedom in Hobbes' contract theory is not the same as it was in Locke, Kant, or Fichte, because the individual, with the possible exception of a very limited right to resist, must transfer all his rights to the sovereign. The fundamental difference, however, between Hegel's and Hobbes' concept of the state lies in the way one reads the substitution of the struggle that ends through struggle in a contract by way of that struggle, and also in the reflection it elicits. For Hegel, the state is not a work of art to protect individuals from each other, but an "absolute substance" wherein particulars exist only as "ideals," as sublated moments, and where they "honor each other as being-for-itself" (233). The state in Hobbes is an artifact, an artful apparatus constructed for the self-preservation of the individual; Hegel's state, on the other hand, is a "communal work," an independent or self-supporting entity or essence demanding that all nonindependent individual moments be put into the service of absolute ethics.

However, the limitation of the freedom of the particular through a contract is still not sufficient, inasmuch as it is much more important to sublate the individual as end-in-itself, which can only take place through a radical understanding of himself as a totality experiencing a positive sublation. For this reason, therefore, the struggle can under no circumstances remain in the service of self-preservation—it must consist in a struggle for honor and be conscious of its intent to risk life. Honor for Hegel requires that one exclude the other, that is, strive for exclusivity, at the same time that one attempts to look at oneself in the other and be recognized by him. The relation between struggle and movement toward recognition conveys no approximation of, or approach to, Hobbes but instead, illustrates the difference with respect to their point of departure.

In the *Vorlesungsmanuskripten zur Realphilosophie* of 1805–6 the theory of struggle for recognition is taken up again and treated in relation to the *Jena System of 1803–4*; furthermore, the stuggle for honor is addressed as a form of transgression in the way it was conceived in *System of Ethical Life*. Was this renewed partitioning of the struggle into various forms, which would eventually arrive at a quite different functioning in the development of the spirit, based on an alteration to the taxonomy of philosophy of the spirit (*Geistphilosophie*)? Any comparison of the *Realphilosophie* with the *Jena System of 1803–4* is impeded by the latter's incompletion. The fragment breaks up after the section on possession and property in the people—only at the end does one find an article that addresses the issue of art included.[15] Missing, above all, is the teaching that assuredly belonged to this outline. To be assumed, however, in such a comparison is the autonomy of the sphere of law and economy in the *Realphilosophie* of 1805–6 that will not allow for a return to a teaching that would imply the existence of a natural or pre-State ethics. The system of "universal work" (214) and its institutions, exchange and contract, and so on, accompanied by the relation of transgression and punishment in which the state is constituted as public violence, that is, "violence-possessing law," achieves a level of spirit that has already presupposed the self-sublation of individual consciousness in the struggle for recognition.

One can see readily accomplished in the unity of individual will, the "to-be-recognized" by all in the universal will. However, being held within this universal will, the particular as a "special will" and "lawful person" still constitutes the object of action of the universal. The

---

15. See *Jensener Realphilosophie I*, Appendix 269ff.

complete sublation of the particular in the universal will brings with it a new form of struggle through which the particular sets itself up against the universal. This is the struggle as transgression that for Hegel also results in the loss of honor and where the transgressor feels the loss of honor manifest itself in force. Only through the repentance of the transgressor, that is, through his separation of particular and universal will in punishment and in reconciliation, is it possible to unite the particular with the "spirit of the people" (242). The decisive level, the self-perception of one's particular will as a totality in opposition to other totalities and the change or conversion of this self-perception in the sublation of itself, is once again, the struggle for recognition. To the extent that the totality of particular will here, too, achieves the unity of its will with that of its counterpart, as well as manifest its freedom as particularity, it will make this struggle the most external expression of a state of nature comprehended as such and simultaneously become its own sublation. Nevertheless, there remain a few differences between the doctrine of struggle for recognition as it is portrayed in the *Real-philosophie* of 1805–6 and in the *Jena System of 1803–4*, which we should be able to illustrate in a brief comparison.

In addition, the struggle in the *Realphilosophie* of 1805–6 seems to contain a real conflict with respect to the family where Hegel begins his discussion with these words: "The family as a whole is an entity that encloses within itself an other whole vis-à-vis itself, otherwise we are faced with completely free individuals for-each-other" (205). Further-more, whether the struggle is a struggle *of* the family or *for* the family, we must ask how this would bear on the struggle of the family in the *System of Ethical Life*. On the other hand, we find Hegel's equal positioning of the relations between free individuals and the of state of nature in the following remark: "This is the customary relation or ordinary with respect to what is called *state of nature*, namely, the free equal being of individuals opposed to each other" (ibid.).

Furthermore, there is also the fact that the struggle of the two does not aim at the family as the whole superimposed upon particulality; instead, it is the will's "for-itself" that is revealed as the "extreme of its particularity" (211). In any case, the consciousness of such a particularity is first revealed in the struggle where the unconscious unity of the individual in the whole of the family is once again disintegrated and the particular will has to stand completely on its own. The unity of the individual that is achieved in the family is a "being of recognition without the opposition of the will" (209); and this is actually a cognition of oneself in the other but still not yet as "free will" (ibid.). In opposition to this "self-denial" (ibid.) of the individual founded on the unity of love, the value of the moment of exclusive self-reference must be introduced: only then can "cognition" in the other become "recognition" (212).[16] The particular must also freely attain to the membership in the family, to "the whole that encloses within itself an other" (205) and as a member must experience itself in this whole as a unity of the opposed drives of external activity and self-reflection, that is, as self-cognition in the love of the other as self and object and through the objectification of love with respect to family hearth and child. The family is thereby a whole of oppositions whose moments themselves comprise a unity of opposites—are, in other words, "complete, free individuals" (205), totalities in line with the *Jena Philosophy of 1803–4*.

In the *Jena Philosophy of 1803–4* struggle also pertains to the achievement of an individual totality within the family and manifests itself in the struggle on the part of the individual to will his totality. This totality is, however, without the "extreme" of particularity—what the individual lacks is not only the consciousness of his totality, as shown in the *Jena Philosophy of 1803–4*, but above all the "selfness" (*Selbständigkeit*) (209), which is a quality of the will. In order to accomplish this, each one must simultaneously pull back from unity with the other. The "movement" of the struggle for recognition does not begin with an unconscious self-knowledge through the other, but "on the contrary, consists of not knowing oneself in the other and much more in seeing the for-itself of the other in the other" (ibid.). That is why recognition does not require loss of possession, as in the *Jena Philosophy of 1803–4*, but rather, taking possession would already suffice where recognition involves taking something that the other person needs. Because "man as a particular has the right to take possession of what he can. . .what he grasps in his mind is that he must be a self; thereby he becomes a power over all things" (207). It is with respect to this right[17] and this power of taking possession of the other, that each person will necessarily be unsettled. Possession also finds itself in a situation, that is, in the state of nature as a necessary cause of conflict where power

---

16. The beginning of this can already be seen in upbringing as the highest potential of the family whereby the individual learns to differentiate between the "for-itself" of the community and "spiritual substance" (p. 204) and will go beyond itself as "whole." Upbringing, therefore, is a "sublation of love." Even in this, however, the individual does not arrive at his extreme moment of particularity.

17. This certainly does not do service to the concept or idea of right, since in the *Realphilosphie*—as in the case of Kant and Fichte—right is not possible in the state of nature.

pertains to power over each and every particular. However, this conflict, as in the *Jena Philosophy of 1803–4*, is itself a moment of the movement of recognition in the way that the self ceases "being this particular" (206) and acknowledges its own identity with that of the other in the universal will. The struggle is transformed as the movement of recognition recognizes the legal aspect of the recourse to natural possession. It is in the relation of the free individual that there arises the "necessity" (205) of leaving behind the state of nature. It is for this reason that Hegel could positively cite Hobbes' exeundum e statu naturae—as he had earlier in his inauguration thesis—yet by it mean something quite different; namely, that the state of nature is not only a struggle through which conquering must be relinquished but rather it is relinquished through struggle or is sublated in the struggle itself.

CHAPTER 16

Self-Sufficient Man

DOMINION AND BONDAGE

Judith N. Shklar

BONDAGE

"Man is born free and everywhere he is in chains. The man who believes that he is the master of others is nevertheless more enslaved than they are." Hegel's political philosophy begins with a restatement of Rousseau's immortal paradox. It was for him the ultimate revolutionary challenge. Rousseau had claimed that he simply did not know how mankind had come to this monstrous state of collective bondage and self-deception.[1] Hegel could not leave it at that. He had to account for the historical fate that the French Revolution had revealed in the moment when freedom was both affirmed and denied. To go beyond Rousseau was no simple task. It required a reconstruction of the entire experience of European "self-consciousness."

Self-consciousness is the second cycle of Hegel's model of the mind in search of knowledge. It begins with the realization that the certainties of understanding are projections of the categories inherent in man's intellect. When one reaches the limits of natural reason one sees that the question, "What do I know?" can only be answered when one knows what one is. In its first efforts toward that self-knowledge the now self-aware ego divides itself so that one half is observed and desired by the other; for desire is awakened by objects that the mind places before itself. And it is the desire to reappropriate its other half, to know it by reinte-

---

1. Rousseau was being disingenuous here, since in the *Second Discourse* he had given an elaborate explanation of how this state of affairs had come about.

gration, which moves the ego. This procedure, however, can yield only tautological self-certainty: the perfect assurance that ego = ego. This is subjectivism in its purity: an unending pursuit of the self by itself. It does not lead on to knowledge. For that, as "we" know, a whole self must confront another entire self in a conscious act of mutual re-cognition, that is, of knowing the self again in an other. This is the final, the erotic act, the equivalent of reproduction. It is the ego re-creating itself fully in order truly to know itself. In this case that does not call for self-reincarnation, but for its intellectual equivalent. In mutual recognition men acknowledge their identity and overtly know each other as one "we."[2] This process is the perfection of communication and even its first steps require more than primitive utterances. It is possible only as part of an already highly articulate culture. The dawn of self-knowledge is Homer's poetry, itself an act of memory. His was the first "universal song" that sets us off on our journey toward self-knowledge.[3]

The epic hero is certain of himself, aware only of his own self-sufficiency and autonomy. Achilles is beholden to nothing and to nobody. He is utterly alone in the knowledge of his own character and fate.[4] The existence of other equally independent beings is for him both a threat and a challenge. Since, as a hero, he must demonstrate his independence to reaffirm himself, he is determined to impose himself upon these others. Each one is driven to challenge the others to a duel to the death. Each one, knowing only his own passive, consuming ego, sees the other as a mirror of that half of his self-divided self. As such the other is a deadly threat that must be subdued to ensure the survival of the active, the self-conscious ego. He must therefore risk everything for the sake of ensuring this independence. The battle of heroic competition cannot be anything less than mortal combat. Hector and Achilles never consider anything else. They do go beyond self-certainty, however. A moment of genuine mutual recognition does occur. For it is peculiarly human to risk one's life for the sake of one's self-image.[5] It sets men radically apart from the beasts. The germ of the freedom of mankind is born in the battle between heroes. But it does not grow or endure. For no common bond

---

2. *B* stands for *The Phenomenology of Mind*, trans. and ed. J. B. Baillie (London, 1949), and *H* for *Phänomenologie des Geistes*, ed. J. Hoffmeister (Hamburg, 1952): B218–27; H133–40.

3. B732–33; H507–8.

4. B229–34, 736; H141–46, 510. In the sections that follow I use the words autonomy, independence, and self-sufficiency interchangeably.

5. H. C. Baldry, *The Unity of Mankind in Greek Thought* (Cambridge, 1965), 8–15.

is forged. Only a sense of a general fate, of inevitable death is shared by these warriors. One recalls that Homer's phrase for men is "mortal beings." Nevertheless there is one fleeting moment of genuine recognition: when Achilles and Priam stand over the dead body of Hector, they suddenly know their common humanity. Here is knowledge, but it is only the act of a passing moment.

The real defects of the self-sufficient self emerge in the inevitable consequences of heroic battle. If one of the warriors is not killed, he is enslaved and reduced to passivity. The new situation is now one that involves no heroes, only the slave and his owner. The latter, considered only as a master, is neither a hero, nor a citizen engaged in the affairs of the city. The Aristotelian master knows that happiness is to be found only in perfect contemplative self-sufficiency. To achieve this he must have a slave to provide him with the necessities of life. He also needs the slave to define himself.[6] Self-sufficiency is the very opposite of slavery not only because the slave is obviously constrained by his owner, but because he toils and produces. He performs wholly degrading tasks that immerse him in the material world of which he is almost a part. At most he is the supreme tool. For to the extent that he is a part of the master, he cannot be called an instrument of production, but one of action. As a true slave, however, he lacks the capacity for deliberation and merely produces, he functions as a "thing." He exists to supply the master with all the objects that the latter desires. The master is a pure consumer. His desires are gratified effortlessly. He need not concern himself in any way with work or creation. Indeed that would only impinge upon his independence. All he must know is to command the services of a slave. What the slave does is of no interest to the master as long as this instrument acts in accordance with his wishes. If the slave were to be considered a human being that would, of course, render this arrangement impossible. Greeks, Aristotle remembered, cannot be natural slaves.[7] That does not render slavery any less necessary. It is not only required for the self-sufficiency of the master. Master and slave are, above all, paradigmatic, a manifestation of a universal principle of order. It would be difficult to exaggerate the importance of the image of master and slave in Aristotle's thought. It expresses the essential character not only of all relationships of superiority and inferiority, but of a pervasive dualism. Mind and body, spirit and matter, theory and practice, contemplation

---

6. *Nicomachean Ethics*, X, 1177a–1178a.
7. *Politics*, I, 1252a–1255b, 1259a–1260b; III, 1277a.

and action, all exhibit the necessity of ruling and subordination that originates in the very constitution of the universe.[8]

These considerations give Hegel's celebrated set-piece "Lord and Bondsman" its central place in the rise and fall of the independent self-consciousness.[9] As a hero, self-sufficient man had a very clear, and within its limits, a true sense of himself. The lord who sees himself solely a master of others is quite mistaken about himself and his situation. He thinks that he is perfectly autonomous, but in fact he relies utterly upon his slave, not only to satisfy all his desires, but for his identity. Without slaves he is no master. That is the implication of reducing the "other" to a mere, part of himself. He has defined himself in terms of the "thing" he owns. The master is also deluded in thinking this toiling part of himself inferior because it works. The belief that producing is a less than human activity is wholly erroneous. It condemns the master to arrested development. Contemplation without creation, thought without learning, is pure passivity. As a pure consumer it is the master who becomes an idle thing.

The active erotic consciousness is that of the slave. By working upon material objects not only does he learn skills, but he also develops an awareness that he dominates the matter that he molds with his hands. He knows the difference between himself and the products of his labor. In his mortal fear of the master he also comes to know what it is to be human. Total fear teaches him self-discipline and self-mastery. Only this mixture of such fear and unremitting productive toil can give the slave his consciousness of autonomy. Work without fear is just vexing, while pure fear merely paralyzes. Together these two experiences make the slave the self-sufficient man that the master so falsely imagines himself to be. The slave now has a mind of his own that goes far beyond stubbornness. He is conscious of himself as a human being and demands that his master recognize him as such.

When master and slave know each other as alike in their autonomy, neither one is liberated. The slave merely adopts the stance of the master as both flee inward. The master gives up his dependence on the slave, and indeed on all external things, while the slave comes to share the master's contempt for productive work. Both are now alike in their independence from the shackles of the entire physical order. This is the stoic consciousness, a state of indifference to the external world that was

---

8. *Nicomachean Ethics*, V, 1138b; VIII, 1161a–b. Baldry, *Unity of Mankind*, 88–101.
9. B234–40; H146–50.

implicit all along in the master's highest aspirations. The ultimate aim of his mastership was to give him the leisure to devote himself entirely to contemplation. He is the hero-as-philosopher. Had not Socrates already compared himself favorably to mighty Achilles?[10] Aristotle's master, the hero-as-philosopher, looks upon contemplation as the perfection of the self-sufficient life. It is the worst of his illusions, for the man who just waits for knowledge to come to him waits in vain. There is nothing out there to contemplate. The contemplative man is doomed to a condition of spiritual emptiness and immobility. This is the stoic. He thinks himself unfettered in thinking and does not realize that his is the freedom of the void.[11] Ratiocination divorced from experience yields only formal platitudes: it repeats intuitions without advancing toward new knowledge.

With stoicism Hegel, for the first time in the *Phenomenology*, chose to refer to speciflc political events directly. The inner emigration of the stoic reflects the spiritless, atomizing, horrible despotism of the Roman Empire.[12] It is a world that repels everyone, from the supreme lord down to the lowest slave. Thought alone, the mind in isolation, seems the only impregnable spiritual fortress. Marcus Aurelius on his throne and Epictetus in his chains share the same philosophy. Both are "wise men" in flight from a crushing external world. That is why Marcus Aurelius quotes Epictetus's remark that man is "a poor soul burdened with a corpse" and pitied the great warrior heroes of the past for suffering from "an infinity of enslavements."[13] Epictetus' own view of slavery is an inversion of actuality, not a liberation. Slavery is not really being owned by another man, but being subjugated to one's own ambitions and avarice.[14] The perfect independence that both these "wise men" seek is really a rejection of otherness. To be sure, both emperor and slave acknowledge their common manhood, but they achieve this sense of universality only by turning their backs on nature and history, labor and action. Theirs is a rationality abstracted from all possible sources of human experience. Their standards of judgment, drawn from this internal reason, is a dogmatism that issues commands directed at all men at all times and in all circumstances. Conduct prescribed for everyone in this way fits no one at all. All this talk about goodness, virtue and wisdom is very ele-

---

10. *Apology*, 28–29.
11. B245, 752–54; H153, 523–24.
12. B242–46, 502–3; H152–54, 343–44.
13. *Meditations*, trans. Maxwell Staniforth (London, 1964), Bk Iv, s. 41, Bk VIII, s. 3.
14. "Of Freedom," *Moral Discourses*, ed. and trans. H. D. Rouse (London, 1910), 200–216.

vating, but it has no specific context or intent. In fact, the stoic always does his painful duty, but for him that is only evidence of his irremediable bondage to the world. In acting he is not independent, for his withdrawal from the world is incomplete.

The stoic uttering his various prescriptions from within does not actively justify the voice he calls reason. Such dogmatism exists, as it were, to be challenged and defied. Where there is intuitive rationalism there skepticism is bound to appear.[15] This is the spirit that denies, that doubts everything, the outer no less than the inner order. The skepticism of Sextus Empiricus is no mere Humean empiricism.[16] It is total uncertainty. It sees that all the objects of knowledge are fleeting. This skepticism knows all the exceptions to the rules, all the contradictions raised by every generality. This is free thought in action.

The stoic's independence was entirely passive. To really assert the autonomy of thought one must deny the certainty of all sense experience. One must doubt everything in fact. That is why the merely complacent dogmatism of stoci indifference to the world calls forth skepticism. The skeptic really means to put the autonomy of thought into action. Everything gives way to its doubts, its whys and wherefores. Facts, moral rules, data, all the certainties are swept aside. The slave is cast out entirely. He is all that toil and desire that a liberated mind denies. For the skeptic has completed the dialectical run from sense-certainty to the limits of understanding and knows all about the flux of appearance on which slaves work so painfully. He is, finally, not taken in by the sophist's faith in man as the measure of all things. Those standards are just as open to doubt as the will of the sovereign or anything else that may present itself as a rule. The world, after all, is full of contradictory regulations. This, in short, is doubt for the sake of doubting. It is not the acquiescence of the baffled understanding confronted by infinity, but a deliberate doubting as an assertion of spiritual self-will.

The skeptic doubts even his own doubts, his own ever-challenging ego, but he cannot altogether annihilate it. He needs it to doubt. That is one difficulty. The other paradox is inherent in the activity of doubting. The mind must always absorb and identify with the objects that it must deny. It must see to deny the certainty of sight, recognize rules to challenge their validity, and hear in order to doubt sound. Such a mind is shackled to the world, because it needs chains to break, since its freedom is just the act of liberation.

---

15. B246–51, 503; H153–58, 343–44.
16. *Lectures on the History of Philosophy*, II, 328–73; *The Logic of Hegel*, ss. 24, 32, 81.

In his awareness of the contradictions inherent in consciousness, the skeptic stands at the gates of wisdom. Precisely because of his despair regarding common sense and "the whole compass of the phenomenal world" he is qualifled to approach truth.[17] However, over and over again, he turns away from this possibility. He does not move on to self-knowledge. This refusal of the skeptic to forge ahead is a recurrent experience of consciousness. The radical skepticism of the Enlightenment, for instance, had been dissipated in the French Revolution, while the even more profound skepticism of antiquity had been succeeded by gnosticism, Neo-Platonism, and Christianity, all expressions of the unhappy consciousness.[18] This is not a logical necessity, but an emotional one. The psychic tension of skepticism is overwhelming and the distracted ego chooses some avenue of escape. It yearns for some point of spiritual peace far from the world of doubt. It flees to some "beyond" where it hopes to be free or goes inward to cultivate a "beautiful soul." In either case the ex-skeptic now accepts self-division, ceases to be defiant, and becomes a permanently unhappy consciousness shifting miserably between the bonds of this world and the ever-receding freedom above, out there, or within.

With this account of skepticism Hegel had not only elaborated Rousseau's resounding sentences; he had gone well beyond them. For Rousseau had identified freedom with self-sufficiency. That is why he was not able to rise above the eternal see-saw between dependence and independence. Not only did he admire the inner autonomy of stoic wise men, but he was also obsessed with securing the external, personal, and social self-sufficiency of ordinary people. *Emile's* model is Robinson Crusoe. He is dependent only on natural necessity, never on other people. The *Social Contract* is a scheme for combining that sort of liberty with the advantages of political society.[19] To Hegel, who identified Rousseau with the most anarchic tendencies of the French Revolution, that arrangement was merely the democratization of the autonomous consciousness.[20] Rousseau's failure, and above all that of the Revolution, arose

---

17. B136–37; H168. *Logic of Hegel*, s. 78. That master and slave taken together add up to nihilism is very ancient wisdom, as the Babylonian "Dialogue between Master and Slave" shows clearly enough.
18. B608, 754–56; H421, 524–26.
19. *Émile*, trans. Barbara Foxley (London, n.d.), 147–48, 436–37. *Social Contract*, I, 6.
20. B602–10; H416–22; *Philosophy of Right*, trans. T. M. Knox (Oxford, 1942), 33, 156–57 (ss. 29, 258); *Logic of Hegel*, s. 163; *Lectures on the History of Philosophy*, III, 400–42.

from an inability to grasp that independence and dependence are indissolubly linked parts of a single, self-divided consciousness, a continuation of the see-saw of dominion and bondage. These are not really alternatives. The one cannot and does not overcome the other. Freedom must be found in a far more radical change of human self-consciousness, in a genuine "recognition" among egos.

Hegel surely was mistaken about Rousseau's social ideas. They may have been closer to his own than he could bear to admit. One subject about which the two surely agreed was skepticism and its psychological burdens. Indeed to illustrate the self-estrangement of the unhappy consciousness, Hegel could have done worse than to quote "The Creed of the Savoyard Vicar."[21] The vicar begins by confessing that in his youth he had been a complete skeptic and a soul in despair. Unable to bear this state of mind, he turned to God, for whose existence he found sufficient proof in the needs of his own heart and in the visible order of nature. The manner of his discovery of God is interesting, but the character of this deity is even more important. For the vicar's God is pure will, omniscient and omnipotent. He is loved not as a benefactor but as a master who must be obeyed unconditionally. Unless the vicar can feel His presence immediately he feels lost. Only when he is certain of his obedience to God is he at rest, and that is rare. Mostly he is totally self-divided, at war with hienself. His life is therefore a constant yearning for the peace that only God's felt presence can give him. The belief that sustains him is that in an after-life he will be eternally reunited with God and so at peace. Until then he feels enslaved ty his lower self, free only when he obeys the voice of God within himself. When he errs, he is a mere thing; when he is good, he knows that he owes all to God's will. At all times he desperately needs God for both moral and intellectual reassurance. For "if there is no God, then the wicked is right and the good man is nothing but a fool."

This is a perfect picture of what Hegel called the unhappy consciousness.[22] It is miserable and self-divided not because it is sinful, but because of the kind of God it has created for itself. All creativity has been vested in an unreachable master. Mind has left nothing but thinghood for itself here and now. This God who is master clearly is the God of the Old Testament. The basic situation is not altered when God is incarnated in a historical person, in Christ, nor when He is universal spirit, as the third person of the Trinity. There is still only *one* source

---

21. *Émile*, 228–78.
22. B251–56; H158–62.

of life and *one* "beyond" toward which the believer aspires. The vicar is a Christian, but he trembles before a God, even though he longs to be reconciled to Him forever. As long as this God remains in charge, the relationship of master and bondsman prevails. What this unhappy consciousness cannot grasp, according to Hegel, is the meaning of God becoming man and dying. God is really dead, and the holy spirit is mankind's own spirit. The limits of a still primitive "pictorial" imagination, no less than self-division, keep the Christian far removed from self-knowledge. By directing all its erotic energies toward a beyond, the ego is deprived of the possibility of integration.[23] The self hatred of the skeptic is simply frozen in this consciousness, but he has been relieved of the anxieties of total doubt. Instead of accepting assertion and negation as part of a universal process he gives up questioning and finds stability in a beyond that guarantees the structure of reality. He also condemns himself to a life of yearning. Half of him is always "beyond" seeking God, the other must live below in the shadow. Although this ensures its misery, the unhappy consciousness needs this beyond and the master too much to return to the wholeness of here and now.

The "figurative" or "pictorial" awareness of God forbids any effort to make Him an object of thought. The believer cannot reach Him and attempts to do so, in any case, appear too self-assertive. Only the humble exercising of pious longing will do. To achieve the desperately desired unity with the divine object of devotion the unhappy consciousness tries at least four different ways of reaching God. All fail, but each one is a step toward ever deeper self-enslavement.[24] That, for Hegel, was the sum of the spiritual history of medieval Europe. First the unhappy consciousness tries to join God by possessing symbolic objects recalling Christ, relics especially. It seeks the tomb of Christ, for example. The Crusades, although they are acts of devotion, are also the occasion of the grossest brutishness. The quest for the Holy Land does not lead to God, but makes the crusader aware of himself and that in the most earth-bound form. The second effort is to toil and labor in the service of God in the hope of self-forgetfulness. However, just like the slave of a human master, this worker discovers that far from reducing the self, work gives him a strong sense of his own powers. Horrified by its pride, the worst of all sins, the unhappy consciousness practices humility and self-abnegation. God is credited with all the good work it has achieved. Whatever is well done is the work of Providence, not of man. The human consciousness

---

23. B778–85; H544–48.
24. B256–67; H162–71. E.g., *Lectures on the History of Philosophy*, III, 45–60.

eliminates itself from its work and thanks God. Even in these thanks there is pride and a sense of achievement. The unhappy consciousness is now so overwhelmed by the sense of its own sinfulness that it gives up toil on God's behalf. Its third effort to be at one with God is through self-mortification and asceticism. The devil is within himself and unconquerably so. For the very suspicion that the devil has been subdued is a sign of pride and proof of failure. This battle cannot be won. Having failed in all its attempts to destroy its own ego, the unhappy consciousness now comes to the most desperate measure of all. It gives up its power of judging, willing, and knowing to another human spirit, the priest of the Church. Now the believer is really a "thing"; he has inflicted upon himself what the Greek master could never do to his slave. It is not quite the end, however. The priest after all knows that he is not God, that the Church is so only implicitly. That is a crack in this destructive arrangement. It is enough to permit reason to enter and eventually to undermine this order.

The drama of the self-sufficient consciousness is now complete. It is not ended, since it repeats itself though in different ways and under other circumstances. In the age of the French Revolution the cycle of stoicism, skepticism, and unhappy consciousness is repeated. From rebellious self-assertion to the flight to a beyond by all sorts of yearning "beautiful souls," the pattern is displayed again. For Hegel these last, the romantics quivering with longing as they turn away from actuality, seemed particularly revolting.[25] In spite of his scorn and contempt he knew these to be the necessary final moments of the consciousness that begins by confusing the autonomy of passive masters with real freedom. The self that depends on its "thing," whether that be another human being or its own body so conceived, is conscious not of freedom, but only of bondage. It must swing back and forth between independence and dependence. The skeptic understands that perfectly well. He does not suffer from the delusion of those who think that self-isolation is really autonomy. The psychological cost of his realism is, however, too heavy and far from escaping both mastery and slavery he sinks eventually into extreme dependence. Hegel clearly thought that he was the first philosopher to have succeeded in going beyond this cycle, and in the works he wrote after the *Phenomenology* he set himself the task of explicitly overcoming it. Here he merely points to that possibility. For this is mostly an account of the experiences of incomplete forms of consciousness.

---

25. B663–67, 675–76; H460–76; H460–63, 470.

FREEDOM

One of the reasons Hegel was able to entertain the intellectual possibility of overcoming the recurring cycle of independence and dependence is that he knew that it had not always prevailed. Neither the epic hero nor the citizen of a free polity in its grip, and these figures from the past allow one to consider the character of free men. The precivic consciousness, though incomplete, did have its moments of undiluted grandeur. The epic heroes, founders of states, and creators of a vision of unbounded personal dominion, were undeniably glorious. Their fate was always lamentable, but they were neither self-divided nor self-deluded. To be sure the age of heroes can never return. They have no place in the civic order.[26] However, as men of action they remain exemplary, a reminder of what men can be. The hero is the very opposite of that consciousness that signs away its own will-power to others.

Hegel had already in an earlier essay compared the freedom of the heroes of Greek tragedy to the self-enslaved consciousness of both the Old Testament and of Kant. The latter are always subject to an external master, responsible to some power outside them. Even moral law within acts like an external master who lords it over the rest of the ego.[27] He rethought and rewrote those passages in his last years, especially in his lectures on art and religion. In the *Phenomenology* the heroic consciousness is singled out, even if only briefly, for its stance in the face of fate, for its ability to act freely even under that shadow. When the hero acts— and it is always on a grand scale, for these are great noblemen—he knows that he is challenging fate. He is the man who risks everything. He knows that he is asserting himself against a power that is superior even to the gods in the epic poems of Homer, and against the established religious and social order in the tragedies of Aeschylus and Sophocles. When he seeks glory, dominion, or revenge, he is defying powers he cannot control. To act boldly is in any case to incur the danger of error and evil. Innocence is not for man, not even for children. Only stones are innocent.[28] The Greek tragic hero knows that he can know only a part of all that is involved in his action. That does not deter him for one instant. For him

26. *Philosophy of Right*, 245 (addition to s. 93); *The Philosophy of Fine Art*, trans. F. P. B. Osmaston (London, 1920), IV, 120–68.

27. "The Spirit of Christianity and its Fate," trans. T. M. Knox, *Early Theological Writings*, ed. T. M. Knox and Richard Kroner (Chicago, 1948), 224–38.

28. B488; H334; *Lectures on the Philosophy of Religion*, ed. and trans. E. B. Speirs and J. B. Sanderson (New York, 1962), I, 272–85; *Hegel's Philosophy of Mind*, trans. William Wallace (Oxford, 1894), s. 472.

the real tension is not between guilt and innocence in any case, but between guilt and destiny.[29] The Greek hero knows that he must suffer unspeakably as a result of his self-assertion. Achilles knows that he must die soon, but he does not shrink from action.[30] Neither do Oedipus, Orestes, and Antigone, who expect to suffer as they do thanks to their inner destiny. The heroes of tragedy, moreover, accept responsibility for the "entire compass" of their deed. They do not limit their responsibility to what they intended and could foresee. Their crime includes all the consequences and unknown aspects of their deeds. It would be beneath them to assume the lesser burden. They are not responsible *to* anyone, but *for* everything, even those circumstances that were beyond their knowledge and control. The acts of tragedy, unlike those of the earlier epics, are not controlled by an outer fate; their actions are compelled by their character, but necessity surrounds them and enhances their guilt. Indeed culpability is part of that necessity which is now called fate.

When Orestes and Oedipus commit their various crimes they are rebelling against fate. They arouse an enemy against themselves. By destroying life they bring the furies down upon themselves. The fury of remorse and grief rages within the tragic hero. He knows that he is faced with necessity and accepts it. He does not deny his responsibility for his acts or the inevitability of what follows. It is so. The sorrow and regret that torment him, moreover, can be shaken off. They can be washed away. There are several things a tragic hero could do. He might commit suicide to find forgetfulness in Lethe. No judging god awaits him and the blot is wiped out. He might expiate his crime and put the furies to rest as Orestes does with Athena's help, or heal himself as Oedipus does in a mystical rite at Colonus.[31] At no time does he receive grace or forgiveness as a Christian might. He heals himself and frees himself from culpability. The age of heroes is gone, but the possibility of thinking of error and evil as fate remains. Not a punitive God, but the inherent structure of reality and of our individual natures make it inevitable. No one need fear action.

The Greek who knew necessity and said "It is so," "It cannot be helped," did not need consolation. For necessity is not coercion and it is not a tyrant or something imposed at all. It is simply inescapable

---

29. B489–92; H334–36.
30. B736; H510.
31. B489–92, 739–43; H334–36, 513–16. In the *Philosophy of Find Art*, IV, 312–26, Hegel made clear that he did *not* think of Oedipus's release as a Christian act of salvation, but as an ethical reconciliation.

reality. It cannot oppress once it is truly accepted. That is why the Greeks were never vexed as we always are. The reverent sense of necessity led the Greeks to create themselves into noble and beautiful characters. They internalized necessity, they made no effort to escape it. We, in glaring contrast, never say "It is so," but always "It ought to be so" and are always petulant-and dissatisfted with ourselves, thanks to bad conscience, to the fear of God and of law—all seen as willful masters over ourselves. Finally, the necessity of Greek fate had nothing to do with the chain of cause and effect. The latter is also experienced as a loss of freedom and thus a source of frustration for which we require continual consolation. Real necessity is not an explanation. It is the sheer "is-ness" of reality as given.[32] Heroic man, in short, is free.

This realism and untroubled acceptance of necessity, which is the heart of freedom, is not limited to heroic figures. It is shared by the far less ambitious and far more law-abiding chorus of citizens. The capacity to act without inner division, the undivided ego, is common to the united citizens of a free polity. The law is their fate. The master is neither an epic nor a tragic hero, but he is more than a mere owner of slaves. He is also a citizen. He shares in the spontaneous inner integrity of a whole people. Collectively these citizens are an individual people, a whole that acts freely. It is a situation that cannot endure. The inner harmony of such a people is unreflective and that is its great defect.[33] When individual rationality asserts itself against the common order the free society crumbles. The sophists shake it and Socrates is both the product and voice of its dissolution. He already speaks for the future ages of personal morality and public disintegration. Not even Plato could restore a civic order once it had been destroyed.[34] Nevertheless, Athens remains our one and only intimation of what a free people might be. As such, the people, far more than the totally defunct hero, is a more relevant example of genuine freedom. As citizens they stand outside the cycle of independence and dependence. They are the only example of a happy consciousness. Their happiness is one that mankind has lost or *maybe* has "not yet attained."[35] In either case it is the "utopia," the nowhere, now which alone illuminates what freedom, in contrast to lordship and bondage, would be. As the only picture of recognition, it shows the self at home

---

32. *Philosophy of Religion*, II, 239–43; 256–67, 286–88; *Philosophy of Fine Art*, I, 214–15.
33. B462–63, 498–99; H317–18, 342.
34. B747; H519; *Lectures on the History of Philosophy*, I, 384–448.
35. B378–80; H258–60.

and the erotic ego satisfied. It is not a state of self-knowledge, but it is its emotional equivalent.

The master is *merely* a slave owner when he has ceased to be the citizen of a free polity. Only then is he isolated. He thinks he is independent because he is not owned by another man and has achieved an aloof spiritual condition. Once, however, he had been an integral part of an ethical culture and a free, rather than a merely independent, man. Without being aware of it, he was an active citizen, integrated into the political life of an autonomous city of people who mutually recognized each other. The relationship among masters was freedom and reason realized. This autonomy of the polis and the freedom of its people had never been regained. The French Revolution had not been a new beginning, but only the prelude to a new cycle leading inward and to the unhappy unconsciousness of romanticism, endemic in modern culture. The culture of an ethical people is nowhere in sight. Yet Hegel thought that it might be in the future. However, prediction was never his business. The *Phenomenology* is devoted to remembrances.

Each one of the cycles of self-consciousness, that is, every section concerned with moral and political phenomena, begins with a lovingly drawn picture of ancient Athens and its free, ethical people. Hegel clearly places these passages strategically to remind us in each case of what had been lost and not yet regained.[36] He uses the Homeric hero, the single free man, to introduce the cycle of autonomy that ends with the unhappy consciousness. The story of the efforts of modern practical reason to develop a viable ethic is preceded by a long account of the happy people of the polis. The tale of the course of the European public spirit up to the age of the French Revolution opens with a discussion of Sophoclean tragedy. And finally, the pages devoted to religion, after a brief review of natural religion, go on to Hellas's religion of art in all its perfection. All these recurrent reminders of the Greek achievement are not just meant to give us an intelligible notion of what a free people would be. They are extreme contrasts that act as illuminations, like searchlights. The Greeks are called on to show us what has not been achieved, the distance between then and now. In each case one is forced to see that every cycle of self-consciousness is remote from self-knowledge. If one puts all these passages about Athens together, one sees that they are not presented as a goal to strive for, but as a judgment. Indeed, even as a young man Hegel had already known that Achaea could never be the Teutons' home, even if they were to forget Judea.[37] They belong neither

---

36. B230–34, 375–79, 462–99, 709–49; H142–45, 256–59, 317–42, 490–520.
37. "The Positivity of the Christian Religion," *Early Theological Writings*, 149.

to Athens, nor to Jerusalem. There can, however, be no mistaking the difference in Hegel's attitude to these two eternal cities. The first was regretted, loved, and recalled as an enduring inspiration; the second was an experience to be overcome.

CHAPTER 17

The Metaphor in Hegel's *Phenomenology of Mind*

Henry Sussman

The program of the following essay is to read the *Phenomenology* in terms of its internal account of its own language.[1] Yet the Hegelian attitude toward language that may be extrapolated from the text is far from unambiguous in itself. It is no accident that the stages through which consciousness first passes in the *Phenomenology*, sense-certainty, perception, and understanding, though organically linked, follow the stratification of the Kantian system (as elaborated in the *Critique of Pure Reason and the Prolegomena to Any Future Metaphysics*). In these texts the locus of the intuitions (*Anschauungen*), appearances (*Erscheinungen*), and representations (*Vorstellungen*)[2] is perception, the lowest common denominator of cognition, a level cultivated by understanding and reason. On the one hand, when Hegel questions the certainty based on sensory experience in the first chapter in terms of the problems attending the notions of meaning and intentionality, he conditions all that follows in the *Phenomenology* by these linguistic concerns. On the other hand, since the higher crystallizations of cognition, culture, and social organization increase primarily in the complexity of the mediation they afford,

---

1. With regard to the *Phenomenology*, citations and page numbers refer to Georg Wilhelm Friedrich Hegel, *Phenomenology of Spirit*, trans. A. V. Miller (Oxford University Press, 1977). German phrases derive from Hegel, *Phänomenologie des Geistes* (Hamburg: Meiner, 1952).

2. Immanuel Kant, *Prolegomena to Any Future Metaphysics* (Indianapolis: Bobbs-Merrill, 1950), 29–31, 39–41, 51, 34–36, 38–39.

Hegel's interest in problematizing language so early in the *Phenomen-ology* could be as much to silence the question as to privilege it.

Hegel's conditioning the *Phenomenology* with the problematization of language bespeaks an ambivalence toward language as much as it does an anticipation of current philosophical and literary interests. What may well emerge with greatest contemporary value from a reading of Hegel is not so much a repudiation of possibly mechanical formal operations but the schizoid break separating the counterimperatives of the text: to read the *Phenomenology* as a nonlinear, discontinuous metaphoric generator and to read it in terms of the presuppositions enabling its formal apparatus to operate. The endurance of this schizoid structure may well constitute the ultimate contribution of dialectical thought.

NOVELTY

The *Phenomenology* functions simultaneously as a novel, an encyclo-pedia, a history of ideas, a genealogy of symbolic forms, and a logic of its own operations. As such, it is of mixed genre.

As a novel, it records the development of a central character, con-sciousness,[3] which in turn breaks down into a group of subcharacters, including sense-certainty, perception, understanding, *Aufhebung*, and *in-itself, for-itself*, and *for-consciousness*. It is the repeatability of these terms, their iterability[4] from context to context, which gives them the continuity of novelistic characters. The first three components of the above list, for example, initially appear as the basic *stages* of cognition. But stoicism and skepticism, the preliminary stages the "unhappy con-sciousness," are negative examples of sense-certainty and perception, which prepared the way for the speculative breakthrough of under-standing. And the narrative of the *Phenomenology* explicitly mentions all three substages of cognition as models for the substages of natural religion, itself a preparation for esthetic and revealed religions.

---

3. The "character" "consciousness" is also the most fully elaborated metaphor in the work.. . .The metaphoracity of consciousness is at once the *Phenomen-ology*'s central and widest category. It is at this point that my reading diverges from those which, like Jean Hyppolite's, regard the work primarily as a develop-ment or genealogy of consciousness through experience. See Jean Hyppolite, *Genesis and Structure of Hegel's Phenomenology of Spirit*, trans. Samuel Cherniak and John Heckman (Evanston, Ill.: Northwestern University Press, 1974), 11–15, 39–41.

4. For an elucidation of the problems attending the notion of iterability, see Jacques Derrida, "Signature Event Context," in *Glyph I* (Baltimore: Johns Hopkins University Press, 1977), 172–97.

Other characters of the *Phenomenology* are so by virtue of function rather than identity. Each stage of consciousness generates its own particular, universal, and *Begriff* (notion or conceptual horizon). The particular, universal, and *Begriff* change from stage to stage, are *relative* to their respective stages. Yet as *functions*, the particular, the universal, and the *Begriff* share in the continuing existence of characters. Infinity, a trope encompassing all of the stages of distinction-making and generalization involved in abstraction, constitutes the conceptual horizon of a not yet reflexive consciousness. Yet beyond the threshold of self-consciousness, on the inside of the reflexive sphere, the once-formal fluctuations of infinity reappear, but under the organic rubric of life (*Leben*). Life is to self-consciousness what infinity was to consciousness, a conceptual horizon. The function has continued while its filling has changed. The existence within the text of functional constants that attain the continuity of characters is in keeping with an ideology of the organic that has repeatedly stressed the importance of process over product and development over rectitude.

The development of the philosophical characters in the *Phenomenology*, whether substantial or functional, is narrated by a narrator. But no sooner do we speak of a narrative voice in the *Phenomenology* than this construct bifurcates. There is a retrospective narrative voice that intervenes from the superior position of absolute knowing. This omniscient narrator often introduces sections and provides summations at their ends, but is also free to interrupt elsewhere: "In so far as it ['self-consciousness which. . . knows itself to be *reality'*] has lifted itself out of the ethical Substance and the tranquil being of thought to its being-*for-self*, it has left behind the law of custom and existence, the knowledge acquired through observation, and theory, as a grey shadow which is in the act of passing out of sight (217). The observations made by this rather sedate self-consciousness are behind it "as a grey shadow"—yet the tone and point of view of this passage could apply to a character recently undergoing an experience in any novel with an omniscient narrator. In the narrative of the *Phenomenology* this particular voice alternates with a blow-by-blow description of consciousness experience presumably as it is taking place. The narrative function providing the ostensibly immediate transcription of events has been designated by critics, at least with respect to the twentieth-century novel, as the *erlebte Rede* or "narrated monologue":[5] "But sensuous being and *my* meaning themselves pass over

---

5. Cf. Dorrit Cohn, "The Narrated Monologue: Definition of a Fictional Style," *Comparative Literature* 18 (1966): 97–112.

into perception: I am thrown back to the beginning and drawn once again into the same cycle which supersedes itself in each monment and as a whole. Consiousness, therefore, necessarily runs through this cycle again" (71). This narrative voice confines itself to the endlessly extended present to which the phenomenological enterprise continually devolves, the present in which consciousness senses, perceives, and understands.

Not only does this philosophical novel pursue characters and narrate, if in different ways. As we have seen, *in-itself*, *for-itself* and *for-conscious-ness* are the text's perspectival constants. They are differentiated according to degrees of purpose and containment. *In-itself* is a perspective of passive self-containment that can be positive or negative. It is negative in excluding otherness and the awareness that otherness might bring (52); positive when the containment consummates a return to the self, the recuperation of a self-awareness that has been lost (138). *For-itself* is a perspective of assertion and purpose rather than passivity. The possibility of actualization that it affords is undercut by the general critique of action (as opposed to thought) formulated, for example, in the reading of Sophocles' *Antigone* in "The Ethical World." *For-itself* enjoys the positivity of assertion (10), but it suffers from the blindness of self-interest (52). The perspective of being *for consciousness* is predicated by a reversal in which self-containment and self-assertion are seen from their *other* sides, that is, from the perspective of what they contribute to otherness, both to the overall development of consciousness and to the philosophical mind composing and reading the text. The pervasiveness of these three perspectival constants provides a trigonometric notation by which consciousness can often, if not always, sight its position and progress.

Just as the *Phenomenology*'s narrative structure vacillates between immediate transcription and omniscient narration, its temporal perspective incorporates both diachronic and synchronic analyses. The text's diachronic purview encompasses the development from primitive hypotheses (e.g., "the ancient Eleusinian Mysteries of Ceres and Bacchus" in "Sense-Certainty," 65) to the sophisticated rationality of modern science. This development is both conceptual and historical: it encompasses the evolution of the infrastructures (force, law, genus) making modern science possible but also situates certain particular crystallizations (phrenology, organic reason) within their wider intellectual contexts.

Closely related to this genealogy of scientific disciplines and symbolic forms is the text's anthropological stratum, accounting for the rise of more or less universal social institutions, most notably of a political and theological nature. It is within this strand of the text that the treatment of the dead preconditions and defines the ethical community. Sophocles' *Antigone* becomes an extended metaphor exemplifying a moment when the law of the natural community (the family) is at odds with that of the state. This moment is also, for Hegel, the genesis of the unconscious: The predicament of an actor subjected to opposing but inescapable sets of laws implies that each action entails the repression of all other alternatives, alternatives fated to haunt the actor in a strikingly Freudian way. Both an anthropological moment (the institutions regarding the treatment of the dead) and a psychohistorical event (the rise of the unconscious) thus join to form part of a historical progression. This moment is preceded by the organization of the city-state and succeeded by the concept of the nation. Similarly, Hegel's fundamentally ahistorical accounts of nature religion and sun-worship will be marshaled in a progression culminating in the historical appearance of Judeo-Christianity.

It is, however, in its synchronic program that the text comes closest to its title, to being a *Phenomenology*, if we define this genre as a profile and dramatization of the structures of a consciousness that is continually asserting, negating, and surpassing itself. There seems to be little that argues against the conclusion drawn by Jacques Derrida in *Speech and Phenomena*[6] that the enterprise of phenomenology never passes beyond the perceptual field—despite the fact that Hegel supplements his "Perception" with the elaborate scenario for abstraction in "Understanding." In its phenomenological dimension, the text observes consciousness as it in turn perceives its own prior crystallizations and the limits that are the product of every stage. It is within the text's phenomenological dimension that there can be at least some reconciliation between its formal tropes and metaphors. As was suggested above, both of these components comprise a metalanguage in which the text accounts for its own writing. The text's formal tropes tend to *formalize* its narrative necessities. The *Aufhebung* and the triad of *in-itself, for-itself,* and *for-consciousness* implement the narrative functions, allowing for progression in time and change of perspective. The text's metaphors, on the other hand, tend to emblematize *conceptual* developments, as electromagnetism embodies a particular type of abstraction. And so both the formal and the metaphoric elements of the text's phenomenological program are descriptive of consciousness development and the constitution of the text. And if these formal and metaphoric components are ever at odds with each

---

6. Trans. David B. Allison (Evanston, Ill.: Northwestern University Press, 1973), 104.

other, it is because they are descriptive of slightly different textual domains.

As a novel, an encyclopedia, a history of ideas, a genealogy of symbolic forms, an anthropology, and a logic of its own operations, the *Phenomenology* is itself a germ, a microcosm of Hegel's writings. The synecdoche that enables this work, in reduced scale, to anticipate subsequent explorations also characterizes the interaction between the *Phenomenology*'s smallest and widest scales of activity. The movements of interiorization and exteriorization, which so often describe developments within the immediate transcription of events, also characterize the relations between the text's widest units. "Self-Consciousness" and "Spirit," for example, may be described as internalized or subjective emanations, respectively, of "Consciousness" and "Reason." This synecdoche, whose organic model is the seed, is one of Hegel's most successful, and for that reason most suspect, modes of coordination.[7]

The general coordination within the Hegelian text enables its narrative, logical, formal, and metaphoric strata to be mutually interchangeable. Where an argument reaches its logical termination—say when it becomes explicit that the increasingly abstract constructs of understanding are based on *apparent* distinctions—the formal level is free to intercede, as when the stages of understanding are collapsed and formalized into the trope of infinity. Infinity *circularizes* the steps of asserting and withdrawing differences that comprise understanding within a single (organically) unified figure. Or when the limit of a stage becomes its formalization—again understanding—a metaphor can be summoned, in this case the theatrical curtain at the close of chapter 3, that "redeems" the formal flattening by reversing it into a self-reflexive moment. In emulation of the *Phenomenology*'s organic ideal, its discursive functions replace one another, complement one another, and compensate for each other's deficiencies.

FORCE

If in "Sense Certainty" and "Perception" Hegel outlines certain structures that will carry through for the rest of the work, it is in "Force and the Understanding" that he completes the battery of formal tools that not

---

7. For the place of the synecdochical relationship between the seed or germ and the living being within the ideology of the organic, see Philip C. Ritterbush, *The Art of Organic Forms* (Washington, D.C.: Smithsonian Institution Press, 1968), 16–27.

only allow for the speculative leap into the supersensible, but also provide for virtually all subsequent operations. Although understanding constitutes an intellectual stage against whose endless distinction-making and abstraction Hegel voices his skepticism, this chapter nonetheless consummates Hegel's program for the *Phenomenology.* In the wake of this chapter, additional substantive material from a variety of different scientific, sociopolitical, and esthetic contexts may be fed into this program, but the deep structures of the readout will have been established. The master-slave conflict will comprise a meditation on the models of reciprocity and inequality completed in this chapter, while the Unhappy Consciousness will expand upon, in a self-conscious domain, the hierarchical configuration of metaphysical strata that the variable appearance (*Erscheinung*) first allows.

The achievement of understanding that completes consciousness detachment from sensation and literally breaks the gravitational field of the empirical world is a conception of force in which the existence of *particular* reciprocally related counterforces does not compromise the existence of the force as a (general) whole. The metaphor of a conceptual force on a higher level of generality than the particular subforces that make it up, a conceptual force somehow above the activities of expression (*Äußerung*) and repression (*Zurüruckdrängen*) to which the subforces are relegated, is a model for abstraction itself. The general, conceptual force derives its structure and motion from the subforces yet is not subject to their limitations (their particularities of valence or direction). The primary metaphor that Hegel selects for the conceptual stage of understanding is from the referential sphere of physics. An electromagnetism that incorporates, assimilates, and supersedes its positive and negative charges yet nonetheless remains structured by them is an apt example for the abstraction bonding two different planes of generality.

Spatially conceived, a bond between lower and higher levels of generality or particularity is vertical. Yet the highest conceptual crystallization suggested in the first two chapters of the *Phenomenology* is a reciprocity whose spatial extension is horizontal. A passage from "Perception" (from p. 76 of the text) demonstrates a self-assertiveness to the extent of being for another (and vice versa) that takes place in the plane of reflection before a mirror. Hegel's formal task in "Force and the Understanding" is to turn a horizontal reciprocity on its end so that it becomes a vertical mutual interrelation between the particular and the universal. This gesture of literal upending constitutes the configuration of superior and inferior horizontal strata basic to all scientific and theological speculation, and registered with particular persistence in the ontology underlying much of romantic literature. As will be discussed in detail below, the shifter of valence that will facilitate the conversion of horizontal reciprocity into vertical hierarchy and of the data of sense experience into the immobility of law is the variable, appearance (Erscheinung). The capabilities of appearance overlap those of metaphor itself: imputation and transference. Appearance is able to *impute* actuality or semblance (*Schein*) to phenomena and to *transfer* the status of actuality to semblance and vice versa. In this manner, appearance converts the almost physical movement of reversal in models of reciprocal action into conceptual terms (semblance and actuality) that harbor metaphysical valences within them. Once the semblance or actuality of a phenomenon is at stake, a vertical configuration has been summoned, with all the hierarchical and judgmental valences that may be attached to the distinctions between truth and appearance, seeming and being. It is the semblance or show (*Schein*) in appearance that makes possible the subtle translation of physical motion into metaphysical evaluation and beyond it. All subsequent crystallizations of theology, culture, politics, and art will be predicated and structured by this bond. Yet appearance, the converter of actuality into semblance, is itself pure shift, pure transference, pure variation. Paradoxically, then, the ontological strata and system that sublimate themselves *above* the level of the sensible rest upon a factor of pure difference.

"Perception" began with a double gesture of recapitulation and deformation; the first phase of "Perception" was a repetition of the stages of "Sense-Certainty," but translated into new and slightly different terms. It is not surprising, then, that "Force and the Understanding" begins with the vacillation between unity and multiplicity that occupied "Perception" (81). But in "Force and the Understanding" the mutually negating moments of inclusion and exclusion are incorporated into a single figure, a term figuring their transformation into each other. This is the figure of forces: "But this movement is what is called *Force*. One of its moments, the dispersal of the independent "matters" in their [immediate] being, is the *expression* of Force: but Force, taken as that in which they have disappeared, is Force *proper*. Force which has been *driven back* into itself from its expression. First, however, the Force which is driven back into itself *must* express itself; and, secondly, it is still Force remaining *within itself* in the expression, just as much as it is expression in this self-containedness" (81). If inclusion and exclusion were the complementary moments that constituted the thing or object of perception, expression (*Äußerung*) and repression (or withdrawal, *Züruckdrängen*) constitute the notion of force that is the object of understanding. Expression and repression: not only is the substantial rhetoric of thinghood (*Materien*) translated into the dynamic interaction of forces, but the linguistic problems touched upon in the commentary at the end of "Sense-Certainty" now occupy the center of the stage. *Expression* constitutes the force that is understanding's emblem and its notion (*Begriff*). While the properties of the thing were themselves *substances*, the activities making up the language-object that is force are *functions* or *relations*. Hence, they are free to disappear into each other.

The form of the interaction between counterforces is the reciprocity introduced in "Perception," but achieving its fullest physical (as opposed to metaphysical) elaboration in "Understanding." This reciprocity was already intimated in the passage cited above, in which an internal necessity dictated that the expression and repression constitutive of the force imply each other ("the Force which is driven back into itself *must* express itself"). This rhetoric of reciprocal interaction reaches its fullest physical or mechanical expression in the following passage:

> From this we see that the Notion of Force becomes *actual* through its duplication into two Forces, and how it comes to be so. These two Forces exist as independent essences: but their existence is a movement of each towards the other, such that their being is rather a pure *positedness* or a being that is *posited by an other*, i.e., their being has really the significance of a sheer *vanishing*. . . .Consequently, these moments are not divided into two independent extremes offering each other only an opposite extreme: their essence rather consists simply and solely in this, that each *is* solely through the other, and what each thus is it immediately no longer is, since it *is* the other. They have thus, in fact, no substances of their own which might support and maintain them. . . .Force, as *actual*, exists simply and solely in its *expression*. . . .This *actual* Force, when thought of as free from its expression and as being for itself, is force driven back into itself. . . .Thus the realization of Force is at the same time the loss of reality; in that realization it has really become something quite different, viz. this this *universality*, which the Understanding knows at the outset.

The reciprocity that describes the interaction both within and between forces is indeed multidimensional. To begin, the general existence of the force, its existence as an abstraction or concept, and its actualization in a particular form are mutually dependent. In order to be actualized, force as an abstraction must be divided into concrete subforces, but in order to be conceptualized, the concrete subforces must be collapsed and unified into an abstraction. In terms of this passage, the real (particular) existence of the form disappears into the thought (*Gedanke*) of a generalization

(*Allgemeinheit*), and the notion (*Begriff*) of force divides into mutually opposed particulars. Not only do the general and particular levels of the force relate reciprocally to each other, but the opposing particular forces into which the abstraction divides in order to be actualized exist "solely through the other."

The reciprocally related counterforces into which the force divides exist purely in relation to each other. They are functional and relative rather than substantial. In a sense, it is the physical and mechanical nature of the counterforces that enables them to disappear without a trace into each other. The pure relativity and functional nature of the counterforces is an effect of the physical and mechanical metaphor of force. Yet it is only a brief step from this reciprocal mechanics to the operating principles of Hegelian intersubjectivity. Purely functional vectors may disappear into each other, but this self-consuming physics lays the groundwork for the recognition of the self in an other and the complementary identification of the other through the self that not only will condition all subsequent Hegelian interactions but will reverberate well beyond Hegel.

The elevation into the supersensible from the sensible depends on the establishment of a continuity between the purely sensible existence represented by the "first generalization" of force and the purely intellectual existence of the "second generalization." The phrase "establish a continuity" in fact falls short of the immediacy with which sensible and supersensible, particular and universal, must give rise to each other. This immediate conversion is effected by the semblance or show (*Schein*) at the etymological heart of appearance (*Erscheinung*). *Schein* is an immediate bond between being and nonbeing: "*being* that is directly and in its own a nonbeing." It is on the basis of this bond that appearance, as a totalization of self-consuming play, fosters an endless and restless conversion between particularity and generalization, "the One immediately into the universal, the essential immediately into the unessential." Already, then, the conversion *to* a superior ontological realm must embody the immediacy and immanence that will define the realm itself. The superiority of the elevated realm will consist in a hypothetical immunity frown mediation and differentiation.

Appearance (*Erscheinung*) is a general rubric for the substitution effected by show (*Schein*), a generic term, even though Hegel has not yet taken up his discussion of biological taxinomy: "appearance, a totality of show." Arising in the between-space of the horizontally aligned reciprocal play of forces, appearance is the sum total of the bond that facilitates a wide-reaching set of substitutions: general for particular, inner for outer, negative for positive. The superior realm that precipitates out of appearance is not a mystical otherworldliness whose principles are inherently arbitrary and inscrutable, but a transformation of relations that have been painstakingly anticipated in this organic text. The relations modified in the course of the overall or systematic conversion that the term "appearance" both facilitates and emblematizes are particularity and generality, interiority and exteriority, and positivity and negativity.

So it is in the above passage, then, that as a totalization of the physical and therefore external play of forces, appearance opens up a reflexive *interior*; in its particularity and self-consumption the play of forces is relegated to a negative status, but this merely particular negative will harbor the operating principles, the positivity, of the superior domain. As the multifaceted converter within the Hegelian enterprise, appearance also claims the privilege of determining the usefulness of the now-superseded stages of consciousness. In reevaluating consciousness, progress in sense-certainty and perception, appearance retracts this experience and assigns it a metaphoric or figurative status. What provided the positivity or certainty of sense-experience now becomes metaphoric for a reflection taking place in an inner world. Appearance thus performs upon the entire two preceding stages of consciousness what was rehearsed during both of their intermediate stages. Appearance interiorizes within consciousness processes that ostensibly took place in an exterior sensible actuality: "The *being* of this object for consciousness is mediated by the movement of *appearance*, in which the *being of perception* and the sensuously objective in general has a merely negative significance. Consciousness, therefore, reflects itself out of this movement back into itself as the True: but, *qua* consciousness, converts this truth again into an objective *inner*, and distinguishes this reflection of Things from its own reflection into itself: just as the movement of mediation is likewise still objective for it" (87).

There is yet another conversion performed by the variable "appearance." Paradoxically, in its context, this substitution of a vertical for a horizontal spatialization is the most radical of apppearance's many shifts; yet it is precisely this conversion that carries the heaviest teleological and metaphysical weight. *Appearance opens up* the supersensible (as Matthew Perry may be said to have opened up Japan) by *projecting* a reflection that occurs in a horizontal plane into a vertically superior space that functions as a heaven.

> Within this *inner truth*, as the *absolute universal* which has been purged of the *antithesis* between the universal and the individual and has become the object of the *Understanding*, there now opens up above the *sensuous* world, which is the world of *appearance*, a *supersensible* world which henceforth is the *true* world, above the vanishing *present* world there opens

up a permanent *beyond*, an it-self which is the first, and therefore imperfect, appearance of Reason, or only the pure element
in which the truth has its *essence*. (87–88)

This passage dramatizes the shift from an *inner* truth to an *over* truth.
In Hegel's first image of the *rise* of the supersensible, the superior domain
constituted by appearance (*erscheinende Welt*) literally imposes or super-
imposes itself ("schließt sich. . .über") over the sensible world as its truth.
There is a truth value attached to the vertically superior stratum, and
this judgment is all the weightier in its descent from a permanent beyond
(*bleibende Jenseits*). So momentous is this rise, this projection upward,
that it heralds the appearance of reason, which is an objectification and
externalization of the knowledge gained in self-consciousness, even
though the text has not yet attained self-consciousness.

In a passage that commemorates the triumphant rise of the transcendental world, the replaceability of vertical for horizontal spatialization reasserts itself in full force:

The inner world, or supersensible beyond, has, however, *come
into being* (*entstanden*): it *comes from* the world of appearance
which has mediated it; in other words, appearance is its essence
and, in fact, its filling. The supersensible is the sensuous and
the perceived posited as it is *in truth*; but the *truth* of the
sensuous and the perceived is to be *appearance*. The supersensible is therefore *appearance qua appearance*. We completely
misunderstand this if we think that the supersensible world is
therefore the sensuous world, or the world as it exists for immediate sense-certainty and perception; for the world of appearance is, on the contrary, *not* the world of sense-knowledge and
perception as a world that positively *is*, but this world posited
as superseded, or as in truth an *inner world*.

In this passage the verb *entstehen* describes the emergence of the "inner
world, *or* supersensible beyond" (my emphasis). The beyond has come
into being quite literally by standing up. It is in this passage that Hegel
most fully elaborates the mediatory function of appearance. Paradoxically, the activity of this term, at whose center stands an *immediate*
bond between being and nonbeing, concentrates itself preponderantly
in *mediation*, both between opposites and ontological strata. Hegel
elaborates this mediation by exploring the resonances of the terms for
filling (*Erfüllung*) and mediation itself (*Vermittelung*). Appearance constitutes both the *filling* (i.e., contents) of the supersensible world and
its *fulfillment*. If the beyond emerges from the intermediate position

of appearance (between the sensible and the supersensible), appearance is both the *medium* of the beyond and its *broker* (*Vermittelung*). The supersensible, is the negated or transformed data of sense-experience placed (*gesetzt*) or taken for truth. (Hegel's term for perception, "*Wahrnehmung*," is a taking of the sensible for truth.)

In relation to the beyond, sense-experience is a figuration of consciousness emptied of any substantive truth or value it might have *appeared* to have. In relation to a sense-experience that never completes this elevation, the beyond can only appear as an elusive, pure appearance (*appearance qua appearance*). Appearance, the almost biological medium out of which the supersensible and transcendental grows, sells sense-experience to transcendence, monopolizing a metaphysical commerce.

Once the initial but by no means whimsical foothold in the supersensible has been secured by means of the complex variable "appearance", the fate of understanding will be to repeat its operations on increasingly higher levels of abstraction. This repetition-compulsion toward generality will spell both the contribution and limit of "Understanding." The law of force will be to force what the supersensible is to the sensible: an abstraction of force's particularity, a totalization of what in the force is negative by virtue of particularity. Yet the law, and the levels of abstraction that succeed it (kingdoms of laws and supersensible worlds), will repeat the processes undergone by force. The initial entity, whether the force, the law, or the supersensible world, will bifurcate into two subentities. But the horizontal division will be turned on its end and the second subentity will be elevated to a higher level of abstraction than the first. In conformity with the model of mediation or brokerage provided by appearance, the relation between the relatively higher and lower levels of abstraction will be one of inversion or perversion.

In the physical field of force, the opposed counterforces simply vanish into each other. In the deterministic representations that comprise laws, expressions or assertions leave a trace. The form of this legal script is that the same-named pushes off from itself; the same becomes different; the different becomes same ("das *Gleichnamige* sich von sich selbst abstößt"; "das *Gleichwerden des Ungleichen*"). Or identity, to use terms employed in this century, produces difference; difference underlies the hypothesis of identity. This notation represents the highest development of the logic and mechanics of reciprocity evolved through the first two chapters of the *Phenomenology*.

The attraction of opposites and the repulsion of the self same comprise the most extreme formal crystallization of the Hegelian reciprocity. This formula arises from the combination of an ongoing structure of *binary opposition* with a relation of *reversal* between successive stages of abstraction. The attraction of opposites and the repulsion of the self-same is an instance of reversal (or inversion) being permanently implanted within a matrix of binary opposition. The examples that Hegel selects for this chapter all demonstrate, in different spheres, this concurrence of bifurcation, abstraction, and reversal. The magnet, polarized yet whole, self-repulsive and opposite-attractive, embodies most concretely the reversal produced by abstraction. This reversal applies both to the relation between opposites and to that between successive levels of abstraction. As a codified writing, the law metamorphoses the traceless and therefore blameless force into an enduring statute of reversal.

Not only does the inverted world metamorphose sweet into sour, positive electricity into negative, or social deviance into rehabilitation. Automated, left to their own devices, the structures of understanding open the space for negativity in itself. They form the frames surrounding Bosch's apocalyptic paintings and set the stage for the "Walpurgisnacht" scenes in Goethe's *Faust*. The possibility of recuperating or rehabilitating this automatic negativity is questionable, as is the finality of the resolution provided by the lifting of the curtain at the end of the chapter. This latter act is a *performance* of resolution, but the laborious effort with which "Self-Consciousness" begins in the wake of the compulsive repetition of "Understanding" undermines the decisiveness of this gesture.

The supersensible world, as well as the law that is one of its subcategories, could not have been opened up without appearance, which, as we have seen, owed its capabilities to formal operations of bifurcation, displacement, and substitution developed in the first two chapters. With this goal attained, however, with the opening of the heavens that sustain transcendental projection, the time has come to contain, close the lid on, and deny those very formal operations. Operations that on the underside of the beyond were necessary to give consciousness any movement at all have now become a mechanistic threat to the transcendental. Hegel's containment of understanding by applying to it a critique of formalism is thus a cover-up, a concealment of the operations that make understanding possible. The necessity of the law is spurious because it is "merely verbal" ("nur im Worte liegt"). The law is a narrative or recital (*Hererzhälung*) of its moments. The law has been kidnapped out of the service of the phenomenon itself ("der Sache selbst") and forcefully impressed into the misrepresentations of language. This corruption can be identified with a name, explanation (*Erklären*), and the most ominous aspect of this language disorder is its mechanical operation. Its moments form the cycle of a machine: "It is an explanation that not only explains nothing, but is so plain that, while it pretends to say something different from what has already been said, really says nothing at all but only repeats the same thing" (95).

Even in the Hegelian text, then, formal operations serve as a convenient whipping boy for the profound ambiguities toward language that occasionally surface.[8] In certain moments of confusion, even Hegel unleashes the general romantic frustration with the *Ding an sich* against the formal operations that he himself had synthesized and that constitute the enduring contribution of the *Phenomenology*. In this text Hegel assumes the double task of accounting, in formal and logical terms, for the movements of philosophical language *and* of legitimizing the thrust of Western civilization in many of its theaters. This ambivalence toward the operations of bifurcation, displacement, and reversal is a sorespot where the irreconcilability of these enterprises is felt most acutely.

Explanation, in the chapter on "Understanding," is a pejorative term, a rubric for the mechanistic processes of abstraction. Yet explanation merely repeats a gesture that was essential to understanding; just as appearance totalized semblance (*Schein*), relativizing the status of being, explanation totalizes the internal operation of laws. The initial description of explanation as a cycle reflects a mistrust of the linguistic processes involved in the formulation of laws. But at the end of "Understanding," infinity (*Unendlichkeit*) totalizes understandiing's activities, becoming a trope for the entire process. And the form that this trope assumes is precisely that of a cycle. Life itself, in "The Truth of Self-Certainty," will not only borrow this cyclical structure, but will appropriate, in *very* slightly different terms, the steps of infinity.

Thus, at a particular moment when the legitimizing function of his program is threatened, Hegel invokes romantic truisms *against* the structures of his own text. But in other contexts, these structures will emerge with renewed force. The unique resilience of these formal tropes is evident both in the rich variety of the operations that Hegel has developed in the course of "Understanding" and in the complex but by no means arbitrary manner in which he has been able to interrelate them in a narrative. A summary of these formal developments would read as follows:

1. The abstraction implicit within the notion of force has for the first time opened a space for mediation that was totally absent in "Sense-Certainty'" and only present rudimentarily in "Perception" (there in the "unconditioned absolute universality"). A space between two reciprocally related counterforces is the setting for this mediation.

---

8. For a discussion of the fundamentally linguistic constitution of both the Hegelian subjectivity and objectivity, see Josef Simon, *Das Problem der Sprache bei Hegel* (Stuttgart: W. Kohlhammer, 1966), 11–47, 55–62, 66–84.

2. The variable "appearance" situated in this intermediary space, shifts the horizontal interplay of forces into a vertical configuration of strata. Appearance imputes the status of nonbeing to being and transforms the certainty of sense-experience into the uncertainty or negativity of speculation. Appearance thus allows sense-experience to be *projected* into a superior transcendental domain, where it functions as a negative basis for speculation.

3. The vertical projection first allowed by appearance, when combined with the bifurcation that is the basic operation of the Hegelian logic, produces a model for abstraction in general. According to this model, an abstract entity will always be bifurcated, and the second subentity will exist on a higher plane of abstraction than the first. The relation between successive levels of abstraction is one of *inversion*. The higher level of abstraction embodies the *form* of the lower one without the content. But since the higher level depends on the lower level for its *form*, the only change that the abstraction can produce is a transfiguration of values.

4. The principle of inversion, when introduced into reciprocal relations, initiates an automatic reversal of values whose magnetic model is the attraction of opposites and the repulsion of the selfsame. This generation of difference out of identity and intimation of identity in difference may assume either a horizontal or a vertical spatialization. "Understanding" tropologizes the stages of abstraction by collapsing them into a single figure. This collapse of multiple operations into a single figure performs the same totalization by means of which sense-experience is projected into the transcendental domain under the single rubric of appearance. Hegel calls the initial totalizing trope, describing the relation between laws and the phenomena they modify, explanation.

REVERSAL

We cast the *Phenomenology*, then, in a well-known literary role. It is the venerable source of assurance and integrity in the community that is also suspect, the standard of value based on a cultural currency that is counterfeit. This ambiguity arises, as I have suggested, from the *Phenomenology*'s twin birth and twin destiny. Divided at birth, this text is *both* the consummation of a civilization, a diachronic account of a panoply of learned disciplines placed in tandem *and* a metaphoric generator, producing the metacritical structures and terms that describe its own existence as a text.

This doubling of aims and functions is *almost* schizophrenic. And indeed, a schizophrenic text, such as Kierkegaard's *Either/Or*, would be one way of pronouncing this tendency while avoiding the sometimes arbitrary resolutions to which Hegel occasionally reverts in order to assure narrative continuity. Many of the accounts and terms in the *Phenomenology* are easily placed on one side of its functional divide or another—on the side of history and teleology on the one hand, or on the side of textual self-dramatization on the other. In the most general of terms we can say that the primary contribution of the first four chapters is to generate the logical terms and formal tropes that will structure the subsequent discourse, and that the accounts of religion, art, and politics in the latter sections of the text presuppose these structures and belong to a history of cultural forms.

Yet in a typically Hegelian manner, there are constructs that cross these lines, that function within both counterprograms, and that save the text from the stark termination in schizophrenia that becomes Kierkegaard's response to the Hegelian formalism. Among these double constructs we would have to number appearance, whose translation of the movements of reflection into a hierarchical configuration is also a translation of *formal* structures into historical and teleological progressions. The notion (*Begriff*) and sublation (*Aufhebung*) also fall into this intermediary category, playing both structural and metaphysical roles. The *Begriff* is both a structural and metaphysical horizon, while the *Aufhebung* translates the mechanics of negation into the teleology of history.

The existence of these double functions that accommodate both counterprograms of the *Phenomenology* is symptomatic of a wider coordination within the Hegelian text. The suspicion lurking behind the text's irreproachable aims is not that it should have provided a successive account of the major crystallizations of Western culture, or that it should have generated a formal lexicon of its own functioning, but that these radically different programs could have been marshaled with such precision and *seamlessness* in support of each other.

The model of abstraction elaborated in "Understanding" contains the lineaments of this coordination. Each time a process is totalized to a new level of abstraction, it is lubricated in the sense that tensions and frictions involved at the lower level of generality are diminished. In "Understanding," appearance figures and totalizes sense-experience, the law of force totalizes the operations of law, the kingdom of laws totalizes the operations of law, and the cycles of explanation and necessity totalize the operations of understanding itself. The tropologizing of a process, the subsumption of a sequence of steps under a single figure drastically reduces, in subsequent stages, the irregularities initially at play in that operation.

According to the omniscient narrator of the *Phenomenology,* the limit of "understanding" is precisely the absence of friction made possible by tropologization. The mechanical circularity involved in the assertion, withdrawal, and elevation of distinctions constitutes the limit of "Understanding," but the resolution of this impasse is precisely the smooth circularity afforded by tropes. Both the crisis and outcome of "Understanding" are defined by circularity, and the nature of circularity is infinity (*Unendlichkeit*).

If circularity is the outcome of "Understanding," the *Phenomenology* has reached a premature dead end. The impetus that the text as a whole needs in order to continue consists in the breaking, or at least the by-passing af this circularity. In terms of the impasse at the end of "Understanding," we may say that when the infrastructure of tropologization becomes locked into an unresolved circular motion, the superstructure consisting of the interior/exterior relations between the largest units of the *Phenomenology* creaks into motion. Or again, we may say that the coexistence of circular and lateral models of movement in the text enables an involuted circle to be broken by a lateral thrust that was from the outset held in reserve.

What is most suspicious about the Hegelian coordination is the endlessness of such possible resolutions. The different models of motion and logical relation sustained by the text are so great in number and variety that each impasse generates its own resolution. The solutions arise after the fact, with the retrospective confirmation of rationalization.[9] The "Lordship and Bondage" section, for example, is so conditioned by an inequality and reversal of positions emerging from equilibrium that it needs no resolution. Upheaval is so deeply implanted in this scenario as an ongoing potential that for once the text can afford to allow the conceptual and narrative outcomes of an episode to dangle. Yet this apparent indirection is more than answered by "The Unhappy Consciousness." If "Lordship and Bondage" establishes an infinite imbalance in an intersubjective relationship projected vertically, the figure of the priest or servant in "The Unhappy Consciousness" sets this eccentricity aright by means of the self-denying but also self-elevating gesture of sacrifice.

"Lordship and Bondage" and "The Unhappy Consciousness" are transitional episodes in which the formal structures of the first four chapter are provisionally translated into intersubjective and historical

---

9. For a discussion of the retrospective self-confirmation performed by the Hegelian text, see Andrzej Warminski, "Pre-positional By-play," in *Glyph III* (Baltimore: John Hopkins University Press, 1978), 98–117.

terms.[10] They are distinctive both in their steadfastness to the text's formal program and in their metaphysical resonances. Both episodes are extensions of moments of "Understanding." "Lordship and Bondage" returns to the reciprocal interplay of forces and explores its intersubjective implications. A hypothetical condition of perfect intersubjective symmetry produces inequality in two forms: the fight to the death and labor, the sublimated product of this conflict. In formal terms, the episode describes the generation of social and historical difference out of a hypothetical state of perfect sameness.

"The Unhappy Consciousness" repeats the projection upward performed by appearance in "Understanding," but once again this takes place within an intersubjective sphere. If "Lordship and Bondage" grew out of the reciprocity of forces, "The Unhappy Consciousness" again turns reciprocity on its end and bonds the mutable to the unchangeable (127ff., *das Unwandelbare*). The middle term is no longer the mystifying variable, *Erscheinung*, but the minister or servant (136, *Diener*), whose acts of renunciation and self-sacrifice bond the higher and lower domains by emulating the former and redeeming the latter. Renunciation and sacrifice translate the withdrawal of a physical force into terms of social utility and hence historical destiny. Henceforth, in conformity with the inversion of value that defines the relationship between successive stages of abstraction, the highest moral values will always accrue to self-restraint, which is the intersubjective and social correlative to being-for-another (as opposed to being-for-self).

These two episodes, then, comprise particularly striking instances of one of the most vibrant forms of the Hegelian coordination: translation. Translation, for Hegel, is a substitution of terms that takes place in conjunction with a structural continuity. "Lordship and Bondage" and "The Unhappy Consciousness" *translate* the dynamics of the physical world into intersubjective relations and the history initiated by them while sustaining the operations that define the text's possibility.

If "Lordship and Bondage" gives the physics of "Understanding" a detailed intersubjective treatment, it remains for "The Unhappy Consciousness" to reinstate in human terms the hierarchical configuration opened up by appearance. In a predictably Hegelian fashion, no sooner

---

10. J. Hillis Miller performs the invaluable task of adapting the arena of intersubjective relations to the dynamics of textuality by exploring the metaphoric specificity and rhetorical implications of linear imagery in certain exemplary novels. See "Ariadne's Thread: Repetition and the Narrative Line," *Critical Inquiry* 3 (1966): 57–78, and "A 'Buchstäbliches' Reading of *The Elective Affinities*," *Glyph VI* (Baltimore: Johns Hopkins University Press, 1979), 1–23.

does consciousness become aware of itself than its danger becomes *excessive* interiority, imprisonment within a hopelessly involuted, self-contained world. Hegel's misgivings regarding the self-containment of which self-consciousness is capable is yet another indication of his suspicion toward the self-referentiality of language. Unhappy consciousness is the discontented child of a *freed* self-consciousness, one not constrained to confront an external objectivity. Unhappy consciousness is an *internalized* form of the reciprocity that takes place, in "Lordship and Bondage" between two ostensibly external subjects: "The duplication of self-consciousness within itself, which is essential in the Notion of Spirit, is thus here before us, but not yet in its unity: the *Unhappy Consciousness* is the consciousness of self as a dual-natured, merely contradictory being" (126). The resolution to this unbearable state of internal division will arise from the capacities for surrender and repression demonstrated by the slave in relation to the master.

The answer to the paralyzing internal bifurcation that is the condition of unhappy consciousness ts provided by the figure of the servant (*Diener*), who is the slave expressed positively and projected into the heavens of speculation. Yet it is a long step from the intersubjective exploration of identity and difference in "Lordship and Bondage" to the theological self-renunciation consummated by the servant. This explains why the chapter on the unhappy consciousness is so schematic. Stoicism and skepticism are invoked as stages of free self-consciousness preliminary to the unhappy consciousness. Stoicism and skepticism occupy in relation to the unhappy consciousness a position analogous to that of sense-certainty and perception in relation to understanding. If sense-certainty comprises a hypothetically unmediated absorption in sense-experience, stoicism is a hypothetically equal absorption into pure thought, thought without substance. In skepticism, as in the thing of perception, a crude balance is reached: the oscillation between inclusion and exclusion in the thing becomes a falling in and out of conceptual unity in skepticism. The unhappy consciousness totalizes and tropologizes these movements, just as appearance totalizes the sensible. If the torment of the unhappy consciousness is an infinite vacillation within a bifurcated subject, the poles of the vacillation are defined by the stages of stoicism and skepticism.

The degree of the tropologization in the unhappy consciousness is equal to the degree of repression involved in passing from the potentially infinite reversal between master and slave to theological self-sacrifice.[11]

---

11. The fullest placement of Hegel within the context and particular crystallizations of Western thought is Jacques Derrida's *Glas* (Paris: Galilée, 1974). Derrida

The structure of this tropologization is complex. Unhappy consciousness is a trope of processes in stoicism and skepticism, which are in turn tropes of the processes of the physical world. The splendid exploration of formal operations *in themselves* in "Lordship and Bondage" is, then, "answered" or retracted by the schematization that resolves the division in the unhappy consciousness with the figure of the servant.

Thus, at the same time that "Lordship and Bondage" and "The Unhappy Consciousness" effect a decisive translation of the physical world into the intersubjective terms of history, psychology, and culture, they are also compelling examples of Hegelian coordination. The former episode effects the initial *translation* of the dynamics of *reciprocity* into intersubjective terms. "The Unhappy Consciousness" *internalizes* this conflict and subsumes its stages into a single trope. The trope, "unhappy consciousness," fashions a doubly involuted *circle* of totalization, encompassing both the stages of consciousness and the prior stages of self-consciousness. It will be a notable and perhaps enduring contribution of recent critical theory to have fostered and promulgated a healthy suspicion toward the speculative system in which the servant's self-sacrifice, at the end of "The Unhappy Consciousness," implies a universal truth and destiny. This organic *inference* of the transcendental from the empirical recapitulates and expands upon the dawn of the beyond out of appearance. Such moments typify the capacity of the Hegelian formal apparatus to be manipulated, to be marshaled into a not thoroughly warranted progress, to *force* resolutions in the interest of an ulterior and encompassing goal. Yet even with orientations and acts that are and must be so suspect, in its wider composition the Hegelian formal apparatus exerts a profound historical and conceptual influence, one not worthy of underestimation.

REPETITION

To attempt, at the end of so technical an elaboration of the formal trope of the early *Phenomenology,* to suggest their wider historical and theoretical implications, is a self-defeating task that can itself only produce spurious resolutions. Yet the particular affinity between the crystallizations of romantic literature and the twentieth-century problematics of shock, mechanical reproduction, the esthetics of adultery, the repetition-compulsion, and psychoanalysis in general arises at least

---

isolates and painstakingly combines the theological, ontological, anthropological, economic, and psychosexual elements of the matrix of Hegelian speculation.

in part from the concern shared by both epochs for the formal operations synthesized and elaborated by Hegel. A vast swath of romantic literature occupies the space of the unhappy consciousness, the setting of an internal, reciprocal division suspended between transcendent and mutable worlds. Even such notable texts as the Keatsian odes and Shelley's "Triumph of Life," which question this configuration, arise within the tragically paradoxical condition that defines unhappy consciousness. The romantic performative gestures of blessing and curse, desire and complaint, and the fascination with intermediary characters such as Prometheus all arise in an attempt to assimilate the differences that the unhappy consciousness both fixes and unfolds.

The psychoanalytical subject is the subject of the *Phenomenology* projected within a personal field or space. The pathology of the psychoanalytical subject consists of the standard operations of the Hegelian subject. Psychoanalytical *disorders* are isolated instances of the formal operations at play within the Hegelian subject. Formal operations are convertible into *pathological* manifestations because of the internal necessity within the Freudian enterprise to construct *positive* models for psychoneurological *disturbances*.

Laws of symmetry prevail within the phenomenological unconscious as it is elaborated by Hegel in his analysis of Sophocles' *Antigone*,[12] and these laws are suspended within the Freudian dream or joke. Yet it is significant that both Hegel and Freud appeal to Greek tragedy, with its unresolvable double-binds, in synthesizing models of an unconscious that is held in check by repression. For Hegel, action is inescapably reductive. The unconscious consists of the actions and principles that the tragic character, in reaching a decision, is no longer free to follow. The alternatives that were excluded by action literally pursue the character until they achieve their retribution, attacking from the back, from the blind side of unconsciousness. For Freud, too, repression defends the borders of "consciousness": "*the essence of repression lies simply in turning something away [abweisen], and keeping it at a distance [fernhaltung], from the conscious.*"[13] A dominant form of repression involved in paranoia is projection, which is defined in terms of the lateral shifts within the Hegelian subject: "The most striking characteristic of symptomformation in paranoia is the process which deserves the name of *projection*. An internal perception is suppressed, and, instead, its content, after undergoing a kind of distortion, enters consciousness in the form

---

12. Hegel, *Phenomenology*, 267–94.
13. Sigmund Freud, "Repression" (1915), *SE* 14: 147.

of an external perception. In delusions of persecution the distortion consists in a transformation of affect; what should have been felt internally as love is perceived externally as hate."[14] Freud links paranoid manifestations closely to homosexual desire, and homosexuality proceeds from the dialectics of sameness and difference and self and other. Rather than making an *other* his object-choice, the homosexual "begins by taking himself, his own body as his love object, and only subsequently proceeds from this to the choice of some person other than himself as his object."[15] The homosexual *takes* the same when a logic of opposition and the repulsion of the selfsame demands that he take an *other*. The disorders of paranoia, then, both the active manifestations and their psychosexual underpinnings, are defined in relation to a philosophical conciousness whose operations, largely with Hegel's assistance, may be presupposed.

The configuration linking the id, ego, and superego is manifestly mediational. "The ego seeks to bring the influence of the external world to bear on the id and its tendencies, and endeavors to substitute the reality principle for the pleasure principle which reigns unrestrictedly in the id. The ego represents what may be called reason and common sense, in contrast to the id, which contains the passions."[16] Here, prefiguring the strictures of the superego, the ego mediates between the instincts and reason, effecting a substitution of the reality principle for the pleasure principle. Such a relatively late Freudian construct as the repetition-compulsion undermines the neatness of such a structure and challenges the subject-object relation that had been previously postulated between the patient (or analyst) and the unconscious. *Beyond the Pleasure Principle* (1920) gives the unconscious an indomitable life of its own, even if death, as the restoration af stasis, is the repetitive message of this life. Repetition, whether it is a "source of pleasure [*Lustquelle*]" as in this text, or whether it produces the discomfiture of uncanniness, is a function of the tropologization and circularization within certain of the formal operations that we have observed.[17] In *Beyond the Pleasure Principle*, the repetition-compulsion is the sign of a restorative psychic economy that functions alongside an acquisitive and productive one. This text, then, whose point of departure is an automatic psychic repetition

---

14. Sigmund Freud, "On the Mechanism of Paranoia," in "Psycho-Analytical Notes on an Autobiographical Account of a Case of Paranoia (Dementia Paranoides)," *SE* 12:66.
15. Ibid., 60–61.
16. Sigmund Freud, "The Ego and the Id," *SE* 19:25.
17. Sigmund Freud, "Beyond the Pleasure Principle," *SE* 19:7–64,

ultimately deriving from the cycles that form within the Hegelian subject, is a major factor in restoring a dualism seemingly lost from the
psychoanalytical enterprise. Predictably enough, the structure of this
dualism is antithetical. *"Protection against* stimuli is an almost more
important function for the living organism than *reception of* stimuli."[18]
The parity between the reception of stimuli and the defenses against
them goes a long way in explaining the curious balance that the death
and life instincts achieve in this Freudian text.

Beyond the Pleasure Principle restores the parity of death, defense,
and regression within a psychoanalytical system that might have otherwise reached too high a degree of completion and development. This
text permanently installs the indirection of dualism with the Freudian
corpus. Yet the metaphors that Freud selects both in order to describe
his earlier efforts and to describe this final indecision are inevitably
dialectical, derived from the formal operations that take place within
the space of the implicit subject of the *Phenomenology*.

Ironically, then, the greatest vulnerability of the formal tropes of
the Hegelian text has consisted in their success, the resilience of their
internal structures and the power of their historical and theoretical
impact. Profound suspicion is an inevitable byproduct of any speculative
system making claims as wide-reaching as the Hegelian claims of progression and resolution. The Hegelian system's elevation and the vertical
strata that it forms are the primary justifications for this doubt. While
the formal tropes of the early *Phenomenology* verge upon a speculative
horizon, this does not deny them their force and suggestiveness in tracing
the generation and structuration of philosophical and literary language.

---

18. Ibid., 27.

Index

Abel, 181–182
Abraham, 19
Action, communicative, 132
Adam, 19, 173, 175–178, 180–181, 242
  and estrangement, 5
  and externalization, 5, 117, 143
Alienation, 5, 37

Bataille, George, 219
Beyond the Pleasure Principle, 327–328
Bible, 19, 175–178, 299
Bildung, 11, 24, 61, 200, 271
Bildungsroman 258, 306
Cain, 181–182
Cogito, 88–89, 96–97
Consciousness,
  and alienation, 38
  and externalization, 41–45
  base, 38
  folk, (*Volk*), 235, 269, 275, 283
  noble, 38
  servile, 83–86, 163, 347
  technical, 57
  theoretical, 57
  unhappy, 38, 55, 72, 295–297, 323–325

De Cive, 275
Death, 217–222
Desire, 6, 70–72, 154, 172
  and domination, 211–217
  and otherness, 72–74
  and submission, 18, 229
  and transference, 230
  animal, 49–50, 156, 227
  anthropogenetic, 17, 50, 228
  appetitive, 16

Deutsch-Franzosische Jahrotoucher, 119–120
Differenz Schrift, 235, 251, 252

Economic and Philosophic Manuscripts, 101
Ecrits, 228, 230
Either/Or, 320
Elements of Law, 275
Enzyklopadie, 14–16, 254, 263, 270
Epictetus, 293
Eve, 173, 175–178, 180–181

Fear, 35, 56, 83, 85, 164–165, 292
Fichte, 68, 126–127, 150, 266–268, 282
Force, 310–320
Freedom, 58, 146–148, 165–167, 284, 299
Freud, Sigmund, 19, 21, 210, 218, 221, 326

German Ideology, 148
Greeting, custom of, 158–159

Hegel,
  on absolute knowledge, 39,53
  on alienation, 5, 40–41
  on appearance, 314–317
  on categories of economics, 39, 118–119
  on civil society, 14, 267
  critique of idealist ethics, 103, 151
  epistemological optimism of, 92
  on family, 243, 248, 279, 286–287
  on fashion, 197–198
  on force, 310–320

Hegel *continued*
  on identity thesis, 30, 68–69, 91–93,
    125, 153, 241
  on labour, 34, 101, 107, 111, 191–195
  on language, 242
  on law of nature, 145
  on love, 128, 234–237, 243
  on machinery, 195
  on marriage, 244
  on money, 120–121, 196
  ontological optimism of, 95
  on particularity, 276–277, 281–283,
    307, 311
  on perception, 312
  on poverty, 114, 188, 197–198, 208
  on property, 190–191
  on sense-certainty, 69–90
  on social classes, 202–205, 240
  on state, 115, 199–202
  on tools, 9, 112
  on understanding, 319–322
  on categories of economics, 39,
    118—119
  on civil society, 14, 207
  on critique of idealist ethics, 103, 151
Hero, 239, 290, 299
History, 13, 23, 60, 260, 267–269
Hobbes, Thomas, 9, 109, 274–278
Humanism, 13, 21, 50, 108

Idea for a Universal History, 103

Jener System of 1803–1804, 242–278,
  285, 286, 287

Kant, Immanuel, 20, 130–131, 149
Knowledge, 22, 39, 44, 53, 104–105

Lacan, Jacques, 223, 227
Life, 78, 79, 93, 152–154, 174
  life and death struggle, 9, 31–32, 51,
    163–164, 230
Lyotard, Jean-Francois, 23

Marx,
  on humanism, 42
  on mirror of production, 18, 24
  on naturalism, 42
  on religion, 45

Mirror image, 17–18, 225
  of humanity, 24
  of production, 18, 24–25

Napoleon, 15, 51–54, 224
Naturphilosophie, 236
Noah, 183–186

On Natural Law, 105, 145, 235, 238
Opedipus, 300
Orestes, 300

Philosophy of Right, 14, 116, 146, 188,
  194, 207, 208, 270
Philosophy of the Spirit (1805–1806), 145,
  147, 243, 249, 285, 286
Political Philosophy of Hobbes, 273
Propadeutik, 254

Realphilosophie I, 82, 187
Realphilosophie II, 187, 189
Recognition, 8, 74–78
  between Adam and Eve, 178–181
  between Man and God, 234–235,
    250–252
  in property, 180–191, 287
  in struggle for life and death, 55,
    78–81
Revolution, 64, 224, 265, 298, 302
Ricoeur, Paul, 21–22, 226–227
Rousseau, Jean-Jacques, 266, 289,
  295–296

Schelling, 110, 150, 236, 241, 268
Schiller, 10
Science of Knowledge, 68
Sein und Zeit, 97–98
Self-certainty, 4, 69, 172, 305–306
Self-consciousness, 29–36, 67–70
  and "being-for-the-other," 31–32,
    261–263
  as desire, 68–70
  as misrecognition, 16, 19
  in Adam and Eve, 178–181
  in Cain and Abel, 181–182
  in Noah, 183, 186
  of master and slave, 7
Skeptic, 8–9, 63, 294–295
Slave, Christian, 63–64
Smith, Adam, 103–105, 113, 116

Social Contract, 295
Solipsism, 62, 87
Spirit of Christianity, 129
Stoic, 8–9, 61–62, 292–294
Story of O, 211, 215, 219, 221
Strauss, Leo, 273–274
Subjective Logic, 125
Subjectivity, 8
   inter-subjectivity, 8, 20–21
   intra-subjectivity, 8, 20–21

System der Sittlichkeit, 82, 188, 189, 237
System of Ethical Life, 239, 241, 245,
   246, 275, 276–280, 282–284
System of Ethics, 105–107, 115, 116
System of Morality, 123

Wissenschaftslehre (1794), 126
Work, 52, 57, 59–61